STATE OF FEAR

Joshua Barker

State of Fear

Policing a
Postcolonial City

DUKE UNIVERSITY PRESS
Durham and London
2024

© 2024 DUKE UNIVERSITY PRESS
All rights reserved
Project Editor: Bird Williams
Designed by A. Mattson Gallagher
Typeset in Portrait Text by Westchester Publishing Services

Library of Congress Cataloging-in-Publication Data
Names: Barker, Joshua, [date] author.
Title: State of fear : policing a postcolonial city / Joshua Barker.
Description: Durham : Duke University Press, 2024. | Includes
bibliographical references and index.
Identifiers: LCCN 2023049696 (print)
LCCN 2023049697 (ebook)
ISBN 9781478030768 (paperback)
ISBN 9781478026525 (hardcover)
ISBN 9781478059752 (ebook)
Subjects: LCSH: Law enforcement—Indonesia—Bandung—History—
20th century. | Vigilantism—Indonesia—History—20th century. |
Postcolonialism—Indonesia. | Indonesia—Politics and government—
1966–1998. | Indonesia—Politics and government—1998 Classification:
LCC KNW3022 .B37 2024 (print)
LCC KNW3022 (ebook)
DDC 363.2/30959824—dc23/eng/20240317
LC record available at https://lccn.loc.gov/2023049696
LC ebook record available at https://lccn.loc.gov/2023049697

Cover art: Illustration based on map of Bandung, N. Visser & Co.,
circa 1950. Leiden University Libraries, DE 29, 3.

For Jess, Sebastian, and Roger

CONTENTS

ILLUSTRATIONS

ABBREVIATIONS

ABRI	Angkatan Bersenjata Republik Indonesia; Armed Forces of the Republic of Indonesia
AKABRI	Akademi Angkatan Senjata Republik Indonesia (i.e., military academy)
ARD	Algemeene Recherche Dienst; General Investigation Bureau
BAP	*Berita Acara Pemeriksaan*; police investigation report
BIMMAS	Bimbingan Masyarakat; Guidance of Society Unit of the police
GDN	Gerakan Disiplin Nasional; National Discipline Movement
GOLKAR	Golongan Karya; Functional Groups (political party)
HANSIP	Pertahanan Sipil; Civil Defense
KAMRA	Keamanan Rakyat; People's Security
KODAM	Komando Daerah Militer; Regional Military Command
PDI	Partai Demokrasi Indonesia; Indonesian Democratic Party
PETRUS	Pembunuhan Misterius; Mysterious Killings

PID	Politieke Inlichtingendienst; Political Intelligence Service
PKI	Partai Komunis Indonesia; Indonesian Communist Party
POLDA	Polisi Daerah; provincial police
POLRES	Polisi Resor; subdistrict police
POLSEK	Polisi Sektor; police precinct
POLWILTABES	Polisi Wilayah Kota Besar; metropolitan region police
POM	Polisi Militer; Military Police
PPP	Partai Persatuan Pembangunan; United Development Party
SABHARA	Satuan Huru Hara; Security and Crowd Control Unit (police)
SATPAM	Satuan Pengamanan; Security Unit
SATPAMSUS	Satuan Pengamanan Khusus; special security guard
SISKAMLING	*Sistem keamanan lingkungan*; environment security system
TNI-AL	Tentara Nasional Indonesia, Angkatan Laut; Indonesian Navy
VOC	Vereenigde Oostindische Compagnie; Dutch East India Company
WNI	*Warga negara Indonesia*; Indonesian citizen (euphemism for ethnic Chinese Indonesians)

ACKNOWLEDGMENTS

While working on this book I have benefited tremendously from the support of numerous foundations, institutions, and persons. Fieldwork in Bandung and archival work in the Netherlands were made possible by financial support from the Social Science and Humanities Research Council Dissertation Fellowship Program, the Social Science Research Council Predissertation Fellowship Program, and the Joint Committee on Southeast Asia of the Social Science Research Council and the American Council of Learned Societies, with funds from the Andrew W. Mellon Foundation, the Ford Foundation, and the Henry Luce Foundation. Additional financial support for writing was provided by the Connaught Fund, the KITLV Modern Indonesia Project, the Swedish School of Advanced Asia Pacific Studies Fellowships, the Social Science and Humanities Research Council Standard Research Grant Program, and Cornell University's Peace Studies Program, with funds from the MacArthur Foundation. In Indonesia, Universitas Padjadjaran and the National Research and Innovation Agency (formerly Indonesian Institute of Sciences) graciously provided me with institutional sponsorship.

Portions of this book have already appeared in print. I am grateful to those who supported these ideas in their earlier iterations. My intellectual debts are many, and sadly, some of these debts are to individuals who have since passed away. Special mention goes to my mentors, colleagues, and friends in Indonesia, who made my field research there so informative and compelling: Suyadi and Eiffel, Nurdin and Ai, Edi Ekadjati and his family, Iskandarwassid, Merlyna Lim, Rini Andraeni, Andar, Ebo, Zaky, Frans, Ebo, Selly, and Indri. Anggie Syach and Tedi provided me with much-needed research assistance at crucial moments in the data collection. I am also grateful for the kindness and hospitality shown to me by people I met in Bandung's police stations, courts, and prison. It was their willingness to talk to me that made this project possible.

Much of this book is an attempt to address problems posed over the years in the context of discussions with friends and colleagues from Cornell University and the University of London, including Anto Nuranto, Andrew Abalahin, Budi Akuncoro, Thamora Fishel, Maja Gilberg, Jeff Hadler, Carol Hau, Douglas Kammen, Smita Lahiri, Sarah Maxim, Hajime Nakatani, John Sidel, Eric Tagliacozzo, Kari Telle, and Amrih Widodo. Over the many years in which this book was in preparation, I have also benefited greatly from my conversations with a number of other scholars, family, and friends, including Jonathan Barker, Nancy Barker, Gillian Barker, Molly Barker, Nicholas Benson, Tom Boellstorff, Deirdre de la Cruz, Dorian Fougeres, Gerry van Klinken, Abidin Kusno, Johan Lindquist, Nicholas Morgan, Shaylih Muehlmann, John Olle, John Pemberton, Vicente Rafael, Joel Robbins, Loren Ryter, Henk Schulte Nordholt, Nico Schulte Nordholt, Patricia Spyer, Rupert Stasch, Mary Steedly, Jaap Timmer, Jacqueline Vel, Andrew Willford, and Emily Zeamer.

This book came to fruition at the University of Toronto. I thank my friends, colleagues, and students in the Department of Anthropology and in the Asian Institute for providing me with such a supportive and intellectually stimulating environment in which to work. I am lucky to work with Jacques Bertrand, Tania Li, and Rachel Silvey, all of whom share a passion for Indonesia. Special thanks are due to Sheri Gibbings, Sharon Kelly, Constantinos Papadakis, Jean Chia, Jesook Song, Anne Brackenbury, and Ken Kawashima, who read and commented on various drafts of the book manuscript. I am also grateful to Michael Lambek for nudging me along at several critical junctures, and to the three anonymous reviewers from Duke University Press, whose thoughtful suggestions so deeply shaped the book's final form.

I am deeply indebted to Jim Siegel, Ben Anderson, and Takashi Shiraishi for their invaluable guidance. Their thoughtful questions, raised so many years ago, remain with me to this day.

Introduction

Fear, Policing, and State Power

I never saw the inside of a cell in the city of Bandung's main prison. I never even made it into the cellblock. It was in the prison yard that my courage failed me. I was with a friend of mine, Tedi, an Indonesian student of history, and we were walking from the prison's cafeteria, just inside the perimeter wall, across the wide and barren yard toward the cellblocks in the middle of the prison compound.

We were both scared to be there. It was the mid-1990s and President Suharto, Indonesia's authoritarian leader, was still in power. We had been allowed into Bandung's Sukamiskin Prison to interview inmates so we could learn more about what I described as "the culture of crime and security" that reigns in the city and the country more broadly. Most of the other students who came to the prison were studying criminology or psychology, so it was unusual for an anthropologist and a historian to be there. Perhaps because I was a foreigner, or perhaps because of Tedi's connections, we were allowed to meet with the inmates in the cafeteria rather than the official visitors' room. This meant we could mix quite freely with inmates in an informal manner, rather than having to make an appointment to interview a specific person under the formal circumstances that govern most prison visits. It was during one of these informal gatherings that a few of the young men we were talking to suggested that we go over to the cellblocks. I was certainly interested; I had been looking out on the cellblocks for the past few weeks and wondering what was going on in there. According to the inmates we talked to, prison guards rarely entered this area of the prison, which was considered under the de facto authority of the inmates, who were themselves organized into a hierarchy of gangs. But while the guards had not expressly forbidden us to go out there, I was still hesitant, in part because I knew the guards were already a bit suspicious of us for spending so much time with the inmates. After a moment's hesitation, we decided to proceed.

The cellblocks were constructed in the shape of an X and were enclosed by a square perimeter structure that served as both prison wall and the site of various administrative offices, workshops, and places of worship. In its architecture, the prison was typical of the high modern period of Dutch colonialism in Bandung, which is characterized by massive structures that mix various local design accents with striking straight lines that can only be fully appreciated from an aerial view. It wasn't exactly the panopticon envisaged by Jeremy Bentham, and which for Michel Foucault served as the visual expression of the disciplinary society, but it was not too far off. Except here—in this postcolonial moment—the disciplinary logic of surveillance had been at least partly disrupted, with many inmates covering their windows with sheets and bits of laundry so as to shield their cells from the hot sun and make it impossible for guards located in the perimeter structure to see inside.

As we left the shelter of the perimeter buildings and started walking across the yard, I could sense that the guards were taking an interest in what we were doing. It was one of many moments during my research in those years when I felt I was moving out onto unknown and possibly dangerous ground. I'm not sure what it was that made me fearful, whether it was the looming cellblocks and their inmates ahead of us or the prison guards behind us. Whatever it was, I felt extremely exposed out there in the middle of the dirt yard in the glare of the midday sun. A whistle from a guard stopped us in our tracks. Tedi went back to see what the guard wanted. When he came back, he explained to me that the guards would not prevent us from going into the cellblocks, but neither could they guarantee our safety if we went there. That gave us pause. Was it a warning or a threat? Should we trust in the protection of our inmate guides and follow them into the cellblocks or remain under the watchful gaze of the prison guards?

It was only later that I came to understand that out there in the prison yard, I had unwittingly become caught up in a strangely structured "culture of fear" (Barker 2009, 270): on the one side, an opaque world of criminality, territoriality, and fighting prowess, represented by the gangs in the cellblocks; on the other, a world of bureaucratic surveillance and policing, represented by the guards in the perimeter structure. Both are menacing in their own ways, and both lay claim to a domain of authority and the capacity to provide us with "security."

When the whistle sounded and I was forced to decide between venturing further into the shadowy world of the cellblock or turning back toward the prison's administrative offices, I chose the latter, availing myself of the more familiar "security" provided by the prison guards.

This book is about fear, policing, and state power. It is about everyday struggles over the authority to define threats and police society. Based on ethnographic research among police officers, vigilantes, and street-level toughs in the Indonesian city of Bandung, it examines how fear and violence are produced and reproduced through everyday practices of rule.

Vigilantism is when citizens take the law into their own hands, either to prevent illegal activity, investigate suspected offenses, or mete out punishments to those deemed to have committed a crime (Bateson 2021, 925). In Indonesia, vigilantism has been evident in high-profile cases involving members of radical Islamist groups who portray their acts as the prevention of, or punishment for, the sins of unbelievers. But it has also long been implicated in a range of more locally directed acts of violence that receive far less media attention: market vendors dousing suspected pickpockets in gasoline and setting them alight, neighborhood watch groups beating thieves, villagers killing those among them suspected of using black magic, and gangs seeking revenge for perceived offenses against their honor. On occasions like these, vigilantes act not in the name of the state but in the name of their neighborhood community, village, gang, political party, community of believers, or ethnic group. On other occasions, those committing vigilante acts are themselves state actors—police officers or members of the military, say—and the line between vigilantism and state-sponsored extrajudicial violence can often become blurred.

Such acts of vigilantism highlight an aspect of postcolonial state power that has been the subject of growing scholarly attention in recent years: the presence of a range of institutions outside the formal state apparatus that nonetheless claim some form of sovereign authority over their respective domains. In Indonesia, these institutions include neighborhood watch groups, gangs of toughs, youth organizations, militias, and private security guards. They are very important, particularly in the domain of policing, as they far outnumber the uniformed police, and their influence extends into nearly all areas of society. Historically, such groups have often been actively cultivated and supported by elements within the state who wish to appropriate their influence and further monopolize the means of violence and social control. However, even when pressured to operate from under the umbrella of some part of the formal state apparatus, such as the police or the army, these groups have often acted relatively independently of their state handlers, occasionally even standing in outright defiance of official authority. When one steps back and looks at the relationship between such groups and the state over time, the picture is of a complex dance of interdependencies, overlapping claims to authority, and shifting jurisdictional boundaries punctuated by periods of rupture and sometimes even violent confrontation.

This study focuses on this complex dance as it has played out in the city of Bandung, a major commercial and industrial center on the densely populated island of Java, in the sprawling archipelago of Indonesia. It is in part an analysis of the array of formal and informal institutions involved in policing—broadly understood—and their changing forms and relationships as Bandung developed from a tiny colonial outpost into a bustling postcolonial metropolis over the course of a little more than a century. During this time, the city went from being a small beacon of colonial modernity to being one among several Indonesian cities to experience intense urbanization and change as the country passed through convulsions of war, anticolonial revolution, ambitious nationalism, counterrevolutionary mass violence, a lengthy period of authoritarianism, and, eventually, democratization. How did the assemblage of institutions involved in vigilantism and policing adapt to these changes and to the city's changing political economy? Answering this question is important because, as I will show, these institutions have played a key role not only in the everyday violence associated with local vigilantism and routine policing but also in more diffuse episodes of violence in which local security concerns became enmeshed with national fears related to state or regime security. In such cases, it becomes difficult to distinguish between state violence and popular violence, with horrific results both in terms of number of lives lost and in terms of the development of an aura of impunity for the perpetrators of such violence.

A core contention of this book is that by looking closely at the assemblage of institutions involved in vigilantism and policing in Bandung, one can discern an underlying dualism and ongoing struggle between two opposing ways of imagining, constituting, and enforcing social order in an urban setting. On one side of this struggle is a modernist vision of urban order, defined and enforced through bureaucratic techniques of policing, surveillance, and social control. This is a form of governmentality[1] that involves the collection of data about the city and its inhabitants in the world "out there," the abstraction and arrangement of such data into fixed representations (maps, identity cards, blueprints, legal codes, etc.), and the effort to make the realities of urban society conform to these abstractions.[2] On the other side is what I call a *territorial* vision of urban order, in which the city is divided into semiautonomous fiefdoms, each overseen and protected by a figure of charismatic authority. This is a form of social order in which new fiefdoms are continually being constituted, existing ones are always open to challenge, and unstable hierarchies are established through demonstrations of superior prowess in the areas of fighting, spiritual cultivation, and mystical knowledge. Most often the modernist vision of urban order is enforced by those institutions seeking to rule over places and populations at a distance—in other words, by centralized states, colonial governments, occupying forces, and transnational institutions. Those seeking to establish and maintain a territorial system of fiefdoms, in contrast, tend to be people deeply enmeshed in the micropolitics of street life, such as gang members, local toughs, members of neighborhood organizations, and local leaders of ethnic groups and religious congregations.[3]

In most cities, the two modalities of understanding and enforcing social order coexist through an ad hoc recognition of the limits of their respective domains of influence. Precisely where that line gets drawn, however, varies. In many European and North American cities, for instance, technologies of modern policing are so ubiquitous and so powerful that the territorial order has been criminalized and pushed almost completely underground. Mafias and gangs are certainly active in some neighborhoods and economic arenas, but most people—especially in the middle and upper classes—can go about their daily lives more or less oblivious to gossip about the latest street-level rivalries. This can, however, change during times of crisis if the administrative and bureaucratic order of the city has been so weakened that the police lose their capacity to control the streets, as sometimes happens following natural disasters or during bouts of civil unrest. In such moments, territorial authority quickly emerges as one of the most powerful means of enforcing social order and community security. In such circumstances, the realpolitik of the street becomes something that even the wealthy can ignore only at their peril.

In cities like Bandung, by contrast, a social order of fiefdoms and vigilantism is not something that appears only in times of crisis. While such an order undoubtedly becomes more pronounced and visible during crises, it nevertheless endures in the fabric of city life, even during times characterized as normal. To understand why this is the case, it is necessary to examine the articulation and disarticulation of bureaucratic regimes of surveillance and control with local, territorially based regimes of community protection and self-defense. In this book, I study these dynamics by examining the genealogies of institutions, technologies, and practices used to enforce order and maintain security. These institutions include the notoriously corrupt Indonesian police, with their modern techniques for social control, as well as an array of "street sovereigns" (Kivland 2020b) who use magic, violence, and fear to establish their own domains of authority within the city and enforce their own visions of urban order.

While this book looks at various historical moments in Indonesia, its core aim is to develop an understanding of the dynamics of authoritarianism during the time of President Suharto's rule, known by the somewhat Orwellian moniker the New Order (*Orde Baru*). President Suharto was an officer in the Indonesian Army who came to power in 1966 on the pretext of restoring order after an alleged attempted coup by members of the Indonesian Communist Party, followed by army-instigated mass killings of up to a million ordinary Indonesians labeled "communists" (Roosa 2006). The New Order regime was in power for thirty-two years, and over this time, it assembled an elaborate security state undergirded by violent repression, ideological indoctrination, the co-optation of civil society, the construction of an enemy other, and the cultivation of fear. Institutions, technologies, and practices of urban ordering such as the neighborhood watch, the police precinct, the identity card, and the community punishment of thieves were key components of this authoritarian state assemblage. Yet if one looks individually at these components, both in terms of their historical genealogy and in terms of their constitutive social effects, it is evident that they have their own life and logic, which is not reducible to the larger assemblage in which they are embedded. In this sense, the authoritarian state should be seen not just as something constructed by the regime's leadership but also as an aggregated effect of the operations and momentum of its constituent components. As such, it both predates the New Order and has proven itself capable of outliving it.

My analysis of the building blocks of New Order authoritarianism has implications for our current global juncture. As this book will show, many of the institutions, discourses, technologies, and practices that were critical to the formation of an authoritarian state—fingerprinting, household registration, social cordons, cleansing operations, to name just a few—were first introduced during colonial times to protect against a pandemic; later, these policing technologies were adapted for use in domains beyond public health and played key roles in the New Order regime's repressive apparatus. Similarly, everyday territorial institutions like the neighborhood watch, which has long served as an embodiment of local solidarity and is by definition "of the people," came to be instrumentalized by the regime, both for coercive purposes and to endow state violence with an aura of legitimacy. At key moments, these different modalities of policing and social control combined with devastating results. While the circumstances today may be quite different, countries around the world have had to grapple with the effects of a pandemic that has led to the proliferation of an array of new surveillance technologies—only now, these are capable of reaching far deeper into the inner recesses of people's lives. And at the same time, many countries are witnessing the spread of militias and populist movements, which often define themselves in explicitly territorial terms. While these dynamics now play out with the amplifying effects of digital technologies, it is illuminating to take a fine-grained ethnographic look at an earlier moment, when technologies were mostly analog yet the same core forces were operative and sometimes came together with frightening consequences.

Vigilantism, Informal Sovereigns, and the State

> The fact is that the state has to be understood as an institution, of the same species as the church, the university, and the modern corporation. . . . And, like its sister institutions, the state not only has its own memory but

harbors self-preserving and self-aggrandizing impulses, which at any given moment are "expressed" through its living members but which cannot be reduced to their passing personal ambitions.

Benedict Anderson

As an institution, the Indonesian state carries with it many legacies of the Dutch East Indies colonial state. In the essay from which the above quote is taken, Benedict Anderson emphasizes how the New Order state was largely an attempt to resurrect the bureaucratic edifice that had been constructed by the Dutch colonial regime during the late nineteenth and early twentieth centuries, after a period in which it had been severely weakened by war, revolution, and the political turbulence of postwar state consolidation. This is certainly the case, as I will discuss, but it is only part of the story. Another part of the story relates to a characteristic of colonial states that has not always been fully appreciated, but which has received greater attention in recent years as scholars seek to understand the dynamics of postcolonial state power in countries across Africa, Asia, and Latin America: the fact that the territorial authority of colonial states was patchy and depended to a large extent on franchising out sovereign authority to other entities (Stepputat and Hansen 2005). This had several consequences, but for my purposes, I would like to highlight three important ones. First, postcolonial state authority does not adhere to the idealized Weberian image of a unitary, sovereign state with a monopoly on the legitimate use of force; rather, its authority can be characterized as "bifurcated" (Mamdani 2018), plural, fragmented, or multipolar. Second, the authority of the postcolonial state is often encumbered with a sense of being provisional and perpetually incomplete; as a consequence, further state building and projection of authority seems always to be required. Third, and relatedly, since sovereignty is something that comes into being only through performative acts, another characteristic of postcolonial states—and, indeed, of their colonial predecessors—is their frequent recourse to spectacular performances, as they seek to suture over their incompleteness and obtain public recognition of their authority.

The idea that the state is unitary and powerful is very widespread. Most of us are accustomed to thinking of the state as an entity that stands above and rules over society through an appeal to a transcendent law. In order to enforce this law, the state exercises, as Max Weber (1968) famously described, a monopoly on the legitimate use of force. A person who breaks the law is punished for their crime. But such punishment is not a form of vengeance perpetrated by the victim of this crime; it is an act performed by an ostensibly impartial state for the purposes of upholding the law. Both law enforcement and punishment are the sole prerogatives of the state, and they take place through its instruments: the police, the courts, and the prison system.

According to this long-standing conception of state power, when people commit acts in which they "take the law into their own hands"—or "play judge themselves" (*main hakim sendiri*), as the Indonesian saying goes—these are understood to be criminal acts. Such acts challenge the authority of the state since they represent the appropriation of violence by private actors. While this idealized view of state power continues to have a good deal of currency, the reality in many postcolonial settings is that the state does not enjoy a monopoly on legitimate coercive force and other groups are routinely involved in everyday policing and the administration of justice. To understand the dynamics of policing and urban ordering in such settings, we cannot focus exclusively on state power; we need to expand the frame to analyze who exercises authority, in whose name, and how (Buur and Jensen 2004, 7). In the case of Indonesian policing, this expanded frame brings into view an assemblage of institutions dispersed throughout all levels of society, including neighborhood watch groups, militias, and the like. Scholars have proposed various overarching terms for these entities, but the two that best apply to the Indonesian context are "informal sovereigns" (Hansen and Stepputat 2006) and "street sovereigns" (Kivland 2020b).[4] Like the state described by Anderson at the beginning of this section, these institutions also have memories and "impulses" of their own.

The fact that postcolonial sovereignty is dualistic or multipolar is due in large part to the fact that colonial state authority was so often delegated to village chiefs and other community leaders through various forms of indirect rule. In some colonies, including in the Dutch East Indies, the dualistic or pluralistic authority of the state was further accentuated by differentiation in the legal system, with "customary law" being applied to certain groups or regions, and certain domains of law, while a version of European law was applied in others (Mamdani 2018). How this differentiation worked, and how "native" or "indigenous" authority was characterized and structured, was itself shaped by the colonial encounter and the ways knowledge about colonized societies—including ethnological knowledge—was collected, interpreted, imagined, reinvented, and represented (Pemberton

1994). Lines were drawn based on some combination of territory, race, culture, ethnicity, or religion and enclaves of authority established accordingly. Sometimes these alternate centers of authority were respected and given an official seal of approval, and at other times, they were criminalized and repressed. Sometimes steps were taken to incorporate them within the postcolonial state, and at other times, they were excluded. In Indonesia, remnants of such dualism remain within the institutional structures of the state, in policing and in law, for instance, but the deepest effect has arguably been an underlying conviction on the part of state actors that effective governance is only possible through partnerships with extrastate institutions that are seen to be more deeply embedded within the fabric of society. While this conviction can create openings for new centers of authority to appear, and even to be accorded a degree of social legitimacy, it can also create a sense that the state has never fully arrived, that its authority is somehow provisional, and that more needs to be done to complete the state-building project, however defined.

Within this context, the performance of sovereign claims takes on added salience. Sovereignty can only come into being through performative claims, and colonial states were continually engaged in such performances, particularly in territories where their sovereignty was provisional and contested. As Danilyn Rutherford (2012, 4–5) argues, such performances are both unavoidable and fraught with risk, for they depend on recognition by others for their legitimacy. Like other forms of public address, such performances therefore invoke and attempt to call into being an audience, but in doing so, they may also find other, unexpected audiences or have their performances interpreted in unanticipated ways. For instance, a sovereign claim meant to induce in its audience a feeling of fear may go awry and cause the performer embarrassment. In postcolonial states, such performances of claims and counterclaims abound, constituting one of the key arenas for deciphering the relationship between states, informal sovereigns, and the wider public. States may use performances not only to assert their sovereignty but also to try to ground their sovereign claims ideologically in particular sources of legitimacy, such as by connecting these to an imagined precolonial tradition or to "the people." Sometimes this might mean identifying themselves with the kind of authority associated with informal sovereigns, while at other times, it can involve characterizing the latter as threats, criminals, or enemies of the state (Siegel 1998). For their part, informal sovereigns often engage in reciprocal performances that characterize their relationship, or desired relationship, to state power (Barker

2013, 260). To express an affinity with state power, they may replicate within their own institutions some outward attributes of the state—for example, its uniforms, organizational structures, idioms, or acronyms. Conversely, they may tell stories that represent the state as a terrifying outside imposition that is fundamentally alien to local mores, thereby seeking to ward off its encroachments. Sometimes what appears as an assertion of informal sovereignty may in fact be a performance designed to draw the state closer. Daniel M. Goldstein (2004, 3), for example, highlights how attempted lynchings of thieves in Bolivia serve as spectacles in which politically and economically marginalized urban residents, normally invisible, assert their forceful presence as a means to garner the attention of the state by publicly showcasing its absence in certain local settings.

When looking at dynamics between states and informal sovereigns, it is evident that postcolonial developments have introduced additional layers to these relationships, sometimes shifting their contours and their meanings. In some countries, the anticolonial struggle itself depended on the organizational capacities and coercive force of informal sovereigns, providing them with a new identity and adding new dimensions to their mythologies of power. For instance, people who in colonial times had been labeled bandits or gangsters became nationalist revolutionaries (Cribb 1991). In other conflicts, as in Liberia, grassroots civil defense groups have been mobilized by the postcolonial state to serve as a mercenary army and deployed across national borders (Hoffman 2011, 16). In Indonesia, similar groups have played key roles on both sides of various secessionist movements, either serving as a base from which to mobilize against the Indonesian state or being instrumentalized by the state as part of its counterinsurgency operations. Other studies have focused on democratization and neoliberalization, showing how these processes can transform the relationship between the state and informal sovereigns. Competitive electoral politics often fragment informal sovereignties as party leaders compete for alliances with brokers of street-level authority capable of mobilizing votes, while street-level sovereigns become more entrepreneurial as they seek out party patrons capable of providing them with something in return (Kivland 2020a; Wilson 2006, 2015). Under conditions of neoliberalization, as state power is thinned out, marginalized communities may assert and perform their sovereign authority in part to attract the attention of the absentee state and to find new ways of connecting with it (Goldstein 2004; Jaffe 2013; Kivland 2020a, 2020b). Another possible outcome is that gangs fill the void created by the retreat of the neoliberal state. According to Dennis Rodgers

(2006, 321), this is what happened in Nicaragua, where gangs were initially seen to provide neighborhood communities with predictability, order, and a sense of local belonging, but then evolved to prey on residents, instituting local "regimes of terror," a shift precipitated by their involvement in the drug trade. This more extreme outcome looks a lot like a neoliberal version of what Mahmood Mamdani (2018, 8) described as the colonial legacy of "decentralized despotism."

These examples show how malleable the institutional formations of informal sovereignties are and how their complex dance with the state is always being redefined as circumstances change. To fully understand this dance, however, it is not enough to trace the changing contours of the overall assemblage; we must also look more deeply at what Anderson called the "impulses" that motivate these institutions, at their internal dynamics and logics. Benedict Anderson (1990c) identified one of these impulses when he described Indonesia's New Order state as an effort to resurrect the late-colonial Dutch administrative state, an effort in which he sensed the impulse to rationalize, bureaucratize, and deploy modern technologies of rule. James C. Scott (1998) memorably analyzed a key part of this impulse in terms of the modern state's project of simplifying and making legible the territories and populations it governed, a logic of social control he described as "seeing like a state." Strangely, this fundamental aspect of state power is now often overlooked, perhaps because it has become so normalized and ubiquitous.[5] As regards the impulses that motivate the institutions of informal sovereignty, it is often through fine-grained ethnographic work that these are best understood. Philippe I. Bourgois's (2003) study of street-level drug dealers in New York City is exemplary in how it delves into cultural ideas of respect, histories of marginality, and street livelihoods and how these in turn shape gang life. Similarly rich ethnographies from other countries show the sheer variety such institutions take—in the scope of authority they assert, in their degree of formalization, in the cultural values that motivate them. But they also show many underlying commonalities—for example, the importance of territory, security, ideas of masculinity, and linkages to street economies.[6]

In this book, I approach the overall assemblage of the state and informal sovereignties as consisting of microregimes, each with its own particular logic, affective investments, ethics, performances, technologies, and repertoire of policing practices. In Bandung, these microregimes include, among others, the *ronda*, or neighborhood watch patrol, with its guardhouse and its slit gong; street gangs, youth groups, and *jegger* (street toughs), with their tattoos and magical powers; police archives, with their maps, identity cards, and blacklists of undesirables; and the police precinct, with its data room, its periodic "cleansing operations," and its holding cells. Some of these microregimes, such as the police data room and the identity card, derive from various modern governmental technologies that proliferated under colonialism, while others, such as the night watch and the tattooed body, lean more toward local and national genealogies.

The myth of authoritarian state power during the New Order held that each of these microregimes was part of a giant whole that was pyramidal in shape and unified in structure.[7] In the realm of policing, this myth was enshrined in official and unofficial government policies and practices that sought to co-opt informal sovereigns and put them to work for the ruling party, the police, or the army. There is no denying that these policies had real effects. The New Order established an "environmental security system" (*sistem keamanan lingkungan*) in which neighborhood watches, local toughs, and private security guards worked in close collaboration with the state. In most cases, these groups offered themselves up to be overseen and supported by elements within the ruling regime. However, even during the New Order, they sometimes acted relatively independently of the regime, or even against it, belying the pyramidal image. For example, it was not uncommon in Bandung for the police to decide against arresting a suspect whose neighbors threatened to avenge such action with a mob attack on a police station. In the wake of President Suharto's resignation, such assertions of local authority reached something of a fever pitch, and while they have moderated somewhat in recent years, they remain an important factor in everyday policing (Herriman 2006; Jaffrey 2019; Welsh 2008).[8] It is thus important to analyze the microregime of neighborhood territorial authority in its own terms, to see how this impulse for autonomy functions internally, as well as to understand how it sometimes comes to be incorporated within the broader state apparatus. The same is true for the other microregimes mentioned above; one must look closely at each, exploring its internal logic and its various structural transformations. By doing so, I will show how the two logics of rule I have identified—territoriality and surveillance—extend across the broader state assemblage, strongly defining some of its constituent elements while only weakly defining others. For both informal sovereigns and the uniformed police, much of what they do therefore involves navigating the tensions that arise between these different modalities of rule.

Policing, Surveillance, and Territoriality

The term *police* is commonly used refer to a public force involved in maintaining order and enforcing laws or regulations, but historically, the word also had a more expansive meaning, referring generally to the power to govern and to those acts aimed at creating an ordered society (Garriot 2013, 4–7). This broader understanding of policing was famously taken up by Foucault, who used it to describe a wide range of regulatory practices, including, among others, establishing spatial order, intervening in health and hygiene, defining criminality and illegality, and controlling populations (Foucault 1995). For this study, I follow Foucault's lead as I am interested in tracing the genealogies of Indonesian policing practices, many of which first emerged outside the institutional context of the police, either in local security practices or in biopolitical and surveillance projects of the colonial state. That said, I also focus part of my study specifically on the police as an institution, and on the practices of police officers during the New Order. As other ethnographers have noted, studying the routine practices of the police can be revealing of the logics of governance more broadly, as they are key mediators in a range of events, institutions, processes, and performances, providing a window into social and cultural orders (Haanstad 2013; Martin 2013). This is also true of informal sovereigns, who frequently position themselves in similar ways: both as enforcers of local order and as brokers between local communities and powerful outsiders.

When I first started this research, in the mid-1990s, Bandung was a city permeated by fear and obsessed with security. The most obvious manifestation of this obsession was the saturation of urban space with security guards. The entranceway to virtually every bank, supermarket, restaurant, factory, or government, university, or office building had a security post staffed twenty-four hours a day by uniformed security guards. In many of these places, the guards noted down information from the identity cards of all who visited; in factories, they body-searched workers at the end of every shift. In places without uniformed guards, one could still be sure that someone was earning money watching over security. Outdoor markets, bus terminals, sections of roads, parking areas, city squares, discotheques, brothels, and cinemas—all had someone whose job was to provide protection. Even spaces with nothing much to protect were usually guarded. For example, plots of land that had been taken out of cultivation but had yet to be developed into factories or commercial centers were often walled off and provided with security posts and full-time guards. Sometimes these secure spaces stood unused for years, empty except for the guards in their posts. The same was true of residential neighborhoods. To varying degrees, every residential area in Bandung was something of a gated community. Some neighborhoods had a surrounding wall and a guarded gate, like those found in the suburbs of many American cities; others merely had a guard post at the main entrance. In poorer areas, these posts were manned not by salaried guards but by residents of the neighborhood working in rotation. These guards spent the night patrolling their neighborhoods looking for intruders. Even with these night watches, however, families were very conscious of the need for household security. Those I lived with not only locked their outer gates and main doors but also their bedrooms, cupboards, and even telephones and refrigerators, if they had them. Nor was it uncommon for people to perform rituals to ward off thieves and other threats, for example, by reciting mantras and fasting so that one's house would be made invisible to anyone with malevolent intentions.

The tremendous local emphasis placed on security, moreover, was doubled by the presence of state institutions such as the police and the army. As a big city and a provincial capital, Bandung is home not only to several police precincts and district army commands, but also to city- and provincial-level police and army headquarters, as well as military training and education facilities. All these institutions are located within the city limits, and many occupy prominent real estate in the city center. Their buildings, many of which were inherited from the Dutch colonial period, stand as constant reminders of the central role the state's security forces play in virtually every facet of national life.

Despite this pronounced interest in security—or perhaps because of it—it was difficult to find someone who had not been the victim of a crime in the recent past. Everyone seemed to have a story to tell. Many of these circulated by word of mouth and focused on crimes that had taken place locally. Indeed, within hours of such an incident, everyone in the vicinity would know about it and many would claim to have the inside story on what exactly had happened and who was involved. Newspapers and magazines both capitalized on and cultivated this interest, giving crime stories a sphere of circulation that transcended their locality. Regional papers carried daily reports on robberies, rapes, murders, thefts, and arrests that had taken place in the city and province; national papers picked out the most shocking of these and distributed them throughout the archipelago. As James T. Siegel (1998) has described, almost all newspapers and magazines had a section entitled "Criminality" ("Kriminalitas"), and those seeking a wider readership often did so by dedicating more space to such coverage. In addition, private television stations often carried special crime bulletins alongside official government news broadcasts.[9] For North American or European viewers perhaps accustomed to a somewhat more sanitized form of crime reporting, these bulletins could be a bit shocking. Not only did they provide direct interviews with those in police custody accused of committing offenses (sometimes even showing police interrogations); they also did not hesitate to show corpses and to interview victims in the immediate aftermath of horrific crimes. These reports served to heighten people's awareness of the threats to their security, making them that much more conscious of the need for protection.

Both the police and informal sovereigns during the New Order justified their existence less in terms of law enforcement than as a matter of maintaining "security." The root word for security in the Indonesian language is *aman*, which can be translated as peaceful, calm, safe, secure (Echols and Shadily 1989, 14). Variations on the word can be used as a verb: *mengamankan*, meaning to secure, place in safekeeping, pacify; or it can be used as a noun: *pengamanan* or *keamanan*, which describe security guards of various kinds. As employed by the New Order state, the notion of "security" was inflected by related terms used by the Dutch colonial state. An overarching ambition of the colonial state was to establish what in Dutch was called *rust en orde*, tranquility and order (in Indonesian, *tata tenteram* or *tata tertib*), which was to be achieved in part through policing and in part by reinforcing certain elements of traditional Javanese statecraft and culture, which similarly emphasized the importance of calm and orderliness (Shiraishi 1990, 5–6, 186). Yet both during and after colonial times, much could be lost in translation. What Nils Bubandt (2005) refers to as "vernacular" concepts of security might mean one thing in the context of local communities and something quite different in the eyes of the government, and this gap often served to undermine rather than reinforce the state's overarching security discourse.

But the instability of this discourse arguably goes even deeper, for it is a discourse that so often seems to self-proliferate in the way it interpellates and affects people. This is illustrated by my opening story about the prison guards, where drawing attention to the question of security triggered in me and Tedi a sense of fear about possible sources of danger (*bahaya*) and thus a feeling of insecurity. (The Indonesian term for insecurity is *rawan*: restless, unsettled, sensitive, or disturbed—placing it in a slightly different semantic field than the English term, but similar in that it, too, may apply equally to a territory and to one's own emotional state, thus highlighting the reciprocal relationship between external condition and internal affect.[10]) The fear that comes with a feeling of insecurity engenders heightened vigilance and alertness (*waspada*) on the part of those affected and often leads to suspicion. As Patricia Spyer (2006, 206) has argued in her analysis of the dynamics of communal violence in Ambon, a city in eastern Indonesia, this sense that something bad could happen at any time can also lead to "a hyperhermeneutic—or a compulsive need to interpret and mine just about everything for hidden meaning, to see any trivial occurrence as a sign or omen of what might come." Under such conditions, people deploy "anticipatory practices" aimed at "short-circuiting" the feeling of unpredictability, and in so doing, ironically, sometimes feed the violence they fear (189). In sum, to understand the security state, it is therefore necessary to untangle this mutually reinforcing circuitry of policing practices and fear, security and insecurity. In doing so, we must also be attentive to domains where "vernacular" concerns about security are paramount and can have a logic of their own.

In the chapters that follow, I use the term "surveillance" to refer to a self-consciously modern logic that seeks to make the world "out there" legible and to make it correspond to an image, representation, or blueprint of order.[11] The city constituted through surveillance is therefore a panoptic city in which spaces and persons are subjected to the perpetual disciplinary gaze described by Michel Foucault (1995) and Michel de Certeau (1984). "Territoriality," in contrast, refers to a logic that seeks to establish an order grounded in a shared, habitual relation to a territory, and to instill in residents a social imperative to defend that territory against outsiders.[12] The city constituted through territoriality, then, is a city of distinctive locales, each watched over by a self-appointed and often charismatic guardian or protector.

By framing my analysis in terms of surveillance and territoriality, I aim to both renew and reframe two strands of late twentieth-century thinking about power and the state in Indonesia that have for a time been overshadowed by a focus on understanding post-Suharto democratization, decentralization, and oligarchic politics.[13] These strands analyzed both "traditional" ideas of power and the state dating from precolonial times (Anderson 1972, 1990a, 1990b; Errington 1989; Geertz 1980; Milner 1982; Moertono 1981; Wolters 1999) as well as modern forms of power associated with the late-colonial bureaucratic state (Anderson 1990c; Sutherland 1979). I view territoriality as an aspect of the type of power and unstable hierarchy associated with Oliver Wolters's (1999) "men of prowess" and Anderson's

(1990b) charismatic Javanese ascetics. This is a notion of inner power (*tenaga dalam*) as something substantial and as something that can reside in people (such as fearless fighters or ascetics), places (the abodes of spirits, say), and things (like amulets). Anderson (1990b) and Pemberton (1994) have described how in Java, such charismatic power was monopolized and endowed with a degree of stability over time by virtue of being overcoded with kinship structures and subjected to reproducible disciplines. They showed, in other words, how charismatic power was appropriated and re-tooled to provide the patrimonial state with added legitimacy. Leaders were charismatic because of who their father was or because they had access to mystical knowledge only available to members of the traditional Javanese court (*kraton*). My analysis, in contrast, looks at what has happened—and continues to happen—to the kinds of charismatic power that were not fully appropriated and remained at large in society. Specifically, I focus on charismatic power that gets invested in bodies and places, or what I call *territories*. To use Errington's (1989) and Keeler's (1987) terminology, I focus on the "potency" of territorial places and persons. Whether in the form of gang members' tattooed bodies or sacred spots within the cityscape, such potency allows for the constitution of social hierarchies that do not depend on recognition by the state for their legitimacy. Such hierarchies can be maintained even as practices of surveillance seek to deterritorialize bodies and places and install them in an abstract, state-controlled order of identities and addresses.[14]

While the abstract logics of territoriality and surveillance are evident in policing practices everywhere, precisely how they manifest varies greatly from place to place. In Bandung, there has been and continues to be a notable dualism in urban policing. The modern, centralized, and bureaucratic police force exists alongside an array of shadowy institutions, most of which are more informal, local, and charismatic in orientation. As indicated above, this dualism has its origins in the colonial period. Up until the early twentieth century, policing was organized locally according to general principles established by the government. Much of the day-to-day work of policing was done by local people who had no position in the civil service and were both unsalaried and untrained. They were local figures in the sense that their sphere of action, their responsibilities, and their authority were territorially limited and also in the sense that, insofar as they had connections to the government, their connections were usually to indigenous officials rather than European representatives of the Dutch colonial regime.[15] In effect, policing was part of a system of indirect colonial rule.

The move to create a professional police force was part of a broader effort on the part of the Dutch to establish more direct control over the colony and its peoples. Techniques of surveillance were integral to this effort and made their way into policing in two ways. First, they were used to reconstitute the police apparatus itself, scrutinizing existing policing practices, comparing them to an implicit ideal of direct, centralized control, and eventually effecting a transformation whereby the police were bureaucratized, rationalized, and subjected to new forms of discipline. This process began in earnest around the start of the twentieth century with the research and publication of several monumental studies about policing in Java and the reforms that subsequently followed. Second, surveillance in the form of mapping, fingerprinting, and the use of identity cards became the principal means of policing populations and territories. Such technologies emerged in a variety of domains—including that of health and hygiene—and only gradually came together to form a loosely integrated police surveillance system. What is now identifiable in Indonesia as the modern institution of the police is best viewed as the result of the combined efforts of subjecting the police apparatus to surveillance and employing surveillance techniques to police the wider population.

While the modernization of policing had profound effects, it never resulted in the elimination of older institutions and practices of policing. Like their colonial predecessors, postcolonial administrations continued to rely upon local figures for much of their policing needs. The Indonesian government has often claimed that this is because Indonesians have a culture of *gotong royong*: cooperation, self-help, and mutual support. Indeed, many of these self-help practices are very old. However, the history of community self-policing demonstrates that since colonial times the state has not merely celebrated such practices but actively enfolded and incorporated them.[16] This was especially true of the New Order regime, which made neighborhood guards an obligatory part of community organization and encouraged a vast expansion of privatized security services.[17] It also increased police oversight of these institutions by making the police responsible for training and integrating these services into the broader state apparatus of surveillance and social control (Barker 1999, 2001; Bertrand 2004).

The result was the "environmental security system" mentioned above, in which neighborhood watches, local toughs, and private security guards worked in close collaboration with the ruling party, the army, and the police. This arrangement had two notable advantages for the regime: it cost the government very little, and it created a citizenry that thought and acted like police. As one officer indicated to me during my fieldwork in a police precinct toward the end of Suharto's rule, under this arrangement, every head of household would learn to fulfill the function of a police officer.[18] With the demise of the New Order, the Indonesian government underwent significant decentralization and democratization, a process that resulted in multiple centers of authority in both governance and electoral politics. In this context, the fragmentation of coercive authority, often submerged during the New Order, became far more pronounced. Existing groups grew more assertive and new ones emerged on the scene, often defining themselves in explicitly populist, ethnic, or religious terms (Herriman 2006; Telle 2013; Welsh 2008; Wilson 2006, 2015). In this context, efforts by the state to mobilize neighborhood groups against perceived national threats, such as terrorism, have not always been effective, and local support has sometimes been made contingent on the implicit conferral of impunity for community-based vigilante acts (Jaffrey 2019).

In the chapters that follow, I try to elucidate the underlying logics of territoriality and surveillance, and how they relate to one another, across this dispersed field of policing institutions. By exploring the genealogy and logic of each modality of rule, I aim to shed light on how a street-level anticipatory politics of fear both interfaces with and diverges from a bureaucratic politics of fear, and how territorial practices of policing variously interact with or disrupt practices of state surveillance. In doing so, I draw attention to the very different kinds of fears and the very different senses of "security" that can underpin vigilantism and policing in the postcolonial city. I also show how, under certain circumstances, a coincidence of fear and violence makes it impossible to distinguish the police from vigilantes.[19]

Bandung: The Development of a Postcolonial City

Bandung is a large metropolis located on a plateau in the highlands of western Java, just a few hours by train or automobile from Indonesia's capital city, Jakarta. With an estimated population of more than 2.5 million people (more than 8 million in the broader metropolitan area), Bandung is the third-largest city in Indonesia.[20] It is the capital of the province of West Java and an important center of Sundanese culture (the Sundanese are the second-largest ethnic group in Indonesia). It is also a highly cosmopolitan city, with a dynamic youth culture and a large population of newcomers from across the archipelago, many of whom came to Bandung to study or work and subsequently took up long-term residence there. The mix of Indonesian cosmopolitanism and local Sundanese heritage is evident in everyday discourse in Bandung, which consists mainly of code-switching between the Sundanese language and the national lingua franca, Bahasa Indonesia.

The pattern of urbanization in Bandung and its environs over the last two centuries directly reflects the major political and economic shifts that have marked modern Indonesian history. For much of the nineteenth century, Bandung was a small town that served mainly as a remote outpost of a dualistic colonial government—Dutch and indigenous—in the middle of a large and highly fertile agricultural region. It was only in the latter part of the century that the Dutch East Indies government opened the region to private investment and wider settlement, leading to an influx of Europeans and ethnic Chinese, an expansion that was further enabled by the development of a railway connection to the coast. The timing of this new stage of urbanization coincided with the high modern period of colonialism, and the European plantation class around Bandung took advantage of the city's designation as a municipality, granted in 1906, to pursue a range of modernizing projects focused on making the city a beacon of colonial tropical modernity. Schools, churches, hospitals, and roads were built, the Bandung Institute of Technology (then called the Technische Hoogeschool) was established, and tourism was encouraged. These efforts culminated in the 1920s with a plan to relocate the center of colonial government from Batavia (Jakarta) to Bandung, which, although only partially realized, resulted in an influx of civil servants as several large government departments moved to the city. These developments, together with the city's growing manufacturing and service sectors, helped support a burgeoning middle class and establish Bandung as thriving cultural and economic center in its own right. Many residents of postcolonial Bandung look back nostalgically on the decades prior to the Second World War as the city's golden age, the "before times" (*tempoe doeloe*) when the city was still orderly and clean. But the legacy of the colonial period was very much that of a "divided city" (Low 2002)—racially and ethnically as well as administratively and spatially—even though the actual people living there, and their manner of living, often did not fit neatly into the boxes of colonial racial categories (Taylor 1983; Stoler 2010).

Part of the nostalgia for the "before times" is undoubtedly a reflection of the turbulence that followed. In Bandung, the period from the 1940s through the early 1960s saw a brutal occupation by Japanese forces, a series of revolutionary battles fought against returning Allied forces, and an influx of migrants from nearby rural areas escaping a thirteen-year conflict

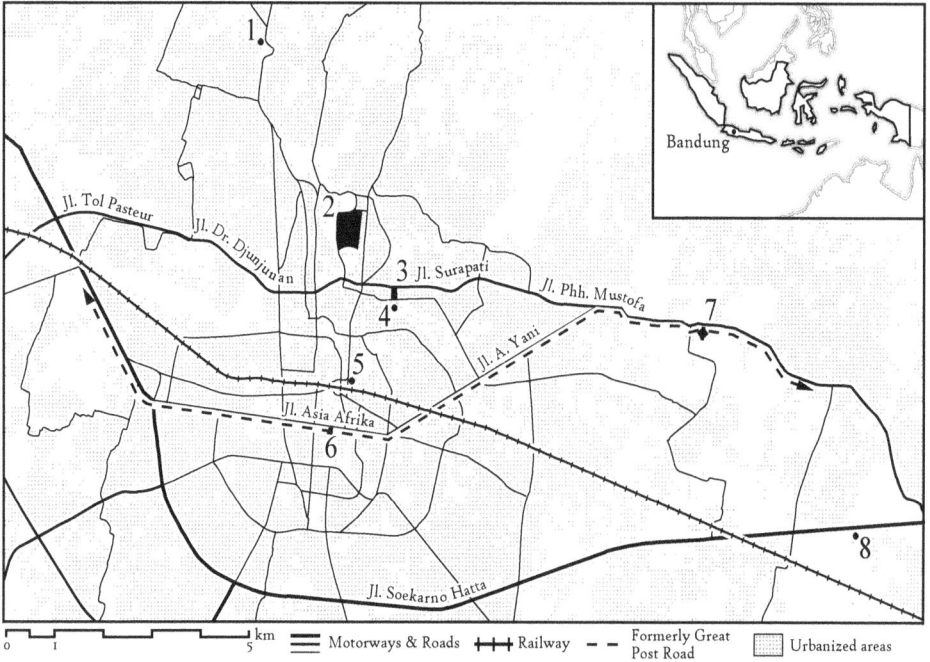

I.1   Map of Bandung. (1) Villa Isola, (2) Bandung Institute of Technology, (3) Gasibu Plaza, (4) Gedung Sate, (5) Metropolitan Police Headquarters, (6) Bandung Central Square, (7) Sukamiskin Prison, (8) Provincial Police Headquarters. Map by Geoffrey Wallace.

between the army and the Darul Islam rebellion. In each of these conflicts new lines were drawn and people were forced to take sides. Yet even in these years the city retained some of its reputation as a beacon of pluralistic modernity. This was perhaps most in evidence in 1955, when Indonesia's first president, Sukarno, chose it as the site for the famous Asia-Africa Conference, a gathering of leaders from newly independent countries in Asia and Africa at which the Non-Aligned Movement was first proclaimed. Sukarno himself was among the first non-Europeans to graduate from the Bandung Institute of Technology, and during colonial times, he had been imprisoned in Bandung for his nationalist activism. The building where the conference was held had been, prior to independence, a social club off-limits to non-European guests. The event thus served to signify the successful Indonesianization of formerly colonized Bandung while reinforcing and renewing the city's status as a beacon of pluralist modernity (Barker 2008).

While Bandung was spared the worst of the anticommunist violence of 1965–66, the city was fully incorporated into the broader push by the New Order regime to consolidate its power, erect a bureaucratic security state, and pursue its top-down economic agenda of "national development." For a time, campus-based politics at the Bandung Institute of Technology provided a platform for critical voices, but eventually even this modest level of dissent was stifled through changes to the institute's leadership and the deployment of a nationwide, antipolitical "campus normalization" policy (Akhmadi 2009; Lowe 2007, 117). More importantly, as a municipal center of government, as well as a provincial capital, the city became a key hub in the expanding military and administrative state. This was reflected in the city's built environment, with significant real estate dedicated to government offices, the military, and the police, as well as to a growing number of schools and universities. All these institutions required personnel, who in turn required housing, so there was extensive construction of new residential complexes, pushing the edges of the city further and further outward. This expansion was also bolstered by the structure of the New Order's state-driven developmentalist capitalism, which depended upon, and enriched, the country's military-bureaucratic elite (Robison 1986). The contractors, suppliers, technical experts, and others necessary to realize the government's developmental goals benefited from their proximity to this elite, and a state-dependent private sector subsequently grew up alongside the administrative state.

The administrative state was not the only colonial artifact resurrected in the postcolonial period. Industrialization also resumed in force, most notably in the textile sector, with large numbers of factories shaping the landscape at the southern edge of the city. These industries depended on a large pool of low-wage workers, mostly women from villages across Java, who migrated to the city and lived in densely packed dormitories and rooming houses in new "urban villages" adjacent to the factories. Migrants also made up the large workforce of construction workers, domestic servants, and drivers, who were needed first to expand the city and then to take care of its middle-class and elite households. A further legacy of colonialism was the ethnic divide that characterized this industrial development. Factory owners—like shop owners—were overwhelmingly ethnic Chinese and their workers almost all Sundanese and Javanese; class divides were thus overlaid by ethnic, linguistic, and religious differences. This led to an underlying social tension—sometimes erupting in anti-Chinese violence—that was productive for the security apparatus, both formal and informal, since owners of capital continually felt under threat and in need of protection.

This overall pattern of urban transformation in Bandung has never disappeared, but since the 1990s, it has seen layered onto it two new dynamics that have significantly altered the city's trajectory: Indonesia's democratization and the city's tighter integration into the megacity centered on Jakarta. Indonesia's move to democratize, which followed the Asian financial crisis of 1997 and resulted in President Suharto's resignation the following year, was spearheaded by a reform (*reformasi*) movement carried out on campuses and streets and helmed largely by students. In Bandung, the financial crisis precipitated a massive increase in the size of the informal sector, and with it the takeover of much public space in the city center by vendors of all kinds. The reform movement and the ouster of Suharto helped reinforce this takeover, at least initially, by pushing the army and the police off the streets and allowing the people to reclaim a range of urban spaces. Democratization also affected government, with competitive electoral politics yielding a more multipolar political constellation in the city just as a nationwide decentralization policy was devolving some powers to lower levels of government.

While over the years these changes had the effect of vitalizing city politics and making them more consequential, they arguably brought about only a modest change in the way state power actually functioned in the city. Furthermore, although in the realm of government the city was becoming more empowered vis-à-vis Jakarta than had previously been the case, this was taking place against the backdrop of a longer trend toward increased socioeconomic integration within the emerging Jakarta megacity region. This closer integration with Jakarta had a long history, but after the New Order it reached unprecedented levels as a flood of large-scale real estate investment transformed large sections of Bandung into shopping malls, outlet stores, cafés, restaurants, hotels, and apartment buildings for visitors, many from nearby Jakarta. The overall effect of this integration has been the economic and infrastructural deterritorialization of more and more areas of the city, even as the older dynamics of Bandung's urbanization continue to play out, albeit in areas previously thought to comprise its periphery.

Organization of the Book

In the chapters that follow I trace a path through a series of institutions and sites that are central to the policing of Indonesian cities, from neighborhood guardhouses to the tattooed bodies of street toughs, from colonial-era brothels and rat-infested homes to late twentieth-century malls and marketplaces, and from the captain's office in a police precinct to the city streets where a paramilitary campaign resulted in the killing of thousands of people labeled "criminals." In tracing this path, I introduce a cast of characters and describe their everyday practices: neighborhood watch guards out on patrol, neighbors relating crime stories, pickpockets policing their turf, toughs running protection rackets, colonial bureaucrats reconstructing the cityscape, vaccinators collecting fingerprints, and police officers taking bribes. I show how these characters use everyday policing technologies—which in the Indonesian context includes slit gongs, investigation handbooks, invulnerability spells, divination manuals, data rooms, and slang—as tools to both maintain urban security and reflect upon what security means.

The core of this book is divided into three sections, organized thematically and chronologically. In part 1, I draw upon a combination of historical and ethnographic evidence to describe how security is defined and operationalized in the territorial mode. Chapter 1 explores the range and flexibility of neighborhood territorial formations, from rather diffuse, egalitarian "societies against the state" (Clastres 1987) to rigid, hierarchical units that function as components of a broader state assemblage. Chapter 2 describes how territorial groups imagine threats to their security—thieves, strangers, challengers, and the state—and shows how they organize themselves to protect against such threats. While my engagement with the territorial mode focuses mainly on its more contemporary manifestations, I understand this mode as having its genesis in precolonial times.

In part 2, I use historical sources to construct a genealogy of police practices of urban surveillance as they arose within the context of colonial rule. Chapter 3 examines the emergence of surveillance in the context of Bandung's founding and subsequent development. It focuses on the way surveillance became a central part of the late-colonial vision of what a modern colonial city should be and traces the peculiar route by which the new conception of urban discipline and order reconfigured and reconstructed the cityscape. In doing so, it shows how Dutch colonists fantasized about the use of surveillance as a way to ferret out contagions and other threats to security, and how colonial subjects were implicated in this vision. Chapter 4 examines how surveillance was used to control populations, tracing the process whereby the police were subjected to surveillance, and techniques such as employing anthropometry, fingerprinting, spying, and using identity cards were integrated into police practices. Together these chapters show how the state used surveillance to control its territory and the general population in a manner that did not depend on local institutions and power structures. They also show how colonial fears often became centered on uncontrollable contagions and on those points where scientific languages and their blueprints of order failed to correspond to the order of things in the world "out there."

In part 3, I examine the development of postcolonial policing practices with a particular emphasis on the various ways that urban territoriality and surveillance articulated alongside each other during the New Order. Territoriality and surveillance involve very different ways of seeing and interpreting the world. To take one example (discussed in chapter 5), tattoos and fingerprints mean one thing within a system of bureaucratic policing aimed at the identification of criminals, and something quite different when seen from the perspective of a gang member interested in assessing the spiritual potency of a rival. Yet the reality of policing is that it involves a constant interplay between these two viewpoints. Indeed, the effectiveness of contemporary Indonesian policing—both in terms of its capacity to enforce order and in terms of its legitimacy—is dependent on a careful management of this interplay. In part 3 I discuss the symbolic and sociological dimensions of such management. Chapter 5 employs historical material to examine a decisive moment in the history of postcolonial Indonesian policing—namely, the paramilitary operation carried out in the early 1980s in which the New Order state sought to kill certain "figures of criminality" (Rafael 1999) on its watch lists. In this way, the state criminalized territorial figures while trying to appropriate their power to help buttress the authoritarian state. In combination with a program aimed at privatizing and regulating local security practices, this campaign subjected territorial fiefdoms to unprecedented state control. Chapter 6 then presents an ethnographic account of life in a police precinct in the mid-1990s. It shows how masculinist networks of corruption—what I call *fraternities*—allow the police to link formal representatives of the centralized, bureaucratic state to figures of territorial authority by a means other than surveillance,[21] and how the police, while continuing to practice surveillance and pay lip service to an "official" notion of security, use these networks to take over territorial power and exploit it for economic gain. Taken together, these two chapters present a picture of a postcolonial police apparatus with tremendous surveillance capabilities, albeit one whose predatory aspects increasingly trace fraternal and territorial lines. In the book's conclusion, I summarize my analysis of these different dynamics and show how postcolonial policing has unfolded in Bandung in the period since the end of the New Order.

Thoughts on Research Process and Positionality

> The ethnographer experiences fear at the same time as he learns how social control works.
>
> Didier Fassin

I conducted most of my field research for this book over a period of twenty-six months between January 1995 and July 1997, while the Suharto dictatorship was still very much in place. I then taught at the Bandung Institute of Technology from 1998 to 2001, where I saw first-hand the reform movement unfolding in the city. In the two decades since, I have conducted numerous shorter stints of fieldwork in Bandung, including a collaborative project on one of Bandung's main plazas that forms the empirical basis for the conclusion.

My experiences obtaining research permission for my initial period of intensive fieldwork helped shape my understanding of Indonesian policing. I received permission for my research only after months of screening procedures and after being interviewed by members of police intelligence at least twice. To the best of my knowledge, I was the first foreign researcher to conduct first-hand ethnographic research among the police. The dozens of hours I spent in various offices of the provincial and national police, waiting for signatures, getting photographed and fingerprinted, and chatting with officers at their desks provided me with my first exposure to the complex procedures involved in bureaucratic surveillance, especially as they were applied to what were then seen to be suspect populations like "foreigners" and "researchers." Being on the receiving end of these procedures gave me an appreciation for how deeply mechanical and routinized they were, and for the extent to which police work was dedicated to building and maintaining the police archive.

Once I received permission to conduct field research, I collected ethnographic data on the police using a variety of formal and informal techniques. At both the provincial- and city-level police headquarters, my interviews were mostly formal, although at the latter site I did have the chance to take part in a good deal of more or less informal conversation with officers from the Criminal Intelligence section. In most cases, I found the officers to be rather careful in their dealings with me. Partly because of this reticence, I did the bulk of my ethnographic work at the Cilengka Precinct.[22] It was there that I spent many long days and nights accompanying the police on their patrols; observing them interacting with complainants, witnesses, and suspects; listening to their stories; and hanging out. This did not mean my access was unfettered. I was aware of several occasions when I was deliberately kept out of conversations or conveniently left behind while officers went about some secret business. Furthermore, certain characteristics of Cilengka skewed the kind of data to which I was exposed. Although at that time approximately 3 percent of Indonesian police officers were women (International Crisis Group 2001, 7), there were no women posted to Cilengka. As a result, my discussion of the banter among men in chapter 6 reflects the deeply masculine and often chauvinist culture present in the precinct at the time. While I believe that this culture is prevalent throughout the police, I would expect that it manifested somewhat differently in offices where women were present on a daily basis.[23]

I faced similar challenges and constraints when conducting research at the Sukamiskin Prison, an experience that informs this study but is not a focus of any of the chapters. I was fortunate in being allowed to simply hang out in the cafeteria and the yard, mixing with the inmates and engaging them in conversation. Here, too, however, I was aware of many instances in which inmates were hesitant to talk and it would not have been appropriate or possible to press them. And again, because there were no women at this prison, I never heard first-hand stories about the violence female prisoners might be exposed to at the hands of the police.

My research outside the formal institutions of rule was subject to fewer constraints. During the time of my main research in Bandung, I lived in three different neighborhoods, all in the southern part of the city. One was an upper-middle-class housing complex that had been built in the 1980s and was home to people from a variety of ethnic groups, religions, and professions. Ethnic Chinese, Sundanese, and Javanese were all represented, and many had intermarried. Most breadwinners were active or retired businesspeople, high-level civil servants, and military types. It was not an exclusive environment like those found in the richer parts of Jakarta, though it was an environment where people left each other more or less alone. The other two neighborhoods, consisting largely of Sundanese or Javanese Muslims, were more typical of how a majority of Bandung's residents live. These were much more tightly knit communities, each centered on an extended family that had originally owned all the surrounding land. The higher-status figures in these neighborhoods were people who had succeeded in the civil service, though most of the inhabitants were factory workers, administrative assistants, mechanics, pushcart traders, or other small-scale merchants.

In addition to my work in Bandung, I conducted a shorter stint of research in Jakarta during the New Order, where I stayed in a boarding house on a back alley in the heart of Kota, which is historically an enclave for ethnic Chinese. The street-side homes in this neighborhood were all owned by well-to-do merchant families, though many of the families who lived in the back alleys were very poor. Dispersed throughout the neighborhood were dozens of boarding houses in which an odd assortment of people—office clerks, hairdressers, single mothers, second wives, night-club hostesses, gamblers, drug addicts, fences, and drug dealers—lived together cheek by jowl. Much of my local ethnographic data comes from observations of life in these four communities and discussions with the people I came to know in them.[24] While these communities are certainly not representative of all of Indonesian society, they are fairly representative of the kinds of communities one finds in many of Java's big cities.

Primary textual sources on postcolonial crime and policing were not easy to come by. Fragmented and incomplete reports produced by the army and the police from all over West Java were available at the provincial archive. This helped me understand how the police fit into the broader governmental and military security apparatus, as it was possible to see how the reports moved up and down through the bureaucracy. With local data I was more fortunate in that the Cilengka Precinct had a nearly complete set of case files for the past six years as well as copies of administrative reports. This archive proved very useful for understanding the anatomy of recent crime in the precinct and for seeing how the police make a case. Secondary published sources based on first-hand research of crime and policing in Indonesia are also relatively rare, though the police college in Jakarta had thousands of theses written on such topics in its library. Some of these are based on personal experience or on first-hand research, and thus were quite informative. Moreover, since they date back to the late 1960s, they provide an unusual glimpse into how police interest in particular problems changed over the course of the New Order period. In a similar but more critical vein, some excellent theses were also available in the University of Indonesia's Department of Criminology. Historical materials about crime and policing, and about Bandung's history, were collected at several local and personal libraries around Bandung, at the National Archive in Jakarta, the National Library in Jakarta, the Royal Netherlands Institute of Southeast Asian and Caribbean Studies, and Cornell University's Kroch Library.

When publishing ethnographic accounts, anthropologists often face ethical dilemmas about how to report on what they have learned. Other ethnographers of policing have noted how this field of inquiry in particular places the ethnographer in a difficult position ethically, as the researcher so often needs to conceal from interlocutors what they are thinking and how they are feeling (Fassin 2017; Herbert 2017). In my research, many of the things I heard about and observed involved acts of violence. In one particularly disturbing case, which I discuss in chapter 6, I was present in the next room during a violent police interrogation of a teenaged boy. At the time, I was frightened and unsure about what to do, and I did not directly intervene. In other cases—discussed in chapter 5—interlocutors told me about past killings they claimed to have perpetrated or taken part in. I have sometimes been told that anthropologists have an ethical or a political obligation to act as advocates or representatives of the people they study. While this may be appropriate for those anthropologists who focus on marginalized and oppressed populations, this does not make sense for a study like this. If anything, my ethical responsibility is to advocate for the victims of violence, including those who are dead, rather than to advocate for the police and others with whom I worked. In this study, I advocate for victims in the way I know how, which is not by uncovering and exposing individual culpability but by analyzing and describing the mechanics and mechanisms of rule that help produce and reproduce cultures of fear and violence.

In order to derive this systemic aspect, I relied on the willingness of countless people to participate in the research by sharing their daily lives with me. To provide them with some degree of anonymity, I have changed the names of interviewees, interlocutors, and research sites. In addition to my use of pseudonyms, this book has a few other stylistic features that should be mentioned. In the chapters that follow, extended textual citations are distinguished by the standard indentation, while field note citations are italicized. Field note citations may include my own descriptions, observations, paraphrases of oral statements, and quotations. Direct quotations within the field note citations are always placed in quotation marks. In paraphrasing people's statements, I did my best to provide a rendition of what people said, in the order they said it. In some cases, field note citations have been modified slightly from the originals to make them grammatically correct and intelligible to English-language readers, or I have included bracketed interjections. In both field notes and textual citations, translations from Dutch and Indonesian into English are my own.

PART ONE

TERRITORIALITY

P.1　　Javanese guardhouse, circa 1853–56. [*Wachthuis = Corps de Garde Javanais*]. By August van Pers and C. W. Mieling. Courtesy of Southeast Asian and Caribbean Images (KITLV) under CC License (https://creativecommons.org /licenses/by/4.0/legalcode). Available at: http://hdl.handle .net/1887.1/item:855331.

1

Ronda

The Neighborhood Watch

Proximity and neighborly contact are the basis for the simplest and most elementary form of association with which we have to do in the organization of city life. Local interests and associations breed local sentiment, and, under a system which makes residence the basis of participation in the government, the neighborhood becomes the basis of political control.

Robert Park

My interest in the neighborhood watch came about as a result of irritation. In the middle-class neighborhood where I lived for several months in the mid-1990s, the night guard would pass by and strike the metal electricity pole just outside my window as I was drifting off to sleep each night, producing a loud clanging noise that would jolt me out of my sleep. For a time, this nightly occurrence came to stand for all my frustrations at living in an environment where peace of mind was so difficult to come by. Then I began to wonder what function this practice could possibly have. As I questioned people, the first thing that became clear was that the electricity poles were standing in for a slit gong.[1] The second thing that became clear was that there was no single answer as to what purpose this practice had. The replies I received included (1) it is music that the guard plays "just for fun" (*iseng*); (2) it is to warn off potential thieves and robbers by indicating that the neighborhood is being patrolled; (3) it is to ensure no one sleeps too deeply by periodically waking them up; (4) it is to communicate back to the guardhouse that the patrolling watchman is still there; (5) it is a call to the owner of the nearest house, who is then supposed to reply with a shout, and perhaps give the watchman something to drink; (6) it is a method of timekeeping. As I will show below, each of these replies speaks to a particular aspect of, or moment in, the constitution of the neighborhood as a territorial subject. This subject may at times have a kind of looseness and playfulness—a relatively soft consistency—while at others it may develop a hardened consistency and exhibit a strong sense of its social purpose and importance.[2]

The culture and history of Indonesian policing is inseparable from that of the neighborhood watch, or *ronda*, its oldest institution. Typically consisting of male heads of households or their sons, the *ronda* is a civilian guard who patrols the environs of a village or neighborhood.[3] Its members take turns participating in the watch, which means that each of them has to perform the service anywhere from once a week to once a month. The number of guards on duty in a given neighborhood on any one night may range from just a few to over a dozen. While the neighborhood watch is not the only means for creating identification among the residents of Indonesian cities, it is important because it provokes a strong identification with a territorially defined neighborhood and calls forth a sense of underlying community solidarity.

There are other means of creating identification among local communities, of course, including attendance at mosques or other places of worship that bring local people together on a regular basis. There are also neighborhood shops and stalls (*warung*), where people buy their daily rations of food, candy, and cigarettes and where they routinely exchange local gossip and news. But while these places could certainly function as focal points for establishing local solidarity and shared opinion, none serve to strengthen the territorial community in quite the same way as the neighborhood watch does. Religious congregations only represent certain elements of any given neighborhood and residents usually have more than one place of worship to choose from. Furthermore, it is not uncommon for people to choose to pray on their own or to join congregations somewhere outside their neighborhood. Some do not pray at all. Similarly, any given neighborhood will have several shops and stalls, each with its own group of regular clientele. These small businesses are in competition with one another and the choice to shop at one stall rather than another is more often used as a means to differentiate oneself from certain of one's neighbors—especially those of a different economic class—than it is to emphasize community solidarity. The neighborhood watch, in contrast, carries with it an obligation that every household in the neighborhood participates. It is, then, the only institution that effectively brings together all the households in a neighborhood, regardless of their religion, ethnicity, or class.[4]

Given how the *ronda* is organized, one might expect that it would lead to a highly gendered form of neighborhood solidarity. As noted above, the people who perform the service are almost always men. Women are neither invited nor pressured to take part in the patrols. However, as will soon become apparent, the formation of a territorial subject does not ultimately depend on personal participation in the patrols. The neighborhood watch is not merely a form of routine association; it is, above all, a form of policing. As with any kind of policing, it aims to produce effects not just among those who participate in it but among everyone who falls within its sphere of authority. In the case of the *ronda*, this means everyone in the neighborhood, both women and men.

The Slit Gong, the Guardhouse, and the Patrol

The *ronda* is a very old institution. The term itself, a loanword from Portuguese, reportedly entered local languages in Java during the sixteenth century (Pinto da França 2000), but it is quite likely that the institution of the neighborhood watch predates the colonial era.[5] The use of the *ronda* for everyday policing, either on its own or in conjunction with a salaried police force, has been a feature of village, town, and city life throughout Java for the entire modern period. While there has been a tendency over the past century or more for wealthier and privileged communities to avoid their obligatory watch service by hiring their own guards, the neighborhood watch is still ubiquitous in rural Java and is still common in the island's urban areas. While since the early twentieth century there has been a steady growth in the authority and penetration of the state's professional police force, the *ronda* and other community patrols remain key features of the policing apparatus.

In modern times, the neighborhood watch has typically been organized at the level of the smallest unit of government administration. During Dutch colonial rule, this meant it fell under the authority of village heads in rural areas and under the authority of the captains or heads of quarters in cities. Since the Second World War, in urban areas, it has been organized at the level of neighborhood associations, each consisting of an agglomeration of several dozen households. These associations, known as Rukun Tetangga (neighborhood association) and Rukun Warga (residents' association), were introduced during the Japanese occupation of Java and were modeled on an administrative system used in Japan (Niessen 1995, 125–27).[6] During the period of my research in Bandung, the person responsible for overseeing the *ronda* was either the head of the neighborhood association or a person designated by him or her to be in charge of neighborhood security.

The heads of neighborhood associations are often people who have earned a degree of respect from their communities, either by virtue of being among the oldest residents of their area, by being civil servants, or by having been to Mecca on the hajj. It was not uncommon for the person charged with overseeing neighborhood security to be a member or retiree of the armed forces. Generally, however, neither the head of the association nor the head of security was likely to be a person with much political or economic clout. Administering the neighborhood watch involved keeping a roster of heads of households and the days they had agreed to fulfill their obligation to participate. In the late nineteenth century, before the penetration of the bureaucratic state, this roster was often memorized using oral poetry or was written on a palm leaf. In addition to keeping this roster, the person in charge of the *ronda* was usually responsible for keeping track of an inventory of tools, making sure the guard post was maintained, and establishing rules for the frequency of patrols and their routes.

Historically, the *ronda* has been composed of a relatively stable assemblage of technologies and practices, and it is defined especially by two core technologies: the guardhouse and the slit gong. Each of these has passed through many incarnations and gone by many different names, depending on where and when it was being put to use. The guardhouse is variously known as the *gardu*, *pos ronda*, *pos kamling*, or *pos keamanan*. It is the post where members of the neighborhood watch gather when they are not out patrolling. It takes a variety of forms, depending on the amount of money or work community members are willing to put into it. In its minimal form, still common in rural areas, it is a small building made from wood planks, lengths of bamboo culms, and a thatch roof. It might measure about two meters by three meters, and it often sits a meter or two off the ground. Usually, it is closed at the back and partially open on the sides and the front. The front has a doorway through which members climb into the structure, and inside there might be a bench for them to sit on; otherwise, they just sit on the floor. In cities, guardhouses are often more permanent and costly structures. Many are made of brick, sit directly on the ground, and are furnished with chairs. Some of the fancier ones are even equipped with televisions and internet.

The slit gong is an instrument that hangs in the doorway of the guardhouse. It goes by various names—*kentongan, tong-tong,* and in some local languages *kohkol* or *kulkul.* It can be made of a variety of materials, including bamboo, bronze, and various kinds of wood. A wooden slit gong is made from a hollowed-out tree branch with a slit down its length. The slit is about one-fifth the diameter of the branch and stops short of the ends of the instrument. The gong hangs from one end in a vertical position. To produce a sound, the instrument is struck with a stick. This sound varies according to the material used, the length or width of the slit, and the size of the gong. Slit gongs can be as long as a hand or longer than a human body. Some are simple while others are carved with ornate decorations. One of the more common variations evident in Java today is a gong that has been carved in the shape of an armless and legless man. Thus, above the slit a head is carved, replete with eyes and a nose, with the body of the instrument serving as the man's trunk. At the bottom of the instrument, beneath the slit, a shallow hole is carved out where the drumstick can be inserted such that it protrudes as an erect phallus.

Guardhouses, with their hanging slit gongs, are important elements of the jumble of structures that compose Indonesian cityscapes (Kusno 2006). Every neighborhood has at least one, and sometimes more than one, placed in a strategic location. In Bandung, residential neighborhoods are commonly arranged such that there is one main access point to a nearby thoroughfare and several minor access points to more distant arteries. When one is given directions, these are described not in terms of an abstract grid but with reference to this main access point, from which one enters *into* the neighborhood. Such entry points are important sites for the mediation and control of movement between neighborhoods and the rest of the city. It is through them that almost all traffic moves, and where rickshaw drivers

1.1   Slit gong in West Java, 1931. *Tong-tong in de Botanische Tuin te Buitenzorg* by Th. Metz. Courtesy of Southeast Asian and Caribbean Images (KITLV) under CC License (https://creativecommons.org/licenses/by/4.0/legalcode). Available at: http://hdl.handle.net/1887.1/item:737954.

and motorcycle-taxi jockeys congregate and vie for passengers. Guardhouses are also generally located at these sites, or at a location from which one can see a couple of different points of entry into the neighborhood. In special cases, they may be located somewhere else. In one place I stayed, for example, residents told me that thieves tended to come from the poor neighborhood across the river. The guardhouse was therefore built along the border of the river rather than at one of the four places where one could enter the neighborhood by car. In general, however, the guardhouse is one of the first things one sees when entering a new neighborhood.

From their gathering place in the guardhouse, members of the watch keep an eye on any traffic that comes within their field of vision.[7] This traffic typically includes residents, visitors, and passers-by, as well as a steady stream of ambulatory traders and performers, among them, people cooking and selling fried rice or satay, recyclers buying old newspapers and books, garbage collectors, vegetable sellers, bird sellers, buskers, clowns, monkey performers, and more. With the aid of strategically located speed bumps (so-called sleeping policemen) and gates, all this traffic is slowed and rerouted to facilitate inspection. The guards I spoke with in Bandung generally had an impressive ability to pick out details about people that might indicate a threat. They might notice a person because he or she was a stranger to the neighborhood (*orang asing, orang tidak kenal*)—that is, someone who was neither a resident nor a regular visitor. They could determine this even though there was usually a fair amount of traffic passing by. More frequently, they described threats in terms of movements that gave cause for suspicion (*gerak-gerik yang mencurigakan*). It could be the way someone walked, or the way a car paused, that drew the guards' attention. One finds similar descriptions in police reports from citizens who have caught a thief red-handed: it was someone's peculiar movements that aroused the witnesses' suspicion in the first place.

The guards extend this way of seeing beyond the guardhouse when they patrol. As they walk or cycle around, they check the streets and each of the houses in their territory, looking to see that everything is in its place. At night, this means making sure things are not left outside a house's fence, gates and doors are closed and locked, curtains are drawn, and there are no strangers skulking about. On these outings, guards may bring along a portable version of the slit gong, striking it as they go. At the time of my research, the hollow sound it produced was one of the few sounds to be heard in the neighborhood at night.

Territoriality and Place

The slit gong, like so many other tools/arts in Indonesia, blurs the line between functionality and expression. Just as the national martial art, *pencat silat*, can be seen either as a fighting technique or a dance style, so can the slit gong be used for both pragmatic and artistic applications; an example of the latter would be Sundanese musical performances (*calung*). But some-times these uses are joined, and it is not unheard of for the slit gong to feature as a musical instrument during the long *ronda* nights. Unlike dur-ing the *calung*, however, this is done "just for fun," as an elderly gentleman with fond memories of the *ronda*'s music once told me.

Such music, although just for fun, is nonetheless important. At night, when the sounds of work disappear and things retreat back into the shad-ows, the slit gong appears as a song that keeps the darkness at bay. The song is little more than a gathering together of sounds into a rhythm, as the slit gong does not produce many tones. Yet this gathering of sounds creates an ephemeral order: a tempo in the night. The player traverses the neighbor-hood, giving coherence not just to a temporality but also to a milieu—a loosely defined sense of place—in which all the nearby dwellings are drawn together by these shared sounds. Following Gilles Deleuze and Félix Guat-tari (1991, 311–22), I call these settings *milieux* because they are only weakly constituted assemblages and do not have the hardness and power of a dis-crete territory. The creation of milieux is playful and expressive, lacking the seriousness and intentionality associated with the creation of territories.

A song played on the slit gong creates a milieu by provoking a new kind of awareness, but it does not necessarily incite vigilance or assert possession. The *ronda*'s milieu only becomes "territorialized" when the sound becomes a mark used to stake out a territory.[8] It might be, for example, that the song or the beats take on a particular character specific or exclusive (*khas*) to that place.[9] The song is *khas* in the same sense that a regional food or costume is *khas*: it gives expression to an exclusive constellation of qualities. Food that is *khas* to the Sundanese ethnic group, for example, is made from local products and cooked using local implements. Music that is *khas* to a given place uses the instruments and styles particular to that milieu. As the music comes to stake out a territory, it creates a sense of both interiority and exte-riority. For anyone intending to intrude, the beats thus signal a territorial claim. It is in this sense that the sound of the slit gong is heard as a warning to thieves and robbers that the neighborhood is guarded.

The slit gong is not the only way of expressing this warning, however. For those who, say, feel themselves to be particularly at risk from intruders, it has sometimes been recommended that they stay awake at night singing and telling stories (Quinn 1975, 50). Indeed, there are particular rhythms and mantras that might be used in such circumstances. One such mantra is found in a book called the *Kitab Mantra Yoga*, and begins as follows: "There is a song to be sung while keeping watch at night, guaranteeing the singer and listeners strength and freedom from sickness, keeping all misfortune at a safe distance, putting fear into spirits and demons and rendering magic spells ineffectual. Criminal acts and the designs of evil men will be as fire extinguished by water, and the rapacious burglar plotting against us will be struck with sudden misadventure and vanish" (quoted in Quinn 1975, 51). The *Kitab* recommends that this mantra be sung in a loud voice using the *Dandanggula* meter, which according to George Quinn (1975, 50), "creates a relaxed atmosphere suitable for easy narrative." Moreover, "if it is sung after midnight its power is much increased, and it will turn back criminals and others of malevolent intent. If it happens that a burglar plans to break into a house, and while on his way there he hears this . . . being sung he is certain to cancel his plans for that night because he knows that if he goes ahead he will meet certain disaster" (quoted in Quinn 1975, 50). Unlike the mantra, however, the beating of the slit gong is not primarily about marking a territory in relation to threats from the outside. Thieves might in fact be helped by the sounds of the slit gong since they would know exactly where the patrolling guard is located and thus would not have to worry about being caught unawares while breaking into a house. The slit gong finds its key territorial function, rather, in being an activator: it activates territorializing forces and keeps them vigilant. It does this by preventing people from sleeping too deeply, by keeping them alert and attentive. A colonial government report on policing from the early twentieth century describes this function of the *ronda* and the slit gong explicitly:

> Almost everywhere patrols traverse the villages at night, making people vigilant or waking them up with all sorts of hubbub, and making certain that all is in order. Frequently such wakefulness is the occasion for the discovery of a thief digging under a house [to steal something from beneath];[10] one time the *ronda* trapped a thief busy digging a hole. Also, people who are under suspicion receive a search from the patrol in the middle of the night in order to see if they are home or off on some obscure adventure. (Dutch East Indies 1911, 158–59)

If Freud is correct that one of the functions of dreams is to prevent people from waking up, the slit gong performs the opposite function: it prevents them from sleeping. But even when they do sleep, and dream, people are not always free of the slit gong and its call for vigilance. During my time in Bandung, many of the dreams people related to me concerned acts of theft.

It would seem that even when they were asleep people remained anxious about the consequences of relaxing their vigilance.

Perhaps because of this function, when one hears the slit gong at night, one does not necessarily feel relief that the neighborhood is being guarded. On the contrary, the slit gong can serve as a reminder of the various threats that could be lurking outside in the darkness. One thus thinks about whether all the curtains are closed, and doors locked, and whether anything has been left outside by mistake. As the *ronda* guard passes through the neighborhood, striking the slit gong, he thus activates a whole series of territorial relationships that might otherwise have slipped into abeyance.

Territories are not only places. In the next section, I will further explore the logic of territoriality by examining local oral and textual sources relating to sacred places, bodies, orientations in space, and periods in time. In each case, it is possible to identify a "territory" that is understood as a domain to be watched over, taken over, or occupied. Specific forms of specialist knowledge pertain to each of these territories, and some people even talk about cultivating a "sixth sense" to help them understand the powers and vulnerabilities particular to a given territory.

The Magical Power of Territories

> Examples do exist of territories conceived in the image of the human body, but the inverse—the body conceived as territory—is very widespread.
>
> Marc Augé

What does it mean to activate territorial relationships? In Bandung, one can identify two examples of contexts in which territorial relationships are fully activated: the invulnerable (*kebal*) body and the sacred spot (*keramat*). The invulnerable body is such by virtue of being protected by specialized mystical knowledge and spells, known as *ilmu*.[11] This mystical knowledge activates territorial relationships by giving the body an interiority that is by definition unmarkable or impenetrable by foreign objects. One becomes invulnerable in one of three ways: by being made so by a powerful person like a curer or sorcerer (*dukun*); by going through a series of rites like reciting mantras, fasting, and submerging oneself in water; or by carrying or wearing an amulet (*jimat*), which might take the form of a magical piece of writing, a tattoo, or an item of clothing that has been invested with mystical power.[12] The result is that if one is shot, stabbed, chopped, or struck, no mark will be made, no penetration of the skin will occur, or sometimes no pain will be felt. A young lawyer, for example, told me that when he was in high school he went to a sorcerer in Tasikmalaya to be made invulnerable. The sorcerer recited some mantra and touched his body. When this was done he took a machete blade and cut a piece of paper with it to demonstrate its sharpness. He then chopped and sawed at the lawyer's arms and chest, which caused pain but left no mark at all. Needless to say, people with such a power instill great fear in their enemies and are shown respect by the people around them.

This fear and respect should not lead one to think that the invulnerable body is invincible. It can in fact be penetrated, but one must master the arts of mystical knowledge to do so. Police and criminals alike talk in terms of "finding the weakness" (*mencari kelemahannya*) of a given art of invulnerability. A policeman I talked to, for example, told of how he had once tried to beat up a robber with a metal pipe, only to see that it had had no effect whatsoever. The policeman then searched for information on which art of invulnerability the man was using. Having apparently gained that information, he consulted a sorcerer who was able to identify the fatal flaw of that particular art. He then returned to beat the robber, but this time, he used the twig of a palm leaf. The robber fell and writhed in pain, later claiming that each touch of the twig had brought a horrible burning sensation.

If the invulnerable body is one example of a fully activated territory, another is that of the *keramat*. As sacred spots, *keramat* are "anthropological places" (Augé 1995, 42) par excellence in that they are animated by a private geography of spirits and supernatural powers. Both within the city of Bandung and its surrounding regions there are dozens if not hundreds of well-known sacred spots, some of them tourist attractions. Usually located on a mountain or off in a forest or in a cemetery, these are places to which pilgrims trek in search of special powers. Often marked by a water source, a grave, or a tree or stone that is unusual in some respect, such sacred spots are activated territories not visible to ordinary people, and for this reason, they are capable of exerting their powers over anyone who passes by. To avoid inadvertently being possessed by a spirit, people in Bandung often recommend that any trip to the forest or cemetery should be preceded by a request for permission to enter (the same term is used upon entering someone else's house: *punten* or *permisi* [if you please]). Otherwise, one's entry will be interpreted as a challenge (*tantangan*) to the power of the resident spirit. Moreover, one should never urinate in these places for that draws the ire of spirits. Most sacred spots are watched over not only by a spirit but also by a gatekeeper (*jurukunci*). This person lives nearby and takes care of the sacred place. It is the gatekeeper who holds the "key" to the place, so visitors who come in search of special powers must ask him what offerings need to be made to the spirit and what requisite actions must be performed to have their wishes fulfilled.

Sacred places and the pilgrims who search them out are the stuff of folktales throughout Java.[13] The Sundanese author Mohammad Ambri relates a number of such tales in his 1932 book entitled *Munjung*.[14] The book depicts conversations between men at a guardhouse during their night on the *ronda*. They are dreamy conversations, following associations, drifting from story to story, and from teller to teller as people come and go from their turns patrolling. Their talk, however, centers on a single theme: how so-and-so got rich or beautiful by making a pact with a spirit. One man, for example, relates a story about a neighbor who turns into a pig and steals loose change from nearby houses. Another tells of a spirit providing money that, when spent, will return double its value. A third describes a man who receives money from a person so tiny he is able to slip through any hole that a ray of light can pass through, allowing him to break into houses to steal money.

The most interesting tale, for the purposes of understanding sacred territories, is that of two men, Istam and Suta. Both went off in search of a sacred spot where it was said one can marry a spirit and become rich. Upon arrival, they met with the gatekeeper, who took them through the forest to the destination of their pilgrimage.

> When they arrived at a large stone, the gatekeeper stopped and said, "Here is Sanghiang Lawang [the name of the sacred spot]. We must first burn incense here while scattering offerings of money, as much as you want, one or two cents if you wish. While I burn the incense the two of you must close your eyes." "Alright," they both replied. Istam really closed his eyes, as the gatekeeper had ordered. But Mr. Suta did not. Rather, he gazed upward, watching two sparrows hopping together as if in love. When the gatekeeper invited them to walk onward, Istam opened his eyes. His view had changed. What was called Sanghiang Lawang was a huge gate, with a straight, wide road leading to an immense palace. (Ambri 1977, 21–22)

The two entered but the spirit received only Istam for marriage. When they left,

Istam was very pleased, because he had got what he wanted, he would be rich. When they had passed out of Sanghiang Lawang, he looked back, but all that was visible now was a thick forest, the straight, wide road to the palace could be seen no longer. All that could be seen in the direction of the palace was a pointed, rocky mountain. As for Mr. Suta, he just shivered, saying nothing to Istam or to the gatekeeper. Since leaving, what he saw had not changed; on the way there and on the way back it was just the same. At Sanghiang Lawang he had not seen the wide straight road. (23)

In this story, Istam was capable of establishing an alliance with the spirit by virtue of his ability to perceive the mystical power of the territory. This form of perception was not available to Mr. Suta, whose attention was distracted by the hopping sparrows. The ability to perceive that a person or thing has been marked by a territorializing power is the result of concentration and an unhesitant will. In each of Ambri's tales of journeys to sacred places, the gatekeepers test the pilgrims' resolve.

In Bandung, training in how to attain this concentration and strength of will forms the basis of many self-defense courses. Those who take such courses are taught how to use this concentration to develop their "sixth sense," one that allows them to perceive whether an object, person, or space is "filled" (*diisi*), and if not, how to fill them oneself. This is akin to having an eye or a nose for territorial power. One guru demonstrated this sixth sense to me by having a friend of mine who was his student "fill" one of two spoons. Out of sight of the guru, the student concentrated his energy on one of the spoons, effectively activating his territorial relationship with it. The guru was then given the spoons; by passing his hand over them, and using his sixth sense, he could identify which of the two had been filled. He explained that the practitioner of this art must be careful because others can sense this power. If one strays into someone else's territory, it may be taken as a challenge. In such circumstances, he advised, one should name one's guru so as to avoid problems. Such advice suggests that students are safest when they display the imprimatur of their gurus, just as a neighborhood is safest when it is activated and marked by the sounds of a slit gong.[15]

In the supernatural realm, if a person wishes to constitute a territory, or to find its weakest point and thereby enter it, they will likely make use of the aid of a specialist. Such specialists can create effects like those found at a sacred spot, or he or she can make spaces invulnerable. A sorcerer, for example, can be asked to perform rites aimed at keeping a specific household territory secure. One such rite makes a house invisible to anyone with the intention of breaking in. Another makes the thief confused after he enters the house, making him wander around in circles until the owner returns and releases him. There are also specialists capable of casting spells, known as *sirep*, on houses that cause their occupants to fall into a deep sleep, making it much easier to remove valuables.

Specialists are not the only repository of mystical knowledge relating to the security and vulnerability of particular territories. Such knowledge may also be available in divination manuals known as *primbon*.[16] *Primbon* are pragmatic tools that emphasize the likely outcomes of particular actions; they can be used by thieves to discover whether or not a burglary on a particular day will be successful, whether there is a danger of being caught or injured, which direction they should escape in, and which mantras or spells they ought to use to increase the likelihood of their success. Householders, for their part, can use such texts to determine the days and times that they are particularly vulnerable to theft, to find out whether or not it will be possible to recover stolen items, and to help them locate items that can be recovered.

While the arts of divination in Java are quite arcane, there is one aspect in particular that I would like to highlight here—namely, the ways in which they conceptualize space and time. When one reads divination manuals, one is confronted with a sense of time that is not linear, singular, and empty, but rather cyclical, multiple, and qualified. Time is measured using a variety of different calendars. In addition to Christian and Islamic calendars, there are various Hindu Javanese ways of tracing time cycles. One is the *wuku* calendar.[17] This calendar, which has no clear ties to either a solar or a lunar cycle, differentiates between ten separate weeks, ranging from a one-day cycle to a ten-day cycle. Any single "day," in this system, thus has ten different names depending on where it falls within the cycles of the ten respective weeks. The system also recognizes and names cycles of five- and seven-day weeks. For instance, there are thirty seven-day weeks, called *wuku*, and each has a proper name. A month in this system consists of a thirty-five-day period during which these five- and seven-day weeks complete a single cycle of their combinations.[18] Moments of cyclical coincidence are central to this mode of reckoning time and are often invested with ritual significance. Even ordinary days, weeks, months, and years have specific meanings. These are sometimes reflected directly in their names, which may refer to deities, mythical characters, prophets, spirits, angels, and animals. These figures are guardians of their particular temporal cycle, and it is they who invest time with its particular qualities. These can be startlingly specific. For example, a *primbon* for burglars provides the following information about the characteristics of the period overseen by the prophet Ibrahim: "[This is] a good time for the execution of any criminal enterprise, success is assured. Good news received at this time will turn out to be true and bad news will turn out to be false. Anyone committing crimes at this hour will leave behind no incriminating clues. The criminal who successfully commits felonies at this time is a professional, polite and unobtrusive in his everyday behavior, of medium build, with a fair skin and a clear but slightly hoarse voice. Goods stolen at this hour will never be recovered."[19]

Guardian figures also inform the meanings attached to spatial orientations. The four cardinal directions, and the eight subcardinal directions, are a common means of dividing up and classifying space.[20] These directional categories are often named after mythical figures or gods whose qualities they are said to reflect. The orientation of different things (houses, fences, slopes in the land, water sources, trees, etc.) with regard to these directions and to each other gives them particular values. For example, a fence built around a house may be segmented into nine units on each of its four sides, and each of these units associated with a figure. The placement of a gate in a particular segment may mean "many visitors," "strong-willed," "troubled by thieves," and so forth (Kumar 1985, 24–25). In a speech to an association of indigenous police officers in 1927, a prominent Javanese police officer explained this way of understanding crime and security as follows:

> My people are Javanese and many express their fear of crime in "social" terms like building a house. First they choose to have their plot of land sloped to the east, which is called moelio manik and "slidono," which means prosperous; land that is sloped to the south is called "glagah tinoenoe" and that to the west "sono ngaloep." A person who lives on that kind of land is certain to be in danger, especially of theft. Also in constructing a fence there are calculations according to the front; if the length of the fence falls "sengoro" then it will certainly be easy for a thief to enter and difficult to get any help. Also the gate of the fence, according to "karang songo" calculations, has to be chosen carefully so that [the house] is safe from catastrophe. (Widjojoatmodjo 1927, 3–4)

One of the most powerful figures to give meaning to temporal and spatial relationships is the *naga*, a dragon-like creature that stands guard over each day at a particular point in the compass. The *naga*'s protection rotates on a daily basis, so each day has a particular, predictable directionality. Quinn (1975, 42) cites a *primbon* that states that for someone planning to commit a crime in a distant area, it is best to travel in the same direction as the *naga* is facing, for if you travel toward it, it will "gobble you up."

The above examples shed light on what a territory is and how it is constituted. In each case, a territory—whether it is a place, a body, an orientation in space, or a period in time—is described as something that is capable of being inhabited, occupied, or watched over. The key relation that must be maintained is between the inhabiter and the inhabited, the occupant and the occupied, the guardian and the guarded. A territorial mark, such as the sound of a slit gong in the night, expresses an active relation between occupant and territory, as does the inability of an outsider to mark or penetrate the territory (at least without being subjected to the adverse effects of territorial power). This active territoriality constitutes a territorial power that is perceptible to those who utilize their sixth sense, who then have three possible orientations toward it: one may submit to it, one may challenge it, or one may search for its fatal flaw. As each territory has its own particular characteristics, orienting oneself in one of these three ways may require the acquisition and mastery of specialist knowledge.

Ethics and Effects of Territoriality

When a territorial relation is not fully activated, it invites challenges. The term frequently used for such a state of affairs is *kelengahan*, or inattentiveness—a condition that thieves and tricksters frequently prey upon. Daydreaming is one of the most common expressions of inattentiveness. As one elderly gentleman explained to me, when a person daydreams (*melamun*) their body is empty of thoughts (*kosong*), "like a car left with its engine running but without a driver." Such emptiness is dangerous because, like the car left running, it invites occupation by another. Possession of someone's body by another spirit is described as an accidental or unintentional entry (*kemasukan*).[21] To prevent this spirit possession, a person who is daydreaming will almost always be chastised for it in a tone of voice that calls them back ("Ei, don't daydream!," or just "Ei!" and a clap of the hands).[22] The same goes for a house: it, too, may be *kemasukan*—for example, by a thief. But the thief will not succeed at breaking in if the house is already fully occupied. The following story, told to me by an engineering student, Ujog, illustrates the relation between inhabitation—or what I would call *presence*—and security:

Last night Ujog stopped by. He and Titik got to talking about ghosts. Ujog told a story about how the house he has in Kopo has a ghost that watches over the house. When he bought the house, the former owner explained that the house was guarded (dijaga) *by a spirit* (mahluk halus), *so even if it were left empty and unlocked, it would be safe. Last week a thief broke in* (maling masuk) *but was caught because the house was protected.*

In Ujog's neighborhood, they have a ronda, *which is organized on a rotational basis. That night, two of Ujog's friends were taking their turn at the* ronda. *One would stay at the guardhouse and the other would patrol around, striking the slit gong as he went. When he passed Ujog's house the first time he didn't see anything unusual. On his second round he saw his friend, who was meant to be on duty at the guardhouse, outside Ujog's house. When asked why he had left his post at the guardhouse, his friend answered that there was a thief in the house, and told him to get the people* (masyarakat) *to surround the house. Ujog's friend on patrol ran back to the post to gather people together. However, when he arrived, he was shocked to see the same friend waiting at the guardhouse. "How did you get here so fast?" he asked. His friend replied that he hadn't gone anywhere—that he had been there the entire time. At this point, Ujog's friend on patrol figured that it must have been someone else who had warned him. The two friends then got people out to encircle the house. Some of the people went in to catch the thief, who was then beaten by the crowd. When he would try to get up someone would come over and say, "You're a thief, yeah?" and then hit him again. By the end of it the thief's face was completely wrecked* (hancur). *After the incident, Ujog's friend on patrol started wondering who it was that had given him the warning. There was nobody else on the* ronda *that night, and he was sure he had recognized his friend at the time. He realized that it must have been a spirit taking the form of his friend in order to warn him, so that he wouldn't be afraid.*

Here, the slit gong in the hands of the patrol does for the house what "Ei, don't daydream!" does for the body: it calls forth the occupant, pulling them into a state of vigilance by making them fully occupy their territory. Hence, when the guards make their rounds, people wake up and think about their house and its security, or sometimes, ghost-guards appear and express their awareness of a thief. In the case of Ujog's house, the guarding presence was strong enough that the thief who entered became confused and sleepy:

When the thief was handed over to the person in charge of security (ke-amanan), *a man from the armed forces, the thief described how he had gone in with the desire (niat) to steal but quickly became confused. He had entered through the roof, but once he was inside he could not figure out how to get out again as the door was locked. And then he got really tired and wanted to go to sleep. Finally, when he was about to try to leave he looked out and saw that the house was surrounded. At this time however, Ujog recounted, the people hadn't even yet arrived. It was the spirit again.*

What I find particularly striking about territoriality in the Indonesian context is not so much its supernaturalism as the impermanence of the territories activated. It is as if territorial claims do not "take" very well to things, tending instead to fade away if not repeatedly renewed. This can be seen in a number of very different circumstances. Take, for example, the case of movable possessions. Although laws of private property provide for ownership until such property has been legally transferred, there is a strong custom that goods not attended to may rightfully change hands. It is not unlike the kind of ownership that pertained to swidden rice fields in the time before freehold land tenure: one's possession of a field depended on one's keeping it cleared. If it were left fallow and began to grow out again, someone else might come along and take it over. Similarly, in contemporary Bandung, if one takes insufficient care of one's things—for instance, leaving them out in the living room rather than keeping them hidden in a cupboard in one's room—they may well go missing. And one can only blame oneself for being careless. In addition, if one lends something to someone, one cannot expect that it will be returned. It could well be that it receives great care from the borrower and ends up de facto becoming theirs (I know of cases in which goods as large and as valuable as cars have changed hands in this way).

Anna Tsing (2003, 32) refers to this sort of ownership claim as a "charismatic claim," in contrast with a bureaucratic claim. In the forests of Kalimantan on the island of Borneo, charismatic claims on honey in the wild depend on repeated visits, maintenance, and the telling of stories about one's journeys to the particular bees' nest to which one is staking a claim. Without this constant care, maintenance, and narration, one's claim of ownership will be "forgotten" by others. In the terms I have been using here, this kind of charismatic claim is what defines territorial relations. The primary territorial relationship can be described as one of *presence*. This presence may be rendered in natural or supernatural terms, but its structure remains the same. On a day-to-day basis, this presence makes itself felt through qualities that evidence a care for, or attentiveness to, one's surroundings: responsive eyes, a well-groomed garden, "things in their place," and so forth. In this regard, it is suggestive of a certain kind of ethical relation to the place one inhabits and the things or people one considers one's own. If these territorial marks and this relation are not maintained and cultivated, presence dissipates and the territory loses its consistency. The ringing of the slit gong, in keeping people vigilant, functions to prevent this loss of consistency.

Interpellating the Territorial Community

There are times when the slit gong, in addition to activating relations of territoriality, also demands a response. These can vary. As the *ronda* guard passes in the night, the inhabitant of a house might reply with a shout—"On guard!" (*jaga*) or "At the ready!" (*siap*)—to indicate that he or she is awake and alert. Some *ronda* guards also hope that their ruckus will be answered with an offer of some coffee, cigarettes, and snacks. On the one hand, such interactions can be understood as a form of surveillance in which those inside the house are themselves deemed suspicious. For instance, during the colonial period, ex-convicts used to be subjected to special monitoring by the *ronda* to make sure they were in their houses and not out making trouble.[23] This monitoring was done first of all by the placement of a special black mark on the ex-convict's house to distinguish it from those nearby. Second, each time the neighborhood watch passed by ringing its slit gong, a reply from the occupant would be noted by placing a token on a board by the house to indicate that it had been checked and that the occupant was home. Village regulations would dictate how many times the *ronda* had to pass by the house each night, and the village head would check these tokens in the morning to make sure the job had been done. On the other hand, these interactions can be read less as an effort to surveil the occupants of the house (or, from the opposite perspective, the *ronda* guards) than as an expression of a suprahousehold territoriality. That is, as long as the neighborhood watch serves only to activate territorial ties, and does not demand a response, the neighborhood as a whole has the characteristics of a milieu rather a discrete territory; it is little more than a clumping together of household territories (as when the *ronda* music was just for fun, and had not yet become a *khas* song). But when the slit gong demands a response, the households are made to signify their belonging to a larger territory. In this sense, the slit gong serves the same function as the standard policeman's hailing—"Hey, you there!"—described by Louis Althusser (1971, 163). This act of acknowledgment or recognition places the individual in a subject position. The call of the slit gong likewise interpellates the household and its members, establishing them as territorial subjects. The response indicates that the household, as an element of the neighborhood, is being cared for (just like the trimmed lawn indicates a certain level of care). In this new configuration, the territory of the household is functionally subordinated to the larger territory of the neighborhood.

The subordination of the household territory to the neighborhood territory is expressed in the form of a debt relation. The neighborhood watch is not the primary mechanism for extracting this debt, but it does play a part. For example, we have seen how the call of the slit gong demands a response from occupants of the household and that the response may be in the form of a shout, or it may comprise an offer of coffee, cigarettes, or food. But on special occasions, the call may demand more—say, cooperation in refurbishing the guardhouse, paving a street, or dredging a canal. Indeed, the slit gong is sometimes used to call forth the population in extremely elaborate ways. A particular pattern of strikes might bring people out with particular tools, or it might indicate the presence of a specific threat for which residents ought to prepare (Ahadiat 1994). In some parts of Java and Bali, the pattern of codes has at times been extremely sophisticated, with a particular signal for every imaginable danger. I've been told that in Kediri, Java, there is a special signal for a danger that can be sensed but whose form is not yet apparent. Henk Schulte Nordholt (1991, 84) provides an interesting example of such coding from the nineteenth century, when village heads used the slit gong to warn villagers about government officials or police who were coming to search for stolen goods. Hearing a particular signal, local people would know which goods ought to be hidden away to avoid confiscation. In this case, the slit gong functioned to protect local thieves by providing a language through which they could warn one another of the danger of the colonial state.

The more specific the slit gong's warning, the more it functions as a medium of communication rather than purely as an activator of phatic territorial relations. When used as a wake-up call, the sound of the slit gong serves the latter function, leaving the determination of threats and the character of responses to individual territories. As an instrument for conveying warnings and orders, however, the slit gong is capable of calling forth very particular forms of collective action.

The use of the slit gong for communicating calls and warnings need not be restricted to a single neighborhood. Long before the introduction of clocks into peoples' homes, for example, villages and neighborhoods throughout Java and Bali were using the slit gong to mark the passing of an abstract and universal time. Similarly, before the advent of the telephone, news of a fire could be carried almost instantaneously across long distances by way of the slit gong, which was used to relay messages from village to village and from neighborhood to neighborhood. The efficacy of such communication should not be underestimated. At the turn of the century, for instance, a Dutch official found the slit gong to be a most effective way of catching water buffalo rustlers. Within a very short time of a theft being reported, as many as ten thousand people could be mobilized to catch the culprits (Dutch East Indies 1907, 8).

At certain historical junctures, the slit gong, the guardhouse, and the *ronda* have also functioned as instruments for the mobilization of a broader sense of political or territorial belonging. Many nationalist groups either grew out of *ronda* associations or made use of these associations to help recruit and mobilize their followers. Takashi Shiraishi (1990, 43–46) has documented how the Sarikat Islam, one of the earliest nationalist groups in Java, emerged out of *ronda* organizations. In this context, policing techniques used by the *ronda* were put to use in new ways. For instance, the system of placing signs on houses, previously used for the surveillance of criminals, was refashioned into a system for indicating which Sarikat members were quarreling and thus in need of a mediator. The Sarikat Islam also used the slit gong to call people out to political rallies and to disseminate messages. Near Surabaya, the group set up its own guardhouses and established patrols on farmer-occupied lands as a means to support their claims against European businesses (Bloembergen 2004, 2007).[24] John Smail's (1964) analysis of the revolutionary struggle in Bandung shows a similar pattern. He notes that many Indonesian youth paramilitary groups, seeking to prevent the Dutch from reclaiming the city from the departing Japanese occupiers, originated in *ronda* associations. One of his interviewees described it thus: "It was a spontaneous thing, a product of banging on the gong at the ward office and shouting 'Siaaap!' [Ready!] Those who came were the [defense force]" (93–94). More recently, during the post-Suharto period of democratization and political reform, political parties of various stripes took to constructing new guardhouses throughout the country in the lead-up to elections (Kusno 2006). These guardhouses, dubbed communications posts, served both as gathering places for local party activists and as a means of staking out territorial claims within neighborhoods and villages—guardhouses were often painted in party colors and covered in the party logos. All these examples suggest that the neighborhood watch, the guardhouse, and the slit gong, with their capacity to mobilize people and to relay communications across distances, have the capacity to provoke individual identifications that transcend the village, the hamlet, or the neighborhood. While not of the same scale as the "imagined community" of novels and newspapers (Anderson [1983] 1991, chaps. 2–3), the materialities of slit gong communication do allow for the formation of a sense of translocal territorial belonging.

When the slit gong functions as an instrument of communication rather than an activator or marker of territoriality, it enters into a whole new series of relations. This difference is reflected in the choice of two, quite divergent, designs. The first, called a *koprek* in Sundanese, is a small instrument that the *ronda* guards carry around on their patrols. It is used to ward off thieves by flagging the territory and to activate multiple household territories by bringing them into a rhythmic relation with one another. It creates a soft or more loosely integrated territory with less consistency and no obvious center. It also serves to keep people awake and vigilant, but does not bring them out of their houses. The second design, called a *kohkol* in Sundanese, is a body-sized instrument that hangs in the guard post or in front of the village head's house. This instrument creates the center of a hardened form of territory with a strong interpellating function. When used for communication, it can also serve to link adjacent territories. Yet, being fixed and immobile, this instrument is in a sense "deterritorialized," meaning that its significance is defined by its place in a system of communication and power operating on a different plane. It is capable not only of relaying and distributing messages but also of utilizing a language of charismatic power to consolidate territories and to call forth their inhabitants.

Territoriality and the Neighborhood

In its "simplest and most elementary form" (Park 1968, 26), neighborly association gives rise to a loose gathering of people and their environs into a particular type of social setting. The sense of looseness and playfulness that can characterize this kind of social setting—what I am calling a *milieu*—is evident in the form of neighborly association established by *ronda* guards when they play songs on their slit gongs. They activate a sense of collectivity and shared place without giving it a definite shape or claiming exclusive possession. Such a place takes on the consistency of a territory only when a clear zone of interiority and an occupying presence are evident. An occupant creates this sense of interiority by activating or establishing a relation with "something" specific,[25] a relation that is evidenced by marking, care, and attention. It is an impermanent relation, and lack of regular attention will allow the territory to lose its coherence and dissipate or perhaps be taken over by another occupant. There is thus a purposefulness about the territory that the milieu lacks.

Despite their differences, however, territories and milieux do not oppose each other, but rather respond to each other. The territory represents an insistence that the milieu take on a firmer consistency, just as the milieu is constantly breaking off pieces of territories and loosening them up to create new milieux. Those who plant and care for a garden may do so to indicate they are fully present in their household, but the garden can take on a life of its own, sending its seeds beyond the confines of the fence and engendering new relations between territories. Similarly, people may turn on exterior lights in front of their house to show that it is occupied at night, but seeing all the lights along a street may give someone the idea of putting together a whole light show, with multicolored lights hanging from bamboo poles all the way down the length of a street. The lights thus break off from the territory and gather together to create an expressive milieu. Just for fun.

The technologies and practices of the *ronda*—the guardhouse, the slit gong, and the patrol—are constitutive of people's sense of the relations between individual, household, neighborhood, and nation.[26] They help define how people in the city situate themselves within the broader urban and social fabric. There are times when neighborhood-level territorial sentiments in Indonesian cities have been very strong, and times when they have been somewhat weaker. Generally, however, people's sense of belonging to a particular neighborhood—with all the obligations this implies—is strong in Indonesian cities.

One reason for this strong sense of belonging may be that territorial claims of rights and obligations tend to enjoy a level of legitimacy that other kinds of claims, such as those based on citizenship, gender, ethnicity, religion, class, or political affiliation, do not.[27] To put it in philosophical terms, there is in Indonesian cities a "metaphysics of presence" (Derrida [1974] 1998) that privileges territorial over other forms of subjectivity. Territorial subjects are seen to be more basic and primordial than other subjectivities and therefore more natural and more legitimate.[28] There is no reason why this needs to be the case. However, as long as the *ronda* remains a core institution of neighborhood life, it is more than likely that the metaphysics of territorial presence will be maintained.[29]

2

Neighborhood Fears, Vigilantism, and Street Toughs

The territorial subject created by the neighborhood watch is not benign; it is prone to fear and prepared to commit acts of vigilante violence. In most cities in Indonesia, it is not uncommon for ordinary citizens to take the law into their own hands or to "play judge themselves" (*main hakim sendiri*). The archetypal form of such vigilantism is the beating or lynching of suspected thieves by members of neighborhood watch groups and passers-by. Other common examples of community vigilantism include the public stripping and humiliation of adulterers, the murder or expulsion of local people accused of witchcraft, and the violent defense of the neighborhood against criminals, gangs, the police, and other perceived threats. Not all such violence is perpetrated by the neighborhood watch or local residents. In some neighborhoods, particularly in those areas where there are business interests, those who take the lead in community policing and protection may also include local toughs, gangs, youth groups, or militias.

To understand why ordinary urban residents are willing to take part in vigilante violence, it is necessary to look more closely at the fears that animate neighborhood life and capture peoples' imaginations. As Teresa P. R. Caldeira (2000) has shown in her ethnography of postauthoritarian São Paulo, one way of learning about cultures of fear is by analyzing everyday discourse. Through the "talk of crime" and other kinds of speech, people name their fears, thereby reducing their anxieties by making certain threats legible. At the same time, such talk may also serve to relay fears from person to person, particularly in cases where the name given to such fears is incapable of containing or displacing the full force of the anxieties it represents (Siegel 1986, 272–75). As in any kind of othering, the names or figures people use to objectify threats—like "terrorist" or "criminal"—rarely if ever represent exactly what it is that frightens them. Rather, they function as convenient containers for any number of phenomena that challenge or undermine the prevailing logics of social and symbolic ordering.

Such names and figures are much more than discursive constructs, however, because they are inseparable from regimes of policing and punishment. Just as the identification of the "juvenile delinquent" as a category of criminality in eighteenth-century France was inseparable from a whole series of practices aimed at normalizing and resocializing delinquents (Foucault 1995), local constructions of threats are also only comprehensible when situated within regimes of local policing. It is not that threats are created through discourse and are later subjected to policing; rather, policing is the means by which these threats get defined.

In this chapter, I consider two figures representative of outside threats that stand at the core of neighborhood policing practices: the thief and the phantom state. It is against these two figures that neighborhood vigilantes often define the sovereignty and autonomy of their territorial communities. The thief is a figure made to stand at the center of a spectacle of collective violence that performatively constitutes a realm of informal neighborhood sovereignty. The phantom state is a figure that graphically highlights the perceived dangers of surrendering neighborhood autonomy to outside powers. An examination of these two figures sets the stage for consideration of a third figure, the street tough, or *jegger*, who comes from outside the neighborhood and installs himself as its informal sovereign.[1] For those in the neighborhood, the *jegger* is an ambivalent figure—someone who is worthy of fear but who may also serve as a guardian against outside threats. He may be a vigilante, but he is *their* vigilante.

The Thief

The thief is arguably the most talked about criminal figure at the neighborhood level, and it is above all the protection against thieves that provides the neighborhood watch with its raison d'être. The full interpellative power of the slit gong is thus most evident when it beats out the rhythm signifying that a thief has been spotted: people of all kinds come out of their houses at a run. Even just the sound of someone shouting "thief!" (*maling*) will yield the same effect. Indeed, thieves are the most despised of creatures in the neighborhood and on the streets. According to a number of inmates I spoke with at Sukamiskin Prison in the mid-1990s, it is easier to return to one's community after serving time for murder than it is after serving time for petty theft.

Thieves may operate individually or in gangs. A sense of how such gangs are formed and organized is provided by Marlan Akip's (1991) case study of a gang of pickpockets in Jakarta founded by four migrants from Kayu Agung, West Sumatra, as a form of mutual protection.[2] Its members denied having leaders, but it did have two people whose tasks were to coordinate thefts and to divide up the booty. The first coordinator started stealing in primary school and eventually became a market thief in his hometown before migrating to Jakarta in 1968. Prior to forming the gang, he was a robber in Jakarta, Bandung, and Yogyakarta. Known for being wise in the mystical sciences and having had friends who were killed in the so-called Mysterious Killings of the 1980s, he was the only one in the gang referred to as "elder brother" (*kakak*).[3] The other leader started off stealing fruit, chickens, and cows. The group was active at certain bus shelters and on certain bus lines at Blok M, a huge complex of shopping centers, shops, and informal street markets in the wealthy neighborhood of Kebayoran Baru. On the buses, for example, they would only work until the bus got to the attorney general's office and then they would get off. There were two other gangs of pickpockets working Blok M at the same time and they all knew each other and did not infringe on one another's territories.

By the 1990s the gang had grown to thirty-one members. All were from Kayu Agung; whenever members went home, they would bring back relatives who wanted to join. New members were the responsibility of those who brought them into the group, and initially, they would be given a little training and then told to pick someone's pocket. These novices were often caught and beaten and would only be made members if they could take such a thrashing without reporting the gang to the police. At that point they would be given real training in pickpocket techniques and communication codes. For example, they would learn how to touch the target's body repeatedly before picking their pocket so the person gets inured to such touch, that you never look at the pocket you are picking, and that a wink of the eyes means it is safe to steal and a furrowed brow means it is not.

The group was divided into subgroups of four to six people, including a coordinator. If one member of the subgroup was found out, another member would always be the first to give chase before finding a way to let him go. The remaining members would intimidate meddlers. If members were caught by the police and could not be freed with a bribe, the gang would see to it that they received money while they were in prison. Relatives who took the time to visit them in prison would also be paid. All problems between members had to be reported to the founders, who would then find a solution. Members were expected to keep their profession completely secret; if they failed to do so, they would be ostracized or killed. They were also expected to fight other gangs that infringed on their territory.[4]

While gangs of thieves can be organized territorially, theft is also a crime against territory. Thieves enter a territory unnoticed and uninvited, remove some of its elements, and leave.[5] According to a pensioned police officer I spoke with, up through the 1970s Bandung's thieves were almost all organized into gangs. If a theft took place, the police could tell that the thief was a member of a particular gang—not just from the location of the crime, but also from the particular manner in which the gang member would enter and leave the territory. Some would enter through a window and leave through the front door. Others would operate only at night, digging under the exterior fence and coming up under the house (when houses were on stilts or piles). Still others would enter through the roof and would always defecate on the roof as they left. In some cases, as we have seen, the modus operandi might be informed by mystical knowledge, with very specific instructions about how and when to enter and leave. If the police recognized the modus operandi of a particular theft, they could immediately reduce their list of suspects to a couple dozen people. Whether or not thieves used magic, what defined them as thieves was that they entered a given territory—a pocket, a house, a yard—unannounced and without permission, left a mark (the absence of property, defecation), and exited again. What identified them as individuals among their peers, and among the police, was where they did it and how.

When people in the neighborhood hear the shout "thief!" they are not interested in who the thief is, or in the thief's modus operandi. When people hear such a cry and come rushing out of their houses, they are interested, first of all, in catching the rascal (*bangsat*). What might have been an ordinary day, with people going about their regular personal business, is suddenly transformed into a swirl of communal activity. People run after the thief, get in their cars and give chase, or, if the thief has already disappeared, set off to search nearby hiding places, like fields and ditches.[6] Once a thief has been captured, they are often subjected to a spectacle of collective violence: swarming (*mengeroyok*), pummeling (*menggebuki*), or eradicating (*menggulung*).[7] As James T. Siegel (1986, 43) has pointed out, what is important about this punishment is that the thief's face or body shows the marks of the beating. The bruises and swelling are always mentioned in stories afterward. To quote Ujog (see chapter 1), *When he would try to get up someone would come over and say, "You're a thief, ya?" and then hit him again. By the end of it the thief's face was completely wrecked.* It seemed from his story that it was not enough to have others mark the thief; everyone needed to get in a punch of their own. In one neighborhood I lived in, the punishment did not end there. The thief was then stripped and given a sign to wear that said "I'm a thief" and was paraded around the neighborhood for everyone to see.

What is the order restored by this beating? Siegel (1986) offers a compelling answer to this question. He notes that in Solo—and the same could be said of Bandung—the neighborhood's sense of "community" is expressed not through ties of kinship or through shared economic interests but through a shared concern for security. When people distinguish their neighborhood from those around it they always say the same thing, which is that it is "a safe neighborhood, one that thieves are afraid to enter" (39). For residents, especially *ronda* guards, the figure of the thief thus provides a name for that which stands "outside" the neighborhood and threatens the community. In beating the thief, the residents describe a way of relating to this outside and a way of addressing it. Siegel compares the beating to a language that expresses a social hierarchy: whereas it is proper to speak a Low Javanese dialect to one's neighbors, and a High Javanese dialect to one's superiors, "it is proper to beat a thief" (48). What defines both security and neighborhood identity, then, is an adherence to a proper order that is at once linguistic and hierarchical. By speaking to the thief in the proper way, residents of Solo seek to restore the hierarchy that the thief had offended. The success of this restoration is achieved when the thief behaves in a way that in Javanese society indicates respect; he feels something (the pain indicated by the bruises) that terror and respect make him hold back (he remains silent during the beating). He has, as people frequently say, "learned his lesson" (*kapok*).

From the standpoint of territorial community and power, an analogous process is at work. One can distinguish two moments in the beating. First, the naming of the thief is followed immediately by a punch, a succession of actions whose cumulative effect amounts to a sort of word-punch. In this sense, the punch does not differ greatly from the act of striking the slit gong or clapping to startle someone who is daydreaming. It territorializes the thief, using the alertness caused by pain to call him back from a place beyond the social pale. Second, the reaction of the body to the word-punch is evaluated by the spectators' eyes, which "jump" back and forth between the bruise and the body or between the sign and the face.[8] The "success" of the word-punch at territorializing the body is evidenced by the spectacle of the bruised face, the bruised face showing that the body can be marked. What is "eliminated" in this beating is a body on which a territorial mark did not take: the possibility of failure in establishing a territorial relation. Replacing this feared, nonterritorial body is a body that is fully territorialized in the sense that it is fully alert to, and marked by, a territorial power. Thus, the beating of the thief is simultaneously a gesture that locates the threat the thief represents and one that manages this threat by expelling him from the community.

In the immediate post-Suharto years, as the state security apparatus saw its legitimacy wane and its authority became more fragmented, assertions of territorial identity and power by means of vigilantism reached what seemed to be new extremes of violence. In the past, people captured as thieves were subjected to beatings and they might well have been killed in such attacks; now, however, they were sometimes doused in petrol and burned alive. Danang Kukuh Wardoyo (2004) reports on a number of incidents in which suspected thieves and criminals were killed in this manner. He also describes personally witnessing the following incident: "On one occasion, I observed a crowd dispensing street justice to a pickpocket in Pejompongan, Central Jakarta. As I stood there, a number of those in the crowd called for the pickpocket to be burned: 'If this was Bekasi that pickpocket would be burned for sure!,' 'Just burn him, so he'll learn his lesson!,' 'In Tangerang there'd be no messing around, he'd be burned for sure!'" (n.p.). In this instance, bystanders are inciting the territorial community to violence by suggesting that a lack of violence signals a kind of territorial weakness that would not be found elsewhere. This indicates that such violent spectacles are directed not just at an audience of locals and prospective thieves but also at residents of other neighborhoods and cities.[9] When directed at the latter audiences, such spectacular violence becomes part of a competitive display of territorial community power.[10]

Spirits and the Phantom State

If the unpunished thief constitutes one threat to neighborhood territorial power, a second threat is represented by the figure of the powerful outsider. Powerful outsiders are considered a threat in part because territorial power always involves debt relations. In return for the enjoyment of territorial security, residents of a neighborhood must offer something of their own. In areas watched over by the *ronda*, for instance, residents offer their labor for patrols, respond to calls for vigilance, and provide patrolling guards with coffee, cigarettes, and food (see chapter 1). There is an implied egalitarianism in this system as debt remains diffused among all members of the community and is restricted to the neighborhood territory. But there is always the fear that this egalitarianism will be undermined and that some greater power will seek to take over the territory and collect on its residents' debts. Various figures are used to represent this kind of danger, but one of the most common in Sundanese folklore is that of a powerful spirit residing outside the neighborhood or village to whom residents become indebted. In the following story, written by Mohamad Ambri, this powerful spirit is explicitly identified with the power of the state.

Like the Ambri story discussed in chapter 1, this one focuses on a conversation among guards out on the *ronda*. It involves an older guard by the name of Mang Uham relating a tale to two younger colleagues, Wirja and Arta. It is a cautionary tale about a pilgrimage to a spirit's abode in a forest near Cirebon. The pilgrims aim to enter into a pact with the spirit in order to get rich, a practice known as *munjung*.[11]

> MANG UHAM This is someone else's story, not my own experience. The place of *munjung* is Koromong Mountain. In the month of Mulud, we depart to Cirebon along with a mass of people. Upon arriving there—Cirebon is large after all—we separate from the group. Some go to see the Sultan, to meet with the prince, to go to *Keramat*, but we go to Koromong Mountain. First we meet the gatekeeper, and

then continue to the place of *munjung*. There, the fullness of our determination is tested. What had been a forest changes and becomes an astonishing state. Its fences are humans that have been skewered like satay. The raja's house has a foundation of human heads, their tongues sticking out, their eyes bugged out, their bodies sticking out underneath the house; the stairs, too, are made of humans, stacked and then fixed together with wood. Even the roof is made of humans, stacked orderly as shingles, their heads down and their feet tied down to laths with palm-fiber string. The ridge of the roof is made of a line of humans sitting with legs apart as if horse riding, who knows how many dozens, all arranged to fit tightly together. Their necks and hips are fixed together with wood, pegged, and then tied with palm-fiber string; their chests and torsos nailed to the rafters. Humans are even used as carvings for the pillars, four nailed to each pillar, those chosen only women; their backs squared with the pillar and their chests nailed to it. The nails used are square iron nails the size of an index finger, intentionally not sunk all the way in, but pulled out just enough to hang something on.

WIRJA That's really horrific, Mang. I wouldn't be brave enough to open my eyes. Oh, *audzubillah* [may God protect me].

MANG UHAM Then you wouldn't pass if you wanted to go *munjung*, Wirja.

WIRJA Goodness, I'd rather not get rich than go through that.

ARTA Children aren't treated like that, are they, Mang?

MANG UHAM No. Children are made servants and have to do whatever the others order them to.

WIRJA So after that, what happens?

MANG UHAM Now we are invited to move around, to look at things. Footbridges and larger bridges, both the pillars and the struts one steps on, are all made of human bodies. So that they don't come unattached, they are variously skewered, pegged, nailed, and of course, tied with string.

WIRJA Ugh, enough of that. What happens then?

MANG UHAM After looking at the Raja's house and its grounds....

ARTA A Raja's house is called a palace, Mang.

MANG UHAM A Raja's house has to be beautiful, right, not like this.

WIRJA Arta, don't interrupt. We accept that a palace is something else again. (Ambri 1977, 31–32)

In this story the sacred abode of the spirit takes the form of a horrific phantom state, represented here by a raja's palace constructed out of corpses. The palace is built with tremendous attention to detail. It is a meticulously designed and crafted horror. But what makes this engineering disturbing is that it is working with human material: human bodies are substituted for shingles, pillars, decorative carvings, and so forth. We are thus forced to think of the bodies not as people but as things that are defined by their place in a functional arrangement. The transformation is analogous to the change the slit gong undergoes when it moves from being an activator of territorial relations to a communication device (see chapter 1). It is a process of deterritorialization and reterritorialization. However, in this instance it is the human body that is deterritorialized from its original place and reterritorialized within the architecture of the state, and we get a sense of the terror that may accompany this process. The human body's reterritorialization is not merely a neutral transformation; it is the creation of a technology out of something that should not suffer this fate.

In order to get what they desire the visitors must not only face this horror; they will have to make sacrifices to the spirit residing in this palace.

MANG UHAM After looking around, we are invited to eat. *Tumpeng* [a ceremonial dish of yellow rice] has been prepared for us. The chickens are even slaughtered in front of us. "Keok! Kek-kek-kek" is what chickens usually sound like when they are slaughtered. But not this time. This time they sound like our kids, calling us like they usually do: "Dad!" or "Father!" Of course we are startled to see a chicken slaughtered yet have it cry like the children we love. After the chicken is slaughtered, it is skinned and chopped up, without being plucked first. It is not even washed. The whole of it is then placed in a rice steamer, used as filling for the *tumpeng*, cooked until ready. For firewood, human arms and legs are used. After cooking, the rice is served. We eat, and have to finish it all up, not leaving even a single crumb. As we are about to eat the last bite we come across a piece of meat that is nothing less than the hand, finger, foot, or other part of our child's body. We can't hesitate though, even that must be eaten.

WIRJA *Audzubillah*, Mang, that's too much, it makes me want to throw up.

MANG UHAM If you're going to whine like that, don't *munjung*.

ARTA People like Wirja would be turned back before even arriving to that point. (32–33)

Here we see that entering into a relation with the outside power represented by the phantom state involves making a sacrifice of one's own kin (and, as we shall see below, of oneself too). Those unwilling to make the necessary sacrifices would be turned back and would receive nothing in return.

MANG UHAM After finishing the *tumpeng* rice, what remains is to promise when we will return to give ourselves up. Different people ask for different things. There are those who ask for a life as long as that of a hoe, a machete, or various other farmers' tools. The hoe is then only used once a year when the first rain falls, and then is stored well, wrapped in a white cloth so that it lasts a long time. The same is true for whatever tool is used for the promise: it is used sparingly, and cared for like the hoe.

When we return home from the place of *munjung*, we find that our child has already been buried, sometimes three or seven days ago....

The people who go *munjung* at that place only bathe once a year and this only during the month of Mulud. If they defecate, they place their feces in bamboo, in a sack, or perhaps in an earthenware jug. That is what then changes into money—but if it is stolen it will change back into what it was originally; and although it may have been there for a really long time, it still smells so much it makes you sick.

As many of the people who *munjung* are thoughtful, many also end up dying before their promises are up. Their corpses are buried as usual, but at night they are sure to return as the earth refuses to accept them. If a corpse returns, its family doesn't make a scene; they simply cut up the corpse and stick it in a leather sack, sew it closed, and wrap it in striated bamboo. They then carry it en masse to a large river and let it be swept away. (33–34)

To say that a corpse is chopped up, bagged, and cast into a river is to say that it is treated like garbage that must be expelled from the community.[12] Thus, although the person who has entered into a pact with the phantom state does receive money, he or she will never receive a proper burial. Even if the person manages to pay off their debt to the phantom state, their corpse will be spirited away.

> MANG UHAM If the promise is up before the person dies, an envoy from the place of *munjung* comes to collect the person, bringing along a zebra. It is said that as they are taken away, many meet a friend on the street and give them a message to give to their family, but when the messenger gets to the family it turns out that the family is crying because the person [whom the friend just met] has died and been buried. However, what was buried was really just the tool that had been used for the promise, it just looked to those who saw it like it was a corpse.
>
> If many people in a neighborhood *ngopet* [a type of *munjung* that involves sacrifice], eventually God is sure to destroy the neighborhood: the world will turn upside down, it will be covered by landslides and volcanic eruptions, or if it is by a river, it will be washed away. Those who don't *ngopet* will not be spared, because they are willing to live together with those who *ngopet* in the same neighborhood.
>
> Thus is the story. Because of that, it's better to live in poverty than to *ngopet*.
>
> WIRJA Perhaps you have been there, Mang?
>
> MANG UHAM Thank the Lord, no. There hasn't been a child or grandchild of mine who has died. My nine children are all alive, as are the six offspring of three of these. Where is the proof that I *munjung*? (34)

Ambri's story serves as a morality tale, a warning about what can happen to a neighborhood or a kin group when it surrenders itself to state power. It teaches those who read it, and perhaps those on the *ronda* in particular, that entering into an alliance with the phantom state is to take on a debt. Such a debt is equated with the sacrifice and consumption of one's family and neighbors. Those who submit themselves to the phantom state thus do so at great peril to their communities. For although things may seem to go along more or less as before, with people burying their dead as usual, this apparent continuity masks a fundamental social transformation signified by the fact that the corpse buried is actually nothing more than a tool of production. However, there is a benefit to be derived from making a pact with the spirit. One makes a gift of bodies to the spirit and gets back money: a gift to the phantom state returns exchange value. The tale is cautionary, however, because subordination to the phantom state and the creation of exchange value are closely associated with a sense of horror, made manifest in the palace architecture and the meal.

Along with the horror of this story, however, there is also a strong element of desire. As a genre of folktales, *munjung* stories are all about getting what one desires.[13] Indeed, in Ambri's book, the telling of *munjung* stories comes out of a discussion about how to get rich, something the poor farmers who populate the book all want. And the people who *munjung* do get rich; moreover, men sometimes also get beautiful wives, and women an ageless beauty. To get these, however, a person must have a firm resolve, as it is this that is always tested by the spirits. If one is halfhearted, one will see nothing and get nothing. Desire must thus be directed and unrestrained. For those in the neighborhood, expressing such a desire is one thing, acting on it another. While it is acceptable to tell the stories and to express one's wish to get rich, one's neighbors, and God, will always be watching to make sure these wishes are not acted upon. Throughout Ambri's book, as in the passages above, the characters telling the stories are playfully accused of being the protagonists of the stories they tell. Merely expressing their wishes gives cause for suspicion. But Mang Uham, in the final passage above, is able to demonstrate that he is not cavorting with spirits, his proof being that there are no unexplained disappearances in his family. He has good reason to say such a thing because in many regions of Java people associate unexplained appearances (of money) and disappearances (of people) with the work of spirits. Rumors about such things can lead to a person becoming suspect in the eyes of their neighbors. They may also sow the seeds that lead community members to resort to vigilante justice.

Why is cavorting with spirits thought to bring ruin on the territorial community? Perhaps such relations are ruinous because they introduce outside mediators into the workings of desire. As long as the pathways of desire do not lead out of the territory, the community can maintain its strong sense of autonomy and sovereignty; but when desire follows paths to outside mediators, such as the phantom state, the territorial community risks wholesale indebtedness and deterritorialization. In the folkloric discourse of Ambri's story, this state of affairs is represented by a nightmare world where human bodies take the place of shingles and boards and where children are slaughtered like chickens.

In his study of Amazonian societies, Pierre Clastres (1987) describes how myths can help constitute what he calls a "society against the state." Such a society is one that has always already—in its social structure and its culture—anticipated and warded off state formation. A similar dynamic is at work in the case I am describing here: the territorial community defines itself against an imagined outside state and seeks to ward off the threat of subordination to this state by promoting fears of outside powers. By promoting such fears, *munjung* stories have the effect of shoring up the neighborhood's moral economy.

Street Toughs and the Force of Territorialization

In Indonesian cities, where the modern state is omnipresent and the cash economy is the primary means of social reproduction, one might expect that all neighborhoods would be subordinated to state power and that deterritorialization would be a fait accompli. In fact, this is not the case, partly due to the emergence of a figure that both internalizes the state within the neighborhood and *represents* the force of territorialization. This figure is what the press, public, and police in Indonesia refer to as the *preman* or *jago*, and what many Bandungers refer to as the *jegger*.[14] In Java, these "boastful and pugnacious" strongmen used to be associated primarily with rural banditry and were particularly powerful in socially and ethnically diverse regions where there was a lot of trade, such as along the northern coast of western Java (Smail 1964, 88). However, over the past several decades this rural type has increasingly been eclipsed by the rise of an urban variant whose importance seems to have grown in direct proportion to the expansion of Indonesia's burgeoning cities.

Ayip Muflich (1979) has written an account of a young man from the western Javanese region of Banten, called Mardy, whose life followed a fairly typical trajectory for an urban *jegger*.[15] The son of a civil servant, Mardy was born and raised in a relatively closed and endogamous part of Banten, a region known for being rich in mysticism. In his neighborhood there were youths who liked to engage in "mass fights" (*perkelahian massal*) with their rivals from nearby quarters.[16] This fighting tradition had been passed on from generation to generation, and the neighborhood had made its name as a place of *jegger*. In the mid-1960s, after Mardy finished primary school, he convinced his parents to let him go to Jakarta, where he stayed with a relative in an army complex and attended middle school. There, he joined the youth group responsible for protecting the school against communist threats, while in his neighborhood he quickly became known as a leader among his friends and formed a local gang. Recruitment to his neighborhood gang followed a common pattern: challenging someone to a fight, beating them, and then making them a member. For example, Mardy told of walking down the street and greeting someone he thought was a friend. However, the guy just stared back at him without saying anything. "Oh, you think you're a *jago* now," Mardy said to him, challenging him to a duel that night. Later, the guy approached Mardy to ask for forgiveness, and eventually became one of Mardy's followers and underlings (*anak buah*). One of the reasons people were afraid of Mardy was because he used mystical arts to make himself invulnerable. For neighborhood Independence Day celebrations he liked to give public demonstrations of his invulnerability. Once he even invited a group of his friends back to Banten to seek invulnerability magic, though most of them lost whatever protections this afforded because they could not keep to the requirement that they refrain from sexual relations.

Mardy's gang made its money at a nearby bus terminal, where it collected protection money from restaurants, and where members worked as scalpers and go-betweens (*calo*), helping broker—and extract rents from—relations between businesses, members of the public, and officialdom. For example, in return for a fee, a go-between might direct potential passengers to board a particular bus or might facilitate a small bribe of a police officer to allow the bus to take on passengers in a prohibited location. Such go-betweens have long figured prominently in the nexus between the formal and informal sectors of the Indonesian economy, and in urban settings, transportation hubs and marketplaces have presented fertile grounds for such brokerage work.[17] Mardy and his gang's involvement in the political economy of the local bus terminal had evolved slowly and was usually based on oral agreements between Mardy and the owners surrounding businesses. For instance, some of his friends would make trouble at a restaurant and then the owner would come to Mardy asking for help in preventing them from hanging out there. Mardy would oblige in return for a payment each week and a right to borrow money. This arrangement worked until the terminal was moved to a larger location, at which time another gang tried to take over Mardy's business. The result was a series of turf wars utilizing guns and knives. Eventually Mardy's gang organized an assault on the neighborhood base of its competitor, destroying residents' cars and houses in the process. Parents of members of the rival gang invited Mardy to make peace. After some discussion, Mardy agreed not to bother them any longer, as long as the rival gang admitted they were in the wrong and had lost the battle for control of the terminal.

Mardy's story is not unusual. When I asked inmates at Bandung's prison what a *jegger* is, they gave the following characterization: a *jegger* is usually (but not always) male, originates in provincial villages and towns, and makes a name for himself before moving to the big city. He can be young or old, large or small, but he frequently sports tattoos (*otat*) and is said to have mastered the mystical art of invulnerability.[18] Upon arrival in Bandung the *jegger* picks a site to plant his flag (*mendirikan benderanya*), usually the central square (*alun-alun*), a bus terminal, a train station, a market, or some other location with lots of commercial traffic. He finds out who controls that area (another *jegger*), and then challenges him to a duel (*jantan*). The duel usually involves the use of handheld weapons, such as machetes (*golok* or *ulak goman*), samurai swords, knives (*sikim*), or sickles (*clurit*). The winner's name circulates within the surrounding area so people know who it is that "owns" or "holds" (*pegang*)[19] that area, and therefore who it is that must be respected (*disegani*).

In owning an area, the *jegger* establishes or takes over the right to collect on what I have described as the debt that people owe simply by virtue of living or doing business there. This debt is paid with a piece of the action on any commercial activity that takes place in the *jegger*'s territory. People who operate businesses in the area pay protection money, transportation vehicles pay a fee for use of the roads, parking attendants pay a portion of their take, and street vendors pay a rent. According to the inmates I spoke with, even pickpockets who successfully extract a person's wallet feel obliged to pay the *jegger* a tenth of their take, although the *jegger* is not their boss. The money that is collected is called "tribute" (*upeti*) or *japrem* (*jatah preman*, the *preman*'s allotment) and is generally collected not by the *jegger* himself, but by his underlings (*anak buah* or *kronco*). Indeed, tribute is the right name for it: it is the fee paid under duress for the right to live or do business in the *jegger*'s domain.

The people most frequently targeted for this fee are people deemed to be foreign. As they are not considered "natives of the land" (*pribumi*), their debt to the territory is greater. This is especially so for members of the ethnic Chinese minority, as they are often considered to be both outsiders and deeply dependent on local commerce. But non-Chinese, too, can be considered alien to a territory. The following story, drawn from my notes on statements to the police by a mugging victim and suspect, provides an impression of how basic this orientation is, especially for small-time *jegger*. First, from the victim:

> At first me and Dani went out for a ride on a motorcycle. When we were finished we headed home by way of Veteran Street but were caught in the rain. So we stopped and took shelter at the scene of the crime, and as we were sheltering there at the side of the road, a person called Idang showed up and asked us something and stood by our motorcycle. Then he disappeared and returned shortly with Ewit, who asked Dani, "What are you up to?," to which we replied we were taking shelter. They then introduced themselves and asked where we were from and "Do you like to use drugs or not?," to which we answered no, and then they offered us cigarettes, but we said we had some. Then they advised us not to take shelter there because it is dangerous, with lots of drunk people, so you could be taxed. They advised us to move the motorcycle into the alley, at which point we became suspicious and Dani immediately started the motorcycle and invited me to go but I couldn't 'cause Ewit already had me in a strangle hold. [His wallet is then stolen.][20]

Ewit describes what his accomplice Idang does after first seeing the two guys: "Idang came to my house and invited me to go out and explained that there were two strangers [*orang asing*] taking shelter on Veteran Street. Then he suggested we tax them, saying, 'Urang pajek we' [Sundanese: Let's just tax them], so with that intention I grabbed my Carter knife, and we went out." Like the neighborhood watch guards, these *jegger* take a special interest in strangers. For them, however, strangers are not so much a threat as an opportunity to collect rent; in this case, the rent that was implicitly being charged for the shelter that the two guys used to get out of the rain. The fact that the two were non-Chinese Bandungers who lived just a kilometer away from where they were mugged did not prevent them from being classified as "strangers."

For the *jegger*, the territory is defined very much in terms of land. Thus, one might infer that his power would be limited to things like charging rent for the "taking of shelter" and so forth. But what is impressive about the *jegger* is his ability to territorialize any activity that takes place in his domain. No matter how deterritorialized such activity is, he always manages to find the points at which it must touch down in his ambit, and he uses these as his points of leverage. Even forms of commerce that are assumed to be national in character or controlled by multinationals cannot avoid dealing with him. For example, the expansion of the telephone system, an activity that obeys a logic of blueprints, capital, and bureaucratic power, and which treats places only as nodes in a larger web of relays, has historically been territorialized by the *jegger* at two points: public phones and cable installation. In the age when public phones were common, the man who came to collect the coins from the pay phone would frequently be charged a "parking fee" that amounted to a significant percentage of the income from the phone. Similarly, even now, when the phone company wants to lay down cables in an area, these cables may be tampered with if a fee to the local *jegger* is not paid.

While the *jegger* is a territorial power in the literal sense that his domain of action is defined as a plot of land, or perhaps a particular bus route, he is also territorial in the more general sense I discussed in the previous chapter. That is, he occupies his territory, developing relationships with its elements, and taking care of them. If the police detain one of his underlings, it is the *jegger* who pays the bribe to spring him. If someone disrupts one of the businesses from which he extracts rent, it is the *jegger* who comes forward to protect its interests and provide security. This is why the public's relation to him is always somewhat ambivalent. The following comments by an itinerant street vendor about *jegger* in the region of Tanah Abang, Jakarta, are typical in this regard:

> To sell here you really have to be good at dealing with *preman*. If they already know you, they don't ask for too much, and not everyday. And there is an advantage to having them around. Now no pickpockets have the guts to operate here.... If we are good to them, they don't hassle us. People say that they used to be quite tough. They used to order one of their underlings to collect protection money. If it wasn't given then the seller would be called or taken to the back of the market and be beaten up. (Purwanto and Subroto 1997, 34)

On the one hand, the *jegger* is resented for the extra economic burden he places on people, while on the other hand, people generally attempt to keep up good relations with him and may appreciate the protection he provides. Sometimes they might even seek him out when they are in need.

In sum, the *jegger* takes over a territory by challenging those within it and then appointing himself guardian of its households and businesses.[21]

Because he "owns" the area,[22] anyone who passes through, lives, or does business there is forced to acknowledge his presence. Such acknowledgment usually takes the form of paying a rent. This rent is higher for people who, by virtue of their ethnicity or their place of residence, are deemed to be outsiders. But in theory everyone in the neighborhood is subject to these debt relations. As a result, the political economy of the neighborhood under the authority of the *jegger* can come to take on the overall appearance of a protection racket, much like those found in other parts of the world.[23]

Embodiments of Territorial Power

The *jegger*'s power is derived from his ability to exert a centralizing and unifying force on the multiplicity of forces that might otherwise characterize the organization of territorial power under the neighborhood watch. This is evident in the mythology that surrounds the competitive duels through which he performs his fighting prowess and acquires much of his authority. It is also evident in the debt relations that constitute his protection racket. There is, however, another aspect of his authority that deserves consideration here: his use of tattoos and other forms of body modification to turn his body into the object of a certain gaze. While in recent years tattoos and body modifications have entered the mainstream of youth culture in Indonesia, for a long time they were closely associated with charismatic *jegger* and criminals. Indeed, in many cases tattoos have been seen as repositories of mystical power in their own right, much like amulets. In this sense, charismatic *jegger* derive some of their authority and power from their tattoos. While I take up this topic in more detail in chapter 5, there is one aspect of such body marking and modification I would like to emphasize here, which is the way it aids in the appropriation of territorial power.

A sense of how such appropriation takes place is provided by an experience I had during a visit to Bandung's prison. I was in the canteen with some inmates who were explaining how they occupy their days while serving time, which led to a conversation about tattoos and other kinds of body modification.

> *One young man was quite eager to show his tattoos, but before lifting his shirt he checked to make sure no guards were looking. When I was suitably impressed with the tattoos on his chest, he went one step further, showing me something he assured me only prisoners know about: plastic pellets made from sanded-down pieces of ballpoint pens. When I asked what they were for*

*he promptly opened his pants to show that they were inserted just under the
skin along the shaft of the penis. He had several of these implants and one
could make out the colors of the pieces of plastic through the skin. He showed
that they could move under the skin and assured me that they drove women
crazy.*[25] *Once, he said, he visited a prostitute who liked it so much that later
she came searching for him at his home. This led to a ruckus with his wife.*

Alfred Gell (1993, 37) writes that any "tattoo—indeed a mark of any
kind—on the skin, is a registration of the causal factors which produced it,
and hence a symbolic residue of the totality of causal factors, events, social
obligations, individual and collective relationships impinging on the social person." With this in mind, we might thus pose two related questions:
What are the tattoos and penis implants of the *jegger* in the example above
registers of? And what do they say about his social person?

One way to answer these questions is to compare this kind of body marking with the marking of the thief by people "playing judge themselves." The
most important difference is that the scars that mark the thief are inscribed
on his body by numerous inhabitants of a neighborhood, and that the force
of their impact is evaluated by a multiplicity of eyes, while the tattoos on
the *jegger*'s body are inscribed either by his own hand or by someone of his
choosing, and are evaluated first of all by his own eyes. Thus, the thief's
scars are comparable to the types of tattoos and marks that are given during
initiation ceremonies in many parts of the world, since they are inscribed
publicly by the community, while the *jegger*'s tattoos and penis inserts differ
in that they are meant to be measures not of a community's territorializing
power but of his own personal power.[25] It is as if he has appropriated territorializing power and centered it on his own body. But this appropriation
is only successful insofar as others behold it. If the tattoos were merely to
produce narcissistic pleasure and the power the *jegger* derived from them
was purely private, he would leave the tattoos hidden. He does not leave
them hidden, however, except when he is afraid of being recognized by the
state—here the police, or if the *jegger* finds himself in prison, the guards—
as a "criminal."[26] Rather, his power is derived from exhibiting his tattoos
and thereby making others see his territorializing power. Implicitly, such
exhibition is always social since it demands a response in the form of recognition of the *jegger*'s territorializing power (just as the slit gong demands
a response from those who hear it).

As Gell explains in reference to Polynesian tattooing, tattoos mark a
person's relationship to an "external social milieu" and activate a series of

relationships particular to that milieu; even the "apparently self-willed tattoo always turns out to have been elicited by others, and to be a means of eliciting responses from others" (1993, 37). The relationships established by the self-willed tattoo reflect the *jegger*'s appropriation of territorial power. Perhaps this is why the *jegger*'s tattoos are frequently associated with the art of invulnerability: they signify a body that has already appropriated the power of marking to itself and is in a sense therefore self-territorialized.[27] To try to mark such a body would necessarily involve challenging the strength of the prior territorializing force by asserting another force against it. It is precisely this kind of challenge that leads to duels between *jegger* for control of an area.

While monopolizing the power to mark is one additional way the *jegger* unifies and centralizes territorial power, monopolizing the power to see and be seen is another. To some degree, the *jegger* already satisfies this goal when he makes a spectacle of his tattoos, but his use of spies (or "eyes") is also important.[28] The *jegger*'s underlings are his spies, keeping a lookout for challenges to his territory, for debts that may be collected, and so forth. People are worried about such spies and therefore careful about what they do and say. One is, of course, never certain who these spies are, so the multiplication of the *jegger*'s eyes can seem almost infinite. By making sure people see the territory as he sees it, and that its inhabitants see him as he sees himself, the *jegger* consolidates his power and ensures that he will be the representative of territorial power in his particular area. In many respects, the power of the *jegger* to mediate territorial relations gives him a status not unlike the *munjung* spirit: people fear him, pay off their debt of existence to him, and tell stories about him. Yet the *jegger* differs from the phantom state in that he does not threaten the territory's existence in absolute terms; he is not its "outside." Rather, he comes from outside but makes a place for himself by building up his authority from within.

That the *jegger* is capable of unifying and representing territorial power means that he can be very useful to the state apparatus. Although he is often portrayed as independent of state power (coming from the provinces, acting autonomously), the *jegger* or *preman* is not necessarily a free man (*vrijman*).[29] Precisely because he is so good at keeping a grip on an area, and at extracting tribute from its inhabitants, he has often been put to work in the maintenance of state power and the collection of wealth.[30] The relation of *jegger* to the state is often expressed as one of *bekking* or *dekking*, which refers to the way in which *jegger* receive protection from members of the police or the armed forces in return for regular payments of rent (*setoran*). There are some who have such *bekking,* and others who do not. Thus, like the slit gong, the *jegger* may in different times and places serve either to mediate the relation between state power and the neighborhood or to constitute a territory beyond the reach of formal state power.

The Territorial City

While a territory often has creative and expressive qualities, fear of the "outside" can make it hunker back in on itself. I have identified two figures of the neighborhood's outside, the very notions of which cause the neighborhood to adopt a defensive posture: the thief and the phantom state. While thieves may in fact have their own territories and recognize the authority of their own *jegger,* the neighborhood views the thief as an almost primordial threat to its territoriality, an animal-like figure who does not yet accord the neighborhood the respect it deserves. The phantom state represents another limit of territorial power—namely, the threat of a state that will displace neighborhood territorial relations by introducing external mediation of desire, thereby effecting a deterritorialization of the neighborhood. Insofar as these two threats can be anticipated and eliminated before they are actualized—by punishing the thief and by telling stories about the dangers of *munjung*—the neighborhood territory can maintain a fragile autonomy and sovereignty. The *jegger,* in contrast, introduces ambiguity into this autonomy: he makes a place for himself in the neighborhood but he originates from outside; he makes a name for the community but he also seeks a monopoly over territorial violence; he takes on responsibility for the community's protection and security but demands tribute from those who live and do business there; and he territorializes "foreign" intruders even as he seeks out the backing of powerful outsiders. The *jegger* cuts an ambiguous figure because he is both a means for the territorial community to defend itself against outside powers and a means for outside powers to exert control over the territorial community.

Vigilante violence is normally justified by the claim—whether explicit or implicit—that it preserves or defends community norms and rules. Vigilantes in Indonesia are no exception in this regard: they regularly justify their violence by claiming that it is directed against people who have offended some law, moral code, or religious edict. More important than these rationalizations for vigilantism, however, are the means by which such "everyday policing" (Buur and Jensen 2004) takes place. Most everyday vigilante policing in Indonesian cities takes place at the hands of neighborhood watch groups, *jegger* and their gangs, youth groups, or militias. While these various kinds of informal sovereigns may interpret the law and define their morality in diverse ways, ultimately all express their power primarily through street-level territorial claims.

The overall effect of such claims is to constitute Indonesian cities as territorial cities. A territorial city is a city seen through the eyes of a *ronda* guard or a *jegger*; this is in contrast to those eyes that see it "like a state" (Scott 1998) and thereby rule it from a distance. Using the *jegger* optic, a city like Bandung is revealed as consisting of thousands of nested and sometimes overlapping territories. Some of these are whole neighborhoods, markets, malls, or bus terminals; others are merely a street block, a row of stalls, a single business, or a set of buses that ply a particular route. In each of these territories, whatever its size or domain, a struggle is going on for who will occupy it and provide it with protection. Will territorial power remain distributed among different members of the community, as it is in communities whose security is provided for primarily by the neighborhood watch? Will a powerful *jegger* emerge to dominate the territory and mediate its relations with powerful others? Who will the *jegger* be and what kind of morality will he claim? Or will the phantom state finally materialize and deterritorialize the city once and for all?

PART TWO

SURVEILLANCE

P.2 Sukamiskin Prison, an aerial view, circa 1930. (*De gevangenis Soekamiskin bij Bandoeng*). Courtesy of Southeast Asian and Caribbean Images (KITLV) under CC License (https://creativecommons.org/licenses/by/4.0 /legalcode). Available at: http://hdl.handle.net/1887.1/item:787024.

3

Urban Panopticon

Perhaps you know, that I am obsessed by the vision of a European colony and a great city laid out on the Bandung plain. There are those who disagree with my view, calling it an illusion and a fantasy, far too idealistic. But I know that these ideals will someday materialize.

Assistant Resident **W. R. van Hoëvell**

To understand the dynamics of contemporary policing in postcolonial Bandung, we must move beyond the particular forms that territoriality takes. While the neighborhood watch, *jegger*, and gangs play an important role in defining and policing threats to urban order, they are only a part of the picture. The other part is the modern police force. In this chapter and the next I consider the origins of modern policing in Bandung by tracing the development of a "scopic regime"[1] (Feldman 1997), a gaze that seeks to define and impose urban order through routinized, bureaucratic practices of surveillance. This gaze defines problems of urban order in terms of opacities, unsurveyability, visual disorder, contagions, and a lack of correspondence between images or representations of order and the reality of things in the world "out there." Surveillance is crucial to this gaze as it is both a means for creating representations of order—through the collection of data about the people and spaces that make up the city—and a means to try to discipline the city and its inhabitants such that they conform to these representations.

The genealogy of this gaze in Bandung can be traced back to the late nineteenth century, when the region was abruptly integrated into the global economy and the government was reorganized along bureaucratic lines. One of the earliest Bandung officials to adopt this gaze was R. A. A. Martanagara, a Sundanese regent appointed by the Dutch who was widely credited with modernizing the growing town and its environs in the late nineteenth and early twentieth centuries. An analysis of Martanagara's autobiography provides insights into how he came to adopt a self-consciously modern, scientific gaze, and how this gaze shaped his efforts to remake the region he presided over so as to integrate it more deeply into the circuits of a swiftly developing capitalist economy.

One of Martanagara's greatest accomplishments was the building of roads and railways, which provided colonial officials, among others, with a new way to travel through and look out onto the landscape. This view from the carriage, as I call it, was an important step in the development of a scopic regime that sought to police city life. Initially focused on the orderliness of city surfaces, the regime incorporated tall buildings and airplanes as prosthetics for establishing a commanding aerial view of the city as a whole. It then extended its view into the depths of urban spaces through municipal programs aimed at maintaining health and hygiene. In this chapter I trace these developments in an effort to elucidate the character of the modern bureaucratic gaze, its blind spots, and its ambitions. As will become evident in subsequent chapters, this aspirational panoptic regime, developed in a context of colonial rule, has come to underpin much of the work of bureaucratic policing in Bandung in more recent times.

Surveillance and the Colonial Economy

The modern city of Bandung has its origin in Governor General Herman Willem Daendels's 1810 decree that the capital of the Bandung Regency be relocated eleven kilometers to the north of its original location. The goal of this relocation was to place the city on the route of the Great Post Road, the first highway in the Dutch East Indies, which stretches a thousand kilometers from Anyer in the west of Java to Panarukan in the east. Planned by Daendels and built with forced labor, the highway was designed to increase the speed of postal communication and facilitate the quick movement of troops to defend against a feared British invasion. To facilitate quicker travel, the road was made as straight as possible, ferry crossings were replaced with bridges, and posts were placed every five to six kilometers so that those traveling on government business could change horses.

According to legend, while the road was being built, Daendels came to the district to supervise the construction of a bridge over the Cikapundung River. When the bridge was finished, Daendels was the first to walk across it. Accompanied by the regent (the highest non-European official overseeing the district), he then continued on along the road a bit further and stopped. Planting his staff in the ground, he declared, "See to it that when I return here a city has been built." And to mark that place, a post was then erected with a sign that read "Kilometer 0." It is there that Bandung's main square (*alun-alun*) is now located.[2]

When Daendels made this mythical gesture, the region he was standing in—known as the Preanger Regencies—had already undergone profound transformations as a result of its integration into the colonial economy. The region had constituted an important source of revenue for the Dutch East India Company (Vereenigde Oostindische Compagnie, or VOC) and, according to Mason C. Hoadley (1994), the eighteenth century had seen a gradual shift in the VOC's use of extractive techniques to generate revenues. In essence, a method that relied on the appropriation of surplus using existing relations of production gave way to a method whereby production relations were redefined in increasingly feudalistic terms. Hoadley identifies several policies that account for the rise of a feudal economy: the introduction of new cash crops such as coffee, the encouragement of dry terrace and wet-rice production techniques and the discouragement of swidden cultivation, the introduction of laws aimed at sedentarizing the seminomadic population, and the establishment of a form of rule based on control over a discrete geographic territory rather than a geographically dispersed population. In these ways the VOC attempted to stimulate the production of goods for export, thus effecting a transformation whereby social relations were redefined in feudal terms.

Daendels's Great Post Road did not in the end prevent the British from taking over the colony, and his vision for the Bandung plateau was to remain unrealized for almost a century. Instead, when the Dutch returned in 1817, it was decided that the highly productive lands in the Preanger Regencies would be kept in government hands, and its produce exploited through a monopoly. This plan, part of the colonial government's *Cultuurstelsel*, a system of agricultural production that sought to encourage greater exports from the colonies, involved preventing the emergence of private farms and alternative markets for produce by severely restricting the number of Europeans, Arabs, and Chinese who were allowed to settle in the region and by performing public hangings of "smugglers" who tried to circumvent the Dutch-buying monopoly. As a result of such policies, the Preanger Regencies saw few changes for much of the nineteenth century, and what changes there were amounted to refinements of the existing economic system. For local rulers, from the regent down through the village heads, the central problem remained how to maintain a captive, sedentary population that could meet its forced-labor obligations and pay its taxes of coffee and rice. This was accomplished by placing restrictions on travel. Henceforth, a person who wished to travel outside the region required a passport issued by the regent. Furthermore, village heads were made responsible for keeping track of people's comings and goings.

The latter regulation, which would remain the most important means for policing people's movements for more than a century, was first communicated to the local population in the following terms:

RULES OF POLICE PUNISHMENTS FOR THE PUBLIC

A fine of one to fifteen roepiah for:

No.1. He who moves from a *kampoeng* to another *kampoeng* and does not let the head of the first *kampoeng* know.

No.2. He who moves to a *kampoeng* and does not let the head of the *kampoeng* know his name, work, and place of origin within 24 hours of arriving in the *kampoeng*.

No.3. He who within 24 hours does not let the head of the *kampoeng* know that someone not from the *kampoeng* is staying over in his house, that is, by telling the *kampoeng* head the name of the person, his work, and place of origin. And he who does not tell the *kampoeng* head upon the departure of this person.

Because in each and every region [*negri*] it is appropriate for the heads, or persons in charge, who are responsible for defending public security [*kaslamettanja orang banjak*], to be informed when people are coming and going. It is included in these regulations that breaking the rules results in punishment, so that no one will be reckless enough to leave his place or bring another person into his place without informing the area's leaders or their police. It is also to make searching for evildoers or others easier. (Mayer 1889, 4–5)

The sedentarization of the population was not entirely successful. The Bandung plateau was still sparsely populated and escape from tax obligations was not impossible. Well into the nineteenth century, Dutch reports of *overloopen* or *wegloopen* were still common; these were the terms used to describe the Sundanese practice of simply leaving a region and thus avoiding forced labor. Known locally as "bird people," many of these elopers were in fact merely continuing the tradition of seminomadic swidden cultivation but in a context where its practice was now considered illegal. According to laws instituted by the Dutch in 1778 and 1805, offenders who took flight could be punished by six months of hard labor in chains (Svensson 1991, 16–17). As a result of these isolationist policies the town of Bandung remained somewhat of a backwater compared to the more cosmopolitan centers of Batavia, Semarang, and Surabaya. Whereas the latter were all important gateways for overseas trade with Europe, Bandung remained a small town whose main function was as a seat of local government. This is not to suggest that the region around Bandung was stagnating, however, for it was in fact economically booming, at least for the rich. Indeed, the regents of Bandung were reputedly some of the wealthiest local rulers in Java. But the town itself was little more than an administrative center and marketplace.

Several important developments provided the conditions for the demise of provincialism in the region and the realization of Daendels's vision of a city on the Great Post Road: the opening of the Preanger Regencies to European, Arab, and Chinese residents in 1852 (a move encouraged by van Hoëvell's letter to the governor general, quoted at the opening of this chapter); the relocation of the Preanger Regencies' capital from Cianjur to Bandung in 1864; the decision to allow private plantations in the region in

1870; and, in 1884, the opening of a railway connecting Bandung to Jakarta (then called Batavia) via Cianjur (Ekadjati, Hardjasaputra, and Marlina 1985, 39–41). The combined effects of these developments were far-reaching: as outsiders took up residence in the town, traffic to and from other areas increased, and a class of wealthy European plantation owners emerged to share power with state functionaries. These transformations coincided with a concerted attempt by the colonial government to restructure local power relations. An indirect system of hereditary rule gave way to a system of direct rule and bureaucratic office. Together, these changes established the preconditions for Bandung's eventual emergence as a modern colonial city.

A New Bureaucrat and His Scientific Gaze

The person who best exemplifies this early phase of colonial modernization is Martanagara, the regent of Bandung from 1893 to 1925. Born in 1845 to a district chief (*wedana*) in Sumedang, he was among the first of the Sundanese aristocracy to be schooled in Central Java. Raden Saleh, the great Javanese painter, sent both Martanagara and a friend to Semarang. Saleh thought it appropriate that Martanagara attend a Javanese school so that he could later "be employed by the Government in both the Sundanese and the Javanese areas" (Drewes 1985, 407).

In their first year in Semarang, both boys met only one other Sundanese, a fact that demonstrates the separation of Javanese and Sundanese societies in those years. In his autobiography, Martanagara describes his time at school as follows:

> We were taught reading, writing, and arithmetic, just as in Batavia, but also drawing and geodesy. In 1858, during the period we were at Semarang, the "cent" was introduced as legal tender, and the *duits* which had hitherto been used as currency had to be handed in in exchange for the new currency. This measure caused quite some excitement in the marketplaces, as only a few people were capable of doing conversions from *duits* to cents. At every intersection in the marketplace an officer was posted, who, guarded by two soldiers, acted as money changer. There were scores of places where such an exchange could be effected.
>
> When we had successfully attended school for about two years and were quite good at speaking Javanese, Ence Dimah received a letter from Raden Saleh to the effect that the two schoolboys should

be sent back to Batavia in the charge of a dependable person whom he knew well. That year the first steamships had put in an appearance in the Archipelago. . . . After a voyage of two days and two nights we arrived safely at Batavia harbour. (Drewes 1985, 408)

After a brief stint as a clerk in the western Javanese town of Sumedang, Martanagara's uncle decided he should enter public service. Martanagara reports,

> I was appointed to the position of assistant teacher at the school of Sumedang at a monthly salary of ƒ10.- (Dutch florins). The subjects I had to teach were: 1. Malay language; 2. calculation in compound fractions—at that time people in Sumedang only knew about halves and quarters; 3. geodesy. People were unacquainted with measuring in metres. The linear measure was the *tumbak* (3.7674 m.), numbering 12 feet (Dutch "Rijnlandse roede"). Nor were the villagers acquainted with the square measure *bau* (7096m²). If one asked a landowner, "How many bau of *sawah* [wet-rice fields] do you possess?," the answer would be "Four or five fields, and the yield is one to two *caeng*" if the man was not rich, or "Ten to twenty *caeng*, and ten or twenty fields" if he was. (409)

Martanagara's life took him on a complete tour of duty through just about every office open to "native" officials at the time. After working as a schoolmaster, he was charged with advising Sumedang district chiefs (*wedana* or *wadana*) on matters related to irrigation. Martanagara was then named head (*camat*) of the subdistrict of Cikadu, followed by an appointment as *kaliwon* of Sumedang. As *kaliwon*, or secretary to the regent's assistant (*patih*), Martanagara trained for a subsequent appointment as a *wedana*, in which capacity he was responsible for overseeing and maintaining what were then the key installations of government authority: the residences of the regent and the Dutch assistant resident, the state-owned coffee warehouses, and the district jail (Drewes 1985, 409–10). Eventually, Martanagara was promoted to *patih* of Sumedang, and finally to regent of Bandung.

It is clear from Martanagara's career trajectory that the bureaucratic rationalization of government was already well under way. Each office that Martanagara occupied involved responsibility for a set of specialized tasks. The chain of offices he passed through was no longer rooted in a single locale. And most importantly, he was a salaried official since, as a result of the Preanger reorganization, government officials' incomes were no longer taken directly from the population but were instead extracted indirectly through taxation (Drewes 1985, 410).

The form of the late-colonial state can be traced through two major developments that paralleled Martanagara's life. The first was the advent of bureaucratic government and the gradual deterritorialization of prior systems of rule. This deterritorialization occurred first in geographic terms, as Martanagara traveled to Central Java for his education and was eventually appointed regent of Bandung, a position that had hitherto been reserved for members of Bandung's aristocracy. It then occurred in economic terms, as he came to depend on a government salary for his income rather than on revenue extracted from the people he governed. The effect of this deterritorialization was the replacement of local aristocratic lineage with a line that had deeper functional segmentations and fewer ties to any particular place or people—a line derived from state administrative structures rather than from kinship and birthplace. The transformation was effected by a form of rationality that Michel Foucault associates with modern discipline: "In discipline, the elements are interchangeable, since each is defined by the place it occupies in a series, and by the gap that separates it from the others. The unit is, therefore, neither the territory (unit of domination), nor the place (unit of residence), but the rank: the place one occupies in a classification, the point at which a line and a column intersect, the interval in a series of intervals that one may traverse one after the other" (1995, 145–46). The spread of this type of rationality would provide the basis for the gradual bureaucratization of rule along Weberian lines.[3]

The second major development was that which took Martanagara from the study of mathematics, language, geodesy, and drawing to his being regarded by the Dutch authorities as someone whose technical knowledge approached that of a trained engineer. As he moved in this direction, Martanagara adopted a perspective on the region under his control that reflected colonial ambitions to modernize life in the Bandung Regency and to stimulate a new age in the traffic in commercial goods. Martanagara's description of his work as the newly installed regent of Bandung provides a sense of the forms this ambition took:

> The first matter demanding my attention was the manufacture of roof tiles. Only a quarter of the houses had tiled roofs, and thatched roofs were in the majority. Furthermore, I stimulated

cassava growing, since tapioca was very much in demand on the world market.... I also gave my attention to building bridges. On my inspection tours throughout the regency I had to cross the Citarum, the biggest river in the region, here and there. But bridges there were none, and one had to be taken across the river by ferry. This caused considerable inconvenience; therefore I asked permission to build some simple bamboo bridges which could be constructed by the villagers themselves. So within a short time the Citarum was bridged in five places.... Two years later these five bamboo bridges were replaced by iron ones for the convenience of everyone. (Drewes 1985, 415)

As a boy, Martanagara had already taken an interest in the power of mathematics to convert an old currency into a new one. As an administrator he used his mastery of this scientific power to convert "fields" into square measures, forests into irrigated rice fields, bamboo into tiles, and ferries into bridges. His tremendous aptitude for surveying and engineering won him recognition from the Dutch authorities and explains his speedy rise in the colonial hierarchy. Moreover, the projects Martanagara was involved in are indicative of the form the modern colony was beginning to take. On the one hand, there was a continued attempt to bring more people into the colonial economy by sedentarizing them and putting them to work. Thus, a roof tile industry was established in town and irrigated rice farms were introduced in rural areas. On the other hand, there was the attempt to bring disparate areas into communication with one another by increasing the volume and efficiency of traffic through the construction of bridges and roads and the transition to a cash economy. While the former practices tended to capture the flows of people and goods, the latter released these flows but only along certain specified and controlled pathways. An earlier colonial economy, characterized by stasis, and especially feudal modes of agriculture and economic organization, was now giving way to capitalism, characterized above all by its dynamism.

At times, this increased traffic threatened to overwhelm the channels laid down for it. In the following case, Martanagara describes how the government responded to the spread of a cattle contagion that occurred while he was still a *wedana*. The response was to try to contain the contagion by constructing a great fence down the middle of the island in order to block unsanitized flows of people and livestock from one region to the other.

In 1879 West Java was seriously hit by the plagues of rinderpest and epidemic malaria. The cattle plague started in Ujung Kulon and spread eastward over almost the whole of West Java. The symptoms were a swollen neck and loss of appetite, followed by death within three days. Numerous veterinary surgeons were sent from Europe, but they were powerless against this contagious disease, for which there seemed to be no cure. When the plague had penetrated as far as West Priangan, off Kandangwesi, large-scale measures were taken. It was decided to construct a dividing wall from south to north for the purpose of dividing Java in two. Two parallel fences were to isolate West Java from the rest of the island in the manner of a sanitary cordon, with no cattle from West Java being admitted in the space between. . . . Where a carriage-way or a minor road crossed the fence, a gate was constructed. These gates were each guarded by two soldiers. Lanes were simply closed off. Anyone wishing to pass through a gate had to be disinfected before; the carbolic solution used for that purpose went by the name of *kobokan,* "dishwater." (Drewes 1985, 411–12)

Having presided over these and other changes, each aimed at facilitating a regulated traffic in produce, people, and livestock, Martanagara was the first regent to inhabit Bandung as Daendels had envisioned it—that is, as a city uprooted from its place and reinstalled on an abstract line that had been engineered into the landscape. Being both an administrator and an "engineer," Martanagara inhabited this line to the extreme, and from his position at "Kilometer 0," acted to extend it further and further into the districts he ruled.

The two great lines of the modern colonial state—bureaucracy and traffic—were not laid down in a vacuum, and their encounters with the world beyond were not unproblematic. Just as the imposition of a feudal mode of production had given rise to the "bird people," so, too, did the engineered release and channeling of human and capital flows give rise to its own problems. Accounts of these problems do not take the form of history so much as local stories. The two accounts that follow come, respectively, from Martanagara's autobiography and the biography of Lie Kimhok, a contemporary of Martanagara, who was a journalist and publisher. They appear as digressions from their respective narratives and are marked by a shift to a more informal discourse, as if both authors are finally getting to what really interests them.

Martanagara's digression occurs as he reflects on the moment he was confirmed as regent of Bandung. He recounts how he was summoned to the residency late one evening, where he was informed of a criminal plot:

> The Resident himself came to meet me on the steps and said, "Let us go inside." We entered the reception room, where two men were already present, a lower-class European, Van Woesiek by name, and a certain Iksan, who was unknown to me. . . .
>
> Addressing Mr. Van Woesiek, the Resident then said, "Come on, Mr. Van Woesiek, let us hear your story; but tell it in Sundanese, so that Iksan, too, may understand you." Thereupon Mr. Van Woesiek told us that there were plans for an attempt on the Resident's life by means of dynamite. On the next Saturday afternoon a charge of dynamite was to be hidden in the Resident's carriage, so that, when the carriage was set in motion, the dynamite would be detonated and the carriage destroyed, and everyone in it would be killed.
>
> I was ordered to have a search instituted in the houses of all suspected persons according to the information supplied. . . . In the early morning of the next day six houses were searched. Dynamite was found underneath the house of one R. Nata Anbia, a relation of the deceased Regent, but a further police inquiry brought to light that he was not to blame for its presence there.
>
> The inquiry into this affair continued for four months. Every cooperation was given by the Regents of Cianjur, Garut and Sumedang, who put their police spies at my disposal. The Regent of Sumedang even came to Bandung every Saturday evening. The protracted investigation brought to light that the plotters had intended to murder not only the Resident, but also the Assistent-Resident, the Controleur, and myself. Ten people, among them four *priyayis* [members of the nobility], were a party to the plot; however, the matter was not taken to court. The reason given by them for their conspiracy was their utter dissatisfaction at the appointment of a Regent who was not of the stock of the Regents of Bandung. So the affair was settled by the political measure of their banishment from Java for a period of twenty years. (Drewes 1985, 414–15)

This was not the first time government officials in Bandung had been targeted for assassination. In the 1840s, the assistant resident was murdered—the regent narrowly escaped—in a plot not unlike the one described above. The differences between the two cases are instructive. In the earlier case, the two culprits were a Chinese trader, named Munada, and the chief prosecutor (*jaksa*) of Bandung. Munada harbored a grudge against the assistant resident because the latter had jailed him for failing to pay back money he had borrowed.[4] The *jaksa* had a grudge against the regent because the regent had failed to take his daughter as a wife; he also hoped that by doing away with the regent, he would be appointed as a replacement. Together the two plotted to set a fire near the marketplace, and then to kill the officials in the ensuing commotion. In the event, while Munada was able to fatally stab the assistant resident with his ceremonial dagger (*kris*), a bodyguard protected the regent from harm. Whereas in the Munada case the motive for the assassination attempt was largely apolitical and was located firmly within the realm of kinship and debt, the motive in the Martanagara case involved defending the system of kinship and debt against a new system of government imposed from without. Given this difference, it is perhaps appropriate that the earlier plotters used the traditional weapon of assassination, the *kris*, while the later plotters planned to booby-trap the resident's carriage, a key symbol of the new, traffic-oriented state.[5]

Although this dramatic event shows the extremes to which Bandung's elites were prepared to go to resist the imposition of a ruler from outside their stock, it also shows that it was not just the conspirators who saw Martanagara in terms of his heredity. It was, after all, the regent of Sumedang, where Martanagara hailed from, who took the greatest interest in the subsequent investigation, making the trip to Bandung every Saturday to keep abreast of developments. And although Martanagara was in many ways a representative of the new bureaucratic state, he, too, seems not to have forgotten older ties. When he retired he chose not stay in Bandung, although he had been living there for the past twenty-five years. Instead, he returned to Sumedang, his "place of origin" (Drewes 1985, 417).

The second story, taken from the biography of Lie Kimhok, concerns resistance not to the bureaucratic line of the modern state but to the lines being engineered into the landscape to facilitate the new age of traffic. This was not so much a political or social resistance as a resistance to a mode of perception. The story involves the siting of the land near Bogor for the construction of the Preanger line, a railroad that would link the Preanger Regencies to Batavia. Its protagonist is Prince Aquaboachi, a man who lived in Bogor toward the end of the nineteenth century. According to Ie Soei Tio (1958, 30), this is one of many strange stories about Aquaboachi that circulated for decades after his death in 1903:

Prince Aquaboachi came from Ashanti (West Africa) and was educated in Europe. After completing his studies at the Technical High School in Holland, where he had become a mining engineer, he came to Java. . . . After retiring he lived in Bogor, where he bought some land in Sukasari and built a beautiful palace in Tadjur. He was a huge man with an angry face and harsh customs, but he was friendly and was known to possess skills in the occult arts. Among those who received help from him was a surveyor [*mantri ukur*] who suffered a difficulty in his work near Batutulis, between Batutulis and Tandjakan Empang. The surveyor was surveying land for the installation of a railroad (the Preanger line) when suddenly he couldn't use his theodolite because in front of the measuring instrument—which was in excellent condition—all that could be seen was thick, billowing black smoke, which obscured long-distance visibility. He and many others were astonished by this problem, and it could not have been solved except by asking for Prince Aquaboachi's help.

The prince-engineer came and inspected the place of the incident and was in fact able to solve the problem. He explained that not far from the place the *mantri* was working, in the direction he was surveying, an old grave was located. That grave was the grave of Rangga Gadung, an important man in the Padjadjaran kingdom, and it was that grave that was producing the smoke as an obstacle. Smoke that was only visible in the theodolite and was not visible to the ordinary eye!

The building contractors, Thung Siong Kie and Koan Djin An, paid ƒ300.-, then a large slametan ceremony was performed during which a water buffalo was sacrificed and the Rangga Gadung's grave was shifted to a place across the Tjisedane River. The cost was low when compared to the benefit, for after the grave had been moved, the work of surveying could continue and the Preanger line did not have to change its direction. (Tio 1958, 30)

In this story, the failure of the surveyor's instrument is not due to some technical problem on its part; rather, it stems from the very nature of the place it was trying to survey, which obstructed the gaze of the mediated eye. The eye mediated by the surveying instrument sees more than the naked eye does; it is capable of seeing an obstruction that does not appear as such to the naked eye. However, it is incapable of seeing the source of this obstruction—namely, the grave of the royal figure. For this, Prince

Aquaboachi's occult powers—powers I described in chapter 1 as a kind of "sixth sense"—are necessary. In the end, the problem presented by the obstruction is resolved by a displacement. The grave does not prevent the construction of the railroad, or even prevent the line from following its original course; rather, through a ritual movement (the *slametan*), the grave itself is shifted from its original location (just as the conspirators above were expelled from Bandung to allow for the extension of the bureaucratic line). The act of uprooting is allowed to progress, but the power of the grave still exists, albeit in a displaced form.

By the end of the nineteenth century, the increase in traffic and the deepening of government in the Bandung area had led to notable changes to the town itself. In 1852, when the government first produced a plan for the town, the layout adhered closely to what was then typical for regency capitals.[6] It showed a main square on which were located the regent's building, a mosque, and a jail. Scattered around this main square were a number of hamlets interspersed with gardens and rice fields. The population of the town was only a little over eleven thousand people at this time and included just nine Europeans (Kunto 1993, 142). A half century later, the town was home to two schools, one for training teachers and the other for civil servants (Lubis 2005, 132). North of the Post Road a train station had been built, along with an installation that served as the central repair shop for the state-owned railways. Near the train station was a large new home and office for the resident, the highest-ranking European official in the town (Brand 1958, 230). Shops, hotels, markets, and other services had become more numerous. The city's population had also grown significantly with newcomers arriving in search of work and the town gradually spreading out and absorbing the surrounding villages (Reerink 2006, 4). By 1901 Bandung had a population of nearly thirty thousand and counting (Kunto 1984, 94).

Reordering City Surfaces: The View from the Carriage

Although Bandung was modernizing and growing, it was only at the end of the nineteenth century that the city began to come into view as an object of more sustained and intensive bureaucratic surveillance and control. The new regime of control did not come into being all at once. It emerged gradually through a step-by-step extension and refinement of the bureaucratic gaze into all the dimensions of urban space. In general terms, one can think of this extension as both following from and expressing the shifts in perspective available to the city's political and economic elite. The gaze took as its first object the roads themselves and all the surfaces of the built environment that would have been visible from a carriage or a car passing through. It then extended to incorporate the view from above, a perspective enabled by the lay of the land, by architectural innovations, and, eventually, by the use of airplanes. Finally, using a regime of inspections and data collection, the bureaucratic gaze sought to extend its reach into the depths of the city's *kampung* (neighborhoods) and homes in an effort to make even the darkest corners of the city visible.

As a result of this gaze, the lines that planners, administrators, and inspectors would come to lay down in Bandung would follow certain ethnic distinctions, and in this sense were physical manifestations of the colonial divide. In the north of the city, up on the hill, a European enclave would take shape, providing a place from which the city's colonial elite could look down over the southern section of the city, where the *pribumi*, or indigenous population, lived. The division between these communities would be marked by two great slices across the middle of the city, the Great Post Road and the railway tracks, between which a thriving community of Chinese, Arab, and a few Jewish traders would live. The northern, southern, and middle sections of the city would be further divided into *kampung* (Sundanese: *babakan*) with an even more local affiliation. For example, the western portion of the middle section of the city was where the Arabs would live, while the *pribumi* part of the city would include Babakan Bogor (where people from Bogor who had moved to Bandung as railway builders lived), Babakan Surabaya, Kampung Jawa, and Babakan Ciamis.[7] However, it was in the center of the city, around the main square, where the city's cultural life would emerge. This was the region where, to some extent at least, the different ethnic groups could mix. In respect to its overall plan, Bandung would thus roughly follow and perfect the model then prevalent in other cities in the Indies—the model that John Furnivall would later describe as the "plural society."[8]

The first major thrust to order the city anew arose among the emerging elite of Bandung, the European planters who had taken advantage of the end of the *Cultuurstelsel* and the opening up of the Preanger districts by leasing huge tracts of lands from the government and establishing lucrative plantations. Between 1898 and 1906, these planters worked in concert with the regency administration to institute a number of changes: new roads were built; existing roads were widened, paved with cobblestone, and provided with ditches; sidewalks made from wood and bamboo were paved over; oil lamps were installed for street lighting; fences were constructed to divide the road from people's yards; traditional houses that lined the roads (on stilts, made from bamboo and wood without nails so as to facilitate disassembly and relocation) were converted into permanent structures with brick walls and tile roofs; a market was built to house street-side vendors; the shop fronts along the Great Post Road were renovated in a uniform style; two new cemeteries were built to replace the single one then used by Europeans and Chinese; and, finally, the use of water-buffalo-drawn carts for transportation within the town was replaced by the horse and carriage (Kunto 1984, 74–75).

These developments indicate a change in the line of sight. Whereas the construction of the Great Post Road and the Preanger railway had involved a segmented line cut through the land, displacing and realigning territories in its wake, Bandung's first urban planners were beginning to look more closely at the surfaces they passed as they traversed that line. The horse and carriage on the paved roads would have provided a smooth ride, a kind of hovering movement, relatively free of the bumps and jerks that characterized the older modes of transportation. It would have allowed passengers to feel at one with the line and to overcome the sense of friction that characterized past attempts at mobility.[9] It was with this "view from the carriage" that an aesthetic of urban order was formulated: traditional, seminomadic houses would be sedentarized and made over, shops would be given a face-lift, street vendors would be rationalized and collected together in marketplaces. It was a view that focused on surfaces, establishing order on the face of things. The new boundaries defined functional positions in space: a road for carriages, a sidewalk for pedestrians, a ditch for water and refuse, a fence for the yard, a wall for the house, a cemetery for the Chinese dead, another cemetery for the European dead. Separate and integrated, everything had its place.

The new aesthetic order was not embraced by local people everywhere, of course. When a similar program was introduced in the coastal town of Serang, a colonial official found that police violence was necessary for its imposition:

> A kampong has 15 houses, disorderly and close together, which is detrimental to the health of the inhabitants. Twelve of the inhabitants place their houses such that they are in the middle of their respective compounds with the front facing the roads, while the distance from one house to another is not less than three Rhineland birches. The three other inhabitants nevertheless categorically refuse

to change the stance of their houses in their plots because their present stance has provided them with luck and will continue to do so.... In the territory of belief, the Inlanders in general are holding very fast.... So it is with the three people mentioned above that it happened that one by one they were physically taken by a strong *oppasser* to a dark corner and given the necessary kicks. (Dutch East Indies 1911, 142–43)

The beliefs this official refers to in disparaging terms related to the locating of houses according to geomancy rather than a Euclidean geometry. Whereas the former implied a notion of space in which things were oriented relative to the qualitative features of temporalities, directions, and landscapes (spirit abodes, the lay of the land, water sources, trees, etc.), the latter implied an abstract and quantified space in which things were oriented in relation to the observer. In the late nineteenth and early twentieth centuries, the policing of cities and towns sought to impose the latter kind of order to the surface of things.

A Prototypical Colonial City: The View from Above

The period from 1906, when Bandung was granted municipal status, to the onset of the Depression in the early 1930s saw tremendous growth in the city. The population more than tripled, from under 50,000 people to over 160,000.[10] In this same period the number of European residents increased from just a few thousand to almost 20,000, making Bandung the city with the highest proportion of Europeans in the Dutch East Indies. As a consequence of this growth, northern Bandung saw an explosion of construction, as housing complexes were built to absorb this influx of people.

One of the main reasons Europeans moved to the city was the climate, which was much cooler and thought to be much healthier than those of Batavia or Surabaya. It was this consideration that led to Bandung being chosen as the site for the first technical college in the Indies, what is now known as the Bandung Institute of Technology. Similarly, the combination of the city's healthy climate and its elevated position, which made it more secure from foreign invasion, was what led to a plan to move the seat of colonial government from Batavia to Bandung.[11] Indeed, many government offices and enterprises did move their headquarters to the city, including, among others, the post, telegraph, and telephone service, the Department of War, the state railway, the Department of Public Works, the munitions factory, and the geological museum. Due to a lack of money, however, the People's Council (Volksraad), the governor general's palace, the Department of Internal Affairs, and Department of Education remained in Batavia.

The change in architecture that accompanied this period of growth was profound. While many of the houses took the old and familiar shape of box-like structures dominated by huge, sloping roofs, there were a growing number of experimental designs for both houses and public buildings that self-consciously emphasized a modern style. There were, for example, a large number of tropical art deco and art nouveau buildings, both homes and commercial buildings. The most exemplary of these was the Villa Isola (Island Villa), located at the extreme north of the city, high on a hill overlooking the entire Bandung plateau. Built by an Italian millionaire as a private residence, the building is now part of a university campus. It is four stories tall and layered like a wedding cake, with curved walls on all sides. It appears to have been designed for the express purpose of providing a panoramic view, as on each side of the building, and on each floor, there is a line of windows running along the entirety of the curving walls. Indeed, if one looks out these windows, one is met with the peculiar sensation of looking at a panoramic photo collage, with the window frames forming the point of overlap between each respective image. Part of the reason for this impression is that the short windows and turret-like architecture give the building a strong sense of interiority, as if those on the inside are entirely separate from the outside view they are beholding.

The other architectural style that made its appearance in this era was the so-called Indo-European style. The prime example of this is the building that housed the Department of Public Works, one of only two buildings that were completed for the giant square that was intended to constitute the colonial center of government. Now known as Gedung Sate (Satay Building), after the skewer-like spears on its roof, this structure was built several years before Villa Isola. It is of monumental proportions and highly symmetrical, with the strong horizontal and vertical lines that characterized much state architecture in Europe at that time. It shares with Villa Isola a layered quality and a commanding view in all directions, especially from the small tower at the top. However, it differs from the latter building in that it has an "Indies accent," with the roof resembling those found on mosques of similar vintage. The overall effect is peculiar, for the sheer size of the structure and its location on an open expanse make it appear impervious to its surroundings, but it is nonetheless meant to signify local "tradition."

3.1 Villa Isola, Bandung, circa 1933. Courtesy of Southeast Asian and Caribbean Images (KITLV) under CC License (https://creativecommons .org/licenses/by/4.0/legalcode). Available at: http://hdl.handle.net/1887.1 /item:786052.

The thrust of development in the European part of Bandung during this late-colonial period was indicative of two contemporary trends. The first trend was a growing concern with developing a point of view that could capture the totality of the city, a commanding view from above. This was achieved in some cases by constructing buildings with a view over the city; in others through the use of aerial photography, which was quite popular in this period.[12] The second trend was the increasing tendency to use architecture and building design as a means to provide concrete representations of the prototypical "tropical" or "colonial" city. This was to be a healthy and modern city that incorporated aesthetic styles from the East as well as the West. But who was this colonial city for? Was this a demonstration to the colonized peoples that "we" can all be modern? Were non-European Bandungers supposed to look at the Indo-European structures and see themselves reflected in them? This seems not to have been the intention. In the domain of architecture, the privileged audience was European and consisted primarily of visitors from other Indies cities and from Singapore, India, and Europe. The local tourist club, Bandoeng Vooruit, encouraged visitors to write about their impressions of the city. Appearing as regular features in local newspapers and magazines during the 1920s and '30s, such writings played an important part in shaping Bandungers' own perceptions of their city and their views about how it ought to be transformed. Even the Indo-European style got its major impetus from the critical comments of Hendrik Petrus Berlage, a respected architect who, after visiting Bandung, wrote that its architecture did not show enough local accent. It was Berlage who suggested that Bandung ought to be constructed as a "prototype" for colonial cities everywhere.[13]

Urban Hygiene and the War on Rats:
The View in Depth

At the same time that colonial architects were developing a line of sight that could capture the totality of the city, the colonial state was also beginning to penetrate beyond the surfaces of *kampung* life. What had begun as an aesthetic of order that applied only to those things glimpsed from the carriage, as it were, became something quite different: an eye that searches out disorder, investigates the depths of things, exposes things to knowledge, and makes this knowledge the basis of a new order. It was this view in depth that saw the first large-scale European penetrations of, and interventions in, the "native" neighborhood.

The emergence of this panoptic gaze was driven by an intensified interest in the problem of social welfare in the Indies and particularly the problems of health and hygiene. This was a period in which government officials and other members of the colonial elite were starting to pay more and more attention to the problem of welfare in the colony, evidenced by the growing number of detailed investigations and reports focusing on the social, economic, and health conditions of the populace.[14] The problem of disease had always loomed large in the Dutch East Indies, where outbreaks of smallpox, influenza, beriberi, syphilis, cholera, bubonic plague, and other diseases were common. Addressing this problem had been a central concern of Dutch colonists since they first began to settle in the region. Some of the more drastic measures were taken by Daendels, who in the early nineteenth century had Batavia's city walls torn down along with many of its fortifications to facilitate the circulation of fresh air. But by the early twentieth century, medical science had trained a far more microscopic sight on the problem of contagion and had determined that disease was best battled through a systematic and comprehensive control of "hygiene."

3.2 Gedung Sate, Bandung, circa 1920. *Het hoofdgebouw van het Departement van Gouvernementsbedrijven te Bandoeng* [The Main Building of the Department of Government Enterprises at Bandung]. From the album of B. Coops. Courtesy of Southeast Asian and Caribbean Images (KITLV) under CC License (https://creativecommons.org/licenses/by/4.0/legalcode). Available at: http://hdl.handle.net/1887.1/item:913979.

The new discourse on hygiene had its origins in attempts to combat disease in the teeming industrial cities of Europe, where poverty and illness were rampant. In the Indies it began with a similar urban focus, but it came to be imbued with a distinctively racist logic. The early part of the twentieth century was a period of heightened awareness and anxiety about the instability of racial boundaries, particularly among newly arrived Europeans.[15] In urban settings, where people of various social groups might live in close proximity to one another, the boundaries between European, native, and Chinese were becoming increasingly fraught.[16] In its focus on the dangers posed by the permeability of such boundaries, the discourse on hygiene dovetailed with emerging racist discourses. Writings by hygiene experts emphasized that diseases claiming European lives might well have originated in the squalid and unsanitary conditions of non-European slums; they also emphasized that high levels of disease would adversely impact the supply of labor power and the economy. Accordingly, colonial interventions aimed at improving hygiene in urban *kampung* are best viewed as a matter of enlightened self-interest (Coté 2002).

This concern for hygiene provided the overarching rationale for greater state involvement in regulating and controlling the urban environment. This was evident in a whole series of plans, ordinances, and programs of "improvement" (*verbetering*) aimed at reshaping the cityscape according to a new ideal of urban order.[17] And these are largely responsible for the visual order that neighborhoods throughout Java display to this day. This fact was of course not lost on my interlocutors. These are the chain of associations an elderly gentleman in Bandung made when asked about what the architecture of houses in southern Bandung was like before the revolutionary era:

> In the Dutch period, the houses were off the ground. The floors were made of wood, and the sides and top of bamboo. At first the walls had two layers with a space in between, and the roof was made with whole pieces of bamboo, open at the end. The problem with this was disease, because bedbugs would come from the chickens underneath the house (when they had a new chick). But then the problem became the "pest" of rats in the walls and the bamboo. So the walls were made with only one layer and the roof bamboo lengths were closed off. If a family experienced a death they would be taken away and placed in barracks with other families of victims to prevent it from spreading. They would then place a police guard on the house to prevent theft and the spread of the lice. The kids at school would have to line up to receive their injections, which in those days were given in the chest, not in the arm. It would leave a red mark.

The penetration and reconstruction of houses to prevent rat infestation presents a good example of how the panoptic gaze sought to police the city. To understand how this gaze developed it is helpful to examine contemporary reports on hygiene. What follows is a citation from a report on the control of endemic diseases produced in the late 1920s by the Netherlands Indies Medical and Sanitary Service. It provides a step-by-step account of how the logic of a penetrating eye led to the reconstruction of the residential environment. The citation concerns the campaign against plague.

> The danger to human beings emanates exclusively from the rats and the fleas which parasitize on them and thus a rational campaign must be directed against the rats. As, however, experience has taught us that a direct war against the rats i.e. their extermination by mechanical means (traps, etc.) or by chemical or bacterial poisons, only provides very temporary results, the war can only be waged on indirect lines i.e. by making the distance between human being and rat as

great as possible and by maintaining it, so that the contact between the two is broken. . . .

The clearing of the house of rats, theoretically the most radical measure, turned out to be feasible, within certain limits, in practice. De Vogel and van Leghem, who were the first to make a study of the way to prevent nestling in so many different places in the house, showed the way in which to arrive at a solution. . . . By depriving the rat of its favourite nesting places in this manner, it was successfully driven out of the houses and it appeared that the fight had been won. (Netherlands Indies Medical and Sanitary Service 1929, 36–37)

The tone of the report is confident. Military metaphors are used to buttress an approach to hygiene that is firmly based in rigorous scientific reasoning and technical ingenuity. At the same time, a bit of fear collects just below the surface, and the report's authors are clearly anxious about the long-term efficacy of the barriers they had put in place against infection.

However, although the problem of combating the plague had been reduced to a housing problem, it soon appeared that the final objective—the breaking of the contact and maintaining it—was by no means achieved. . . . Even the improved houses still provided nesting possibilities. Every hole which, through bad workmanship, had remained open or was insufficiently closed, was used to full advantage by the rats, which could now nestle, hidden more than ever from the human eye, in the bamboo or ridge purlin through the undermined cement. The rats were also quick to take advantage of the so-called *trontongan* (slits made in the bamboo between the knots, from 1.5 to 2.5 centimeters wide, for joining purposes) and therefore it is understandable that bamboo was more and more replaced by wood, in order to do away with the blind space in the bamboo. Even then the rats had not been driven out of the house; where hidden nestling places were no longer available it was found that the rats were content to build their nests on the horizontal beams, the ceiling etc.—thus in completely visible positions. These technical improvements, therefore, only deprived the rat of not visible nestling places, so that if the success which had already been gained was not to be lost again it would be necessary to wage a continual war against the rats, as soon as they returned. An inspection service was therefore indispensable to the maintenance of the technical improvements and also to drive out the rats as they returned and if possible to destroy them. (37, italics in original)

In this passage, the rats, which had hitherto been treated as predictable creatures, turn out to be quite devious, using nooks and crannies to their "full advantage." While it is possible to drive them out of the house, it remains necessary to continually police the house to make sure they do not return. Nonetheless, the rats somehow manage to return. This was true even of what the report's authors described as "houses of perfect technical construction."

> A systematic investigation of the reasons for this state of affairs brought to light that the improved construction of the houses, which was mainly confined to the architrave and the roof, usually resulted in a migration of the rats to a lower part of the premises where in the dark bedroom, under the *bale-bale* [bed made from bamboo] and also among the litter of household goods and stores etc. there was still plenty of opportunity for nestling. The improvement of the house, both as regards the living quarters and the outbuildings, had therefore to be followed by an improvement in the living conditions. In the same way as the upper part of the house had been made more surveyable by making changes in construction, it was now necessary to apply this system to the floors; in the first place by an efficient arrangement of the household goods, especially the *bale-bale* and by providing more light. It was not until this combination of technical and household improvements was applied that the house inspection was successful in its efforts to maintain the broken contact and, as a result, to stamp out the plague. (37–38, italics in original)

The explicit object of this campaign's surveillance is not a thing so much as a relation: the relation or connection between humans and rats. This connection is objectified in the idea of the house-nest, and it is against this that an operation aimed at eradication is mobilized. The effects of the operation, however, are far more profound than the simple eradication of house-nests, for the attempt to prevent contact brings whole new objects into view. This is the result of a kind of tracking movement, in the sense that a camera tracks an object: from the fleas, to the rats, to the roof, to the bamboo, to the walls, to the rafters, to the floors, to the bed, to the household stores, and out into streets, neighborhoods, and the city as a whole. As each of these objects comes into focus, it is redefined. At first this redefinition is simply in relation to its appeal as a nesting place for rats, but this quickly gives way to a more general redefinition based on each object's "surveyability." It is in reference to this putative surveyability that each thing is then physically reconstructed and provided with a new order. Spaces that do not meet the requirements of surveyability are "chaotic," seemingly "constructed without any thought of order or rule," as the report's authors write (38–39).

The reconstruction of things from the standpoint of their surveyability was what led to changes to the architecture and urban plans of Indonesian cities, changes collectively known as *kampung verbetering*, or neighborhood improvement.[18] In Bandung, *kampung verbetering* took a number of forms: municipal regulations were introduced prohibiting the construction of houses closer than two and a half meters from the boundary of one's land, thus ensuring that houses were separated by at least five meters (to provide more "air" and "light");[19] electric street lighting was introduced; roads and fences were straightened; houses were renovated; surveyors were hired to produce a highly detailed map of all the houses and roads in the city; and a house certification program was introduced in which each new or renovated house was given a certificate that provided a map of its layout (*Bandoeng en de hygiëne* 1927, 34–53). Such changes often implied not just a visual ordering but a linguistic and an archival ordering. As a result of house registration, for example, the "house" became something that existed in the state archives as well as on the street; it was given, as it were, an address, but this number corresponded to both the house's physical location and its location in the archive. Yet for non-European inhabitants of the city, this new order was still represented as something foreign. As Haryoto Kunto (1984, 74) notes, houses that had been inspected and certified were called *woning* (Dutch for "house") by the locals, rather than by the Indonesian word *rumah* or the Sundanese word *imah*. A *woning* was a new thing, existing alongside the *rumah*, but maintaining a foreign connotation.

The transition from the focus on nests to the focus on the general "surveyability of the house and its interior" is not a seamless one. The operation begins with an assumption: that nesting is something rats prefer to do out of sight, in the dark, in the "blind spots" of buildings. The attempt to eliminate darkness has the unintended consequence of actually making what darkness remains that much more impenetrable to surveillance, so that if the rats can access it, they are that much more invisible. This, however, is a technical problem that can be solved. The more profound and scandalous problem is a conceptual one, noted by the author in the anxious recognition that the rat is perfectly "content" to nest on the rafters "in completely visible positions." The work had been conducted on the peculiar assumption that light would in itself sever the contact and bring order. In a sense, this was the great fantasy and fetish of colonial surveillance: the dream that light would itself penetrate the depths of the colony's darkest corners and render them ordered, that "enlightenment" would obfuscate the need for inspectors. As it turns out in practice, however, there is no necessary relation between light and the willingness of rats to nest; light in itself is not capable of severing the contact. At least in the case of rats, order still requires the existence of a surveying eye—in this case, the inspector. The fantasy of total surveillance thus gives way to the more modest goal of institutionalizing a form of surveillance that comes to rest firmly on a subject.[20]

When relocated on the subject, surveillance becomes less of a technical problem and more of a social one. It is necessary to put in place enough inspectors such that any rats that reappear will immediately be detected and eliminated. To this end, the Public Health Service created a Division of Medical Hygiene Propaganda, which was responsible for educating the populace about the necessity of hygiene (Honggare 2021, 101). Unlike earlier hygiene programs, however, which had been applied without concern for local conditions, this new method emphasized the importance of enlisting the support of the masses. It also recognized the need for a more flexible, pragmatic approach.

> An attempt to carry *out hygienic measures by beginning with the use of force gives rise to active and passive resistance* which always accompany the enforcement of any law which is not supported by public opinion. Therefore any attempt to bring people to a more hygienic manner of living should be made not by means of laws, but by educational measures. . . .
>
> There would be no objection whatever to the use of coercion if its use could secure permanent results. But it has been tried so often without success, and it is so much more difficult to secure the cooperation of the people after a failure due to the use of coercion that it is not advisable to begin with the use of force. Work should be begun with educational measures and coercion should be added only after the educational measures have built up a public opinion which is strong enough to give support to the measures of force. (Hydrick 1939, 7–8; italics in original)

The aim of these educational measures was the formation of a governed subject that would take an active interest in hygienic living, making the costly use of coercive inspectors unnecessary. Foucault (1980, 155) has described the logic of this form of discipline in the context of prison control: "There is no need for arms, physical violence, material constraints. Just a gaze. An inspecting gaze, a gaze which each individual under its weight will end by interiorising to the point that he is his own overseer." With the Dutch colonial hygiene program, the interiorization of this gaze was pursued actively through education.

> Experience has shown how subtle this work is, how carefully and tactfully one must set to work, and especially how every precipitate action and every inconsiderate interference from without, can ruin everything in a short time. The purpose of the work is to add to the manner of living and the customs of the people something which will benefit their physical welfare. This must really become an essential part of their way of thinking, an imitation which is chosen not as a result of coercion or persuasion, but indeed as a result of their own conviction that it is necessary and that is also for their own good to follow this example. (Hydrick 1939, 8)

But as the author of this work makes clear, the people "*should be lead, not driven. They should be stimulated and lead to express a desire to live more hygienically. It is the task of the health worker to create this desire*" (3; italics in original). Not only must everyone become inspectors, then, but they must be stimulated to desire that which the inspectors desire.

And yet stimulating this desire was not an easy task. In the beginning, the propaganda service worked by publishing and distributing booklets about hygiene in local languages, but this only met with moderate success. Rather, it was found that "plastic instruction" (Hydrick 1939, 7) was more effective, so the propaganda service, with funding from the Rockefeller Foundation, instituted a massive education campaign. In three years (1926–28) they conducted "no less than 462 000 house demonstrations, 15 500 public lectures, 1 366 school lectures, 1 639 microscopic demonstrations, 762 special lectures and 564 worm demonstrations" (Hydrick 1939, 35). The first targets of this education were the health workers (*mantri*) themselves. An elaborate system for training these workers was developed, which, in addition to teaching them about hygiene sciences, taught them how to speak and how to sit during their house visits so as to avoid coming across as figures of colonial authority. In these training courses, prospective *mantri* had to live as the people did, making their own toothbrushes, growing their own vegetables, and so forth. Having completed their training, they were then expected to live among the people whom they were educating. This created a problem of supervision, which was solved in the following manner:

> Each mantri, midwife, or other worker has at his house in the village or at the house of the village head, a sketch map of the village showing every house with its number, the roads and paths, rivers etc. Each morning and each afternoon a small paper flag with the date and "A.M." or "P.M." is placed on the map in the area of the village where the person plans to work so he can be easily found by the doctor if he visits that village for inspection or checking.
>
> At each house the mantri has a small card which is fastened to the doorpost or somewhere in the front gallery of the house. On this card he notes the date of his last visit and the subject or subjects discussed and the number of the members of the family who understand the subject. This gives the doctor an opportunity to check the mantri's work at any house even if he can not find the mantri. (Hydrick 1939, 33)

While the ultimate aim of this campaign was rather mundane forms of education, it was found that modern visual technologies were useful for stimulating people's interest and desire. During the daytime public lectures, charts, models, photographs, and drawings were used; at night, it was lantern slides and films. Particularly in rural areas, such visual technologies were new, and according to Hydrick, required varying degrees of explanation.

> To the village man a photograph or a drawing has no depth. Therefore the lines and other details have very little meaning for him until they are thoroughly explained by the health visitor. After the photographs and drawings have been explained, their meaning becomes clear.
>
> The image thrown upon a screen from a lantern slide has more depth and is therefore more easily understood....
>
> Since the film shows moving objects, living persons, animals et cetera, the projection of the film on the screen, in as far as it concerns the number of people, houses, trees, et cetera which are shown,

is still more easily understood, but the scenes of the films pass so quickly that the lesson which should be taught by the film is not so well understood. . . .

Since the projection from a lantern slide can be kept upon the screen for several minutes, the mantri has an opportunity to explain the projected picture in detail. It is for this reason that, where the work is in the beginning stage, the lantern slide is of more value than the film.

Microscopes are useful for giving demonstrations to small groups of people, but these demonstrations must be preceded by a very careful explanation concerning magnification. The people are first taught to put small objects behind a glass of water to see how the glass of water magnifies these objects. They are then shown how one magnifying glass magnifies, and that a set of two magnifying glasses has a much greater effect. Then they are shown that a microscope consists of many magnifying glasses and is therefore able to make visible bacteria, which are invisible to the naked eye. They can then understand that they can not see the bacteria which they have on their hands. (1939, 21–23)

Educating people to see the world as the inspector sees it is a complicated process. It involves the acceptance and comprehension of a way of seeing that is mediated by the lenses of cameras and microscopes. When combined with the transmission of knowledge about what is being seen through the lenses, the process presumably aims to facilitate a kind of identification with the mediated eye of the camera or microscope. This identification allows for the mediating technology to "disappear" so that in place of two-dimensional lines, one sees an image in depth. In the hygiene campaign, the formation and reproduction of a subject of surveillance was thus inseparable from the development of a new type of vision that was mediated by a combination of lenses and knowledge. One can imagine the *mantri* standing by the lantern slide with a pointer, showing those looking at it which constellations of light and darkness were people and which were houses or latrines, teaching them at once how to read an image and how to evaluate it within the context of hygienic practices. It is unclear, however, how effective the campaign was at establishing this identification. The films drew huge crowds, but the interest people showed was very short-lived, particularly if the subjects of the films were from other locales. It seemed that people were more desirous of the spectacle the films and slideshows provided than of their intended "meaning."[21] In fact, the best results in this campaign were found to occur in cases where the effects of hygiene were demonstrated to be visible and immediate. For example, sufferers of frambesia (which disfigures the skin) would be gathered from a region and treated. They would then be shown to the population a month later (each in a different stage of the cure) as "living evidence" of the positive effects of intervention (Hydrick 1939, 62). These types of "before-and-after" images were central to all the hygiene operations, since they stood as proof that progress had been achieved. Photography was essential to this proof, as it allowed for the immediate juxtaposition of the two moments. Yet what the photos illustrate is that the results sought were as much aesthetic as scientific.[22]

To the colonial administration, the image of an order in which everything was surveyable was just as important, if not more so, as the reduction of disease. Moreover, it is ambiguous what it was about the images of "before" and "after" that made them so effective. Was it that people learned to identify with an image that embodied the inspector's perspective? Or was it the juxtaposition of the photos that gave them their effect? Whereas the former would imply the propaganda service's success at disciplining the population to see the environment as inspectors see it, the latter implies something quite different—namely, a different way of looking, one that "jumps" back and forth between the two photos, not so much identifying with the lines of sight as appraising the transformative power of the force of scientific modernity that intervenes between them. If the force is strong, it produces a spectacle.

Urban Panopticon

The colonial city of Bandung was the product of a vision. In the beginning, this vision had the character of a dream: the dream of a place that would come into being not through a gradual process of evolution but through the effects of a plan. Or rather, two plans: one for a healthy European city and the other for a node in an elaborate traffic network designed to facilitate the regulated movement of people and the extraction of goods from the highlands of western Java. For economic and political reasons, this dream of the city only began to be realized toward the end of the nineteenth century, at a time when scientific principles were providing the basis for a rationalization of colonial administration as well as the technical know-how for constructing bridges, railroads, and buildings. The fantasy of a city on the Bandung plateau thus became closely linked to the scientific and technological fantasy of a world that was completely knowable and fully susceptible to reconstruction.

The chief mechanism for making the Bandung environment known, and for reconstructing it according to an image of order, was surveillance. This mechanism did not come into being all at once but evolved gradually through an extension of lines of sight along the axes of Euclidean space: the view from the carriage followed by an aerial panorama and a view in depth. As it evolved, the surveillance apparatus tended more and more to exceed its practical objectives of facilitating the regulation of traffic, spectacularizing the modern, or creating a healthy environment, and took on the more general ambition of establishing an order based entirely on the aesthetic principle of "surveyability." The attempt to establish this order involved a campaign to educate the population in the new aesthetic both by stimulating among the colonized peoples a desire for surveyability and by giving them the habits to match that desire. The use of education rather than repression to achieve this aim resulted in part from a wish to reduce costs and in part from the conviction that repression was a less effective means of changing habits and desires than was education. Education meant first of all an internalization of scientific knowledge to the point that it would become the basis for social behavior. More importantly, it meant establishing an identification with the surveying eye, adopting the inspector's way of seeing. The colonial vision was thus to be realized through the production of a society of surveyors, each probing and patrolling the environment, exposing shadows to light and eliminating its most dreaded threats: contagions, contaminants, and eyesores.

The formation of an apparatus of surveillance was not completely untroubled. With each extension of its line of sight there was the possibility that it would encounter other forms of seeing and knowing that would resist its organizing principles. We have seen a number of such encounters: the resistance of lineage to bureaucracy, of a powerful grave to the surveying gaze, of geomancy to geometry. From the standpoint of the history of surveillance, such encounters were "resolved" through a combination of force and displacement. (In another type of history, there would be no resolution at all, just a series of stories about encounters and their effects.) In addition to these encounters, the formation of the apparatus of surveillance was troubled by something else: the possibility that it would take on a repressive and spectacular form rather than an educational and mundane one. While the hygiene operations tried to guard against this possibility, their greatest "successes" were nonetheless conceived of in spectacular terms.

Despite these troubles, some Bandungers did come to imagine their city in terms of an all-seeing gaze. This is evident in the opening to a novella by Soe Lie Piet entitled *Bandoeng di waktoe malem* (*Bandung at Night*), which appeared in 1931. The novella captures the sense of power and foreboding that accompanies the realization that the city and its inhabitants have been rendered visible to a panoptic gaze:

> Thousands of electric lamps were shining brightly, especially at the cinemas and at other places for spectacles. Under the moonlight and the rays from the lamps the entire city of Bandung looked joyful and smiling!
>
> The roads were busy with all sorts of vehicles and just as many pedestrians. Everyone who was out at that moment was overjoyed, their faces filled with sweet expressions. People could be seen on each and every one of the wide streets of that city known for its beautiful women. . . .
>
> But . . . Oh, Bandung apparently did not know that from a place of silence and darkness far above the bright and shining city, for some time now there had been a pair of sharp, serene eyes quietly surveying every movement in every last corner of this classy Paris of Java. (Soe 1931, 2–3)

4

Subjects of Surveillance

The control of habits and the reconstruction of the living environment was only one prong of a two-pronged surveillance apparatus;
the other concerned the control of persons. As with its counterpart, the system for the surveillance of persons emerged in large
part as a response to fears of contagion. The contagion was varied:
it was at times disease, criminality, or political ideas. This chapter
traces the formation of this apparatus from a time when the central government was quite unable to recognize the people of Java as
"individuals" to a time when each person was not only theoretically
recognizable to the government but also identifiable and registered
in its files. In tracing this history, I focus on two questions. First,

according to what process and under what conditions were people "out there" in the world rendered recognizable to the central state? Second, how was the surveillance of individuals generalized to the entire population? In addressing these questions, I will situate new developments in technologies of surveillance, like anthropometry, fingerprinting, and identity cards, within the older regime of human surveillance that formed the backbone of policing practices aimed at the non-European population, such as neighborhood watch patrols and spy networks. These latter institutions employed techniques of surveillance that focused on the continual monitoring of undesirables in order to gain access to local knowledge about crimes rather than on the problem of trying to fix individual identity in the body. Both approaches to surveillance would remain important in the postcolonial era.

Vaccination and Individual Identity

One of the first contexts in which the colonial state found it important to conceive of the individual as a discrete unit was that of disease prevention. Unlike taxes, which were levied against villages and other political-territorial units, or censuses, which were initially concerned more with aggregates and categories than with the individual members of those groupings, the prevention of disease depended on every last potential carrier being isolated and accounted for. This was particularly true of vaccination programs, where individuals who slipped through the vaccination net unnoticed might render the program less effective, if not altogether useless.

The first experiments with vaccination in Java date back to the early nineteenth century and were conducted on a strictly local basis. For the most part, these experiments occurred in response to epidemic outbreaks and were intended to prevent the further spread of disease. In this sense, they were not unlike the physical sanitary cordon that Martanagara described in the previous chapter: they attempted to limit contagion by localizing it. But eventually, these programs came to be utilized on a preventive basis. The first person to instigate a widespread vaccination campaign at a time when there was no immediate threat from an outbreak was Andries de Wilde, a planter and doctor who made his home in the countryside near Bandung. Andries de Wilde trained "Javanese priests," or religious leaders, to vaccinate the population in their respective districts against smallpox, and he was reportedly able to reach a good portion of the population in the Preanger districts of highland western Java (Schoute

1937, 97). Attempts to apply such a program to the whole of Java began in the 1850s with the invention of the so-called Waszklewicz "circle system," according to which Java was divided up into a series of overlapping circles, each with its own vaccination center (Schoute 1937, 153). The idea was that no individual would have to travel more than 5 *paal* (approximately 7.5 kilometers) to reach a center. Trained vaccinators in a district would then tour from center to center, and local authorities would be responsible for making sure those needing vaccination came to the center on the appropriate day.

While the first of de Wilde's vaccination campaigns was wildly successful, he encountered problems when it came to revaccination. A single inoculation was not enough, but while the first dose left a permanent scar on the recipient's skin, the second did not, and people would avoid revaccination by sending others in their place. Moreover, because the government had no record of individual births, it relied on estimates of the population's birth rate and the region's population count to ensure vaccination among newborns. Local leaders were required to deliver up the number of babies that corresponded to such estimates. Often this meant children who had already been vaccinated were given third doses simply to meet the quota. That it was possible to trick the system was a cause for concern among Dutch officials. It showed that the colonial government had not yet developed a system capable of monitoring individuals on a wide scale.

The government had already had some success at developing systems of surveillance capable of isolating and identifying individuals on a smaller scale. Prisons, hospitals, army barracks, and poor houses, for example—these were contained societies that utilized either more or less elaborate forms of spatial surveillance and population control. But if mid-twentieth-century colonial administrators looked back to the previous century in hope of finding a surveillance prototype applicable to their own time, these were not the types of institutional spaces that would have caught their eye. It was, rather, the middle ground between such directly administered, closed communities and the indirectly administered world outside (organized, as we've seen, into ethnic blocks administered by local heads) that proved most attractive.

An example of this middle ground can be seen in the way prostitution came to be organized as a result of Dutch efforts to combat the spread of venereal disease. In the first half of the nineteenth century, brothels began to be "localized" and subjected to government control.[1] In some areas, this meant setting up semiofficial brothels, while in others it meant restricting brothels to a particular neighborhood in the town.[2] Once localized, brothels were subject to "vigorous bylaws and placed under constant supervision of the armed force and police, by day and by night" (Schoute 1937, 156).[3] According to Dirk Schoute, in 1852, the practice of localization was generalized, and a system of monitoring was introduced that was based on practices used in France at the time. This system focused less on the brothel owners and more on the women working there. It involved the registration and compulsory health examination of all sex workers and, whenever possible, their relocation into brothels. In addition, "every prostitute was now provided with a card which had to be produced at each examination and would be kept back in case of an infection" (Schoute 1937, 157). Often, women who were found to be ill would also be confined in special hospitals or, if there were none in the area, in prisons. Needless to say, the women did not like these controls, and often found ways to circumvent the rules and to escape confinement.

Anthropometry and Criminal Identification

The success of both campaigns depended on isolating and controlling individuals by creating identities for them. In the first instance, the individual's identity was established by leaving a mark on the body at the site of the first injection; this mark amounted to nothing more than a sign that that particular body had already been vaccinated. In the second case, the mark was not physically imprinted on the body but had to be in the possession of the person who practiced prostitution. The identity card included a record of the medical inspections the individual had undergone.[4] In this respect the prostitute's card was not unlike the passport discussed in the previous chapter; it provided a record of a person's encounters with the authorities (i.e., village heads of the districts passed through in the former, doctors in the latter) and acted as a form of permission allowing the individual to engage in a particular type of activity (i.e., travel and sex work, respectively). Because vaccination left a permanent mark on the body, the person did not need to remain under surveillance. However, for both the identity card and the passport, surveillance by police or village heads was necessary to ensure that the document and the person holding it matched. As with revaccination, Dutch administrators feared that impostors would foil these otherwise rational systems.

The fear of impostors in the Dutch East Indies was not restricted to the domains of health and travel. In the military, desertions were common and the authorities worried that new enlistees might also be former deserters;

in the courts, there was a concern that those accused of crimes might be repeat offenders posing as first-time felons to get a lighter sentence.

Why did the government find impostors so threatening? Impostors undermined the emerging regime of social control by challenging assumptions about the relation between bodies and signs. Their existence suggests that there is no natural relation between the world of bodies and the world of signs: that language is not necessarily referential. As long as signs were literally imprinted on bodies, this problem did not arise. But if the signs on the body were indistinguishable, or if they were inscribed on paper instead of flesh, the risk of impostors presented itself and a supplementary system of surveillance was necessary to ensure that the "proper" relation of a particular sign to a particular body was maintained. It was toward the policing of this proper relation that the surveillance of individuals was initially directed. In this regard, the rise of surveillance was closely tied to the state's wish to control the population through laws, contracts, and regulations. Only by making bodies accountable to language would such texts carry any force. Impostors represented in no uncertain terms the threat that the language of colonial authority could not fully grasp its object.[5]

The solution to the problem of impostors came in the shape of formal systems for the identification and classification of individuals. The first of these systems, known as anthropometry, was developed in France by Alfonse Bertillon and was used primarily for the identification of criminals. Bertillon's American translator summed up the system's broadest aim as an attempt "to fix the human personality, to give each human being an identity, an individuality, certain, durable, invariable, always recognizable, and always capable of being proven" (Bertillon 1977, 15).[6] Bertillon was unsatisfied with the subjective character of descriptions of criminals according to their height, eye color, and so forth, and proposed instead a system that would allow for the mathematical measurement and identification of criminal bodies. He argued that the precise measurement of the size of a person's head, the length of their arms, their feet, and so on, revealed that virtually no two individuals were exactly alike. Moreover, the measurements taken from adults showed no variation through time, so the effects of aging would not change an individual's mathematical identity. Bertillon's system had all the trappings of high modern science. It claimed not only to prove that individual identity was mathematically observable but also to provide a rigorous method for others to repeat these observations for themselves.

The text in which Bertillon described his method was a handbook entitled *Instructions for Taking Descriptions for the Identification of Criminals and*

Others by the Means of Anthropometric Indications. The handbook takes the reader step-by-step through the act of measuring a human subject, a procedure that involves a peculiar interplay of measurement tools, light, a docile subject, and a probing "operator." The "first movement" in this procedure is the measurement of the head. Bertillon specifies that the subject should be seated on a stool, with their "face turned toward the light, but slightly inclined toward the floor" (1977, 22) The operator must follow a complex positioning process in order to obtain precise measurements. Bertillon instructs, for example, that the operator must "place the left point of the calipers in the cavity at the root of the nose, holding the rounded extremity between thumb and forefinger ... the other fingers, being slightly bent toward the palm, should hold the calipers in a semi-oblique position, in such a way that the light from the window strikes directly on the millimetric graduation" (22–23). Here, the fingers and the calipers probe and penetrate, but the eye remains focused on the calipers' millimetric graduations as revealed by a light source. Even under conditions in which the operator must look the subject in the eye, as when he examines their eye color, his gaze is completely dispassionate and objectifying. "In analyzing in a uniform way the color of the iris the examiner should stand opposite his subject, at a distance of about 30 centimeters, his back to the light so that the eye to be examined is struck by a full strong light (not the rays of the sun, however). Then he orders the subject to look him straight in the eye, and lifts lightly with his right hand the middle of the subject's eyelid" (49). The subject is unable to alter the results of this particular procedure, but at other times, the operator must take precautions to ensure that he is not tricked by the subject. Such trickery again raises the specter of the impostor and must be anticipated by the operator. "As a rule the operator must never let the prisoner suppose that deception can be successfully practiced. He must correct the trickeries, or execute movements that will prevent them, without any explanation whatsoever" (19). In the measurement of height, for example, the subject is made to adopt a soldier's posture to prevent the possibility of slouching or knee bending, which could conceivably result in different measurements at different times. "In taking the height, the subject should be barefooted and standing in the position of a soldier, as it is defined in military tactics; the heels joined and touching the foot of the measure, the feet in a little more acute than rectangular position and turned symmetrically outward, the knees stretched, the body straight and plumb, shoulders back, and of even height, the arms hanging naturally along the body, the chin drawn slightly inward, the eyes looking straight ahead" (44). By keeping the body perfectly still and by standardizing its posture, the operator is able to determine its identity. (That Bertillon describes this standard posture as that of a "soldier without weapons" [76] is not entirely accidental, for the power of this identification system is precisely to disarm populations and to subject them to scientific rule.)

The scientific way of seeing embodied in this form of surveillance could not be more different from the *jegger*'s territorial way of seeing (described in chapter 2). To look someone in the eye in a territorial fashion would imply a challenge full of risk, whereas here, it is a completely dispassionate procedure. The difference derives from the fact that the eye of modern surveillance is always trained on a system of signs that exists prior to its encounter with the body. Rather than the body being evaluated for its power, it is triangulated by a system of signs. As a result of this triangulation, the status of what was previously a territorial mark changes. From a territorial perspective, the mark is an expression of power, individuality, and possession, while for the science of identification it is a form of signification whose real power is reference. Consider, for example, Bertillon's procedure for the "description of particular marks, scars, etc." on the prisoner's body:

> Every individual mark should be described with respect to:
> 1 Its nature (or designation)
> 2 Its direction (or inclination)
> 3 Its dimensions
> 4 Its situation with regard to one or two specified points of the body. (72)

One looks at the mark not to measure the force of the blow that created it but to give it a name and mathematical coordinates. Scars are thus no longer treated as traces of discrete encounters, each with its own particular story, but as signifiers whose meanings are defined by their place in a larger signifying system created by the state.

Bertillon's system was novel not only in demonstrating that each individual body had a set of fixed and unique dimensions but also in showing that these dimensions were susceptible to simple classification and retrieval. At the time Bertillon was developing his system, the French police were using photographs to identify criminals. But the problem with photographs was that they were difficult to retrieve from a large archive if one did not know the name of the suspect. They thus provided a representation of individual identity (one that was temporary in that it was based on a facial appearance that changed with age) that could be used to verify the face of an individual whose name one knew but could not be used to discover the identity of someone suspected of posing as a first-time felon. Anthropometry, however, was developed with the problem of classification and retrieval in mind. The system it used was one of progressive differentiations, so that body parts would be measured in a specified sequence and then classified according to preestablished divisions, subdivisions, sub-subdivisions, and so forth. By using just three size divisions for each body part, a measurement of eight body parts would thus allow sixty thousand records to be divided into subgroups of just eight or nine records. Retrieving a single record was thus a simple process—not unlike using a dictionary, as one observer put it.[7]

Despite the fact that the anthropometric system of identification and classification surpassed that of a purely photographic archive, Bertillon and his acolytes never did away with photography. Indeed, it was made an integral part of an individual's file, in the form of the mug shot. The reason for this may have been that witnesses of a crime would be hard-pressed to recognize individuals by their mathematical formulas alone. But one suspects also that even for the police, a purely mathematical representation of bodies did not allow for the satisfaction of recognition that photos undoubtedly provided. The photo supplemented the mathematical formula, reinforcing its referential power by juxtaposing it with an image of what was signified. Or, conversely, we might say that the mathematical formula supplemented the photo, ensuring that the image was assigned a determinate linguistic address so that it did not disappear into the archive of images.

"Bertillonage" was introduced to the Dutch East Indies by G. J. P. Valette through his 1896 book entitled *The Recognition of Criminals by Anthropometrical Identification According to the Laws of Alphonse Bertillon and the Desirability of Their Application in the Netherlands Indies*. Valette had been assistant resident in charge of the police in Semarang for three years, and in 1894, he had taken a trip to Europe during which he made a study of policing techniques in Britain, the Netherlands, and France. In Paris, he learned about anthropometry and its successes in identifying recidivists in various countries, including colonized regions like Algeria and India. Valette argued that anthropometry should be used in the Netherlands Indies because existing forms of identification were inadequate. For the most part, according to Valette, the police relied on subjective descriptions by "natives" who had, for this purpose, their own "vague" vocabulary. Photographs were used only very rarely, and these were usually of very poor quality. And in cases where the verification of a person's identity was necessary, the police had to enlist the services of village elders, a costly and time-consuming process. Moreover, the "natives" tended to shield their own from police investigation, a problem against which Europeans were powerless since, as Valette explained, they had such difficulty identifying persons of other races.[8] This state of affairs had given rise to various problems: recidivists not being recognized as such, deserters avoiding punishment and sometimes even reenlisting under a different name, fugitives avoiding capture, and forced laborers exchanging identity papers. To solve these problems, and to provide a basis for a statistical tracking of criminality, Valette recommended the establishment of three anthropometry centers: in Batavia, Semarang, and Surabaya. Through government decrees in 1898, 1901, and 1905, his recommendations were put into law. Anthropometry, along with photography, would henceforth be integral to the identification of criminals in the Dutch East Indies.

Techniques of Local Surveillance

While anthropometry was designed to allow Dutch officials greater powers of surveillance over the local population by standardizing identification and registration procedures, and thus eliminating local leaders' monopoly on information about the criminal underworld (especially the power to recognize criminals), it was only partly successful. In his monumental study of policing in Java during the years 1906 and 1907, Boekhoudt (1908, 47) lamented this fact, although he did note that many subdistrict and village heads had started keeping registers of notorious figures. Such registers might include the offender's name, age, birthplace, and physical description, along with the crime for which he had been tried and the names of his family members and friends. For the most part, however, these registers were wanting in detail, as the heads knew who the offenders were and thus saw no reason to provide intricate descriptions of them.

The failure to keep detailed registers is evidence of the fact that local leaders did not face the same problems that Dutch officials faced when confronted with crime. Colonial administrators felt they could not see what was going on in the colony and they wanted to extend their lines of sight and means of direct control.[9] This feeling derived from their fear that what they could see was not necessarily "real," that it might be just an appearance put on by "native" deceivers. Local leaders, on the other hand, already had an elaborate apparatus of surveillance in place, one that relied on spies and the neighborhood watch rather than on technologies of identification. To understand the problems local leaders faced, it is necessary to take a closer look at how this apparatus functioned.

The people most systematically surveilled by local leaders were figures of criminal notoriety. They went by different names in different regions: *semoet gatel* (itchy ant) in Bantam and Old Japara; *djoeara* (champion) in Bantam; *djahat* (evil) in Bogor; *kenong-kenong* (gongs) in Preanger; *koenang-koenang* (fireflies) in Cirebon; *badjingan* (squirrel, scoundrel) in Pekalongan; *moetawatir* (inherited) in Banjoemas; *bengseng* (bastard) in Old Bagelen; *boeroeng* (bird) in Kedoe and Madoera; *weri* (evildoer) in Semarang and Madioen; *letjet* (blister, scratch) in Rembang; *kesitan* (quick, hasty) in Old Probolinggo; *bromotjorah* (bandit) in Kediri, Surabaya, and Pasuruan; *doersilo* (unethical) in Krawang, Besuki, and Madura (Boekhoudt 1908, 46–47). According to Boekhoudt (1908, 47–53), such people were kept under surveillance in a number of ways. First, they were required to report to village or *kampung* heads at regular intervals, sometimes weekly, sometimes monthly. Second, any time there was a festive event, they might be rounded up and placed in prison until the event was over, since it was during such events that burglaries often took place.[10] Third, neighborhood watch patrols were obliged to check to make sure the "fireflies" were at home during the night and not out and about.[11] To facilitate such inspections, fireflies were sometimes obliged to sleep with their doors open and with lights lit so that their presence could be easily verified. Finally, if these fireflies did have legitimate cause to go out at night, they were forced to carry lanterns so that—like their insectile namesakes—their perambulations could not go unnoticed.

Sometimes the obligation to carry a lantern was imposed not just on suspected criminals but also on the general population. In writing about his travels in Java during the mid-nineteenth century, William Barrington D'Almeida claimed that the practice was universal:

> In no town or village of Java are the natives allowed to walk after seven in the evening without a light. Some make their rambles with torches of small thin split bamboo, made up into bundles, and lit at the end. Others carry about a tumbler filled halfway or two-thirds with water, and the rest with oil, upon the surface of which floats a wick made of pith, and pierced with a couple of sticks having corks at the end. I saw many carrying these tumblers in white pocket handkerchiefs, through which the light shone. How they kept them from lighting was always a mystery to me, unless it be that the handkerchief

has been previously dipped in some incombustible solution. Some natives carry torches of damar and rosin, the extract of some indigenous plant, or sticks of wood tied in a bundle and rubbed over with ignitable compounds, which generally give the most glaring but least durable lights. (1864, 271)

This system of surveillance, no less than anthropometry, depended upon the control of appearances. However, the way it sought to control them was different. Whereas anthropometry set up an equivalence between appearances (photos, bodies) and language that was designed to give language a point of purchase on appearances and to give appearances a place within language, the surveillance of fireflies worked almost entirely through a routinized and direct control of appearances. To keep these individuals under control did not mean naming them and giving them a fixed identity in the state archive; it meant making them appear again and again, before the neighborhood watch, before the village or subdistrict head, and before any passerby who might see them glowing in the night. The assumption appears to have been that if they were not constantly monitored, made visible, fireflies would fly away into the darkness, disappearing from view. Whereas anthropometry depended on a scientific vision that sought to recognize fireflies in a definitive sense, to fix them as criminals once and for all, this local regime of surveillance depended on a system of monitoring that would keep them in constant view.

Surveillance at the local level was not restricted to the control of known fireflies but was also an integral part of investigative practices. Consider, for example, the *Patih of Pandeglang*, a short text about policing written in 1898 by Soeropringgo and one of the first modern Melayu-language texts to outline a technique for policing. Its focus was on dealing with thieves and those who trade in stolen goods. In addition to explaining how to conduct searches and arrests, Soeropringgo discusses the problems one faces when dealing with thieves and spies. Thieves, according to Soeropringgo, can be classified into four categories: professional thieves (*maling doerdjana*) who steal and then sell the goods to a fence; swindler thieves (*maling tipoean*) who steal goods, stash them on communal property, and then approach the victim offering to find them in return for a fee;[12] slandering thieves (*maling pitnahan*) who steal goods and then put them on someone else's property to frame them; and revenge thieves (*maling sebab sakit hati*) who steal goods from someone they have a grudge against and then burn the goods or throw them in a river (Soeropringgo 1906, 1372).[13]

This manner of classifying theft illustrates the variety of motivations that might underlie an apparently simple event. It shows that nothing can necessarily be taken at face value. The "victim" might turn out to be the perpetrator, the "perpetrator" the victim, or the "police" the perpetrator. That this was the case meant that police, according to Soeropringgo, had to be very careful about producing an official explanation (*katerangan*) of a crime. The investigation had to be conducted as "fast as lightning, as sharp as a razor, but in a manner more subtle than the wind" (Soeropringgo 1906, 1370). Any suspect, according to Soeropringgo, had to be "watched day and night, followed wherever he goes, his behavior observed" (1370). For this task, spies were indispensable, though choosing the right spies was not an easy task. "The police must search for someone who is of the same ilk as the thief or the fence [i.e., a criminal himself]—but only choose someone *who can speak and will not be seen*" (1370; italics added). One or two such spies were enough, but they had to be "trustworthy," both to the police official and to thieves. An untrustworthy spy was dangerous, not only because he would be unable to convince suspects to talk to him, but also because he might use his connection with the police to blackmail or slander others.

In contrast to anthropometry, the use of spies was aimed not at discovering who the person who committed the crime *was* (i.e., what his or her "real" name was, who the person had been in relation to the state) so much as who was who when the crime took place (Was the "victim" the perpetrator? The "perpetrator" the victim? The spy the perpetrator or the witness?). In the former case, a "real" identity was masked by a false one and the problem was then to determine who the "real" one was. In the latter case, there was a circulation of roles one had to enter into (as, say, a thief-spy) in order to understand the situation at play. Crime provided the occasion for the police to step in and halt the circulation of roles, even if only for a moment. Once stopped, all sorts of things were revealed about the players: their desires, their debts, their conflicts, their envies. Such revelations were only available to spies. What were spies exactly? Spies were thieves who spoke and eyes (*mata-mata*) that could not be seen. Spies were thus somewhat analogous to spirits, since they, too, were capable of speaking through silence and seeing from an invisible place. But unlike spirits, which in Java are known for their tricks and deceptions, spies were to be chosen based on their trustworthiness. Spies who could be trusted were capable of being thieves as well as overseeing events and relaying information to the police or local authorities. This was not a form of supervision, in the sense that police would oversee traffic, but was rather akin to overhearing. Spies overheard what people said, oversaw what people saw; they partook in such observation and passed on what they learned. Once passed on, the police or local leaders could then successfully recognize the players for who they were.

In certain respects, the local regime of surveillance based on the neighborhood watch and spies can be seen as complementary to the science of anthropometry. Local surveillance determines people's motives and roles in a crime, and keeps watch on shady characters, while supralocal surveillance ensures that people who move outside a locality do not just disappear from sight. Yet the apparent complementarity of these different systems of surveillance should not blind us to the fact that the notions of "identity" they are working with, and the forms of recognition they use to establish that identity, are very different. The fears these two systems sought to address are different as well. Anthropometry provided a mechanism for fusing language to appearances, thus equating linguistic recognition with seeing. This method of seeing amounted to a form of supervision in that it presupposed an order of fixed individual identities. The fears anthropometry responded to were thus associated with the failure to equate seeing and recognizing, as occurred with impostors. Local surveillance, in contrast, established "identity" by locating people within roles. Insofar as individual players' roles were not yet known, surveillance was a matter of *overseeing* (in a manner analogous to overhearing). The instrument for overseeing was the spy, who relayed appearances and stories to the police or a local official. The latter then established who was who when the crime took place, based on an understanding of possible motivations and scenarios. Once the roles had already been established (as with known fireflies), local heads instituted a form of surveillance that controlled appearances by keeping suspected persons in sight. Fear in the local surveillance apparatus thus centered on two things: on the one hand, the trustworthiness of the spy, whose dual role meant that he might "deceive" the wrong people or use his connection to the police to further his criminal objectives, and, on the other, the possibility that fireflies might disappear from view. Local and supralocal surveillance thus show some complementarities, though they also show a possible source of instability. Although crime provided the Dutch with an occasion to try to eliminate the possibility of impostors, it also provided local leaders with an occasion to expand their use of spies, which in effect meant increasing the numbers of impostors.

For a time, the Dutch colonial administration believed that anthropometry would provide a way to do away with local systems of surveillance. W. Boekhoudt (1908, 84), for example, argues that keeping track of notorious figures was far too costly and time-consuming an effort for local police and that a good system of identification and registration would unburden them of this task. But more than the economic costs, one suspects that the primary reason driving the Dutch desire to establish a new system of surveillance—one that could reduce the central government's reliance on local leaders—was the fear that much of the crime in the colony was actually being masterminded by local officials and carried out by their spies or by recidivists under their control.[14]

Anthropometry seemed to provide a mechanism for reducing Dutch dependence on local officials and their forms of knowledge insofar as anthropometry might supplant the use of spies and the neighborhood watch, and eliminate the local character of power altogether.[15] As it turned out, however, anthropometry did not replace spies or the neighborhood watch. Rather, the two systems of surveillance continued to function relatively independently of one another, although both did undergo transformations that served the Dutch desire for more direct control of the population.

Refashioning Colonial Policing

In the realm of policing, the government instituted a number of important changes that had the effect of establishing an organization of local agents and spies under the control of the central government. Until 1912, policing in each of the various districts of Java had generally been under the formal control of the resident and assistant resident, but police personnel themselves were recruited and maintained by the regent. On a day-to-day basis these *mantri polisi*, as they were known, and their assistants, the *opas*, answered to either a *camat*, a *wedana*, or directly to the regent. It was largely through these agents that the regent developed his network of spies. In addition to this network of police and spies, the indigenous administration also oversaw a set of neighborhood watch patrols. While the exact system varied in each region, the general pattern was that each *kampung* had a guardhouse and conducted a neighborhood watch that was overseen by a higher, village-level *ronda* (*ronda desa*). The latter was also responsible for maintaining guardhouses at the entry points to the village and for watching over communal property such as the village hall (*bale desa*). A district patrol answering to the *camat* or *wedana* oversaw the village *ronda* and was entrusted with maintaining a watch at the district capital.[16] Policing was thus largely under the authority of indigenous officials, or *pangreh praja*, but those involved were themselves not part of the civil service. Neither the *mantri* nor the *ronda* patrols received any formal training from the government, although there was an emerging body of popular handbooks on criminal procedure and investigation for them to learn from.[17] Participation in the *ronda* at the lower levels was one of several obligatory services that households were called upon by village heads to perform (other obligatory tasks included road building, irrigation maintenance, and similar communal projects).

This entire system of policing, which was mainly under the authority of indigenous civil service officials (*pangreh praja*, or "rulers of the realm"), later came to be known by the overarching term *polisi pamong praja*.[18] Despite successive waves of police modernization and reform, the *polisi pamong praja* was never completely done away with. Instead, other units were added that answered more directly to the Dutch administration. The most important of these were the Armed Police (Gewapende Politie) formed in 1912; the City Police formed in 1914; the Political Intelligence Service, or Politieke Inlichtingendienst (PID), formed in 1916; and the Field Police (Veldpolitie) formed in 1920.

In rural areas, policing was first brought under control of the Armed Police.[19] The Armed Police were a redeployment of what had once been the *prajurit*—that is, a body of armed men responsible for maintaining security in rural areas. While the *prajurit* had been recruited locally by the regent (although like the *mantri polisi* they were ultimately under the authority of the resident), the Armed Police were directly responsible to the Department of Internal Affairs and thus to the colonial state. With many of its members drawn from the army, and all its members living in barracks, the Armed Police were organized into detachments and brigades that could serve as mobile forces for putting down local rebellions and riots. The Field Police replaced the Armed Police and were organized along similar lines, except that agents were seconded from other police units. The Field Police were directly responsible to the resident, and secondarily to the Department of Internal Affairs (they also had ties to the attorney general). Their orientation was less repressive than the Armed Police, and they were expected to cooperate with the *polisi pamong praja* by providing training, helping organize *ronda* patrols, and providing support when necessary. As Sutherland has pointed out, however, there was a distinct overlap in duties between the Field Police and the indigenous officials overseeing policing, leading to tensions between them: "The [indigenous officials] felt that there were damaging tendencies [when Dutch officials used] the police to intervene directly into local affairs and [trusted] them more than their Indonesian subordinates" (1979, 93).

Before 1914 (and 1917 in Bandung), policing in urban areas had been the responsibility of police working under the authority of indigenous officials.[20] Similarly, the organization of neighborhood *ronda* in the "native" quarters of the city was in their hands. However, in the European quarter it was organized by Europeans and in the Chinese quarter by the head of the local Chinese community. The patrols were meant to be conducted by members of the quarters themselves, but in practice *pribumi* residents were often hired by the Dutch and the Chinese for this purpose. With the formation of the City Police, a permanent, trained, and salaried police force was introduced that was responsible to the resident and assistant resident rather than to the regent.[21] On a day-to-day basis, however, the City Police was run by a commissioner and by unit and subunit heads. While the City Police included some members who had worked under indigenous officials, for the most part they were trained agents under salary from the Department of Internal Affairs. Each City Police headquarters was organized into four units: the secretariat, investigation (*recherche*), public surveillance, and traffic. Under the command of the central office were two or three *Afdeeling* (regional units), each with its own office; and beneath these were varying numbers of subregional sections. The latter were responsible for maintaining guardhouses throughout the city, including those located at each entry point to the city proper. They were also responsible for coordinating and conducting *ronda* patrols. Thus, in the city, the professional police effectively took control over policing out of the hands of indigenous leaders, while retaining indigenous police officers in the force.

Perhaps the most important of these changes, however, was the formation of the PID, or what would later become the Regional Investigations Unit (Gewestelijke Recherche) and finally the General Investigation Bureau, or Algemeene Recherche Dienst (ARD).[22] Ostensibly formed to deal with external threats during the First World War, the PID became the central body for surveillance of political groups during the late-colonial period. Under the supervision of the attorney general and with spies throughout the Indies, the PID became an important source of information on the local population for the Dutch central government. In its incarnation as the Armed Police, it was primarily responsible for addressing problems of crime in rural areas. As this was a period with a great number of political organizations and protests, many related to the nationalist struggle, the

PID tended to focus on these, leaving problems of nonpolitical crime to the Field Police. But from around 1930 (as the ARD), it provided a central clearing house for intelligence from both urban and rural areas. To facilitate information gathering in the cities, a branch was added to the central office of the City Police forces (in Bandung, this branch went by the name of Afdeeling Vreemdelingen en Inlichtingendienst). The agents of this intelligence service were drawn primarily from the indigenous civil service, which meant that *wedana, mantri polisi,* and their networks of spies were now providing information directly to the Dutch resident and to the central government, bypassing the regent altogether.

The reorganization of the police provided a means for the Dutch administration to establish its own network of agents and spies on the ground and to co-opt agents and spies who had previously been under the exclusive control of indigenous officials. The presence of agents of the Field Police and the City Police, along with a host of other agents with more limited authority (Forest Police, Market Police, Building Police, etc.), served to make government laws and regulations an unavoidable part of everyday life. Unlike the *mantri polisi* who had preceded them, these agents were trained in the letter of the law and were themselves subject to all sorts of disciplinary controls. They were thus an important instrument for establishing the forms of "public order" described in the previous chapter. The presence of police spies also had profound effects, though of a very different sort. Spies, it appears, had the effect of generalizing the colonial administration's fear of impostors to the entire population. According to G. H. Bousquet (1940), who wrote a witty and cutting appraisal of the Dutch colonial system entitled *A French View of the Netherlands Indies,* "There are more suspicions floating about than one can shake a stick at. The whole system of Dutch colonial Government depends at least at present upon police informers. Naturally the part they play is not mentioned in the law books, but their existence is far more vital than that of the books themselves. The native world teems with these informers; people speak of nothing else, and they see them in every strange face—often no doubt without cause" (35).

Insofar as the police were in control of such spies, one might say they had successfully solved the problem of impostors. Spies effectively reversed the power relation that had once characterized the relationship between the central government and local authorities. An impostor, after all, was someone who was locally recognizable but who posed as someone else before the state, while a spy (or informer) was someone who was recognizable to the police but who posed as something other than a spy locally. The failure to recognize this figure, and all the fears and suspicions such a failure entailed, would thus be a problem not for the government but for the people. However, the situation was more complex than this. In the first place, as Bousquet's own spies seem to have informed him, the Dutch did not enjoy a monopoly on networks of spies. "Opponents of the government, moreover, have their own information service, if I may judge by what I have heard and am inclined to believe. In any case, I have seen persons in their own homes reading administrative documents marked 'confidential: for the department.' This little scene of home life, worthy of the brush of a Dutch master, gave me food for thought" (35).

More radically still, there was always the possibility—often portrayed in Melayu popular literature—that spies were not tied to any authority at all, that they simply circulated, seeing and listening, always escaping recognition by the government and its opponents. This latter possibility was already an indication that the straightforward distinction between local authority and central Dutch authority had by this point broken down. The rise of a lingua franca, conveyed through film, newspapers, and other mass media, meant that everyone was "overhearing" and "overseeing" everyone else. Such communications were giving rise to new forms of recognition that surpassed those available to either Dutch or local authorities, including political movements like international communism and Indonesian nationalism.[23] Spies and impostors were indeed everywhere.

The proliferation of spies provided an even greater impetus to Dutch efforts to generalize a system for the identification of individuals. "To fix the human personality, to give each human being an identity, an individuality, certain, durable, invariable, always recognizable" (Bertillon 1977, 15), seemed all the more imperative. The system of identification that was generalized was not Bertillon's body measurements, however, but the more microscopic science of fingerprinting. The fantasies surrounding fingerprinting did not differ greatly from those that had attached to anthropometry but, if anything, they generated even more enthusiasm.[24] Rudolf Mrázek (1997) has shown that Dutch officials were fascinated by the possibility of recognizing the "natives" mathematically and of finding a way to make them stand still; they dreamed of generalizing the system so that all traffic between Java and the rest of the Indies would be "strained" through a giant "dactyloscopic sieve" (Mrázek 1997, 16–18).[25] Indeed, fingerprinting, even more than Bertillonage, seems to have been concerned with regulating movement—that of discrete bodies in space, and, on an individual level, between identities.

In Java, fingerprints had long been used in place of signatures and seals. Made using ink or a dye from the *sirih* plant, they were known as *tjap doemoek* (touch stamps) (Boekhoudt 1908, 86). Insofar as *tjap doemoek* were interchangeable with signatures and seals, they functioned as an expression of commitment or ownership. By placing their mark on a document, one was consciously and voluntarily establishing a relation between oneself and the text; the relation amounted to a direct contact that left a recognizable trace. Some early terms used to describe fingerprints in Melayu maintained the idea of the trace: *bekas jeridji* and *bekas jari* both meant finger trace.[26] The term that took hold, and that is still used today, emphasizes neither the touch nor the trace, however, but the act of examination by the police: *sidik jari*, or finger examination.

Fingerprinting was first used as a tool of population control in British India during the nineteenth century, where, as Michael Taussig (1993) has pointed out, state officials consciously played up the "magical power" that such prints seemed to have over subjects.[27] It was used first to prevent the repudiation of contracts, but by 1877, it was being used on an experimental basis to identify people in criminal courts, for the registration of deeds, to prevent sham death in prisons, and to stop the impersonation of pensioners after their death (Lambourne 1984, 28). The use of fingerprinting for state surveillance in other countries began in earnest only after the practice was wedded to a system of classification similar to Bertillonage. This system, which formally recognized the unique contours of a print (the so-called arches, tented arches, radial loops, whorls, accidentals, etc.) and their measurements, was developed in Britain by Sir Edward Henry and came to be used throughout the world. In the Dutch East Indies, the "Henry system" was first introduced in 1902 by the Department of Justice, in which capacity it was used primarily as a supplement to Bertillonage. But as Boekhoudt (1908, 86) argued a few years later, fingerprinting had the advantage of being both cheaper and more user-friendly than Bertillonage. Not only did it require less equipment, but it could be done by almost anyone. Moreover, fingerprinting could identify children while anthropometry only worked on adults. For these reasons, the Department of Justice decided in 1911 to abandon Bertillonage and base its entire system of identification on fingerprinting (Meijer 1926, 928–29).

Although fingerprinting replaced Bertillonage as a science of identification, its potential uses were not restricted to this purpose. It also provided the possibility of identifying perpetrators of a crime by the physical traces they left behind. Insofar as fingerprinting was comparable to Bertillonage, it identified individuals by representing their bodies in the language of mathematics. These representations allowed for direct comparison with representations of other bodies, and thus for individualization. As a science of traces, however, fingerprinting established "identity" not through representation but by tracking a line of contagion. The difference between the two approaches is important. In tracking a perpetrator, it is perfectly possible to determine "who" they are by following the contagion of substances from the scene of a crime while still having no idea as to their name, their address, and so forth. In Bertillonage, all individuals may be labeled with names and addresses, but this information says nothing about their interactions.[28] In Europe and America, fingerprinting's apparent ability to provide a bridge between these two ways of knowing has made it such a powerful tool of policing. We are led to believe that a fingerprint in the archive is like having a piece of the body on file[29] and that finding a fingerprint at the scene of a crime is like finding a label with the name of the perpetrator.

In the Dutch East Indies, fingerprinting never provided such a bridge. In a study of fingerprinting published in 1926, D. H. Meijer noted that it was being used in the Indies for the following purposes: in place of a signature in some banks and in government permits, for the identification of workers by the Java Sugar Syndicate, and more generally for the identification of coolies, foreigners, recidivists, and politically "restless" elements (930-31, 947). Meijer (1926, 930) concluded that although fingerprinting had been widely used for administrative purposes, it seemed never to have been used successfully at the scene of a crime. Investigations, rather than relying on fingerprints—what one early handbook referred to as "mute witnesses" (Hesselink 1911)—continued to rely on spies and informants "who can speak but cannot be seen." Meijer himself was far more concerned with fingerprinting's value as a tool of identification rather than investigation. He advocated for the modernization of dactyloscopy so that a single print could be used for identification and its "formula" codified and transmitted by wire to distant regions. In making his case, Meijer raised the specter of the Indonesian communist movement's master spy, Tan Malaka, who traveled the globe under various assumed names: "If it were the case that a long-distance identity of Tan Malakka existed, and it was in the possession of the police in Singapore or the police in the places that [he] embarked over the past year, there is a very good chance that he would have been arrested" (Meijer 1926, 946).

Pressed forward by these fears and fantasies, the use of fingerprinting for identification flourished, and was eventually generalized to the entire population, though not in the domain of policing, which focused only on criminals and spies, nor in the domain of work, which focused only on laborers; rather, fingerprinting's use as a tool of identification was to take place chiefly in the domain of hygiene. The broad focus of hygiene programs meant they were unusually capable of assimilating surveillance technologies from other domains, including geography, medicine, engineering, architecture, or policing. The function of fingerprinting within this broader surveillance apparatus was to monitor births and deaths in the population. At birth, each child was supplied with a certificate that included their name, their parents' names, their address (regency, district, subdistrict, village, and compound or street), a registration number, the certificate holder's thumbprint, and space for recording immunizations. One copy of this certificate was kept by the regency health authorities, one by the village or *kampung* head, and one by the individual. The certificate had to be kept indefinitely, and if the individual changed their name, this would be recorded and a second thumbprint would be added to the first (Hydrick 1939, 43–44). Through the birth certificate, which everyone in the colony would come to possess, the Dutch were able to realize their dream of a world made up of distinguishable individuals, each with a card on their body and a file in the archive. No longer were such cards confined to prostitutes or recidivists. Everyone had them. By the late 1930s, it was possible to vaccinate the entire population, not as parts of an estimated total, but as individuals localized by their names, their parentage, their addresses, and their bodies.[30]

Fear, Surveillance, and Colonial Authority

The history of surveillance in colonial Java is inseparable from the broader development of communications in the region. Roads, railways, bridges, spies, communicable diseases—each is central to understanding the forms surveillance has come to take. The role of surveillance in communication is one of regulation and control; it attempts to capture flows of persons, things, animals, goods, and even identities, to fix them, and then to release them along particular channels under particular constraints. The explosion of communications in Java in the late nineteenth and early twentieth centuries was thus accompanied by a corresponding growth in the surveillance apparatus. As roads and railways were built, allowing people to move around in unprecedented numbers, so, too, were the mechanisms that could fix the human identity once and for all, making a person recognizable to someone who had never set eyes on them before.

Michel Foucault (1995) has shown that in Europe, surveillance must be understood as two independent processes, one pertaining to laws that "administer illegalities" (89), the other pertaining to the disciplining of bodies. In focusing on the difference between these two processes, he shows with precision the genealogy of bodily disciplines, like those we saw in anthropometry's "soldier without weapons," and demonstrates the relative independence of such disciplines from legal concerns with delinquency and the like. In the Dutch East Indies, a similar disjunction was at work, but the Dutch had little control over the day-to-day disciplining of bodies. For this, they relied primarily on local rulers, informal sovereigns, and their spies.[31]

What drove the tremendous extension of the surveillance apparatus in Java was the desire of colonial authorities to achieve a correspondence between signs and referents. They wished to bridge the gap between the colonial state's language and the world "out there" in order to give their laws and regulations a grip on the population they ruled. That they feared the nonreferentiality of their language was undoubtedly a result of the monopolization of indigenous customary law (*adat*) by local leaders, which, as John Pemberton (1994) has shown, had the effect of circumscribing Dutch authority and limiting its effects. In this regard, the early efforts at surveillance were intimately tied up with the turn-of-the-century policy of imposing a more direct form of colonial rule. And it was therefore no accident that the language the Dutch chose to extend through surveillance was precisely the one they could claim as their own: science.

Yet it was not just the presumed European origin of scientific language that made it so appealing; it also seemed capable of directly linking the world of objects to the world of signs. Mathematical formulas were taken to be true representations of individual identity just as maps were taken to be true representations of distance and location. In itself, this was already an astounding belief, but it was made even more astounding by the fact that the Dutch believed that by controlling the representation they would be able to control the world "out there." We have seen this again and again in our examples: the assumption that simply exposing rats to light would make them behave in an orderly fashion, that having recidivists on file would make *ronda* surveillance unnecessary, that showing people photographs would make them desire surveyability. This fetishization of the tools of surveillance was sometimes so extreme that simply exposing the world to light (and the "natives" to Enlightenment precepts) was expected to bring order to the colony.[32] Thus, the extension of the surveillance apparatus in Java was an effect both of the Dutch wishing to extend colonial power over the whole of the archipelago and of their belief that they possessed the almost magical power to do so.

The greatest threats to surveillance, and those that pushed its extension into new domains, were the threats of impostors and contagion. Contagion may be defined as communication that escapes control, overflowing the channels laid out for it. We have seen that surveillance attempted to stop contagion by preventing dangerous contacts, for example by separating the dwelling places of rats from those of humans, and by separating recidivists and prostitutes from the rest of the population. There were also all sorts of mechanisms for preventing contacts between nationalists, such as the ordinance preventing open-air meetings and the strict censorship of the press. Impostors posed the problem not of excessive communication but of "false" correspondence. For the Dutch regime, impostors were deceptive because they falsified the relation between signs and their referents, thus undermining the power of laws and regulations to find their "true" objects. More importantly, the existence of impostors raised the question of who had the power to mediate identities and highlighted the unwelcome fact that those in control of procedures for scientific identification did not have a monopoly on this power.[33] As long as the state could control the power of mediation, as it did in the case of police spies, the question of "truth" was less pressing. The real danger to colonial power had less to do with the failure of science than with the failure of the colonial state to control mediation.

PART THREE

ARTICULATIONS

P.3 Police "cleansing" street vendors in Bandung, 2015. Photo by Frans Ari Prasetyo.

5

State of Fear

In the old days you would catch a thief by going to someone who was a kind of paranormal. He could tell you when the thief would appear again, bringing with him the stolen object. And sure enough the thief would actually come and surrender himself. You could say that people like that don't exist anymore. But when they did there was no need for police to go hunting people down. The transition to the new form of dealing with thieves took place in the early 1980s with the "cleansing" or Petrus, in which all the people with that type of power were cleaned up.

Mr. Asep, an elderly Bandung security guard

The New Order regime, in power from 1966 to 1998, was dominated by the army, which had its roots in the anticolonial struggle, so it was familiar with the notion of using parastate groups to shore up its authority.[1] At the same time, the New Order regime's approach to developing a machinery of rule departed very little from that of the late-colonial state. It, too, relied on surveillance as a means of establishing centralized control, and, initially, it also depended on informal sovereignties to extend its power into the fabric of society. However, as we shall see in this chapter, starting from the 1980s, the relationship between the state and informal sovereignties was radically restructured. This restructuring was effected largely through two initiatives that sought to use surveillance to eliminate and discipline representatives of territorial power: Petrus and Siskamling. Petrus is the abbreviation given to an early 1980s paramilitary operation known as the Mysterious Killings (*Pembunuhan Misterius*)[2] in which thousands of people labeled as criminals were murdered in a number of Indonesia's main cities. Siskamling, or *sistem keamanan lingkungan* (environment security system), is a term that was first coined by the head of the Indonesian police in the early 1980s to describe a new way of organizing the local security apparatus so as to give police the responsibility for coordinating and supervising neighborhood watches and for training and supervising private security guards for use in commercial and public settings.[3]

Both of these initiatives were means of dealing with the fears generated by a wave of violent crime that peaked in the early 1980s. At a policy level, the two initiatives moved in different directions, since one implied the eradication of the criminal element through what the government referred to as "shock therapy," while the other implied the development of a better system of law enforcement through an extension of the reach of the police. According to David Bourchier, government officials were divided over which strategy to pursue: some advocated the rule-of-law approach represented by Siskamling, others the extrajudicial approach of Petrus (Bourchier 1990, 183). In retrospect, however, it seems clear that the two solutions to the crime problem were effectively part of a single process whose object was the deterritorialization of local security practices in a manner that was conducive to central state control. In the case of Siskamling, this was largely an institutional question, the answer to which depended on subjecting gangs, security guards, and "criminals" to surveillance. For Petrus, it was a matter of appropriating the territorial power that "criminals" and gangs represented, a complex process that involved imitation as well as surveillance.

I begin this chapter with a brief account of urban crime, security, and state power in the period immediately leading up to Petrus and the introduction of Siskamling. I then describe the changes to local security brought about by the implementation of Siskamling—changes that would only really get underway once Petrus had scared competitors away or killed them— before turning to analyze Petrus itself: its lists, its ambivalence in defining the "criminal," and its attempts to recuperate the power that gangs and their leaders represented. Finally, I describe the lasting mark that Petrus and Siskamling left on the contemporary relationship between local security and state power.

Specters of Criminality

> The raging crime at the beginning of the 1980s, especially armed robbery directed at gold shop owners and bank clients, was a hot story in Bandung's media. The news was consumed by the people via the mass media so that it quickly spread to the public, and became a specter [*momok*] that caused people fear. The criminals' actions were performed not just at night but even in broad daylight and in the middle of public crowds.[4]
>
> W. P. Nainggolan

The criminal specter came out of the shadows and into the light of day at a particular time: the early 1980s.[5] It appeared first in the mass media, then among the crowds, and soon after in police theses like the one from which the above quotation is taken. There are several ways to explain why criminality appeared as such a pronounced threat when it did. In the broadest terms, one could point to the fact that, in the history of the New Order regime, the early 1980s was a watershed period in both economic and political terms. Economically, the period from 1973 to 1981 saw a tremendous oil boom, which gave the state unprecedented revenues and leeway in pursuing policies of economic nationalism.[6] By 1982, however, the first signs of the oil bust began to appear, leaving the state in a weakened position with respect to its access to foreign capital. As a result, 1982 and 1983 saw the introduction of liberalization policies, significant cuts in subsidies of energy and food, and a 27.6 percent devaluation of the currency (Robison 1986, 125, 382–84). Politically, the regime was also beginning to show signs of fracture.[7] Student demonstrations in the late 1970s were followed in mid-1980 by the Petition of Fifty, in which many former supporters of Suharto expressed their opposition to the regime. Proponents of human rights and legal reform also managed to push through a new Code of Criminal Procedure, which—on paper at least—curtailed some of the powers of the police. In addition, beginning in 1979, a new, more professionally trained generation of military officers started to be appointed to command positions, a development that had the potential to undermine Suharto's monopolistic control over the military (Crouch 1988, 357). Finally, enough time had passed since the killings of 1965–66 that the idea of a reemergent Indonesian Communist Party (Partai Komunis Indonesia, or PKI) had begun to lose some of its currency; threats to public order were increasingly portrayed as being "purely criminal" rather than as being manifestations of underground "political" opposition. Against the backdrop of these wider developments, the criminal specter can be seen both as the symptom of a structurally weakened state and as a convenient excuse for actions aimed at trying to overcome this weakness.

When the specter of crime appeared, it took very particular forms: *gali-gali* and *preman*. The former term, an abbreviation of *gabungan anak-anak liar* (gangs of wild kids), refers to organized gangs of people involved in criminal behavior, while the latter term refers to a professional criminal or a *jegger*.[8] Taken separately, there was nothing new about these fears and their objects. *Jegger* and their ilk had been a source of fear in Java for many generations, as numerous studies have demonstrated (e.g., Onghokham 1978; Smail 1964; Kartodirdjo 1973; Schulte Nordholt 1991). Similarly, during the New Order, the existence of youth gangs in urban areas had periodically aroused concern.[9] With the rise in violent crime at the beginning of the 1980s,[10] however, so-called *preman* and *gali-gali* came under increasing scrutiny by the press and the government.[11] Attracting particular concern were those among them who were active in businesses or gangs providing "security services": debt collection, bodyguard or security guard rentals, and the like. Such groups were thought to be taking crime into a new, more organized and supralocal realm. Both Siskamling and Petrus took these organizations as their object of attention.

Policing Local Security

Siskamling was started in 1980 as an offshoot of a larger government program called Kopkamtib (Komando Pemulihan Keamanan dan Ketertiban, or Command for the Restoration of Security and Order).[12] It represented an attempt by the New Order government to impose overt state control over local security practices by taking them out of the hands of organized private gangs. Awaloedin Djamin, the chief of police and founder of the program, explained in his autobiography, "We definitely did not want to have the same thing happen in Indonesia that happened in other countries. In Japan, for example, the Yakuza forced protection on businesspeople. Such a situation can give rise to excesses that are difficult to overcome. The same was true in the early days of the mafia in the United States" (Djamin 1995, 240).

The Indonesian "security" groups Awaloedin was likely referring to were mainly of two types. The first were local, territorial gangs based in residential districts that had, over time, spread to adjacent bus terminals, markets, or shopping centers (see chapter 2). In most major cities, there were dozens of such gangs, and turf wars between them were common.[13] Many of these gangs were formed in the early days of the New Order and had provided local "defense" in the context of the anticommunist pogroms.[14] Some derived their authority from charismatic leadership, some from the fact that their members' parents were prominent officials in the government or military, and others from their successes in turf warfare.[15] By the beginning of the 1980s, some of these local gangs had actually become quite large and, as their members grew older, had become rather professionally minded in their provision of "protection" to local businesses.[16] The second type consisted of legal organizations rather than gangs. One of the most prominent of these was Pemuda Pancasila (Pancasila Youth), the nationwide youth group described by Loren Ryter (2001).[17] Others included foundations and businesses formed by ex-convicts and others with few job possibilities. These groups—like Prems, Massa 33, and others—provided security services to shops, transport companies, wealthy businesspeople, and so on, by hiring out "guards" for the protection of particular locales, individuals, events, or traffic routes. Some of the larger groups, like Massa 33, claimed memberships of as many as fifty thousand people, almost all ex-convicts and street people.[18]

For the police, the growth of such private security services constituted a serious threat to their authority. Along with "protection," the pursuit, capture, and punishment of suspects was increasingly being entrusted to these groups rather than to the police. This raised the possibility that the balance of power between the state and informal sovereigns would tilt in the latter's favor. Siskamling aimed to counteract this tendency by establishing clear controls over such nonstate security businesses. It was hoped that greater police control would prevent them from becoming mafia-like protection rackets (or at least ensure the police would have a stake in such rackets). But Siskamling did not just target security businesses. It also aimed to establish a system for centralized monitoring and control in the domain of volunteer residential security. One of the intentions here was to discourage acts of communal violence against suspected thieves, sorcerers, and adulterers (and, undoubtedly, the police themselves, as they were often targets of such violence). Moreover, Siskamling had purposes beyond just the monopolization of violence and the recuperation of police repressive powers. Both gangs and neighborhood watches were extremely effective tools for day-to-day surveillance of the population, and Siskamling provided a rubric for integrating these informal sovereigns into the bureaucratic surveillance machine. In all these respects, Siskamling was viewed as a handy tool for increasing police powers in the context of an extremely low police-to-population ratio, and to do so at little added cost to the state.

Siskamling's system of control worked by dividing local security guards into three types: Satpam, Hansip, and *ronda*.[19] Satpam were uniformed guards employed by private businesses or government agencies to protect a particular space, such as a bank, a mall, a gated residential community, or some government building. Hansip patrolled residential neighborhoods, wore uniforms, and received a small salary, which was generated from the fee charged to each of the households under their watch. The *ronda* was a far older institution for neighborhood security. It was still based primarily on community obligation and its guards did not wear uniforms. All three elements of the security system were brought under the control of the police's so-called Guidance of Society Unit (or Guidance Unit).[20] Because the police did not pay the guards, however, the Guidance Unit's sole functions were surveillance and training. This new system, which was centered on private security guards, was explicitly meant to represent a departure from older forms of territorial security like the *ronda* and the *jegger*. The head of the Guidance Unit in Jakarta described the new approach as follows:

> A Satpam has two "heads"; the firm, house or office at which he or she is employed, and the police, from whom he—or she—gets training. . . .
>
> *Being a Satpam is a profession. A Satpam is not just a simple night watchman [tukang ronda malam], nor are they thugs [centeng].[21] They don't just open the door for people. . . .*
>
> *What Satpam basically do is the police's job, that's why we train them and are responsible for them. (Jakarta Post, October 13, 1996)*

Satpam were defined by what they were not: thugs, old-fashioned voluntary *ronda* guards, or servants of some kind. Like the police, they should be treated with respect and should consider themselves professionals.

In the new system, the Guidance Unit would ensure, in the first place, that all schools, neighborhood associations, markets, businesses, and offices had an individual or committee responsible for overseeing "security"; this would facilitate coordination between the police and those who paid the guards' salaries. The police would also, however, watch over the guards themselves. As part of this surveillance, Satpam and Hansip guards were to be counted and classified according to the education and training they had received. There were to be three-month and one-month courses provided for Satpam by the police.[22] These would include training in military formation, marching, self-defense, how to guard certain vital industries, and a combination of lessons on how to make reports to the police, how to keep track of the identities of those coming and going from offices, factories, or housing complexes, and the procedure to follow in the apprehension of suspected criminals. Those who passed this basic training would be allowed to possess knives; those who went through a special screening process would be eligible to have guns. Although Hansip did not have such a special training course, in principle, its members were to join Satpam guards at the local police station each week for training. Moreover, all three types of guards—the *ronda* included—were to be "controlled" at their posts on a regular basis by patrolling members of the Guidance Unit. On these more informal occasions, the police would make sure the guards were well organized, gather information about threats for their intelligence reports, and give advice. Finally, to distinguish them from the public and from other security services, Satpam and Hansip guards were to wear standardized uniforms and carry identification issued by the police. The Satpam uniform consisted of black pants and a smart, white shirt with logos on the arms and a label on the front saying "Satpam"; the Hansip were similarly outfitted, though in army green.

It was not just the guards themselves who were to be revamped. The guardhouses of the neighborhood watch, which used to be known as *gardu* or *pos ronda*, were to become *pos kamling* (security system posts). These were henceforth counted, inspected, and classified according to their facilities; it was noted, for example, what building type the *pos* was (i.e., from what materials it was constructed), and whether it had weapons, maps, flashlights, beds, and so forth. Based on this information, the police could then work together with Hansip and *ronda* guards to improve the facilities by making recommendations to the heads of neighborhood associations (the Rukun Tetangga and Rukun Warga) about what had to be purchased (it was they who had to find a way to pay for improvements). Through a process of *kentonganisasi*, or "slit gongization," every *pos kamling* would be obliged to have a slit gong and a standardized code for warning of danger, as well as a schedule outlining who was responsible for guarding at what times. Ideally, each *pos kamling* should also have handcuffs, weapons, and a phone, along with maps of the area its members patrolled, lists of important residents, lists of so-called *residivis* (recidivists),[23] and rules for the patrols.[24] These materials would mimic those found at the local police station. Similarly, the security posts usually found in the parking lots or lobbies of commercial establishments were to be subject to the same sorts of monitoring and recommendations made to employers if Satpam facilities were lacking.

The economic backdrop for these ambitious changes was the wave of industrialization and commercial growth that swept Indonesia in the 1970s. On the one hand, this meant the deepening penetration of the cash economy, making the unpaid *ronda* a bit of an anachronism. On the other hand, it meant a dramatic change to the composition of urban spaces, as a growing number of banks, factories, department stores, parking lots, chain restaurants, and housing complexes appeared on the scene. Siskamling envisioned a future in which every one of these new locales—along with virtually every other territory of the urban fabric—would have at least one designated guard and an individual or committee responsible for working with the police to supervise and organize the watch as well as any other security measures. The guards themselves—through their training and use of police modes of surveillance—would act as local representatives of police authority.

The only real problem with this plan as it was first introduced in the early 1980s was that people tended not to choose freshly minted Satpam and Hansip over existing commercial security services run by ex-convicts and gangs. Ex-convicts and gangs instilled more fear not just in potential robbers and thieves but in businesses and communities as well, who thus felt that these illicit figures were capable of offering greater protection than more "official" groups. In its earliest manifestation, then, Siskamling tended to work directly with the sellers of security services—namely, those who controlled the gangs—rather than the buyers. Agreements were made with many of the emerging businesses run by ex-convicts and other shady elements, all of whom undoubtedly liked the idea of being legitimized by the state in return for submitting their members to training and guidance. For a brief period in 1980 and 1981, the police, local government, and businesses created by gangs and ex-convicts thus enjoyed an openly cooperative arrangement that was probably economically beneficial for all involved. It was probably also politically beneficial to the ruling party, Golkar (Golongan Karya, or Functional Groups), which reportedly made use of these businesses' strong-arm tactics in the run-up to the 1982 elections.

The honeymoon was short-lived, however. In June 1982 the national chief of police, under the banner of Kopkamtib, put out an order that effectively banned private security businesses.[25] While these businesses could still legally offer security consultation to other businesses, train prospective security guards, and sell security devices, they were prohibited from renting out employees as guards. Furthermore, those businesses that continued to operate in the more restricted domain set out for them were subject to increased regulation. One regulation held that employees must be able to provide a "letter of good behavior,"[26] meaning that no ex-convicts would be eligible to work in such firms; another forced firms to receive permission for their businesses from the commander of the Provincial Police, and, if they intended to serve areas outside that command, from the national chief of police.

As a result of this new policy, many of the newly established private security firms shut down or were driven underground. Prems Surabaya, for example, which in February 1982 had met with members of the provincial congress (the Dewan Perwikilan Rakyat Daerah) and optimistically claimed that it anticipated a membership of fifty thousand people, about 60 percent of whom would be ex-convicts, officially disbanded less than a month later.[27] Prems Jakarta, on the other hand, restricted its official activities to providing legal aid and job training to ex-convicts, while nonetheless continuing to offer illicit debt-collection and security services (Husein 1983). In Bandung, where the first official security guards were known as Satpamsus (Satuan Pengamanan Khusus), the new policy had the effect of reducing the powers of the *camat* (head of the subdistrict). Initially, Satpamsus had been under the control of the *camat* and the heads of the Rukun Tetangga and Rukun Warga, with some oversight from the police and army. Under that system, the *camat* and Rukun Tetangga and Rukun Warga officials had profited from commercial security since they collected money from shops and factories in their areas and hired out security guards. With the new regulations, however, the *camat* and the Rukun Tetangga/Rukun Warga were restricted to involvement in residential security, while control over commercial security came under the purview of an alliance of business owners and police.

Perhaps the most interesting case, however, was Massa 33, which had been started in the early 1970s by a gang of *calo*[28] operating out of

Surabaya's main bus terminal but grew to be one of the largest of the ex-convict organizations, with branches throughout East Java. It continued to operate illegally for a time but was eventually the target of a police operation. As a result of this operation (and with permission from the army and Surabaya's mayor) the police, working together with the head of the bus terminal, took down personal data on all Massa 33 members, supposedly screened out the most hardened criminals among them, and arranged for some of the others to undergo training as Satpam. These reformed gang members were then mixed in with an equal number of non–Massa 33 Satpam, and all became employees of the terminal.[29] In other words, the original Massa 33 structure was destroyed, but its reformable elements were integrated into a new organization based on the cooperation between the police and the terminal head. To ensure that the gang did not survive as a force within this new organization, it was diluted with nonaffiliated members. Furthermore, since the remaining members of the gang were considered to be employees of the terminal rather than members of an outside organization, they could be subjected to all sorts of governmental and firm-based controls.

In sum, the overall result of the government's policy was to deny gangs and private security firms their economic and legal bases and to appropriate, and subject to police surveillance, their reformable elements. This policy—in combination with the "systematization" and regulation of existing *ronda* practices—set the stage for a massive expansion of Siskamling into all domains of urban life, a process that would continue throughout the 1980s and '90s, and indeed into the 2000s.[30] It also created a situation in which gangs that continued to operate were criminalized (with notable exceptions like Pemuda Pancasila), while those that disbanded saw their members divided into two separate groups of people: corrigible and incorrigible. In other words, it set the stage for Petrus.

The Killings of Criminals

According to Bourchier (1990, 185), who analyzed the unfolding of the Petrus campaign, the killings of "criminals" began in earnest in March 1983 in the Central Javanese city of Yogyakarta and lasted for at least two years.[31] During this time, at least five thousand (and perhaps more than ten thousand) people deemed *preman* or *gali-gali* were killed. The killings were concentrated in the larger cities, like Jakarta, Surabaya, Bandung, Medan, and Semarang. Although international human rights groups condemned these acts, many press accounts were more or less approving of the government's methods for much of the campaign's duration. While there were critics who complained that such extrajudicial punishments would undermine the rule of law, press interviews with people "on the street" almost invariably indicated a certain relief that "criminals" were being eliminated from city bus terminals, train stations, markets, and squares.

Structurally and discursively, Petrus was rooted in the tradition of surveillance outlined in the previous chapters. It depended first of all on a process of identification, which provided a representation of the "criminal" element in society, and second on "operations" that targeted particular people in the world "out there" based on the labels that had been attached to them. It was planned and organized centrally, most likely by General Benny Murdani, who then had control over the armed forces, Kopkamtib, and military intelligence. It also employed a discourse borrowed from hygiene operations, aimed as it was at "cleansing" the nation's cities of the criminal "cancer" that threatened them (Bourchier 1990, 184). Bourchier describes a typical killing as follows:

> Criminals, gang members, or ex-prisoners, frequently tattooed and almost always young and male, would be met in their houses or in the street by a group of four or five heavily built men. In many cases they would shoot their victim where they found him. More often they would bundle him (or them) into a jeep or Toyota Hardtop and drive off into the night. The victim would be taken to a quiet place and shot through the head and chest at close range with .45 or .38 caliber pistols. His corpse would then either be tossed into a river or left in some public place outside a cinema, a school or on a footpath of a busy street. Victims frequently had their hands bound, and often bore marks of torture. The following day there would be a short report about the finding of a "*mayat bertato*," (tattooed corpse) in the local paper, usually accompanied by grisly pictures. (1990, 186)

Bourchier goes on to note that there were also a number of mass graves to which large numbers of people were brought and killed and in which their bodies were then dumped. This was done on a highly routinized basis: on every Friday and Sunday, for example. In the early part of the campaign, people living near the graves were permitted to witness these killings.

From this description of the killings, it is clear that they followed a pattern very similar to many of the less violent operations that were a prominent feature of New Order life: operations against trishaws, drugs, prostitution, vagrants, women's fertility (i.e., family planning), and the like. As in operations aimed at drug dealers, for example, the agents descended on their targets and removed them from the scene in order to maintain an image of order.[32] The removal was then followed by the staging of a spectacle in which the targeted objects or people were shown to have been truly eliminated (the dead bodies displayed for all to see and the drugs crushed or burned).[33] Furthermore, like those operations conducted under the rubric of family planning, the solution Petrus posed for the criminal contagion was not simply elimination but also heightened surveillance. Bourchier's description of the mechanics of Petrus in Yogyakarta highlights these two objectives:

> The procedure in Yogyakarta appears to have been that Police Intelligence supplied the garrison commander (Komandan Kodim) with a list naming hundreds of suspected criminals and ex-prisoners in the region. The garrison then put together a black list and issued a public ultimatum to all *galis* (without, however, naming names) to "surrender immediately" to the garrison headquarters. Those who did, and these numbered several hundred, were required to fill out detailed forms, providing their life history as well as data on all their family members and friends. They were also required to sign statements agreeing to refrain from criminal activities or face "firm action" from the authorities. Each *gali* was obliged to carry a special card and report to the garrison on a regular basis. Those who did not turn up to be registered, or did not keep their appointments with the garrison, were hunted down and killed by squads of military men. (1990, 185–86)

In making its ultimatum to the public, the garrison was saying that it had already completed the process of identification and had a list of "criminals" in its possession. How were these criminals identified? Bourchier notes that the source of this list was the police. In fact, there was nothing new about this since police and village heads had been compiling lists of "fireflies" or recidivists in their regions since the early twentieth century (see chapter 4). With the Petrus ultimatum, however, these lists took on a new significance. In the past, recidivists subjected to heightened surveillance were clearly listed by local authorities and the rules of reporting were explicit. There was no mystery about such lists, and there was even a fair amount of flexibility about who was included since a person who behaved well in his community might well see their name left off the list because of an "oversight" on the part of a local official. Moreover, the lists themselves served what was primarily an administrative function, with the work of actual surveillance being carried out by the neighborhood watches and spies. This meant that a "firefly" was kept aware of his status as a suspect by being subjected to repetitive monitoring by his peers. The Petrus ultimatum changed this state of affairs in three ways. First, it said that the lists had already been compiled and so there would be no flexibility in the process of identification. Second, it made a point of keeping the contents of the lists secret. Third, it proposed an unprecedented equation: an unsurveilled "criminal" was equivalent to a dead one.

One of the more striking things about the blacklists was the idea that they could not be changed. In Indonesia, the proposition that a government decision cannot be changed is usually greeted with cynicism accompanied by statements to the effect that anything is possible with money and influence. Indeed, one of the more common mantras recited by everyone from coolies to elite lawyers is that, in Indonesia, "everything can be bought." Yet when speaking of blacklists, such an attitude was far less prevalent; even people who were otherwise unimpressed by state power showed a certain anxiety and respect when the topic came up. Consider, for example, Mr. Yanto, an older man living in Bandung who fits very closely with the definition of a Petrus target. As a youth he was a member of street gangs, became known as a fighter, and finally joined a group of armed robbers. Just after Petrus, he completed a seventeen-year prison term for murder and armed robbery, and when I met him, he was working as a bodyguard for an ethnic Chinese businessman. He was a gruff man and prone to sudden outbursts of anger, but he was also past middle age, a bit weary, and not as good at hiding his kindness as he undoubtedly had been at one time. Nonetheless, he was always extremely self-confident and felt capable of manipulating all sorts of outcomes in his relations with the police, judges, and others. When I raised the topic of Petrus, he mentioned the lists and became visibly frightened by the possibility that he might be on some sort of post-Petrus blacklist. When I suggested that he might be able to pull some strings to ensure his name did not appear on such a list, he responded that that was impossible: "Once your name is on that list, it's done. You can't do anything about it."

That blacklists might be taken to be immutable—and could actually be so in many cases—shows that they emanated from somewhere close to the heart of state power. At stake for the state in such lists was something far greater than the fate of the individuals in question and even greater than the benefits derived from establishing interpersonal debts through bribery. The lists were important enough that to subtract a name from them would constitute a threat to state power of the first order.[34] A clue as to what such a threat might be is provided by a story, not about the Petrus blacklists, but about their political counterpart. It was related to me by a wealthy businessman in the private sector. As a person with some influence, he had gathered together some high-level military men in the hope of getting politically sensitive criminal charges against an old friend from his hometown dropped. Accustomed to dealing with such figures in the context of his business, he thought he might at least be able to make sure that his friend was charged with something more minor. But in the meeting, when he explained that his friend did not pose a threat and that his offending actions had been a mistake, they asked him, "Do you know who [your friend] really is?" They then proceeded to ask him questions about his friend's daily activities, which he could not answer. Finally, they refused to do anything in the case, saying, "Even if you've known [*kenal*] him for a long time, you can't be certain you really know [*tahu*] who he is." That this event made a lasting impression on the man is indicated by the fact that he related this story to me on two separate occasions; moreover, the way in which he related the story suggests that the questions had genuinely caused him to doubt whether he really knew his friend.

The story shows that what was at stake for the state in its blacklisting was nothing less than the power of recognition. The state needed to privilege its own "truth" about people's identities over competing claims about *who* people really are. By making the lists immutable, state representatives established a domain where the authority of local knowledge, familiarity, and the like were ultimately denied and where the knowledge produced using state surveillance techniques was rendered truthful. In the years before Petrus, it might have been possible to use one's own perception of oneself, or that of one's neighbors, to influence the way one was identified by the state. Certainly, it was possible to maintain a local identity that did not directly correspond to that on file in the state archive. In this respect, many "criminals" were actually regarded as heroes in their local communities. With the Petrus ultimatum, however, other sources of recognition outside of the state were denied. In the end, the ultimatum served to assert that the state knew people better than their own friends did, or indeed better even than they knew themselves. Although all other sorts of "truths" dictated by the government may be subject to localization and corruption, this particular domain remained untouchable.

The Petrus lists were not only immutable; they were also secret. This was important because it asserted the exclusivity of state knowledge while also demanding that all citizens ask themselves if they might be "criminals." In principle, at least, the situation was not at all different from that which obtained during the killings of "communists" in 1965–66, when people were forced to ask, "Am I PKI or non-PKI?" The difference with the Petrus campaign was that they were forced to ask themselves about their "criminality."[35] To answer this question, they had to imagine what the state perceived criminality to be and how the state imagined them to be. And since the contents of the lists were not made public, the implicit demand was that anyone who had ever been remotely suspected by the state, had been in prison, or had committed a crime should voluntarily recognize themselves as suspect, even if they immediately found themselves to be innocent in this regard.[36]

Failing to recognize oneself as the state did could prove fatal: if one's name was on the list and one did not submit to heightened surveillance, one could be killed.[37] This was especially the case for those people who hid from the state or, even worse, asserted another identity against that given to them by the state. Lieutenant Colonel CZI Mohammad Hasbi, the Acehnese head of Yogyakarta's garrison, put this in the starkest terms when explaining why the shootings were necessary: "Why shoot? Basically we want to work in a humane way. But there are those who want to fight back. They want to show off their self-identity [*identitas dirinya*]" (*Tempo*, May 14, 1983). It was these types—those who refused to submit to registration and monitoring, choosing instead to "show off" their own identities—that the campaign targeted. The state was thus reserving the ultimate power of recognition for its surveillance apparatus: the power over life and death. In theory, at least, agreeing to suspect one's own criminality, not just one's politics, was the new condition of survival under the New Order state.

The Tattoo and the Fingerprint

That Petrus identified its "criminal" victims through blacklists and that the campaign was designed to demonstrate the overwhelming power of surveillance is only one side of the story. The other side, interesting but less straightforward, concerns a quite different impression that developed in many quarters regarding how victims were identified. In brief, it was the impression that targets for the killings were identified not by hidden lists but by the very visible markings on their bodies—in this case, their tattoos. Certainly, many ex-convicts had tattoos, but rumors seemed to suggest that the presence of tattoos was in itself enough to identify the bearer as a criminal, and that the mysterious shooters were simply hunting down anyone with tattoos. Such rumors might well have originated in press reports about the discovery of corpses, which frequently made reference to the victims' tattoos. In any case, the rumors were taken seriously enough that many people with tattoos were sufficiently frightened that they tried to get rid of such markings. During a period of just two weeks in June 1983, two hospitals in Bandung recorded a total of sixty-three people who paid to have their tattoos removed by way of plastic surgery. Others tried to remove their tattoos themselves. Many inmates at Bandung's prison cut their skin off with razor blades or tried to burn their tattoos off using caustic soda; others outside the prison used hot irons (decades later, one could still see bus conductors and the like with huge scars where their tattoos used to be) (*Surabaya Post*, June 18, 1983).

How are we to understand this alternate explanation for how Petrus targets were identified? What is the relation between visible tattoos and hidden lists? As a method for identifying "criminals" and targets for killings, the relation between lists and tattoos can be understood to be an unproblematic supplemental relation. This is, at least, the gist of the following remarks, which were made toward the end of the Petrus campaign in 1983 by a member of Reserse's (the Criminal Investigation Unit of the police) Identification section in Jakarta:

> It is clear that a tattooed person is not [necessarily] a criminal, but as I often handle the various types of criminals there are, there has at last arisen an indirect impression when I see a tattooed person, such that my inner voice says, "Why, it's just like a criminal." And the majority of those who often wear tattoos are those who really are criminals, which is to say, those who have been in and out of prison or who have been blacklisted by the police. And in connection with my work, it is clear that tattoos are special signs that have to be noted in people's identity files, particularly those who have business with the police. And as a matter of fact, historically, before the discovery of a fingerprinting system, tattoos were used as a means for identification just like brands made with hot iron.[38]

This police officer, at the center of the nation's criminal identification and registration apparatus, conveys his belief that tattoos are an "indirect" sign of criminal identity.[39] Someone like him, he suggests, who has had countless occasions to look back and forth between the lists of convicts and the bodies before him, can pretty safely say that there is a correspondence between "criminals" defined by technologies of surveillance and bodies with tattoos. In this initial comment, we see one possible way in which tattoos might have functioned to support the state's claims that its lists and its operations were very precise. As soon as doubts about precision emerged, people could be reassured by the indirect evidence that the bodies turning up in rivers and on the streets were not just any bodies—they were tattooed bodies. For him, the reassurance came not just through experience but also through a chain of associations that allowed him to get from criminals to tattoos via identity cards and back again to criminals via fingerprints. This chain of associations went as follows: criminal → prisoner→ blacklist→ identity file→ tattoo noted in file→ tattoo on body→ brand on body→ fingerprint→ criminal.

Yet two things about the policeman's statements suggest that he is giving tattoos more significance than the files would. First, he notes at the end of the chain of associations that brands and tattoos historically preceded identity files (fingerprints, lists, etc.) as a way of signifying the "criminal," thereby giving the former a primacy over the latter. Second, he says that whenever he sees tattoos his inner voice (*hati*) says, "Why, it's just like a criminal." These statements would seem to undermine his initial claim that tattoos signify criminality only by virtue of a statistical correlation. Rather, it turns out that they are "special signs" that provoke in him an immediate equation with criminality, even when they appear on someone not being processed for heightened surveillance. If this is the case, might it not then be possible that the lists used in Petrus had a similar reinforcing effect on what had been a prior suspicion of tattoos? Consider the statements of a food seller at a market in Jakarta:

> It's clear that people with tattoos are criminals [*penjahat*], sir, or at least that their hearts and actions aren't good. Before, almost every night the small traders here were asked for money. It's true it wasn't a lot, sir, but that money meant a lot to us. After a time I came to know the person, but didn't know him really well. He turned up only asking for money and then left again. Indeed, he and his friends had

tattoos as their distinguishing marks. So that this gave rise to a hunch that tattooed people are criminals. What's more, when meeting those guys, at least I had to be careful, maybe they could be criminals [*jangan-jangan orang ini penjahat*]. My hunch was strengthened after I read in the papers that lots of tattooed people were shot to death, and they said all of them were criminals. But now we here are all calm because those guys who asked for money each night are no longer. Maybe they ran away or were shot by someone. (Sumarwoto 1984, 75)

Here, one finds what is probably the most ubiquitous local description of a *preman* or *jegger*: someone who is known by the wider community, but to whom one would not admit being close, who wears tattoos, is fearsome, and who turns up asking for money. With respect to the tattoos, this food seller's answer shows a movement from (at most) a hunch to near certainty that the tattoos he sees reflect their bearer's criminality (and therefore someone whose death is meaningless). One can see in the *jangan-jangan orang ini penjahat* that the recognition of whether this person is a criminal, rather than simply being "not good," is something that derives from outside (or perhaps, that if it came from inside the local sphere the man would already have been killed). The confirmation of his suspicion comes from the reports he reads about Petrus.

In sum, while the explicit targets of the Petrus campaign were professional and violent criminals, the way in which these criminals were identified was subject to two interpretations. One suggested that identification primarily followed the logic of surveillance. In this interpretation, tattoos were merely a supplemental form of identification (found on corpses) that could have the effect of containing fears about who criminals were: you could see with your own eyes that not just anyone was being killed. Another interpretation suggests that the targets of Petrus were not ex-convicts and repeat offenders, as defined by law and by the surveillance apparatus, but people with "special signs" on their bodies. In this interpretation, tattoos were already cause for suspicion about someone's "criminality," and the state's lists and the growing tally of dead criminals acted to confirm what—in retrospect at least—one already knew. The fact that tattoo wearers might be the real targets of Petrus caused Arief Sumarwoto, the policeman who wrote the thesis from which the mentioned quotations were taken, some consternation. As part of his research he interviewed convicts, police, and others, and he conducted statistical analyses to determine what percentage of so-called *residivis* wear tattoos and what percentage of tattoo wearers are *residivis*. Writing during Petrus, he was clearly bothered by the fact that Petrus's targeting of tattooed bodies might result in the wrong people being killed. Perhaps he was disturbed by the operations and had to write about these injustices even if, as his thesis implied, they were merely the result of a technical failure of reference. Or perhaps he had a tattoo himself.

By suggesting that blacklists were not the only way "criminals" were identified at the time of Petrus, I am not trying to argue that Petrus in fact targeted tattoo wearers rather than repeat offenders. Although it is entirely possible that Sumarwoto's fears (fears shared, as we have seen, by tattoo wearers) were justified, and that people were killed simply for having tattoos, the centralized, bureaucratic form Petrus took makes it likely that official lists were what actually determined who was killed in most instances. That said, it would be wrong to dismiss the ability of tattoos to act as a form of identification during the campaign. While they may not tell us the names of those who were killed, they provide an important clue as to what and whom people believed the campaign was targeting and what the symbolic importance of the campaign was. For the state, tattoos were additionally offensive because they seemed to assert an identity that could not be traced back to state systems of identification. They were precisely not fingerprints or brands, both of which would be stamped using the hands of the police under the watchful eye of the state. Tattoos, rather, were self-inflicted, and in prisons at least, were done in hiding from the guards since such practices were against regulations.

With Petrus, however, all this changed. By virtue of the lists of criminals, the corpses displayed for all to see, and the hundreds of newspaper headlines emblazoned with the term "tattooed corpse," tattoos were now both criminalized and indelibly associated in people's minds with a form of death that clearly led back to the state. They had become brands or, as the inmates called them, stamps (*cap*). The people who found themselves unexpectedly recognized by the state, that eye of eyes, had either to accept the omnipotence of that eye by submitting to perpetual surveillance or to risk death. Some tried a different tactic: ridding themselves of this stamp. The scars they created in the process were perhaps the most vivid reminders of what battles over identities entail when they are fought on the surfaces of bodies. And although these scars necessarily pointed back to Petrus, they did so in a way that led back not to death but to survival; they indicated someone who was confronted by the state (at least in their thoughts) and who lived to have their scars tell the story.

While tattoos may assert "self-identity" against the state, this only scratches the surface of their apparent power. As indicated in chapter 2, tattoos are often associated with something far greater, like invulnerability. In this regard, they make greatest sense when inscribed on the bodies of *jegger* who are known for their courage and fighting skills. That tattoos could offend or even horrify some of those who are exposed to them fits well with what the *jegger* stands for. This power of tattoos to cause fear is a constant theme in Sumarwoto's interviews. Some, indeed, craved this power. As one inmate told him, "My attitude has always been that I want to be considered a *jagoan*, so not long after entering into prison I often stood out in various activities, and in tattoos, too, I made as many as possible. With so many tattoos on my body many people pay attention to me" (Sumarwoto 1984, 65). Here, tattoos are part of a larger strategy of acting tough, or like a "game cock" (*jagoan*).[40] The inmate's tattoos make him stand out and thus make people pay attention to him. Not all people wanted this extra attention, however. One of Sumarwoto's respondents actually feared that he would be recognized as someone who was too powerful: "I felt scared [coming into prison with so many tattoos] that I would be stamped as the most tough [*jagoan*]" (66).[41] Those who did want the power tattoos provided them, however, got many and put them in the most visible places. Magically, these were not merely seen as attributes of the *jago* character, however, but as powers in their own right. Another inmate stated, "Those inmates who truly are not bad/criminal [*penjahat*] usually they only wear a few tattoos and these are in hidden locations. It's like after having tattoos there arises a feeling of pride so that it gives off an impression of being admired [*dikagumi*], respected [*disegani*], and all this gives a push to increase one's daring to be determined no matter what [*keberanian untuk berbuat nekad*]" (66). Having visible tattoos, by giving an impression of being admired, actually pushes one to be *nekad*, or intensely determined. It is as if the person has a force of their own that creates a boundless determination. This force, or "capital," as one of Sumarwoto's interviewees calls it in the following quotation, referring to the power one accumulates from having acquired tattoos, comes from the ability of such markings to capture others' attention, to implicate their desires in one's own. The appropriation of such power begins with a process of mimicry:

> It felt good to have tattoo capital on the body [*modal tatoo di badan*], there was a feeling of being respected, especially by those who just entered the prison. I remember the first time I entered prison, if I saw

someone with lots of tattoos, in my gut I felt fearful too, and even more so if his body was big. After I got out of prison for the second time, the capital I had from having been in prison, along with the large number of tattoos on this body of mine, added to my confidence to do crimes. (63)

Seeing himself (and others) fearing and paying attention to tattoos, this inmate wants this attention for himself. He imitates them so that he, too, will have the power he desires: the fear and respect of new inmates. The power that he appropriates is a form of capital that gives him the courage to commit more crimes, which makes more people admire him, which presumably makes him commit more crimes, and so on. By implicating others in his fetishization of tattoos, he has established himself as someone who is fearsome and worthy of respect. And insofar as they share his desires, he has acquired a kind of charismatic authority.

State Mimicry of Territorial Power

When the specter of crime appeared in the light of day in the early 1980s, its effect was not unlike the effect tattoos had on new inmates. Or at least that is how the media and the government portrayed it. The *preman* seemed *nekad* in their audacious crimes, and through the press everybody was looking at them, admiring and fearing their power. Their organization of protection rackets, moreover, seemed to give their power currency, which they could trade for economic gain. It was as if a hierarchy based on tattoos, duels, and territorial authority was taking shape alongside established hierarchies based on kinship, office, and rank. This was not merely a question of "self-identity" but a question of political power. Of course, it is difficult to imagine that these organizations posed any genuine threat to President Suharto's authority; most were more like unions of the disenfranchised than powerful mafias. Furthermore, even those organizations that had not been formed under the auspices of the military were quickly subordinated, through Siskamling, to police and government authority. So why did President Suharto opt for Petrus? It may have been, as Bourchier has suggested, that such organizations were tied into a particular faction or fraternity[42] within the military and that Suharto felt threatened by this alternative power base, or that their ties to local authorities threatened to undermine Jakarta's ability to control the regions (Bourchier 1990, 195). Whatever the immediate political reasons, we shall see below that Petrus did indeed have consequences, both for the state and for local communities. In different ways, both were implicated in, and transformed by, the killings, whose overall symbolic effect was to appropriate, and deterritorialize, the power represented by "criminals" and embed it within the hierarchy of the state.[43]

Exactly how this appropriation worked on a local level is apparent in the following summary of what happened during Petrus in a neighborhood in Bandung. It was told to me by a young man who was familiar with street culture in that neighborhood.

> *In this area alone there were three killed (during the Petrus campaign). Everyone knows who the preman are because they have their own place (lokasi) from which they collect money. If they aren't paid, they will stab people, burn the store, and so on. They will often ask people for their watches. People are scared of them and do what they say. To find the preman the military used lists of ex-cons (residivis). The usual way of picking them up was with a Land Rover. If kids saw a green Land Rover with yellow on the door enter the neighborhood they would run in fear. The military would then go to the preman's house and haul him out into the car (he repeats "Land Rover" as it clearly stood out in his mind). It didn't matter if the preman had already stopped doing bad things, lived with his family, prayed, or whatever. He would still be hauled off. One was even a head of a Rukun Tetangga. When they started turning up dead, people talked about how they were being killed. Some of them were shot but wouldn't die because they had magical powers (ilmu). If they were shot the bullets would enter and they wouldn't be able to get up, but they wouldn't die. The only way to kill them was to tie their feet with plastic string and to tie their neck with plastic string, and then to pull (or tie one end to a tree) so that they were held off the ground. It was said that if they touched the ground they wouldn't be able to be killed. Kind of like electric wires, which must be suspended in midair. The corpses were then always put in a rice sack and dropped in the river or at the outskirts of the city.*

This local perspective on Petrus betrays a sense of powerlessness in the face of agents of death that come from without. We must assume that when he says, "Everyone knows who the *preman* are," he is referring not only to local knowledge but also to state knowledge, for when he then describes the victims that were chosen, it turns out that some were viewed locally as being good and respected members of the community (praying, having family, etc.). The official blacklists are portrayed as having an inevitable referentiality about them that the local sphere can do nothing about.

As soon as this misgiving is out of the way, however, the story turns to how these powerful figures were killed. Here, as in other stories we shall hear later, the killers are said to believe they are confronting someone who is invulnerable: "If they were shot the bullets would enter and they wouldn't be able to get up, but they wouldn't die." The victims do not die ordinary deaths. Rather, their deaths come from outside the local sphere and result from the state's ability to find the weaknesses in their magical invulnerability. (In this story, this comes when the victim is literally lifted *off* his territory, or deterritorialized.) Had it been the case that the victims simply died ordinary deaths, this fact alone might conceivably become grounds for questioning the very existence of their powers of invulnerability and charisma. But what the story shows is that in fact, the people being killed *were* invulnerable in relation to ordinary death; it is just that the type of death they experienced was supernatural. The killers had confronted the magical power of their victims with a magic of their own.

It is the continued existence of the supernatural power that makes the story worth repeating, for an ordinary death would be of little or no interest so long after the fact. But as James T. Siegel (1998, 120–24) has shown in an analysis of stories surrounding the discovery of Petrus corpses, the logic of such stories—and therefore, perhaps, the "reason" for making the killings themselves into public spectacles—was such that it shifted the focus of interest from the *preman* back to the state. Rather than being fascinated by the criminal specter, people became fascinated with the power of the killers; rather than tracing the source of power back to gangs and other forms of hierarchy, people traced this power back to the state. At least, this was the case for as long as the corpses of "criminals," like the tattoos we saw above, had the effect of powerful signs.

Besides identifying itself with the power attributed to the criminal specter, the state also used Petrus to identify itself with the power of territorial communities or "the masses." This identification was more explicit and was based on the supposed similarity between the Petrus killings and cases of "playing judge oneself" (*main hakim sendiri*) that preceded Petrus and that continued both during and after the campaign.[44] As discussed in chapter 2, "playing judge oneself" is the term used to describe members of a community taking the law into their own hands and beating or killing people they have defined as criminals or undesirables. In many of these cases, the targets of such vigilante violence are the same as those who were victimized by Petrus, and sometimes the victim's body is even disposed of in a manner analogous to Petrus victims. Vigilantism of this sort has also often been reported in a very similar way to Petrus cases. Consider, for example, the following case, which occurred during Petrus and was reported under the headline "Recidivist with 'Sweet Memory' Tattoo Killed after Being Mobbed by Inhabitants of Kampung Krendang" (in Indonesian; my translation): "The brain of a criminal gang in the area of Kampung Krendang named Miming (25 yrs), just released from Cipinang prison, was killed as he was discovered to be about to commit a crime in the same area last Saturday. The suspect, whose body was full of tattoos, was sprawled out bathed in blood in front of Gang Janda in East Krendang" (*Harian Berita Buana*, July 25, 1983). Such cases of vigilantism are subject to the sometimes loose notion of catching people in the act of committing a crime. Petrus, on the other hand, targeted people at any time in any place. Nonetheless, the similarity with Petrus in the reporting of such cases is unmistakable. Indeed, an article in the national magazine *Tempo*, citing Lieutenant Colonel Hasbi's explanations for the targets of Petrus in Yogyakarta, appeared next to a report on all the recent cases where *kampung* in Central Java had punished "criminals" to death. The reasons analysts gave for these cases were "the culture of violence among the people," "letting emotion speak rather than rationality," and "an excess of solidarity" (*Tempo*, May 14, 1983). It was an identification that did not escape critics of the government's policy. Adnan Buyung Nasution, who was then head of the Legal Aid Institute, rhetorically asked, "If the people act to play judge themselves it's considered anarchy, but if it is the security forces that do it?" (*Tempo*, May 21, 1983).

While the earlier story about Petrus in Bandung throws doubt on the degree to which this identification was successful, there was a sense in which Petrus could be interpreted as the government acting on the behalf of territorial communities, disregarding the law as they did in an effort to establish an "excess of solidarity" with the people. At the same time, for symbolic effect the state's violence needed to be distinguishable from that of territorially based vigilantism. Otherwise, one might really have anarchy, since the violence would appear as a contagion with no clear source, and the state would be seen not as representing the violence but as merely participating in it. This could explain why the state, in many cases, found it necessary to claim authorship of the killings and why the killings were conducted in a manner that left no doubt as to who was behind them.

Insofar as the killings did involve an identification with communal violence, they would be comparable to Siskamling's process of *kentonganisasi*, which, as we have seen, was meant to bring together all the local territories into one giant security system that derived meaning from the state. With Petrus, however, it was not just the community's solidarity that was identified with the state, but its violence and its power.

Within the state itself, the degree to which the power associated with such killings achieved currency, and the tendency to trace the source of that power upward through the hierarchy to some higher authority or power, varied. This is evident in two stories I was told about Petrus-like killings. The first was related to me by Prasetyo, a mid-ranking police officer in Bandung.[45] Prasetyo himself was probably the most ambitious, and also the most successful, young officer I met in Bandung. In contrast to the jaded Reserse agents at the precinct, for example, he was radiant in his appearance and gave the impression that he was someone who worked hard and did things by the book. It was thus quite disturbing to hear him tell this story in a tone of youthful exuberance and pride. The killing he describes was not part of the Petrus campaign itself, but one of the many that have followed in its wake.[46]

> *Prasetyo and I sat on the couch in the unit head's office and the two of them discussed whom I should talk to from the unit for my research on mystical knowledge. Suddenly Prasetyo remembered a story about a case he handled during one of his former postings. When he first started telling the story he was directing it to me, but as he went on, he increasingly looked expectantly for responses only from his boss. The story was about a man who was being held in a lockup by the police for having committed some crime (he didn't say what). He was known to the locals as an orang pintar (a person with special powers), and indeed it turned out that he was able to use these powers to talk the police not only into letting him out of his cell, but even into giving him a gun and letting him go. When the police realized (sadar) what had happened they called for help in finding him. This is how Prasetyo got involved, as he was part of the team that was sent to search for the man. The police who had let him escape told Prasetyo to be careful of his ilmu and also said that this man was famous for his huge penis. They caught him at the home of one of his many wives. And it was true, his instrument (alat) was bigger than anything that could be imagined (he showed with his hands).... Almost as an afterthought, but conveying a sense that this is what really made the story*

important (not the magic), Prasetyo then looked knowingly at his boss and said in a soft voice (so I wouldn't hear) something that sounded like, "It was a 486." His boss didn't catch it and asked, "What?" To which Prasetyo repeated, "486. We got an order."[47] As he said this Prasetyo made a cutting motion at his throat. "Had to be separated [dipisahkan]," he said, still speaking softly.

In this story, the potency of the victim is described in overtly phallic and phallocentric terms. Not only does he have a huge penis, but he can control language, disarm a policeman, and enjoys a certain power over women. An order is received for the man to be killed but the killing "had to" be done in a particular way, namely, the man must be beheaded. It is common lore in Indonesia that someone with magical powers will not actually die unless their head is detached from their body and the two buried separately. In Prasetyo's story, this beheading seems to take on the significance of a castration. It is as if the state, for fear of its own loss of potency, is responding not just by killing the victim but also by emasculating his power.

That Prasetyo took part in this castration could well have been a source of personal pride quite apart from the recognition that he received from his superiors. But the way Prasetyo told the story suggested that he himself did not lay claim to some superior phallic power. His task was not a personal accomplishment but something that "had to" be done because that is what the orders were. Insofar as the killing was a feat of superior potency, it represented the state's potency, not his. This is not to say that the killing did not serve a purpose for him. One could see that he felt a certain pride, but this pride was the result of having been entrusted with such an important mission. It was as if telling the story was a way of showing off about his successes—not in terms of the killing itself but in terms of the recognition it implied he enjoyed from his superiors. This showing off was not for my benefit at all but solely for that of his boss, whom he kept looking to for approval as he told the story. This culminated in his use of the coded term for an order to kill, which had the purpose of acting both as a euphemism and as a way to establish solidarity with his boss by highlighting a "secret" that they shared (and from which I was excluded). In this regard, the story seemed to be part of the currency of "secrets" that helps constitute shadowy hierarchies in institutions like the army and the police.[48] Interestingly, his boss did not give Prasetyo the reward of recognition he sought; rather, he chose not to look directly at Prasetyo and to "not understand" what he meant by the code. My impression was that this failure to recognize the killing as deserving of recognition was not caused by his feeling that Prasetyo had committed an indiscretion in front of a foreign visitor but was, rather, Prasetyo's boss's way of quietly refusing to use that particular form of behavior as any measure of success. Without explicitly opposing such killings, he was nonetheless implying that his underling was not going to improve his status through such an "accomplishment." Other officers, of course, might be far more responsive to Prasetyo's desire for recognition; it is easy to imagine how such killings, by virtue of being clandestine and risky ventures, could become an important currency in more informal fraternal alliances among officers.

The second story I shall recount also concerns post-Petrus killings. It was told to me by Joni, a person quite different from Prasetyo. Joni claimed to be from military intelligence, rather than from the police, and moonlighted as a debt collector who dealt especially with persons working in the military. His elder brother was a commander in the military police. Joni was born in the late 1960s, the son of an Indonesian general and a Dutch woman. Speaking with Joni, one had the impression that the quotidian aspects of life had receded entirely from his awareness. He looked at everyone as if they were strangers, even his wife and child. He lived in fear, and in an unsettling though not overt way, he imparted fear to those he met.

> When Joni was young his father used to insist that he arrive home right on time. If he was even a few minutes late he had to do push-ups. His father was said to have some mystical powers—his mother told of how when he was fighting against the Dutch he could run across water. When his father died some years ago, his teacher in ilmu started taking care of Joni. Joni and the rest of his family are from Surabaya, but the teacher was from Banten. Now Joni's mother lives in Bandung.

> Joni went to the military academy and from there went to East Timor. At the academy, they were given really tough training, like making their way through ditches filled with shit. He graduated in 1987 and probably soon after went to Timor, later returning for a second tour of duty. In Timor, he was commander of a battalion that wore long hair and tore its signs of identification off its uniforms because the Timorese would kill them if they knew what unit they were from. He twice led battalions into ambushes, with most of his men being killed. In one of these cases, the Timorese were waiting up in trees at night and shot at them with bows and arrows. Some got it through the head, others through the throat. Joni then told his men to be quiet and not to move. They waited until they could see where their attackers were and shot them out of the trees with their AKs. Joni captured the leader, who was the tribal leader

(kepala suku), and cut off his head. He still has a photo of himself holding the man's head. He says that the Timorese have powerful magic and that they can even shoot through bulletproof helmets. Joni was given a tiny Al Quran by his father's guru. Because he has a Dutch mother he never really believed in it. But he brought it to Timor anyway. There were others who said that when he slept they could see two tigers guarding him. He never saw them but once he pretended to be asleep and he could smell them.

When he returned to Surabaya he was made a commander and he and his underlings did some tough things like swimming to Madura from East Java. This is an area known for sharks, so he was pretty worried. Having returned from Timor he says he knew nothing about mercy, feeling like he was still back in Timor (which he attributed to "trauma"). Thus, for example, one night he was walking along and a man came up behind him and held a knife to his throat saying that if he moved he would kill him. He wanted money. But he didn't make Joni put his hands up so Joni was able to pull out his gun. He then held the gun to the man's head and told him that if he moved he would be shot. Joni then tortured him, beating him and then shooting his kneecap. He always had extra bullets so he could refill his gun, pretending none had been fired.

While in Surabaya, he also got at least one special order to kill a dangerous criminal. One of these was a man whom the police were scared of because he was invulnerable to being shot. Joni's order was to shoot him and put him in a rice bag (dikarungin). The man had tattoos all over. When he did it, Joni still had long hair and a beard because he had just come back from Timor. He was wearing a long gray jacket. His relatives had told him to make sure to say a prayer before shooting so that the bullet would penetrate (menembus). Before going he made sure to "fill" the bullet by saying the ayatkorsi (a prayer). The man was in a market when Joni ran up and shot him in the head, saying, "In the name of Allah" (bismillah). And the bullet went through. Everyone around ran away and he put the corpse in a bag and dumped it.

Even more than Prasetyo's account, Joni's stories emphasize the incredible power of his adversaries, be they independence fighters in East Timor or *preman* in Surabaya. Attributed to all of them is a magical power that makes doing battle with them an almost supernatural affair. In this case, however, Joni is quite clearly using the power of his adversaries to demonstrate his own: the mystical knowledge passed down from his father that allows him to sleep safely in East Timor and to kill someone in Surabaya who had, until then, been considered invulnerable. Unlike Prasetyo, the authority to which he lays claim has nothing to do with the recognition he receives from his superior officers[49] (in fact, he was ambivalent about the military hierarchy since he had been court-martialed for striking a superior and thus had lost prospects for much advancement). Rather, it relates to his survival and killing skills, and the *ilmu* he inherited from his father. It is especially the latter—his use of a shaman, his being guarded by tigers, his "filling" of the bullet, and his reciting of the *ayatkorsi*—that gives him power over death. This is also what distinguishes him from others in the state (his comrades in East Timor or the police in Surabaya) who do not possess such power.

Taken together, what these stories show is that the appropriated phallic or magical power of the *preman* or *jegger* is not always given an undifferentiated locus in the "government" or the "state." Rather, individuals and groups within the state, through their actions and stories, may seek to control the circulation of this power for themselves.

Joni's story also shows, however, that there is an inherent danger in laying claim to such power for oneself, as it can lead to a cycle of revenge.

> *He is glad not to be in Surabaya now because during the trial of that case the family of the dead man said, "Oh, this is the man who killed my brother. No matter where he goes in the world we will find him and kill him, and if not us then our children will do it." And indeed, a younger brother did appear once and stabbed him in the stomach, and Joni then pulled out his gun and shot him. If he hadn't been helped by some bystanders right away he probably would have died. (He lifts his shirt and shows the scar.)*
>
> *Recently, Joni got an order here in Bandung to kill a big-time criminal named Rudi. Supposedly Rudi had robbed a bank in Bogor and got away with it; he had committed rape as well. He is now in Bandung. The other people in Joni's team are all older men in their forties, so they don't want to do it. They passed it on to Joni. Joni is not sure he wants to do it, though, because he now has a wife and kid. It's been a week since the order came down and he hasn't done anything yet, but he probably will have to soon. He is worried that his victims will seek vengeance and his family will get it. This happened to his elder brother after he had killed a criminal. They came and killed his family, chopping off his wife's legs. Now his brother is known for his toughness. Every criminal who is caught in the area he controls leaves with his legs broken or maimed.*

The phenomenon of revenge, in which "criminals," kin groups, or territorial communities seek to recuperate the power they lose when the state—or persons or groups within it or acting on its behalf—kill, beat, or imprison people, is a common one in post-Petrus Indonesia. It is evident, for example, in the numerous cases in which communities reassert their own power to "play judge themselves" against the power of the police in cases of sorcery, theft, sex outside of marriage, and extortion. In cases such as these, the police usually do not risk charging suspects for fear that they themselves will become objects of the community's wrath. When the police do overstep this line, the usual response is not actual killing but the spectacular destruction of police precincts by crowds of upset people. The most explosive examples occur when the police are said to "play judge themselves" against someone who is respected locally. This can even trigger full-scale riots, as happened in Tasikmalaya in 1996. In this case, according to one of the rumors circulating after it occurred, a police commander had sent his son to an Islamic boarding school (*pesantren*) for disciplining as he had been caught stealing. At the school, he was caught stealing again and received punishment from the headmaster, an Islamic leader. The boy was angry and reported to his father that he had been tortured. Upon hearing this, the commander sent some of his underlings to extract revenge for the beating. Word of this got out to students, and in the riot that ensued almost all the police stations in the city, as well as shops and churches, were burned and destroyed. However, even with these types of extreme reactions, it is exceedingly rare that communities will actually avenge the crime directly and proportionally and so genuinely reassert their power. Rather, they will restrict their violence to property so as not to directly challenge state authority. Nonetheless, their actions are a powerful reminder to representatives of the state that there are other sources of power that count.

At other times, the revenge against the government is more direct while remaining confined to the realm of fantasy. One man in Bandung's Sukamiskin Prison who claimed to be doing time for fraud offered the following explanation:

> *All you have to do is a bit of arithmetic. In the time of the PKI, how many people were killed? A million? Now, if all those people had children, how many people is that? Two million? Remember, all those kids grew up without their parents and cannot get jobs because they are stamped PKI. Now add the hundred thousand people killed during Petrus.*[50] *All their kids grew up without their fathers, and they know who it was who killed them. They ask, "Why don't I have a father?" And they blame the government. That's why the government here is so scared. They know that there are so many millions of people who want to seek revenge.*

The man who expressed this fantasy of revenge was an unusual character. He could perform magic to make money disappear and told fascinating stories about his criminal history that stretched the limits of credibility without ever quite breaking them. Among other things, he claimed to have been a counterfeiter, a shaman, and a fraud artist. But one thing about him was clear: when he spoke, people listened. Whereas the prison's canteen was usually filled with multiple conversations, when he was there, everyone else fell silent. And when he spoke about the inevitability of revenge, one almost started to believe it. The revenge he had in mind was not the personal or local forms feared by Joni and local police precincts, however. It was collective, implicating not just *preman* but all those who had been criminalized by the New Order's repressive regime.

If the appropriation by the state of the power associated with criminality and territorial authority ran the risk of reterritorializing the state by drawing it into cycles of revenge and reciprocal, competitive violence, it also had the effect of creating a whole new type of *preman*, and even a new type of tattoo. Consider the following newspaper story:

> The Malang court last Tuesday sentenced S. (29 yrs) to seven months in prison for having committed fraud by claiming to be a commander of Pomal [Navy Military Police] working as a mysterious murderer and extorting [money] from a person who sells games.... Evidence included a TNI-AL [navy] membership card, a Kodam 0802 [army] membership card, and a number of threatening letters and lists of names of people who were going to be Petrus-ed....
>
> *On Friday, October 28, [the victim] was visited by S., an unknown man who claimed to be the commander of Pomal and working as an agent of Petrus. S. showed him a list of names who he was going to Petrus, among them two of the victim's younger brothers.*
>
> *Because he was worried and afraid, the victim did what S. asked and gave him Rp. [Rupiah] 17,000. On Tuesday, November 1, the victim received a letter from S., the contents of which demanded Rp. 35,000 in order to have the names of his two younger brothers erased from the list of people who were going to be Petrus-ed.*
>
> *[After that, the victim reported this to the police, who then arrested S.]*
> (Surabaya Post, January 25, 1984)

In this story, an extortionist claims power for intimidation not by showing tattoos but by showing lists and identity cards. He imitates Petrus imitating "criminals" like him. The difference, of course, is that the identity cards and lists this man possesses derive their power not from a territorial inscription but from state language and its power over life and death. This language has a source in the state and a claim to referentiality. The importance of this fact became apparent in the extortionist's trial, when the judges asked him about the military identity card, and he told them he found it on the street. Knowing that there was no such thing as a Kodam with the four digits "0802" in the world "out there," and therefore that the man's identity cards were counterfeit and his claims false, the judges were able to dismiss the man for his apparent incompetence, secure in their conviction that they possessed the truth.[51]

Not all such identity cards and lists are so easily dismissed, however. Certainly in the mid-1990s, in the press and on the streets, one was always hearing about *surat sakti* (magically powerful letters) that would clear a business project through any bureaucratic office, people who were *kebal hukum* (invulnerable to law), and malefactors who were not white-collar criminals but rather *preman berdasi* (former street *preman* impersonating civil servants). Ordinary people, moreover, were always going out of their way to show anyone who was interested their own special signs, which, without exception, traced their power back either to an institution like the military or to a fraternity. Stickers on cars with the emblems of Kopassus (Komando Pasukan Khsusus, or Special Forces) or Pom (Polisi Militer, or Military Police), name cards from important officials, and identity cards and paraphernalia from the local Harley Davidson club (which was known to be headed by an army general) were in a sense all examples of a new type of tattoo. They could all be used to intimidate villagers, to avoid fines and exactions if one was stopped by the traffic police, or simply to impress one's friends. Periodically, the institutions would try to reexert their control over the circulation of these special signs in order to distinguish the "originals" from the "fakes"—for example, by conducting operations to remove army stickers from cars driven by people who could not produce an army membership card. However, the circulation of these special signs or tokens beyond the particular groups of people who could legitimately hold them was ultimately a minor point. The important thing was that they derived their invulnerability and magical power from their connection to the state's institutions rather than their connection to some other source of power (like territorial gangs, illegal political parties, outlawed religious sects, etc.). In this respect, Petrus might be called a watershed moment as it marked the point at which territorial power became deterritorialized from the figure of the *jegger* and reterritorialized within the state and its shadowy, fraternity-like hierarchies. That is, it marked the point at which the power that was once associated with tattoos became subject to a whole new set of disciplines rooted in surveillance and bureaucracy rather than in bodies and localities.

The Power of the Police

Taken together, Petrus and Siskamling changed the face of local security. On a strictly institutional and demographic level, this change was evident in the explosion in the numbers of Satpam and Hansip guards. With *jegger* killed or scared away, businesses, bus terminals, markets, malls, and so on all came to hire Satpam; and many neighborhoods hired Hansip.[52] That every Satpam and every Hansip guard had a particular overseer among the police, and that the police coordinated with the guards themselves, not just with their bosses, meant that local security practices were subject to much more direct control on the part of the state.[53] In this respect, Siskamling provided for the extension of police surveillance into the local sphere. Much of the time, this additional surveillance also served as the premise for a far greater involvement of the police in local protection rackets than had previously been possible when such rackets were under the control of either gangs, heads of Rukun Tetangga or Rukun Warga, or the army.[54] While there was always a tendency for the type of petty criminals that Petrus targeted to return, the police dealt with this by launching operations much like the ones that preceded Petrus. In these operations, everyone on the streets was rounded up and fingerprinted; some were charged, some were given "guidance" by the police, and some were sent off to Islamic boarding schools or foundations for reform.[55] In this way the police maintained their local domination (except in relation to gangs with backing, or *bekking*,[56] from the army) despite their extremely low numbers. None of this would have been possible without Petrus.

Petrus, however, was about far more than just demographic and institutional changes; it was about the deterritorialization of the power associated with "criminals," *jegger*, and territorial communities, and its reterritorialization within the state. Such deterritorialization proceeded by means of imitation coupled with surveillance. Imitation allowed the state to identify itself with said power, releasing it from its locus in "criminals," *jegger*, and territorial communities. Surveillance, through its ultimatum forcing "criminals" to recognize themselves as the state would or face the threat of death, and through its control over the determination of "true" identities, ensured that the circulation of this power would lead back to one source: the state. The process was analogous to that used for *kentonganisasi*, where a long-standing instrument and symbol of the *ronda* security apparatus was uprooted and given a new meaning within a bureaucratic regime. The differences, however, were that nobody was killed in the process of *kentonganisasi*. Slit gongs were not themselves associated with the type of power that the specter of crime evoked, and hence *kentonganisasi* did not attract the attention that Petrus did. With Petrus, the people who were killed were invested with a supernatural power assumed capable of resisting death (their tattoos, invulnerability); and yet, as it seemed through media reports, even the state could control this. That got people's attention.

One of the people whose attention it got was a Satpam in Bandung named Asep, whose words form the epigraph to this chapter. For him, Petrus signaled the end of an era. It was as if the exposure of the *jegger*, the tattooed body, and other paranormal figures to surveillance had eliminated a power from the scene. Asep was an older man and had been working as a security guard in Bandung since the early 1980s, making him something of an expert on the subject. As a youth, he had climbed mountains in Java and Sumatra, sleeping outside for days, always hoping to find some mystical knowledge that would make him invulnerable to machetes and other weapons. One time, he explained, he heard a voice that told him that he already had everything he needed, he already had his mystical knowledge: it was to be good to people. With this he was able to join the army in the forests of Irian Jaya (Papua) and come out alive, while nineteen of the twenty-three people in his platoon were killed. He knew that the best way to survive was to learn the local language and become close to the local leaders by being good to them. He also had many stories about his adventures on behalf of the police. There was the time he spent some months in Jakarta working undercover in a nightclub in order to solve a murder case; the time he married into a village and lived there for months, waiting to catch someone who had been on the run from the police; and the time he had disguised himself as a janitor and befriended students in a university to find out who had been behind a student demonstration. As he told these stories, he pulled out his wallet and showed me the cards of some of the police he had worked with, along with his own police-issued identity card.

When I asked Asep whether or not he worked with the police in the local precinct's Guidance Unit, which was responsible for overseeing the Satpam, Hansip, and *ronda* in the area, he replied, "I *am* the Guidance Unit."

When I objected that I meant to ask about the people at the precinct, he repeated his statement. The people at the precinct, he explained, were "under his guidance." Before there had even been a precinct at that location in the city, he said, he was already there, and it was he who had built the precinct, carting in and laying the bricks that were necessary. Indeed, as I learned at the precinct, successive commanders and the rank and file were indeed familiar with Asep, not only for his help catching suspects and building the precinct, but also for his healing massages.

Despite his experience and expertise, and despite the fact that he was older than the officers in the precinct, Asep always ate apart from them and was ready at their beck and call. Whenever he was in their presence, he was perfectly silent, but from the look on his face it was clear he was listening intently. It was a strange kind of listening, one that often seemed to lead to a wide-eyed, restrained excitement, as if everything he heard confirmed what he knew even if he had not yet known it. Given that Asep was so fascinated by police power, it was interesting that it was he who described the effects of Petrus as having brought about a general disenchantment of crime and policing. It is easy to see how things might have turned out differently. At one time Asep himself might have been considered a figure to reckon with, what with his adventures, his healing powers, his extreme attention to the local sphere, and his mystical knowledge. He could have been an informal sovereign whose authority derived from sources unconnected to formal state power. As it was, however, he laid claim to his authority by identifying himself as the police. And in a certain sense he was indeed the police. Not just because he worked for them as a spy and a helper, but also because he was so interested—far more than they were—in getting close to the source of the power they represented.

This interest, bordering as it did on fascination, was undoubtedly shared by many private security guards, as well as tens—or perhaps hundreds—of thousands of other spies that Siskamling and its related programs brought into the police fold. On the other hand, there were probably even more private security guards who spent their time in utter boredom, waiting for something interesting to happen, or even plotting how to get their hands on what they really desired: the nice bicycles and wads of cash that they were hired to watch over. In any case, Asep's fascination with the police belied his comments regarding a general disenchantment of crime and security. At most, one could say that there had been a shift in the locus of enchantment away from tattoos and mountains and on to identity cards and police stations.

6

The Police Precinct

In the years preceding President Suharto's resignation, international agencies tracking corruption regularly found Indonesia to be one of the most—if not *the* most—corrupt countries in the world. Indonesian observers agreed, arguing that the corruption abetted by their country's "vampire state" had spread through government institutions like a "cancer," creating a "culture" of widespread corruption, even at the lowest levels.[1] According to Ali Sadikin, the former governor of Jakarta, this generalized rot pointed to a deeper moral crisis:

> Corruption is now so troublesome that it can no longer be characterized as only money corruption but is a moral problem in the widest sense. Corruption in the sense of politics and

power. . . . God as the Great Unity is no longer. What is re-membered is only oneself. Someone with faith fears Allah, fears God, considers everything beforehand. This is forbidden [*haram*] or it is permitted [*halal*]. They are religious so they actually know what is forbidden and what is permitted. What is Pancasila, what is the first principle? God as the Great Unity. . . .

This epoch is like the epoch of the Nazis in Germany. The wrong are made right and the right made wrong. (Quoted in Republika, January 8, 1996)[2]

The New Order state, grounded in the principle of faith in God as supreme unifier, was falling apart. It was falling apart as a result of a moral decay in which the distinction between right and wrong had become mundane and open to manipulation rather than a religious one fraught with the fear of divine power. Corruption that had begun with money had become a corruption of power.

The corruption endemic to the state was most clearly represented in the institution of the police, whose claims to legitimacy were met with public derision, both on the street and in the press. People pointed to well-known cases in which witnesses had died in police custody, suspects had "escaped" with assistance from their police guards, or police officers had themselves been charged with crimes. The criticism was so prevalent that even the police leadership had come to see their personnel as tainted. The police commander for West Java, Nana Permana, frequently held interviews with the press in which he admitted that corruption and illegality plagued the force, and he vowed to do his best to eliminate these influences. As he was fond of saying, "Only after the illness in oneself has been cured will it be possible to cure the rest of society's illnesses" (*Merdeka*, June 29, 1996).[3]

This chapter examines those aspects of the Indonesian police that are vampiric, ghostly, and diseased. As I will demonstrate, much of the alterity that inhabits the institution of the police—that which feeds off it, haunts it, and plagues it—actually takes a sociological form: the fraternity. I use the term "fraternity" because it emphasizes these groupings' overwhelmingly male membership, their patriarchal character, and their peculiar combinations of solidarity and rivalry, egalitarianism and hierarchy.[4] It is the fraternity that is the locus of "corruption." In the following pages I examine the institutional origins of these fraternal alliances in the military and police academies, showing how they differ from territorial groups like the neighborhood watch. I then provide an ethnographic account of how fraternal alliances affect the way in which surveillance, law enforcement, and efforts to maintain territorial security are carried out at the front line of police work—namely, at the precinct. In this account, I explain how fraternities bridge the gap between central state power and informal territorial sovereignties in a way that surveillance does not. Finally, I conclude with a consideration of what public perceptions of police "corruption" meant for the legitimacy of New Order state power.

The Precinct House, the Captain, and the Fraternity

The building that housed the Cilengka[5] Police Precinct (known as Polsek, or Polisi Sektor) was set back from a large thoroughfare in the southern part of Bandung. At the time of my research, it consisted of three buildings: a 150-foot-long, single-story rectangular building in front, a small square building behind, and, beside this, a small mosque. Approaching the building through the dirt parking lot—which usually had three or four cars in it—one first came to an open-air foyer known as the picket (*piket*). The picket was an intimidating place for visitors to the precinct; usually several policemen would be hanging out here, either standing or sitting on a bench, joking, watching a small television, and smoking, and they often seemed indifferent if not hostile to prospective interlocutors. In an alcove off this foyer was a desk, behind which sat the officer in charge of the picket. In front of him was a notebook in which he kept a record of any reports of crime that people made during his shift. There was also a telephone that was used sparingly and a two-way radio that periodically sputtered out information from the central dispatcher. The men on duty at the picket were usually extremely tired as their rotating shifts lasted for twenty-four hours. Often during the night, when nothing much was happening, a few of them would retire to their offices to lay their heads on their desks and get a bit of sleep. Otherwise, they would just hang around, doing what they could to stave off boredom. Unlike at provincial headquarters (Polda, or Polisi Daerah), however, the men at the precinct did not usually kill time by reading the newspaper, but instead passed their shifts watching television, conversing, or simply sitting in silence.

The picket foyer opened onto a hallway that ran the length of the main building, with doors leading to various offices on either side. To the right, at the end of the hall, was the holding cell. At any given time, between five and ten suspects were held there in confinement while the police officers prepared their cases for submission to the public prosecutor's office. The cell itself consisted of three small concrete rooms, one of which was open to the sky. For the most part, the prisoners hung out in the room not visible from the hallway, but occasionally they would stand at the bars at the end of the hall, silently watching the happenings before them. On very rare occasions the police would actually turn the television around so those in the cells could watch it instead; or sometimes an angry officer would berate a prisoner for little apparent reason. Once in a while a prisoner was let out to do some cleaning around the station, and there were even times when they were invited to join in conversation with their keepers.[6] But in general, for all their proximity, there was almost no interaction between the police and the prisoners.

The two largest rooms on the hallway of the main building were the precinct head's office and the so-called data room. The former was furnished in the fashion typical of government officials, with a desk at one end and a couple of couches separated by a coffee table at the other. The only paperwork the precinct head did was to sign reports prepared by his underlings, so the desk usually had little more than a small pile of unsigned documents on it. Aside from these items the room was rather bare, with only a few charts and a whiteboard on the walls, and a telephone that shared a line with the one located down the hallway at the picket.

Mr. Andi, the man who occupied this office for most of my time there, was from East Java. As was typically the case for precinct heads in the mid- to late 1990s, he held the rank of captain and he was the only one at the precinct to have graduated from the police academy.[7] Because of this, he was automatically on a very different career track from that of the men below him. Whereas most of them would spend many years here, moving gradually up the ranks from the bottom, Andi's promotions occurred in relatively quick succession and usually accompanied or followed soon after a movement to a different command. The head of a precinct is very often a man in motion, trying to make sure that his next promotion is the optimal one for his circumstances. The rank and file, in contrast, were there for the long haul, with some having spent as many as fifteen years at the same precinct.

Andi put in a lot of hours at the office. Most days he arrived in the morning and stayed until around four, went home for a few hours, came back to the precinct around seven, and then stayed until about five in the morning. During the day, his work consisted mainly of supervision: making sure people were processing the cases at hand, organizing patrols, and keeping on top of the reports that had to be sent off to the public prosecutor and to higher-ups in the police hierarchy. He also attended regular meetings with his immediate superiors at the district headquarters (Polres, or Polisi

Resor) a couple of times a week. But Andi's official workload certainly did not justify these long hours, for he spent much of his day in his office napping or talking with the numerous visitors who came to see him. The important thing, he explained, was his presence at the precinct and that those beneath him were aware of it. This in itself was enough to keep his subordinates in the office and working.

Since for the most part Andi's subordinates did not feel justified entering his office on anything other than official business, the room became the site for a social scene only on the weekends. Almost every Saturday night, his buddies from outside the precinct gathered together in his office and related stories to one another. There might be anywhere from four to eight people at these gatherings, all men of roughly the same age and rank. Andi always introduced these friends in the same way, listing off their names, their current posts, and the year they graduated from the academy.[8]

To have been part of the same graduating class at the military or police academies, or even to have been there at the same time, was probably the most common way of explaining the informal ties between police officers from different regions or agencies. These ties provided the occasion not only for weekend gatherings, but also for simply dropping by someone's office during the day. At the higher levels of the police administration, such as at city headquarters (Polwiltabes, or Polisi Wilayah Kota Besar) or the provincial headquarters, these daytime visits occurred with greater frequency than at the precinct, since at these levels of the bureaucracy, official meetings brought people in from all over the city and province. After these meetings dispersed, attendees would often take the opportunity to call on old academy friends at their offices.

These gatherings between officers highlight the enduring importance of fraternal ties among the police, and their salience well beyond the geographical and temporal confines of the academy.[9] Indeed, such ties are apparent not just among the military and the police but throughout the entire Indonesian state. For the postrevolutionary generations, particularly those who were educated during or after the New Order, these ties can almost always be traced back to an institutional origin, like the academy. In rare cases ties might also be based on a shared *kampung*, or village, of origin, but for the most part such residential connections do not imply the same degree of ideological solidarity as that provided by a shared institutional background. Similarly, although a common local language (e.g., Javanese, Sundanese) can certainly increase the feeling of intimacy between officials, the establishment and maintenance of such alliances do not depend on the use of local languages.[10] The men who gathered at the precinct on Saturday nights, for example, hailed from East Java, West Java, and Sulawesi, and only occasionally did the Javanese-speakers quote a Javanese joke within the general Indonesian discourse. What they shared was a common experience at the police academy, which helped establish a very particular type of hierarchy and solidarity among graduates, one that was neither bureaucratic nor territorial.

To become a police officer in Indonesia during the New Order meant becoming a member of the armed forces. Those who entered the police did so at three different grades. At the first and second grades, recruits were trained in short programs for entry into the lower ranks of the police. At these levels, training took place on a regional basis and was not deeply integrated with that of the other forces. At the third level, however, recruits for the army, navy, air force, and police all received a period of training together at the military academy (Akabri, or Akademi Angkatan Senjata Republik Indonesia) in Magelang, East Java. The aim of this integrated training was to guard against the possibility of political fragmentation within the armed forces, as had happened in the period leading up to the coup and the political killings of 1965–66. The idea was that, for a period of six months, the future leadership of the different forces would share a common experience and system of training. The cadets would then proceed to their respective academies, where they would receive two and a half years of training in their particular disciplines. Police cadets, for example, proceeded to the police academy at Semarang, Central Java, where they received not only physical training but also education in the technical aspects of police work. Entry into the military academy was highly competitive and was restricted to young, unmarried men who had scored highly on the entrance exam.[11] Being unmarried was important because the cadets were said to be entering into a new family: the "extended family" (*keluarga besar*) of the military.[12] In order to maintain the primacy of the cadets' ties to this new family, they were prohibited from marrying during their time at the academy.

Besides the obvious matters of sharing time together and studying the same materials, cadets were subjected to a very special form of authority. This authority was designated in formal terms by the phrase "Elder brother trains and cares for younger brother" (*kakak asuh adik asuh*). According to this idea it was the responsibility of the seniors at the academy to raise the juniors as if they were their younger brothers. Officially this meant that the elder brother must "know in depth the identity of his younger brother to facilitate his education," provide him with a good example, assist in his studies, and help him overcome any professional or personal problems.[13] Unofficially, it meant that seniors were given a great deal of power over younger cadets, a fact expressed among the trainees by the English phrase "Seniors can do no wrong" (Biantaro 1983, 102).

The power of seniors over juniors, ideologically characterized in familial terms, was in a practical sense founded in violence. This violence, first of all, took the form of hazing. As part of the first stage of their training at the military academy, cadets were inducted into the military by way of a week-long orientation that included much violence and humiliation.[14] According to one graduate who later went on to research the matter, "drinks mixed with chilli peppers, food full of salt, bodies smeared with faeces were normal occurrences for Junior cadets . . . [as were] punches, kicks, and other forms of physical torture" (Biantaro 1983, 83). The result of this violence, this author suggests, is that junior cadets "who were conforming to their new environment within the military academy were impressed with the fact that *their new life was going to be completely pervaded by an atmosphere of violence*" (83; italics added). The perpetrators of this violence were both the instructors and the senior cadets at the military academy. The latter tended to be of the opinion that violence is a necessary part of military training, and that since they were subjected to such violence when they were juniors, so, too, should they have the right to subject their younger brothers to it. This violence continued well past the hazing period in both the military and police academies, as seniors felt that it was not just their right but their duty to punish juniors whenever they were deemed to have done something wrong. As frequently occurs in such situations, the criteria by which an action was defined as "wrong" bore little more than a tangential relation to the stated rules of the academy and instead depended a great deal on the seniors' own subjective reasoning. Consider, for example, how one senior, having been tried for beating a junior, subsequently explained his behavior:

> First, there was a feeling that there existed among the 3rd-level cadets a visible decline in the attention [*sikap*] and loyalty given to the 4th-level cadets. . . . Second, as a senior I felt offended by the existence of a belittling attitude on the part of some 3rd-level cadets who didn't want to carry out the orders of 4th-level cadets. . . .
>
> *The aim of the beating was to guide [membina] the cadet. There really wasn't any intention at all to give rise to or cause him pain, but supposing that my actions did indeed give rise to pain, I probably did it in a way that was incorrect and emotional.* (86)

According to the senior, the purpose of his violence was not the punishment of an action so much as the reforming of an attitude. The junior had to learn his lesson about who was in charge.

The central role of violence in the formation of the police "family"—or what I call fraternity—bears comparison to the discussions of *ronda* violence and *jegger* violence in chapter 2. In all three cases, there is a close association between violence and recognition. For the neighborhood watch, the recognition of the thief is achieved through the violence of a beating and is hence inseparable from that violence. For both the *jegger* gangs and the academy, the recognition of new members and their integration into group hierarchies depends on the violence of initiation. However, although all three communities associate recognition with violence, thieves, *jegger*, and recruits have very different relations to the violence they are subjected to. When a thief commits a crime, he risks his life; he knows that if he is caught he will almost certainly be beaten and he also knows that such beatings frequently result in death. For the thief, recognition is thus intimately associated with the risk of death, and he will do everything in his power to avoid such recognition. For the *jegger* who initiates a challenge, recognition is something he desires, and which he can only acquire through competitive displays of violence. He, too, risks death, but his status within the hierarchy he enters is also in play, since the outcomes of fights define that hierarchy. The junior cadet, in contrast, undergoes an initiation that is more akin to that experienced by aspiring members of a territorial pickpocket gang, who must undergo a beating before being acknowledged as members. Both sign up for the suffering they receive, even if they are unaware beforehand just how extreme this suffering will be.

For the prospective cadet, the decision to take the test that enables him to become a junior means entering into an unspoken contract with the academy: it says, in essence, that if he is capable of enduring the violence he is subjected to, then he will eventually become a senior (and later, an officer). Such a contract has the effect of making those who have recently undergone hazing some of the staunchest defenders of the practice. It also has the effect of taking the risk out of the violence, for there is an understanding that the violence will not result in death. That this is the case is indicated by the fact that when deaths do occur during hazing or disciplining—as has sometimes happened—they are inevitably seen as accidents, or as resulting from some inexplicable excess. When the beating of a thief ends in death, in contrast, it is taken as a natural consequence of the community's wrath.[15] The risk of death is removed at the academy precisely because the cadet has agreed to be recognized and has even stated his desire for recognition. The thief, however, desires not to be recognized, for such recognition implies death.

The acceptance of, and desire for, recognition is what provides the foundation for hierarchy. In the case of the neighborhood watch, hierarchy in any meaningful sense is avoided because the thief evades recognition; and even when he is captured and beaten he is recognized not as being one of the community but as someone who stands outside of it, and who is therefore a legitimate target of violence. In the case of the academy, as in the case of the pickpocket gangs, violence is directed against one's own and is intended to initiate rather than to banish. Hazing gives definition to the "junior" who is at once part of the academy community and lower in rank than earlier initiates.

There is of course a sense in which the thief is included in the neighborhood community simply by being made recognizable as the community's "outside," just as one could say the juniors are included in the academy only to be excluded from the ranks of seniors. But unlike the juniors, the "outside" defined by the beating of the thief is not so much "lower" than the community as entirely outside of it, "beyond the pale," as it were. Moreover, even if we were to think of thieves as an underclass, there is nothing in the neighborhood watch that would institutionalize that position. Indeed, the neighborhood evinces a sometimes surprising lack of interest in what happens to thieves after they are beaten; whether they are imprisoned, die, or escape prosecution seems of little concern. Juniors, in contrast, continue to make their home at the academy and to face seniors on a daily basis. In this respect, too, the fraternity is like a gang.

For new recruits, the fact that the desire for recognition implies a desire to undergo violence is mitigated by the promise of future power. It is not unlike the people who sacrifice their family to the phantom state in return for getting rich or beautiful (see chapter 2)—by making such sacrifices, one may get what one desires. But again, the difference is that the academy offers the reward in return for a form of sacrifice that is perceived to be finite rather than infinite. The recruit does not have to sell his soul—he merely has to endure violence for a couple of years. After this period he will transcend his status as junior and will himself become a senior with the power to dispense violence. The cyclicality of the process, based on the promise of transcendence, is what gives the academy's hierarchy longevity.[16]

An important effect of the academy's hierarchy is to diminish the authority of formal, codified law. The law that police learn to enforce is not just the one expressed in the criminal code but also the one expressed in the saying "Seniors can do no wrong."[17] To say that seniors can do no wrong is to locate the source of law in the power of seniors. There is thus no clear distinction between violence and the law since seniors are the source of both (the only law that does not originate with seniors, apparently, is the law that founds their authority—that establishes that they can "do no wrong"—and this law is expressed in English, a language of foreign authority). The identification of violence and the law, and their attribution to seniors, is reinforced through practices at the academy that show disregard for the institution's formal regulations. Thus, for example, rules prohibiting beatings and hazing are ignored in the name of "corps tradition" (*tradisi corps*). As one second-level cadet explained, "Violent measures and beatings are 'cadet corps tradition' and are still felt to be necessary to enforce discipline and to implant the corps spirit among the cadets. If there were no cadets that developed [*membina*] junior cadets in the academy, new members would not learn the true life of military cadets in general, and of police cadets in particular" (Biantaro 1983, 66). Discipline therefore seems to have little to do with regulations and everything to do with the invocation of "tradition." The aim of this tradition of violence is to implant "spirit" in the body (corps). Through this implanting and disciplining of spirit, juniors learn that loyalty to their brothers is more important than following a formal code of conduct.

Already at the academy this "spirit" is evidenced in the tradition of meeting any formal investigation of wrongdoing at the academy with "closed-mouth movements" (*gerakan tutup mulut*); nobody is willing to break the code of silence and jeopardize their standing in the group. According to Teguh Biantaro, however, although there is a strong solidarity among brothers vis-à-vis the outside world, there are nonetheless divisions within the group. These divisions stem from the competition among juniors for the favor of their elder brothers and from the preference some seniors show for particular juniors. The result is that certain subgroups of juniors and seniors enjoy close relationships, even if these are inevitably characterized by rivalry.

In sum, fraternities are hierarchical groups founded in a desire for recognition and sustained by an internalization and regulation of violence. The violence is disciplinary in the sense that its aim is to implant a tradition of recognition, and thus a respect for seniors' authority, among recruits. With its elements of violence and its focus on the body, fraternities resemble territorial groups like the *ronda* or gangs headed by a *jegger*. In the manner in which they internalize violence and use initiations to found hierarchies, they are especially reminiscent of the gangs assembled under *jegger*. However, owing to their roots in modern bureaucratic institutions, fraternities also differ from territorial groups in some important respects: their bodies are not territorial or personal but instead are constituted as a deterritorialized corps; their hierarchy has a stability and predictability that territorial hierarchies tend to lack; their hierarchy depends less on appeals to a tradition linked to mystical or supernatural knowledge and more on appeals to recently invented "corps tradition"; and their members self-consciously attempt to institute and enforce a disciplinary regime.

The Fraternal Economy

In principle, academy graduates have definable links to every other person who has passed through the institution since its inception. In practice, however, the strongest ties are to be found among brothers who are of the same generation (*angkatan*), belonged to the same subgroup at the academy, and came to be posted to the same region. This is indicated, for example, by the group that met at Andi's office on Saturday nights, which consisted of people who not only knew each other at the academy but who had all since been posted to Bandung. It is people such as these who have the opportunity to meet most frequently and who have enough knowledge about one another to keep such meetings informal.

To say that members of fraternities have close ties is to say that they are actively involved and mutually implicated in an economy of exchange. The currency of this exchange varies; information, rumor and gossip, cash, and goods are all central to the workings of this economy. In the Saturday night meetings at the Cilengka Precinct, for example, the central currencies were information and rumor. The following is an account of a conversation at one of those gatherings:

> It was medium-sized gathering at the precinct last night. The heads of two other Bandung precincts were there, as were Andi's two friends from the School for Police Administration, Yus and Heri. It seemed like a lot of people because everyone was speaking so loudly. In this crowd Andi becomes quite the joker, and even though he is the host and clearly is in the best position, he likes to make fun of himself. Yus is incredibly obnoxious, always conjuring up imaginary enemies or people who wronged him in some minor way. When he does this, he threatens them by sticking out his jaw and gritting his teeth while making

a chopping motion with his hand. He is wound extremely tightly and his whole body exudes tension. Andi is the opposite, flopping around in his undershirt and bare feet, getting a massage from Asep, who has been called there for the purpose. Most of the conversation centered on women. There was some talk about a brothel that had been busted and favors the police had received from the prostitutes, but I couldn't tell which area it was in. This inevitably led to the usual questions about whether I like Indonesian women, and so on, and to the semiserious jokes from Yus that he could get me a woman if I wanted (and that I should find him a white woman in return).

The members of informal fraternity groups are overwhelmingly men, and their relationships are highly gendered. In the interactions I observed, women were frequently objectified and treated as little more than a currency of exchange. Even when an actual transaction did not take place, the willingness of two men to consider the idea of entering into a reciprocal exchange of women clearly functioned to cement the fraternal alliance (cf. Levi-Strauss 1969).[18] Julia Suryakusuma (1996, 103) writes that in "Javanese culture, the 'possession' of women is considered a natural attribute of power, and among bureaucrats and technocrats sexual access symbolizes success."[19] Women, outside the kinship networks of the fraternity, thus were used to "reflect masculine identity precisely through being the site of its absence" (Butler 1990, 38–39, cited in Steedly 1993, 184).[20]

Eventually we went out for some food at a Sundanese restaurant out on the ring road. The car was crowded and the music loud. Some mix of house music to which Andi sung along with his own interpretation of the words, which meant something like, "On duty? No," or "Wearing a uniform? No." He also made a show of shaking his head back and forth with his eyes closed in the style of "tripping" (on ecstasy).[21] At the restaurant, they mostly gossiped about promotions—who was moving where, how so-and-so had gotten into trouble, and so on. It mostly seemed to be about Bandung or West Java and to involve people they all knew. Andi told a story about failing a test at a police school and how a paranormal [seer] had told him he would never be able to pass it. So he would just have to be happy with a mediocre career.

On the way back we drove through the southern part of Cilengka and one of the other precinct heads remarked that this was a good area. Andi then pointed to one factory as we drove by and said that it was worth a lot. He followed with a story about a bank in Cilengka that had been getting bomb threats. He told the bank person that they forget about him when everything is

fine, but when they get threats they want to call him. Then they all got to talk-
ing about which precincts are the best. Andi said his underlings are great, as
they do good collections and keep secrets from his wife.[22] *But then he remarked*
that the deputy head of the district headquarters had passed down word that
for the next few months no collections should be made and that police should
steer clear of discotheques. Back at the precinct Andi got out some liquor that
he had received as a gift, but nobody seemed too interested. . . .

> *Later, when there were just four of us left, Yus told Andi that people have*
been saying bad things about him (right after Andi talked about his upcom-
ing promotion). They said he is not loyal enough. At first it remained vague
but gradually it came out who had done the talking, and it was someone con-
sidered "close" to Andi. It seemed to revolve around the fact that Andi didn't
help someone get out of trouble when he should have. It may also have had to
do with payments, but I couldn't tell. But it was clear that loyalty was being de-
fined as covering for each other and going against procedure if necessary. Yus
commented that "It's better to be struck by a sword than to be spoken of badly."
At least a cut can be sewn up, but there is nothing one can do to combat talk.

These conversations illustrate the close association between fraternal ties and corruption. Andi was the chief provider of information, giving the others a sense of how much money could be made from businesses in the precinct, how he went about collecting this money, and so forth. Such information had the effect of securing Andi's position of authority within the group, both because he was the giver of such information and because his precinct was shown to be a lucrative one. It also could help the others should they or their friends eventually end up at Cilengka themselves and need such insider information. At the same time Yus, whose position at the School for Police Administration provided him with little power to control economic resources, conveyed gossip concerning Andi that simultaneously showed he was "in the know" and provided information that might be useful to help Andi defend himself against malicious rumors about his lack of "loyalty"; the gossip also had the added effect of deflating Andi's pride at being promoted.

While flows of information and gossip are typically what's released in exchanges between relative equals in the fraternity, more hierarchical ties tend to set cash, goods, and influence into motion. I learned about a number of different circumstances under which such movement occurred. First, there were the regular payments to one's superiors that the police and public sometimes referred to as *setoran* (rent; deposit). This was a fixed amount and was determined through experience over time of how much money the occupant of a particular police post could extort on a daily, weekly, or monthly basis. The person who occupied that post could then keep any surplus above the rent. The degree to which this system was formalized and prices set varied greatly between different parts of the police apparatus. During my research, the Traffic Unit was widely known to employ a fairly rigid system for fixing monthly payments. In other units, however, such payments reportedly consisted of a percentage of the take rather than a fixed rent. Successfully making these payments was a priority for all police officers. Those who met or exceeded their obligations would be looked upon favorably by their superiors, who might then be prepared to make efforts to secure their advancement and promotion to so-called wet chairs, or positions with a lot of income. Those who did not meet these implicit obligations would be assigned to units and posts where the opportunities for generating such income were few and far between.

In addition to these regular payments there were also the one-off payments that accompanied promotions and the visits of superiors to subordinates' offices. Of the latter type, I saw a number of examples. Once I was at the precinct office late in the evening when, to many people's surprise, a mid-ranking officer from the provincial headquarters arrived unannounced. It turned out he had heard that the police at the precinct had confiscated a truckload of propane canisters, and he needed a couple of them for his house. The police on duty obliged him and he carted them off. On another occasion, I was at the city headquarters visiting with a commanding officer of Criminal Intelligence, Mr. Husain, when Yus showed up.

> As we were talking, Yus dropped in for a visit. I was surprised as I had no idea they even knew each other. He was also surprised as he didn't know I was doing research at the city headquarters. The effect was probably good for all of us as we were all seen to be connected to each other. I asked Yus how he knew Husain and he said they were at the academy together. "The same generation?" I asked, to which he said, "Yes." We sat chatting for a while and Yus told stories about what was happening at the School for Police Administration. After about half an hour, Yus made motions to leave. Husain then rummaged in the drawer of his desk and came out with an envelope, which he subtly passed into Yus's hand as he escorted him toward the door. "Come by often," he said. When Yus was gone Husain explained that in fact Yus was his "elder brother" from the academy. "I gave him help because at the School of Police Administration there's nothing," he said.

These examples illustrate some of the ways fraternal ties linked individuals across very different sections and levels of the police force. For people in Yus's position, who depended on their younger brothers for help if they found themselves in a posting with no possibilities for supplementing their income, such ties provided a form of insurance. The flip side of this, however, is that such ties also provided the possibility for more predatory relations, in which subordinates were pressed to provide cash or goods to their elders with little hope of a return.

In addition to providing links between the heads of Bandung's police precincts and between officers posted at different levels of the police administration, fraternal ties established at the academy also extended downward into the rank and file of police personnel. Such links were extremely important for the heads of precincts because they determined the degree of loyalty shown to them by the men beneath them. At Cilengka, the rank and file consisted of about fifty men. These were divided into three units: the Guidance of Society Unit (Bimmas, or Bimbingan Masyarakat), the Security and Crowd Control Unit (Sabhara, or Samapta Bhayangkara), and the Investigations and Intelligence Unit (Reserse-Intel).[23] The Guidance of Society Unit (which I've referred to elsewhere as the Guidance Unit) was located in the precinct's annex, to the back of the main building, and was responsible for implementing the Siskamling program by coordinating and supervising neighborhood heads, youth organizations, religious leaders, and prominent local figures to ensure the maintenance of local security. The agents of the Security and Crowd Control Unit were for the most part very junior in rank and spent most of their time waiting in the precinct's entryway for something to happen. In the event of an outbreak of a riot or a demonstration, they were called upon to don their bamboo shields and helmets and wield their batons against the masses. Investigations and Intelligence (henceforth Reserse) was the most active and important of the units, as it was responsible for investigating crimes, interrogating suspects and witnesses, preparing criminal reports, and collecting protection money.[24] When Andi first took command of the precinct, he did what most new commanders do, which was to leave the personnel assigned to these various units intact for a few months. After getting to know his underlings, however, he reassigned them to new units. The people he felt most comfortable working with—and those who would form the core of the new precinct fraternity—were the dozen or so agents assigned to Reserse.

Reserse agents have a style and manner of their own. For one thing, unlike their counterparts in the other units, they are not obliged to wear uniforms. And this feeling that they have a more informal air about them is compounded by their cultivation of a tough-guy image. My first impressions of some agents from Reserse at the provincial headquarters were as follows:

> *I ate lunch at the food stall behind the station. The chaps in there happened to be Reserse, plainclothes for the most part. They were all men, aged between twenty-five and their late thirties. Some were Sundanese but there was at least one from Sulawesi and a couple from the Batak region. Their conversation shifted between Indonesian and Sundanese.*
>
> *Although they weren't wearing uniforms, there was a distinct style to them. Most were fairly big guys (muscular), and they all wore long-sleeved shirts, either pinstriped or pseudo-batik prints. They left the top of their shirts unbuttoned and one was wearing a very thick gold chain. There were also a few mustaches there. The overall impression was of something between a cop and a thug. The uniformed guys were more dapper and clean-cut.*
>
> *The style of conversation was extremely crude. They sat around in a sort of circle, mostly very informally splayed about. There was one fellow who seemed to be the more powerful one, and he spoke very loudly. The conversation was a certain amount of banter back and forth and quite a bit of storytelling.[25] The big guy told a story about how he had gone out searching for a man staying at one of the hotels, for instance. There happened to be a great deal of talk about cultural differences and linguistic differences, not for my benefit. The big guy was the only one who carried both a cell phone and a beeper. The others only had beepers. But they borrowed his telephone, although he dialed the numbers for them (and remembered them). Then I was asked if I have foreign women friends here because they want to see what it's like to have a white girlfriend. The man also tried to grab the young server (about twelve years old) and made rude comments to her when she passed. They engaged in such banter even though there was an older woman there who explicitly expressed disfavor with such talk. Finally, an even louder fellow came in, bellowing. The first guy and his buddies made a hasty exit. One big man can't stand being out-bellowed by another.*

The person who played the role of the big man back at the precinct was huge by Indonesian standards and went by the name of Dede. He had a deep laugh and a wide grin, which he used often, displaying long rows of teeth. From his belt he wore a thick chain that looped down beneath his hip and was attached at the other end to the Harley Davidson wallet in his back pocket. His car matched his person: a giant International Scout painted bright yellow, with huge tires that made it hulk over the smaller Japanese cars driven by Andi and some of the others. Everything about this man was big. In his office, opposite Andi's, the chair behind Dede's desk was more like a throne than an office chair.

As head of Reserse, Dede had three groups, each of four or five men, working under him. These groups were crammed into two offices, one on each side of Dede's office. The rooms had small desks with locked drawers in which the agents kept their guns and their private belongings. On top of the desks were old manual typewriters with keys so worn that it was impossible even to make out the letters on them. For all their posturing and stories, the agents spent a lot of time at these typewriters, filling out reports and taking statements from suspects and witnesses. Each page they typed had to be produced in triplicate (if not more), so the agents had become veritable masters at manipulating carbon paper and at finding ways to get the most use out of a single sheet.

Andi liked to refer to the Reserse agents under his command as his *anak buah* (literally, child of the fruit), which implied the same kind of personal loyalty and group solidarity as in the academy's fraternities, though with a more paternalistic edge.[26] For a person in Andi's position, establishing close ties with his underlings was an essential part of the job. In the first place, Andi would ultimately only be at Cilengka for a year and a half and would himself be unable to develop lasting ties with people in the community. His underlings, in contrast, had been there for many years and knew the precinct well. Their ties to people in the community made crime solving possible, provided the network necessary to keep local conflicts from threatening "security," and facilitated flows of money up through the fraternity. Second, close ties to his underlings ensured that Andi's secrets remained well kept, both from his wife, as Andi himself suggested, and from those who might seek to bring him down by circulating malicious rumors about him. By spending almost all his time at the precinct, Andi thus sought to cement his relationships with his underlings and to make certain that flows of gossip, information, and money did not escape his control.

The fact that Andi had to spend so much time at the precinct is indicative of the gap that can open up between a commander on the move and his more sedentary subordinates. The ideology of leadership implicit in the notion of *anak buah* is by itself insufficient to bridge this gap. Even constant supervision does not necessarily help, for it may just be taken as unwarranted intervention. So when Andi was there, he did not spend much time actually supervising his subordinates, but rather made a point of making the precinct his home, even if just a temporary one. While such an effort went a long way toward convincing the rank and file that Andi was a good guy, what ultimately cemented a solidarity between them was money. The central role of money in mediating the relation between police superiors and their subordinates was described very starkly by a former head of the Indonesian National Police, General Kunarto, when he stated that "the only time the leadership and their *anak buah* get along is at salary time" (*Media Indonesia*, December 27, 1995). While this was not entirely true at the precinct, the central role of money in linking Andi to the agents of Reserse was undeniable. At the precinct, however, salaries were only the most obvious of money flows; they were certainly not the most important. Far more significant was protection money. Such protection, which was intimately bound up with the day-to-day work of the police, took a variety of forms. Some were based on the role of the police as enforcers of the law and practitioners of surveillance, others on their role as local protectors.

One purpose of surveillance is to establish a correspondence between an abstract order of signs and the order of things in the world "out there." In principle, one function of the police is to provide the force necessary to apply municipal and legal codes regarding urban order: to impose the letter of the law by acting as inspectors and enforcers. Another function of the police is to gather up-to-date information about crime, security, and threats to security for inclusion in the state's surveillance archive. They do this by acting as spies and bureaucrats. While in the former role, the police aim to change things in the world out there to suit the order of signs, in the latter, they change the order of signs to suit changes in the world out there. In this respect, the police embody the power of mediation on which surveillance depends for both its effects and its legitimacy: without the police, the archival order consisting of codes, laws, maps, censuses, and the like would have no referentiality.

The fraternal ties between Reserse agents, and between these agents and their commander, facilitated the exploitation of police mediatory powers for the purposes of generating flows of money. This exploitation—in which the fraternity effectively appropriated the power of mediation to itself— took the form of demands for compensation in return for either mediating or refusing to mediate in particular instances. For example, although it is their job to prepare reports on lost or stolen goods, to register foreign residents, and to provide "letters of good behavior" to people seeking jobs, Reserse agents I observed did not give the impression that this job would be performed automatically without recompense. Particularly in cases where their actions would have economic consequences, the agents did their best to ensure that their own role in facilitating mediation was acknowledged with money.

The way they asked for this money depended on the situation. When dealing directly with the victim of a crime, or an applicant for an official letter, they usually used subtle tactics like giving people the runaround or finding problems with the request until it became clear that they wanted money. Or sometimes they just did the job and then when it was over asked for an administrative fee. The victim or applicant might then have to guess how much to give or try to obtain signals as to the appropriate amount. But much of the time the police were dealing not with the victim of a crime or an applicant for an official letter but with what is known as a *calo*. The *calo* in a bureaucratic context is a broker who will facilitate the processing of documents by the necessary authorities in return for a fee.[27] Such brokers range in formality from garbage collectors, who will process the driver's licenses of those on their garbage routes, to full-blown businesses with sophisticated computer systems and a permanent staff of agents capable of handling any number of documents, from land certificates to insurance claims to identity cards. When the precinct police dealt with a *calo*, they could be much more open in their solicitation of unofficial fees. Often this led to a kind of bartering, as in the following instance in which a *calo* was taking care of a Korean man's registration with the police.

> *Asep began by asking what the Korean man is doing here and where he lives. The calo explained that he lives on [a nearby street] and is working for a textile factory. Asep was then silent for a while, reading through the information the calo had given him. He then put the papers on the desk in front of him, leaned over them, and told the calo how much it would cost. I think he said 70,000 rupiah (about US$28), which was quite a bit more than the 10,000 rupiah I had managed to pay as a "student." The calo then made some noises about this being a lot, to which Asep replied that the Korean man must have high wages with the job he has. Suddenly Asep changed his manner, shifting into the mode he uses in interrogation: "Who are you?," "How do you know him?," "Where do you live?," "Have you done this before for other people?," he demanded. The man was made a bit nervous by this and explained that he himself had only been given a limited amount and that if he had to pay that much there would be nothing left for him. Asep went easier on him, and they chatted about other things for a while. Eventually Asep told him to come back on Thursday and they would settle it then.*

The interactions between *calo* and police officials were always interesting to watch. At times such interactions effectively "blurred" (Gupta 1995) the boundaries between the state and society as *calo* became so familiar with a particular office that they felt free to walk into areas the public would dare not go and even perform some of the officials' work. And lower officials themselves came to act more and more like *calo*, searching out clients and offering to provide them with mediatory services in return for cash.[28]

As the line between *calo* and the police was blurred, marks of state authority acquired a new significance. Official stamps and commanding officers' signatures no longer simply legitimized a routine bureaucratic process; they came to act as rarefied marks in which the mediatory power of the state appeared to be concentrated. Those who had the power to provide signatures were aware of this and often played upon it by making their signatures extremely elaborate and by behaving in such a way as to impress upon their underlings, *calo*, and clients that it was they alone who held such power. At Cilengka, this power was crucial, for had it not remained exclusively in Andi's hands, his authority might well have been eclipsed by that of Dede, who was the real moneymaker at the precinct. As it was, however, Andi could rein in any efforts Dede made to assert his greater command over flows of money simply by appealing to the authority provided to him by his rank and office; for example, by refusing to sign documents that would allow cash to be collected. Because fraternal power ultimately feeds off bureaucratic authority, its ability to disrupt state hierarchies can usually be kept in check.

Nonetheless, the effects of charging fees for performing routine acts of surveillance should not be underestimated. To complete a report on a stolen car the Reserse agents asked the victim of the theft for 500,000 rupiah (US$200); a similar report for a motorcycle cost 100,000 rupiah (US$40). Given the rates of motorcycle and car theft in the precinct between 1988 and 1994, this would have meant an average income for the police of about 1.3 million rupiah (US$520) per month, or about two and a half times the precinct head's monthly salary of 500,000 rupiah. According to one of the agents who prepared such reports, half of the income was turned over to the head of the precinct and the remaining half was divided among the four members of the Reserse team. If this was indeed the case, the precinct head stood to make more money from these reports alone than he did from his salary; and the members of Reserse, for their troubles, augmented their monthly earnings by about 50 percent. While reports on thefts of motor vehicles were among the most lucrative for the police at the precinct, other reports also generated money, like the "letter of good behavior" people were obliged to provide to prospective employers, foreigners' proof of registration with the police, and reports of lost bank and identity cards. Thus, the actual income from such work was probably significantly higher than many agents' salaries.

Insofar as they were only generating income by charging a fee for performing functions that the police would otherwise normally be expected to perform, the fraternal hierarchy did not jeopardize the bureaucratic hierarchy. The situation became more complex, however, when the police acted outside the law to elicit payments or when they received payments in exchange for abstaining from performing their mediatory function. It is in this context that lack of "professionalism" became a problem as agents overstepped their legal authority.

A common crime committed by the police involved violence against suspects. According to inmates at Bandung's prison, police violence—what is sometimes euphemistically called *diskresi* (discretion)—took many forms: beatings about the face, rape, beatings with a pipe or with a chair, pliers clamped on suspects' genitals, the nailing of their hands to tables, the burning of their genitals with cigarettes, stripping and submerging them in cold water for long periods of time, and the application of electric currents to genitals; these were just some of the violent methods inmates had experienced at the hands of the police. They could also list the precincts that had the most violent reputations and could describe which forms of torture they were known for. They noted, however, that only certain types of suspects received such treatment. Recidivists and suspects brought in for crimes that involved violence or weapons, such as murder, rape, and robbery, received the harshest treatment, while those who committed property crimes like vandalism or theft would also often be beaten but not as severely. Those suspected of economic crimes like fraud, embezzlement, and the like, would almost never be tortured. Police use of violence thus appeared to depend in part on what crime the suspect was presumed to have committed. However, prisoners also stated that money could be used to prevent much of this violence. Sometimes the exchange of payments for the suspension of violence was made quite explicit. One man, a former student who had been arrested for demonstrating while at university, described his experience at a Bandung precinct as follows:

> I was captured and then taken to a room above the precinct where I was
> held for a couple of nights. I myself wasn't tortured but the people I was in the

cell with were beaten with shoes until one of them had no lips anymore (bi-birnya sudah tidak ada lagi) and another had no eyes left (matanya sudah tidak ada lagi). I also saw them carrying prostitutes into the room beside ours, and the police went in one at a time to use them. The Chinese who were there didn't stay long as the police negotiated with them about how many days they wanted to stay, which depended on how much they were willing to pay. My ex-perience there was really horrifying.

While money could be used to prevent detention and reduce the extremity of beatings, police violence was nonetheless often seen as part of the culture of the Indonesian police, as indicated by a conversation I had with a small group of detainees through the bars of the precinct's holding cell.

The guy who was most interested in chatting was a young fellow with a small beard who is married and has a couple of kids. He used to work for a big photography firm that does business with actors and musicians and makes a lot of money. He committed his crime against his boss, he said. After trying to talk to his boss about the bad wages and so on, the boss didn't respond. So he ended up stealing from him. He and the others asked a lot of questions. Most were about how the law differs in America from here. They asked about whether cases get finished at the police level in America, or whether all cases get sent on. They asked about the jury system, and how it differs from the role of the judge in Indonesia. Mostly, they wanted to know whether police in America hit the prisoners during their interrogations of suspects, as they type up case reports.[29] One said that here the police are violent (keras) because the people they deal with are also violent. The bearded fellow was clearly bothered by it, though, and said that even if you confess they still beat you: "Beating here has already become a tradition." They also said that if you have money, you are "safe" (aman), as the police would rather take money than hit you.

The claim that violence is simply an institutional tradition is reminiscent of the statements made by junior cadets subjected to violence by their senior counterparts in the police academy. In that context, violence provided the basis for the formation of a hierarchy that was defined by a debt that one would pay off for the rest of one's career. In this case, however, violence produces a wider range of possibilities. Certainly for those accused of economic crimes, and for those willing to pay their way out of being hit, a similar situation to that of the cadets could be achieved. That is, if the "criminal" indeed managed to escape charges or to have the most serious charges dropped as a result of payments to the police, there was a good chance their relation to the police would not end there. The suspect and the investigating officer would, in a sense, become "friends" and various transactions could continue for some time to come. For example, in the case of people who ran marginally illegal businesses, the police might go on to provide them with "security" in return for a fee. Another possibility is that the police would accept payment, make a promise to drop the charges, but then choose not to honor that promise. Many of the inmates at Bandung's prison felt wronged in this way. They described how the police approached their families with offers to reduce their charges in return for money, only to press the full charges anyway.[30] Some of these people vowed to seek revenge upon being released. Thus, whether payments resulted in solidarity or antagonism, police violence precipitated a tie that was steeped in personal debt.

The Territorialization of Police Power

For police agents, the ideal arrangement was one in which they could establish long-standing ties with offenders. Such arrangements were more common in response to public order offenses than they were in criminal cases. In public order offenses the police did not resort to physical violence in making their threat but depended instead on the economic threat presented by legal violence. This type of threat frequently resulted in a long-term tie between the offender and the police, who agreed to suspend the application of the law in return for payment. I witnessed such a tie in practice one night while on a call with Wawan, an officer from the precinct.

> *After he finished his shift at the picket just before midnight, Wawan invited me to go for hot milk at a street-side café and then to give me a lift home. On the way he said he needed to stop by at a massage parlor because he had a piece of business there. He said that if I wanted I could go for a massage but that he just needed to talk to the owner, whom he has known for some time now. When he was young, he used to like getting a massage, but now he doesn't get the urge as much and realizes that it is better for his family if he stays away from such places. When I asked what his piece of business was he explained that he was low on money and had to go on a trip over the weekend, and since he hadn't been to the massage parlor in a while, the owner would give him some. At the parlor, which was just at the edge of Cilengka . . . we waited in the lobby and chatted for about twenty minutes. It was kind of a dingy place, with soft*

lighting and yellowing calendars on the walls. The person behind the bar seemed to know who Wawan was but didn't make much conversation. When we were going toward the door to leave, Wawan said that he would follow me out in a minute. A few minutes later he came out and we headed to the café down the road. I asked whether the owner had been there and he said he had. The youth who made us the hot milk knew Wawan and we chatted for a while. When the youth left us alone I asked Wawan how he had come to know the owner and why it wasn't someone else who was taking care of security there. He explained that a couple of years ago, there had been an operation against entertainment spots all over Bandung. He had been one of the agents who busted that particular massage parlor and as a result had come to know the owner. The owner liked him because he had arranged to get the charges dropped, and since then, he gave him monthly payments to make sure that the business wasn't hassled anymore. When I asked what laws they had been breaking, he said such places were always breaking some laws. The masseuses are only allowed to wear traditional clothing, not miniskirts, the massage rooms can only be separated by cloth, the women have to be over seventeen years old, they cannot serve beer, and the owner should be paying social security and taxes. If you look you can always find something wrong. So, for the owner, it's good to have someone who they can call if they get in trouble. When I asked if the owner had to make payments to anyone else, Wawan said he might also make payments to the local army command post but he didn't know. Who is paying and how much they are paying is "secret," and only the owner and the recipients are privy to that knowledge. On the way home Wawan told me not to mention the visit to the people at the precinct because they didn't know about this one.

During my time among the police in Bandung, operations (*operasi* or *razia*) of the sort mentioned by Wawan were the quintessential instrument for applying ordinances related to public order. There were two bodies that regularly performed such operations on the city's streets: the police and the public order police, called the *polisi pamong praja*. The *pamong praja* is a body of officers that is under the control of the municipal government and is responsible for enforcing city ordinances. While police operations targeted things like drugs, moonshine, false Levi's, people without identity cards, and prostitutes, the *pamong praja* aimed to increase "discipline" (*disiplin*) by clearing street vendors, trishaws, and squatter settlements out of particular streets. The operations performed by these two agencies took a variety of forms. The police might set up roadblocks and search those who passed through them for drugs and demand to see identity cards. Or they might descend en masse on all the discotheques and nightclubs in a particular region simultaneously, forcing all present to empty their pockets and present identification. The *pamong praja* tended to use the latter method, targeting streets on which trishaws or street vendors were not permitted. Such operations were usually given a name and often the agents wore vests with the name or initials of the particular operation on the back (e.g., "GDN" for Gerakan Disiplin Nasional, or the National Discipline Movement). In Bandung, as in other cities in Indonesia, operations did not happen just anytime but usually preceded the visit of an important official or followed from media attention to a particular problem, such as sex and drugs at entertainment spots. In anticipation of such visits and in response to media pressure, operations were conducted to demonstrate the power of the authorities to produce urban "order."[31]

Yet as Wawan's explanation makes clear, operations were just one moment in a more complex procedure. After the operations were over and it remained to process the cases of those who were snared in the net, the police lost their anonymity and became people with whom one could develop mutually beneficial alliances. In the case he described, the police no longer served the straightforward aims of surveillance, which would have been to enforce the ordinance regarding massage parlors by preventing the mixture of alcohol and women, ensuring that women wear traditional dress, and making people too worried about being overheard and overseen to engage in illicit sex. Rather, those who could have acted as inspectors—such as Wawan—developed relations with those who would have been surveilled and offered to "look the other way," as it were. As a result, the business was allowed to continue its more lucrative trade in sexual services and, in return for the "protection" he provided from the law, Wawan received a supplement to his meager police salary. Under such circumstances the police exercised their mediatory power not by using it but by withholding it. For surveillance to work effectively the police would have to identify with the ideal of surveyability and desire the application of its principles. But as a result of the alliances established between would-be inspectors and the breakers of the law, surveillance became detached from its human subjects of enunciation and was unable to articulate its order in the world. Like the banners that hung in front of the Cilengka Precinct inciting the population to be disciplined and to refrain from social ills, the order of surveillance survived only as empty statements bereft of their points of purchase in the world.

The protection police provided from the effects of surveillance resulted in the establishment of fraternal alliances between agents of the police and business owners outside the state apparatus. Such alliances were couched in territorial terms: a Reserse agent controlled and protected the domain of a particular business; he "owned" (*punya*) or "held" (*pegang*) that business and defended it against others. This territorialization of police power was even more pronounced in the case of legitimate businesses, where the police were providing protection less from their own mediatory power as from the threats of competitors and "criminals." The way in which a Reserse agent first established an alliance with a legitimate business varied, but most often followed from an investigation into a crime, as in this example from the Reserse officer Ujang, who managed to insinuate himself into the security operations of a nearby factory.

> According to Ujang, the task of being a guard for a factory, or being responsible for "guidance" of a particular business, can be the cause of competition between police. He guards a factory that produces winter coats for export to Korea. He originally met the man who owns it after there was a case of embezzlement by one of the man's employees. As the factory is in Cilengka, he reported it to the precinct and Ujang happened to be the one on duty at the time. He managed to find a few different people at the factory who had been in on the scheme and the owner was grateful. But even with this background he has to be careful about making sure he can keep "hold" of the factory. He says that different people have different methods when they act as such guards. His method is to get to know the owners as well as possible. If you can establish a good relationship with them then they will be happy and nobody will be able to edge in on your turf. In his work with this factory, for example, he has built up a "fortification" (benteng) that no one else can get through. Sometimes, for example, police from the district headquarters will ask for a contribution from his factory. In this case he will go himself to talk to the police officer asking for money. His method is not to ask for money from the owner up front for these payments but to pay for them himself out of his own pocket. Only later will he be repaid, and he might not even be repaid the full amount because it would be impolite to specify the exact amount of the payment. Sometimes the competition comes not from other police stations but from other police at Cilengka. Whether someone will try to do this depends on the character of the particular individual involved.

What Ujang provided in this case was not protection from the law but protection from exactions by other police. At least in Ujang's view, he was making a kind of gift to the owner, and while he expected some return on this gift, he wasn't extorting money with the threat of legal sanctions. Whatever the owner chose to offer him as a sign of gratitude Ujang would accept, even if it meant being temporarily out of pocket.

In fact, the police often went quite far out of their way to make sure the relationships established between themselves and those they helped were not construed to be a form of extortion. One of the favored methods of doing this was by requesting contributions from the larger factories, businesses, banks, and shops in the area toward renovating the precinct building, building a new police post, or whatever. Another approach was to extend invitations to the bosses of local businesses to take part in a golf competition, the tickets for which were especially expensive. At Cilengka, Andi himself phoned the bosses to request such "donations" and then sent out some of his uniformed subordinates to make the collections. According to one of his underlings, Andi was not as good at establishing a territorial presence as some previous precinct heads had been.

> One former Cilengka head had a very good method. Monday to Friday were spent doing office business and Saturday and Sunday were spent doing guidance at the various businesses. Each weekend the agents would cover a new region, and after a month the cycle would start again. The business owners really liked this, especially if the police wore their uniforms and took a patrol car. Anyone paying attention could see that the business was being watched over (dikontrol) by the police. As a result, when that precinct head called up businesses to ask for donations to paint the office, for example, he could get much more. They felt that he was watching out for them. But if they do not even recognize the precinct head's name they are not going to want to give.

Establishing a visible territorial presence at the sites of businesses made the owners feel secure, for they knew that anyone paying attention would recognize that someone was watching out for their security. As in the territorial security developed by the neighborhood watch, the important things were that the guards or police were present, that they showed continued attention for the place and its inhabitants, and that this attention had a personal dimension. If the businesses experienced problems with thieves, street toughs, or other police, the owners knew whom to call at the precinct for help; and conversely, if the precinct head needed money his name would be recognized when he called to ask for donations. By establishing such ties, the police were able to generate—and collect upon—a feeling of indebtedness among local business owners.

Although Andi was not terribly successful at developing these ties to businesses in an organized way, such ties were nevertheless extremely common at Cilengka at an individual level. Cases like those of Wawan and Ujang, described above, were the norm rather than the exception. In many instances, the relation was formalized in the sense that the agents did not just receive pay-offs—they were actually hired by the businesses as private security guards. Thus, when they finished their shifts at the precinct they would go to work at a billiard hall or a cinema, where they would keep an eye on things and coordinate the civilian Satpam who were there all the time. To some degree, such cooperation was formalized through the Siskamling program, but it was also done informally to some extent. Either way, such close cooperation between businesses, private security guards, and the police had advantages for all involved: business owners felt secure knowing they had someone to call if they were threatened; Satpam increased their authority through ties to the police; and the police both earned money and established a whole network of people in business and on the street who could prove useful for intelligence purposes.

For an officer in Andi's position, having underlings with these sorts of links to the people in the precinct was absolutely imperative. Without them, he would be unable to collect protection money or solve crimes, and his career depended on his ability to do both these things. On the one hand, the precinct had to generate enough income so that he could make the necessary payments to those above him and around him in the fraternal hierarchy. By making those payments he could cement the alliances necessary to support desired promotions. On the other hand, the precinct had to do its part to maintain a reasonably high crime-solution rate, or about half the total number of crimes reported. This was important in part because higher-ups in the police paid a great deal of attention to statistics, and in part because others in the criminal justice system, such as prosecutors, lawyers, judges, and prison wardens, depended on a consistent flow of cases for their own income.[32] Extending fraternal alliances down through the police hierarchy and into the community was thus a way for Andi to meet his career objectives while also providing a basis for solidarity with his subordinates. Insofar as his efforts were successful, both he and his underlings enjoyed many benefits. Not only were their chances for promotion enhanced, but they also stood to reap significant economic rewards. Of course, there were also problems associated with this approach: illegal behavior by agents, lack of "professionalism," lack of law enforcement, taking part in corruption, and so forth. Such a lack of discipline was a perennial concern of the police leadership, which was worried about the institution's public image.

Dealing with corruption was easier in those units and offices where income was generated from payments whose objective it was to get police to perform their surveillance function. The Intelligence Unit at the city headquarters, for example, reportedly generated some of its income by issuing letters of permission for public meetings of all sorts, including conferences, concerts, and political rallies. People paid bribes to improve the chances that requests for permission would be granted and to increase the speed with which they were processed. Such payments had the effect of reinforcing a certain kind of police professionalism since they provided an incentive for agents to do their work quickly and efficiently. Moreover, since the payments were made directly to the higher-ups they also served to strengthen the fraternal hierarchy since officers were in a position to distribute money to their underlings as informal bonuses for loyalty and good work. At the precinct, however, only part of the income generated by policing was derived from doing the job of law enforcement and surveillance. The rest came from "looking the other way"—that is, by actively working to protect local allies from the effects of surveillance, and sometimes even by committing crimes. Under these circumstances, it was far more difficult to achieve efficiency in the sense desired by higher-ups who had a keen eye for statistics and for the outward signs of order.

The Precinct and the Gaze

At Cilengka, the problem of needing to conform to an image of professional discipline and order was solved by making a special place for that image within the precinct's symbolic world. The order desired by surveillance was allowed to exist, primarily on an aesthetic plane, whereas the actual disciplinary order created by the fraternity was kept secret. As we saw above, the spatial locus for the fraternal order was the precinct head's office, where fraternal nocturnal gatherings provided the occasion for brotherly exchanges. The locus for the order of surveillance, on the other hand, was the so-called data room.

The data room was the same size as Andi's office, but unlike his office it was almost always empty. Furnished with nothing more than a table, the precinct's sole computer, and a small, locked cabinet containing a number of police publications, the main attraction of the data room was its walls, which were covered with charts and tables displaying information concerning the Cilengka Precinct. A visitor examining these charts could learn a great deal about the area from the standpoint of police surveillance. Cilengka in the mid-1990s consisted of 7 subdistricts, 65 Rukun Warga, and 428 Rukun Tetangga. With a total population of 71,071 and an area of 574 hectares, this meant that the population density was about 124 persons per hectare and that the average population of a single Rukun Tetangga was 166 people. The population was divided into various ethnic categories, including "Javanese," "Sundanese," "Batak," and "other." The only ethnic group that was actually quantified, however, was the Chinese Indonesians (so-called WNI, or *warga negara Indonesia*), of whom there were reportedly 554.[33] Overall, men slightly outnumbered women and adults formed two-thirds of the total population. The charts identified three ways of earning a living: "military," "civil servant," or "private/trader," but no numbers were given for any of these. Under the heading "Ideology" the charts indicated that just under half the population was recorded as having already participated in Pancasila (the Indonesian national ideology) upgrading courses. Under "Politics" the charts said that in the last election, 57.7 percent of the Cilengka population voted for the ruling party (Golkar), 25.25 percent for PDI (Partai Demokrat Indonesia, or Indonesian Democratic Party), and 16.79 percent for PPP (Partai Persatuan Pembangunan, or United Development Party). They also showed that of the former political prisoners living in the subdistrict, none were classified as "Band A," 29 were "Band B," and 91 were "Band C" (the different bands referring to a person's degree of involvement in the outlawed Indonesian Communist Party). Other information about the precinct found on the charts included the numbers of mosques (72), public prayer rooms (27), churches (11), Hindu or Buddhist temples (2), Muslims (58,982), Catholics (3,190), Protestants (7,401), Hindus (509), and Buddhists (1,028). The charts noted how many schools there were, and also provided some statistics on crime in the precinct. In 1993 there were 320 crimes per 10,000 people, in 1994 there were 251, and in 1995 there were 270. In 1993 the ratio of reported crimes to solved crimes was 228 to 69, in 1994 it was 179 to 77, and in 1995 it was 192 to 77.

In addition to this statistical information, summaries also provided an analysis of the data's "criminogenic" significance. For example, with respect to "geography" and "demography" it was noted that increases in population put pressure on land and on opportunities for work and housing, which may give rise to demonstrations at factories, robberies, fights, and gambling. Economic development was said to create "social envy" that may result in theft, robbery, and racist attacks at supermarkets or industrial sites; and ideological "misunderstandings" might give rise to strikes and demonstrations on college campuses. Furthermore, specific locations in the area were identified as "hazards," including university campuses, hotels, local government offices, markets, and so forth. Finally, lists were provided of wanted persons, goods reported stolen, former political prisoners, foreigners, and recidivists.

As a cultural artifact and system of knowledge, the data room as I observed it is highly susceptible to an archaeological analysis along Foucauldian lines. On its walls there were several layers of sediment left by successive regimes of surveillance and social control. These included: the history of counting individual persons in censuses for use first in colonial vaccination programs and later for taxation and policing; the history of mapping urban areas, which in Bandung was linked to late-colonial efforts to control pestilence and promote hygiene; the separation of the Chinese and foreigners from other ethnic groups, a colonial inheritance that once dictated residence patterns and dress codes among urban inhabitants; and the lists of individuals considered to be threats to social order, such as recidivists and "communists," a practice that had both colonial and New Order roots.

Virtually all of the layers of knowledge in the data room, with the exception of those relating to crime statistics and recidivism, made their first appearance in Java in domains outside the police apparatus, either in other arms of government or in the work of scientists. If one looked carefully, the fragmentation and layering were still apparent, and one could imagine or recall the contestations, concerns, fears, and beliefs that gave rise to each particular constellation or layer of data. Each of these layers should also be understood as the product of a deterritorialization and a reterritorialization, according to which human bodies, things, and places were transposed into an order of representation—such as the census, lists, and maps—where they achieved a new currency and meaning. While the various layers of knowledge in the data room had diverse origins, there was an overarching logic at work, which Foucault would undoubtedly characterize as that of surveillance, since it was concerned with the alignment of bodies in space according to an optic geared toward social and environmental control. As James Scott has shown, in his aptly titled book *Seeing like a State* (1998), the two main criteria by which such knowledge was selected were that it be legible and that it be amenable to simplification for use in bureaucratic rule.

While the data room may be susceptible to a Foucauldian analysis, for the police at Cilengka it was meant to provide a unified vision of the precinct and its potential criminal hazards. Evidently, hazards were generally seen to occur in spaces where mixtures between social categories were difficult to avoid: universities, as places where people of different political beliefs came into contact; industries, where ethnic Chinese came into contact with people from other backgrounds; and markets, where traders came into contact with government representatives and the military. And then there were the individual contaminants themselves—"communists," recidivists, religious fanatics—who were isolated and identified since they posed a danger wherever they were. Indeed, if we read the data room as it was intended to be read, crime and disorder appear as contagions, analogous to disease. Implicitly, we are taught to adopt a hygienic approach to crime and security: to prevent crime we should prevent or at least monitor spaces and bodies that are prone to contagion; and once a social ill is diagnosed, "criminogens" (i.e., pathogens) should be identified, isolated, and either treated or eradicated.

During the New Order this joining together of crime, security, and hygiene was the dominant discourse employed by the state both to define and to deal with threats. In Bandung, for example, banners in front of police stations or at the entrances to neighborhoods incited the people to "eliminate the five social diseases: gambling, drunkenness, theft, drugs, prostitution." Similarly, operations to eliminate drugs, street vendors, trishaws, illegal prostitution, and other contagions were referred to as "cleansing" operations. But perhaps the clearest case of the power of this discourse was to be found in the treatment of the so-called communist threat. Since the killings of 1965–66, the government spent a great deal of time and money trying to identify exactly which individuals had been members of the Communist Party and who had connections to them. Those so identified were then excluded from careers in the civil service and most private firms. For many years the primary means for establishing whether someone who was not a formal party member had any connection to communism was by asking questions about his or her family. If a parent or grandparent had been a party member, then that automatically made one a communist too. Communism was thus understood as the equivalent of an inherited trait. Increasingly, however, the proof of noncontamination came to focus not just on family but on what was called "clean environment" (*bersih lingkungan*). If one passed the test for noncontamination, which meant that one lacked communist friends, neighbors, or coworkers, one was certified as being "clean of self" and "clean of environment." If not, one was understood to be a criminogen.

The proximity of lists of recidivists and supposed communists to lists of ethnic groups in the data room raises the question of the degree to which the hygienic discourse might be applied to ethnic divisions. From the standpoint of the state, this appeared to be likely only in the case of the Chinese minority. Police surveillance did not distinguish in any systematic way between Javanese, Sundanese, and Batak, for example. But ethnic Chinese Indonesians have always been subjected to special forms of surveillance, even after the explicit policy of their assimilation into the wider Indonesian population. This was indicated in the data room by the continued use of a separate category for naturalized citizens that everyone understands to really mean "Chinese."[34]

The most striking thing about the data room, with its discourse on hygiene as a determinant of crime and security, was the fact that it was hidden away. Although it occupied a prominent spot in the precinct hallway, it was almost always locked and rarely used. Furthermore, the charts and tables were physically hidden by curtains that covered all the walls. Whether these curtains were meant to highlight the exclusivity that the state enjoyed over such information or were meant merely as dust covers remains a mystery to me. What is clear, however, is that the only time these curtains were opened was when the precinct received an esteemed visitor. When I asked to see these charts and tables, the clerk who made them—which was a lot of work, since they were all done by hand on plastic transparencies—recounted to me one such visit that had impressed itself on his mind. The head of the Provincial Police had come to inspect the precinct, and a great deal of effort had been taken to prepare for the visit. All the personnel wore their uniforms and undoubtedly polished their shoes. Upon seeing the data room, the provincial head personally congratulated the lowly clerk on the good work he had done. This was a rare event, and although it had taken place two years previously, the clerk remembered it clearly and was very proud of the recognition he had received.

One can surmise why the official was so pleased by what he saw. At the Provincial Police headquarters, the collection and processing of data on the population, the issuing of identity papers, the taking of fingerprints, and the like formed the bulk of the daily grind. In my experience, this greater administrative function was reflected in a working environment where newspapers were common and where employees paid more attention to outward appearances of orderliness than tended to be the case at the precinct. So when the head of the Provincial Police visited the precinct, the officers there knew what to show him: a representation of what he visualized of Cilengka from his position at his own office—namely, a particular constellation of charts, statistics, and maps. Undoubtedly, seeing the data room provided the visiting official with satisfaction, for it reproduced the information in his files, but in a manner that conformed to his image of the world out there (what the police refer to as "the field"). His idea of the precinct as a real-world copy of what he had in his files was thus preserved. Like the use of numbers on houses in the hygiene program, or the use of photos in anthropometry files (see chapters 3 and 4, respectively), the possibility of recognition failure was avoided. Had the visiting official seen something other than the image prepared for him, he might have had to admit that things were not completely in order, and might therefore have had to initiate a shake-up of the precinct's personnel. Instead, the data room allowed him to recognize the precinct as an orderly one and one therefore deserving of a place in the state's official hierarchy.[35] It is likely that the clerk who made this possible—the one who crafted a representation of order that fit so well with the official's vision—will remember that moment for the rest of his life.

The existence of the data room was enough to ensure that the logic of surveillance could continue to function without friction and obstruction. This pleased everyone in the police, for the officials could go about their business without threatening the continued viability of the whole fraternal structure that underpinned daily activities at the precinct. By creating a kind of camouflage, the fraternal order kept its world hidden beneath an image of aesthetic order constituted by modern techniques of surveillance. At Cilengka this symbolic solution to the conflict between the two types of order seemed reasonably successful, for the precinct was routinely praised and Andi himself was soon promoted to a job he desired.

It is notable, however, that performances of this kind were less effective when designed for public consumption. Consider the aforementioned example of urban ordering operations. Such operations were typically accompanied by great media fanfare. The officer in charge of the operation would hold a press conference in which he described what the targets of the operation were—trishaws, drugs, or moonshine, for example. He would then explain the threat to society such "social ills" represent and name the participating police units. On television, images would then be shown of rows of police standing at attention while they received their orders on how to conduct the operation. As such operations often continued for some weeks or months, the police would regularly update the press on how many people had been netted, and how many items had been confiscated. Newspaper readers might learn, for example, that in the first week of an operation for the eradication of "the devil's pill," 532 ecstasy tablets were confiscated and three people arrested. Television viewers watching the five o'clock news would then be treated to sights of confiscated evidence, such as bags of pills displayed on a table with policemen standing behind them. However, the public often responded to these demonstrations with cynicism. Letters columns in newspapers frequently contained questions from readers regarding what actually happened to all the trishaws, moonshine, and drugs that the police confiscated. Were they destroyed as the police claim? Or—as rumors suggested—were they simply sold again for profit by corrupt members of the vampiric police force?

The police tried to put an end to such rumors and doubts by staging rather bizarre spectacles. These spectacles, broadcast on television, showed scenes of moonshine, drugs, fake Levi's, trishaws, and the like being crushed by bulldozers and steamrollers or sometimes burned. Shots of the destruction were intercut with shots of uniformed police officials and their wives, seated in rows, clapping as the spectacle unfolded before them. Such displays made sense from the standpoint of the aesthetic order the police tried to maintain. Not only did they provide visual "proof" that the police were acting to eliminate traces of disorder in society, but these displays also impelled viewers to identify with the eye of surveillance, and hence appreciate the elimination of these eyesores. Unfortunately for the police, however, this is not what happened. In my experience, viewers tended rather to consider it a waste to destroy perfectly usable things. More importantly, and almost without exception, they noted skeptically that the goods being destroyed were probably only a small part of what had been confiscated, or that the crates being burned were empty, and that the remainder—those things not destroyed—were being sold by the police for profit. They saw, in other words, nothing more than a performance in which state power was being converted into corrupt wealth and money.

Neopatrimonial Dynamics of State Power

The conversion of state power into money depended upon—and sustained— the existence of a semisecret fraternal hierarchy within the police apparatus. I use the term "fraternity" to distinguish this network of alliances from patrimonialism. Admittedly, fraternal ties resemble patrimonial ties in that both involve a feeling of indebtedness and both appeal to a moral economy for legitimization. But equating the systems would be a mistake. In the first place, patrimonialism is generally understood to be a system of ties that extends into the center from the periphery, as when, for example, residential or familial ties penetrate institutions of government. In police fraternities, however, the ties originated in the center and extended outward through and beyond the bureaucracy. Second, the debt underlying fraternal alliances was not individualized to the same degree as is that underlying patron-client ties. Younger brothers owe *all* their elder brothers, even though they might only pay off those individuals with whom they had closest ties. Clients, in contrast, tend to owe an individual or a family, so their debt is highly localized and the rewards more clearly calculable. Finally, although there was an ideological emphasis on a kind of moral economy in the fraternity, it was far less pronounced than in patrimonialism. Fraternities preferred to emphasize shared personal circumstances, solidarity, and egalitarianism as against different personal circumstances, hierarchy, and paternalism.

The broader postcolonial Indonesian assemblage for policing should be understood as an apparatus produced from the interplay between fraternal ties, surveillance, and territoriality. The Cilengka Precinct provides some indications as to how this interplay can occur in a particular institution at a given time. In the first place, the unit of the "precinct" was constructed by way of a surveilling gaze, which imagined the whole of Indonesia as divided into jurisdictions, each with a certain number of personnel whose job was to maintain security and enforce the law within that unit. To a certain extent, the movement of people between these units and between posts was also determined by the demands for an efficient bureaucratic and surveillance machine. Officers who were able to make their precinct approximate the aesthetic of bureaucratic order would be rewarded for their efforts. But officers also had to be active within the fraternal networks that provided allies higher up in the food chain with material wealth. Working with allies usually implied not doing things "by the book," so officers had to do their best to find a way to negotiate between these conflicting aims. At Cilengka, this conflict was "resolved" by giving one or two people responsibility for maintaining an image of order, exemplified by the data room, while the others—particularly those in Reserse—were almost completely subordinated to the demands of the fraternity.

Police fraternities derived their power from their ability to take over territorial units and tie them into a supralocal hierarchy. Surveillance attempted to do the same thing, but the specific manner in which fraternities achieved this effect differed. Whereas surveillance attempted to subordinate localities by allowing locals to see themselves only as the state saw them (via maps, identity cards, laws, etc.), fraternities subordinated localities by collaborating with informal sovereigns and by staking claims to territorial power. The central weapon they used in staking such claims was the threat of violence: the violence of the law, of surveillance, of crime, and of the police themselves. The success of such claims depended in part on the ability of the police to behave in ways that were recognizably territorial: they had to be present in the territory, they had to occupy it, and they had to care for it. For this reason, creating fraternal linkages to administer territorial power depended on the work of precinct-level Reserse agents who, unlike their superiors, had the time to really ensconce themselves within the precinct. To assume territorial power was to assume the role not only of protector but also of debt collector. In return for "giving" the right to live and do business without being disturbed, the police received all sorts of payments. These payments flowed up through the fraternal hierarchy, from business owners to Reserse agents to the head of the precinct to higher-ups in the City Police and Provincial Police and so on. One Reserse agent at Cilengka estimated that the cash income that passed into Andi's hands was about ten million rupiah a month, or twenty times his salary.[36] Flows of such large sums of money provided police fraternities with a powerful raison d'être.

The manner in which territorial power was tied into fraternities was not always direct. When serving as behind-the-scenes backers (*bekking*) of informal sovereigns like gangs and charismatic toughs, the police simply took a cut of any money that gangs and their leaders collected. Working through these intermediaries also gave fraternities additional leverage over businesspeople, for they could become actively involved in disputes without appearing to be. If a factory owner resisted making police protection payments, for example, fraternal ties to street toughs and labor leaders could be used to instigate a strike or an attack on the factory building. The police could then appear to intervene on behalf of the factory owner, thus proving the value of their "protection." The economic power that fraternities wielded was thus supplemented by their power to mobilize people on the ground. Mostly such mobilization was used for economic purposes, but it was also sometimes used to generate a sense of public insecurity through crime or riots, and to infiltrate political demonstrations and to direct them toward violence so as to discredit political opposition.

It might be argued that tying territorial power to fraternity networks should have had a corresponding "localizing" effect on police loyalties; after all, the bulk of the average Reserse agent's income was generated not from his salary but from his ties to people in the community. Even under such circumstances, however, it was extremely difficult for police to stray from the fraternal hierarchy. Agents and officers alike were acutely aware that the almost kingly power they enjoyed in their respective domains was a gift from those on high. Promotions to "wet chairs" were not automatic but depended on one's behavior. Should one's behavior not follow the wishes of higher-ups in the fraternity, one could immediately find oneself rotated to a marginal post. Add to this the threat of being exposed and perhaps even charged for "corruption," and the firmness of the fraternal grip becomes clear.

Policing the City

In sum, if we were to paint a picture of postcolonial urban policing from the vantage point of the Cilengka Precinct toward the end of the New Order, it would resemble in certain respects the system of policing that existed more than a century earlier, before the advent of a bureaucratic state and before the Dutch deployed technologies of surveillance to ensure the population would answer to the linguistic order desired by the colonial state. The resemblance is to be found, above all, in the way police made money: by using the threat of violence—of both the criminal and the legal kind—for purposes of extortion and by taking payments to investigate crimes and enforce the law. Like the regent's spies of old, agents in Cilengka seemed to play whatever role best suited their interests, be it informant, perpetrator, investigator, judge, or punisher. However, they were not connected to local government in the same way as their colonial forebears. Rather than answering to local officials, police above all answered to their fraternities. To meet the demands of these fraternities, police officers and their underlings exploited their official power for economic gain. The legacy of the late-colonial state is important here, for it provided the impetus as well as the tools for police intervention into every facet of people's lives and thus for the generation of income. Moreover, it provided the soil in which the fraternities were allowed to grow. For although such fraternities drew upon the nationalist ideology of "brotherhood" that preceded the capture of the state by nationalist forces, they ultimately owed their power to bureaucratic positions and military posts allocated by a centralized state. Fraternities treated these positions as economic monopolies and engineered their allocation so as to minimize political threats and maximize economic gain. The monopoly enjoyed by the police was the state-sanctioned monopoly of "law enforcement" and—shared with the army—"security." Their ability to exploit this monopoly to maximize gain was facilitated in part by the proliferation of laws and ordinances aimed at "maintaining security" (with the corresponding development of surveillance techniques to enforce these codes), and in part by the ability of fraternities to co-opt informal sovereignties in a way that strictly bureaucratic authority could not. As both the perpetrators of state violence and the defenders against violence, police were in a unique position to prey upon the population, which was increasingly faced with the choice of either being victimized by, or collaborating with, elements in the fraternities.

The police went through the motions of trying to convince the public that they were trying to rid their institution of "corruption." In addition to presenting an image of order to the public through spectacles of public ordering, they regularly punished members of the force who had broken the law. Toward the end of the New Order, such offenders were termed *oknum*, which meant something like "official who acted improperly and thus should not be considered to have been acting as a representative of the state."[37] The idea of the *oknum* allowed the police to give form to the otherwise inchoate corruption haunting their institution and provided the basis for claims that the spectral figure representing such corruption could be—and was being—exorcised. But neither the police nor the public were terribly convinced by these efforts.

In this chapter, I have presented an alternative account of where this ghostly figure might be located. I have argued that it is to be found not in individuals but in fraternal ties that related to the formal police apparatus as its vampiric other. While these ties took a sociological form, ultimately what made them a force of "corruption" was not this form itself but the actions done in its name. These actions can be traced back to the hazing at the police academy and can be seen again and again in the numerous instances in which the police threatened violence in order to shore up hierarchy. On all these occasions the police—acting in the name of the law—suspended the rule of law in order to commit what they regarded as a necessary violence. They committed such violence to enforce another law—that of "tradition" and hierarchy. In other words, the police acted with the authority derived from state law to enforce what was, in effect, an outlaw tradition. The duplicity of this position, and the mixing of two types of power that it implies, is what lies at the heart of police "corruption."

A former head of the Indonesian National Police once remarked that the people's attitude toward the police is one of "hate but [also] longing" (*benci tapi rindu*); people hate the police for their corruption but they long for the feeling of security and protection that police can provide (*Media Indonesia*, December 27, 1995). The remarks of Ali Sadikin which I quoted at the start of this chapter, saying that corruption "can no longer be characterized as only money corruption but is a moral problem in the widest sense," suggest that although people may hate police "corruption," what they long for may not necessarily be security and protection, but perhaps something more difficult to attain—namely, justice. Some may long for justice in the guise of the forgotten law, which is forever suspended to protect hierarchy. For people like these, increased surveillance and transparency promise to encourage democratization and expose the "secrets" of the fraternities to the light of rationality, separating the cancerous disciplines of the fraternities from the wholesome disciplines of professionals, and applying the letter of the law to the former. Others, like Ali Sadikin, who worry about living in an epoch when "the wrong are made right and the right made wrong," may long for something of a different nature altogether: "God as the Great Unity," unadulterated divine justice, and the fear it calls forth.

Conclusion

Panopticism and Prowess
in a Postcolonial City

For the first couple of years after President Suharto was ousted in 1998, the police in Bandung largely retreated from the city's streets. During daylight hours, at least, traffic stops were rare and patrols almost nonexistent. Antipathy for representatives of the state had reached such heights during the antiregime reform (*reformasi*) movement that many police chose to not wear their uniforms when traveling to and from work. As the police receded from view, informal assertions of territorial authority became commonplace. At the far-flung edges of the city, streets were often taken over and blocked by groups of youths who demanded a payment from outsiders wanting to pass by, ostensibly to support the construction of a new mosque or to pave a road. In some areas, idealistic "citizen forums" (*forum warga*) sprung up at the neighborhood level, providing a venue in which local residents could assert their collective rights to the city by organizing for better infrastructure or against incursions by predatory developers.[1] These years also saw a burgeoning of the informal sector, as street vendors and middle-class entrepreneurs took advantage of lax policing to occupy strategically located sidewalks, intersections, and plazas all over the city. There was also a dizzying upsurge in the number of militia-style thugs for hire, who sought to lay claim to the wide array of street-level protection rackets, which for so long had been dominated by a small clique of regime-supported groups.[2] In short, the territorial city had become something of a free-for-all in which competing groups of various stripes struggled to exert their claims.[3]

Reclaiming the Street in Postauthoritarian Bandung

One area where this struggle took place was on the great plaza located in front of Gedung Sate, the West Java governor's office. As discussed previously, Gedung Sate was built at the height of the modern colonial period and was the first piece of monumental architecture to provide a bird's-eye view of the city below (see chapter 3). Both the building and the plaza had been built as part of a plan to create a modern center of colonial government for the Dutch East Indies, a plan that was never fully realized. During the New Order years, the plaza was very much a regime-dominated space, used relatively lightly for recreational sports and military and government assemblies. But during the post-Suharto years, the plaza underwent a striking renaissance that saw it emerge as one of Bandung's most dynamic public spaces. This was in large part due to the achievements of the Bandung *reformasi* movement, which in the late 1990s often chose the street and plaza in front of governor's office as the ultimate destination for its protest marches. In this way, ordinary citizens made a powerful claim to a public space that had been dominated by the regime for decades. While such claims were primarily politically oriented, at least at first, the presence of youthful crowds sometimes gave the plaza a festive atmosphere, and it was not long before it became a magnet for other kinds of public events, like concerts, social gatherings, and pop-up markets.

The changes in the structures of street-level authority that accompanied and followed from this highly visible public reclamation of the plaza are illustrative of the larger changes the territorial city has undergone since the end of authoritarian rule. In the last years of the New Order, the plaza was subject to a pattern of everyday policing similar to that of other streets and public spaces in the city. Although there was a police post located just outside the governor's office, much of the day-to-day policing of activities on the plaza was in the hands of an informal leader, Mr. Ayi, described by one parking attendant as "the one who had power" (*yang punya kuasa*) over the plaza. While clearly a figure of territorial authority, Mr. Ayi also enjoyed close ties with officials in the governor's office. Informal street vendors and parking attendants would pay him a monthly fee, and in return they would be able to use so-called *lapak*, or microterritories, on the plaza, from which they could pursue their livelihoods under the umbrella of his protection.[4] However, just a couple of years after the end of the New Order regime, a shift occurred in the structure of territorial authority at the plaza: Mr. Ayi relinquished control of parking and trade on the plaza in favor of an increasingly lucrative side business renting equipment for the growing number of events being held there, leaving day-to-day territorial control over much of the plaza to others. The result was the proliferation of a patchwork of haphazard local authorities: in some areas, people seeking livelihoods on the plaza could work more or less autonomously without having to submit to a leader or make payments, though this left them vulnerable to police cleansing operations; in other areas, groups claiming to have *bekking* carved out territories for themselves and introduced more routinized forms of organization and collaboration with government and police authorities. In a manner that mirrored what was happening to political authority within the newly democratizing state, territorial authority in the plaza had lost its singular center and was becoming increasingly multipolar and subject to competition.[5]

This more diffuse, multipolar structure of territorial authority endured for many years, even as use of the plaza intensified to unprecedented levels. Near the peak of this intensity, in 2012, I had the fortune to colead a team-based research project that sought to map the uses of space on the plaza and the structures of territorial authority there. Our approach was simple: ensure we had researchers on the ground in the plaza each day for a month, from early in the morning until late at night, mapping activities in the various areas of the plaza and learning through observation and interviews how territorial authority was structured in each area. As it turned out, this was a far more formidable task than we had initially anticipated. Most of the people we talked to who knew the plaza well could point to at least half a dozen distinct territorial zones on the plaza, each with their own authority figures, but how this authority manifested depended greatly on the specific day and time. Territoriality had a temporal, as well as a spatial, dimension. In both dimensions we could identify certain general patterns—

as, for example, in the spatial contours of a territory and the normal cycle of daily and weekly activities there—but the multiplicity of territories and the hyperlocality of their social dynamics made it difficult to see how the various moving parts all fit together.

In the area in front of the governor's office, where protesters liked to picket, it was not uncommon on weekdays to see a range of different protests taking place on the same day, sometimes in a rotating fashion. These were accompanied by deployments of uniformed police officers, who sought to contain the protesters within designated areas so as to prevent them from disrupting traffic flows along the roads bordering the plaza and through the gateway leading to and from the Gedung Sate complex. Along a fence adjacent to that gateway, one could also often find a group of local journalists; some were taking a break from covering the governor's office while others were just stopping in on their motorcycles to have a snack, type out a story on their smartphones, interview some protesters, or exchange information with their colleagues. Experienced protest leaders knew this and would provide journalists with advance warning of a march or bring press releases to share with the reporters gathered there. These sorts of interactions inevitably attracted the interest of security personnel, and among the more experienced journalists, it was regarded as an open secret that a certain older gentleman who sometimes sold them hot snacks from his cart outside the gate was also an undercover intelligence officer. But no journalists seemed much concerned by this fact. The patterns followed by the protesters, the journalists, and the security personnel were generally so predictable and repetitive that the whole routine assumed the trappings of a sort of political theater. Within the broader territorial landscape of the plaza, activists had been ceded a place for democratic expression, but it was understood by all involved that this space was highly circumscribed—spatially, temporally, and bodily—by the police.

On Sundays, by contrast, much of the plaza and surrounding streets were taken over by an enormous pop-up market, reputed to be one of Southeast Asia's largest at that time. Thousands of vendors—many representing shops and market kiosks located elsewhere in Bandung—would gather and offer their wares to throngs of visitors from all over the city and beyond. They displayed their goods on tables or on mats on the ground, built covered stalls using bamboo and tarpaulins, or sold items from the backs of their cars. Pretty much anything that could be easily transported was available for purchase: fresh fruits and vegetables, meat and fish, clothing and shoes, live animals, bedding, books, toys, electronics, accessories, and street

C.1 Demonstration in defense of Pancasila national principles, Bandung, 2017. Photo by Frans Ari Prasetyo.

food. A small amusement park was also set up, and there were areas where one could play badminton. The plaza was so chock-full of people on Sundays that activities overflowed into nearby streets and parks. Attracted by the crowds, small-time gangsters would circulate, drinking liquor and demanding goods from vendors without paying, sometimes with what seemed like the tacit approval of those offering protection. Groups of pickpockets were also common.

Although the market gave the outward impression of being a highly unregulated space, interviews with street vendors, parking attendants, and others on the ground there indicated that the basic structures of informal territorial authority in the plaza persisted on market days. Each sector of the plaza still had an informal leader who would protect the vendors in their area in return for a payment; it was just that due to the increased level of commercial activity, the number of *lapak* up for grabs increased exponentially. And while some vendors claimed that an overarching, unified hierarchy obtained at the plaza, this was clearly a shifting landscape of authority, and contests for control of a given area were often resolved through violence or appeals to one's *bekking*, someone who might be from a mass organization, the police, or the army.

C.2   Demonstration by Islamic Defenders Front, Bandung, 2016. Photo by
        Frans Ari Prasetyo.

In addition to the Sunday market, the plaza at the time of our research
was also a favored venue for large concerts and festivals. Events included
performances by metal bands and dangdut singers as well as film festivals,
product launches, and motorcycle club gatherings. Such events required
government permits and were often sponsored by corporate entities, such
as tobacco companies, beverage companies, motorcycle companies, and
banks. Large stages were assembled and often an area within the plaza
would be fenced off so that attendees could be charged an entrance fee
and crowds could be controlled. Event organizers we interviewed all knew
that the fencing and stage needed to be rented from Mr. Ayi, whose side
business had grown over the years to become quite lucrative.[6] While the
audiences varied, as night wore on, the largest demographics were usually
teenagers and young men. The sound from such events was sometimes so
loud that it could be heard from many kilometers away, providing the city
with a kind of sonic center, territorializing the city in much the same way
the slit gong territorialized the neighborhood.

    Although our research showed that old patterns of territorial authority
were largely able to contain, and give a semblance of order to, the remark-
able reclamation of public space that followed from the *reformasi* movement,

it was not long before the government sought to reassert a more direct form of control over the plaza. In 2014, the then mayor of Bandung, Ridwan Kamil, working together with the local district military command (Komando Distrik Militer, or Kodim), embarked on an ambitious plan to clear the area around Gedung Sate of street vendors by relocating 2,400 of them to the north end of the plaza. The mayor claimed that the government had identified nine groups of *preman*, each consisting of about five to eight persons, who were illegally collecting hundreds of millions of rupiah from street vendors each month.[7] Drawing on language reminiscent of the New Order, he suggested that "the *preman* in the Gasibu area would be accommodated because most of them are prepared to join in making successful [*mensukseskan*] the local government's program."[8] He expressed a willingness to work with these groups to bring order to the plaza, and to employ them in the smaller market planned for the north end, but threatened those who did not comply with military force. The Kodim commander was more pointed, stressing that "there [was] one group of *preman* in particular which often asks for money, but doesn't contribute to the Government. Kodim's capacity will be to help the city government execute its program."[9]

A few months later, the provincial governor announced a plan to renovate and beautify the plaza. He imagined the plaza as a monumental tourist attraction, where visitors would be able to enjoy the bird's-eye view of the city from Gedung Sate: "When visitors climb the tower atop Gedung Sate, they will be able to see the beauty of Bandung City and its environs."[10] To make this vision a reality, the plaza would be temporarily closed so that it could be given a "new face."[11] A spokesperson for the government noted that one of the goals of the renovation would be to straighten out the position of the existing jogging track in the plaza so that it followed an imaginary line running from the tips of the spears atop Gedung Sate to the peak of a nearby mountain, Tangkubanparahu, visible in the distance to the north. "Right now, it isn't [straight]," he observed, "it's tilted to one side."[12] In addition to bringing the plaza more in line with the orderly geometrical aesthetics of the view from above, the renovation was designed to add other beautifying features to the public space, including a fancy new public toilet (five-star quality!), new pavement for the old dirt jogging track, a library, and a themed garden. The significant costs of the project would be covered by Corporate Social Responsibility funds contributed by a local bank, Bank Jabar Banten.[13]

In the end, the revitalization did in fact change the way the plaza was used. As one reporter observed after the plaza was reopened to the public in

C.3   Independence Day ceremony, Bandung, 2018. Photo by Frans Ari Prasetyo.

2016, "From the clean and modern public toilet to the large parking lot, the facilities are quite satisfactory.... The cleanliness is also protected because all the street vendors who used to control Gasibu field have been ordered [*ditertibkan*]. There are no more street vendors on the streets or on Gasibu field."[14] Indeed, the portion of the plaza that had been cleansed of street vendors was now used mainly for jogging, sports, and the taking of family photographs. Large-scale events were still welcome once in a while, and organizers continued to make use of the barricades, sound equipment, and security provided by Mr. Ayi, but the range of what was permitted became much narrower; instead of loud, youthful concerts and raucous festivals, programming mainly consisted of government-sanctioned assemblies, as had been the case during the New Order.

Around Gasibu field the government also installed a new network of CCTV cameras. This was part of a citywide project initiated by the mayor and linked to his signature "smart city" initiative, known as the Bandung Command Center. The Command Center, located in city hall, was very much like the data room at Cilengka Precinct (see chapter 6), only reimagined for the twenty-first century. It was intended as a place where the entirety of the city's data could be accessed in digitized form and connected to real-time surveillance capabilities via the latest cameras and GPS-tracking technologies. In a promotional video, the Command Center is touted for its high-tech panoptic capabilities: we see a space-age room bathed in blue light, designed to look like something right out of *Star Trek*. Employees wearing modern uniforms with Sundanese-inspired accents confidently pore over graphical data about the city on their touch-screen monitors, and CCTV feeds from all over Bandung are visible on a wall-sized monitor. After setting the scene, the video cuts to a woman walking on a neighborhood street at night. Her purse torn from her grasp by a passing motorcyclist, she presses a panic button on her phone; the video then cuts back to the Command Center, where sirens sound and the location of the crime flashes red on a digital map. We see police being dispatched to the scene, followed by an image of the woman indicating via a button on her phone that she is now "safe."[15]

By dramatizing the benefits of such a system, the mayor had hoped to encourage city residents to equip their phones with this same app, and to build public support for the installation of thousands of CCTV cameras around the city, so that the government could respond rapidly to citizen complaints and emergencies.[16] But these efforts met with mixed results; while the police could point to some cases in which CCTV was helpful, more than three years after the project's launch, only a hundred cameras had been installed around the city.[17] Nevertheless, the Command Center became a favorite spot for showcasing Bandung's smart city aspirations to visiting dignitaries and inspired several other politicians to build similar centers in their own cities. As with the Cilengka data room, the Command Center— at least in its early phase of operation—seemed to be more about performing the state's powers of modern surveillance than actually enacting them.

Panopticism and Prowess in Historical Perspective

In this book, I have sought to understand everyday policing in Bandung in terms of a struggle between territoriality and surveillance, two very different modalities or logics of social ordering and governance. It is a struggle that plays out at the level of practices, technologies, and institutions of everyday policing, both formal and informal. It also plays out in symbolic terms, as state actors and informal sovereigns alike lay claim to the power associated with one or the other kind of logic.

The logic of territoriality constitutes entities as territorial domains, often under the authority of a responsible sovereign, whether a person or collectivity. Mild territoriality constitutes milieux that loosely cohere, while strong territoriality constitutes discrete turfs with hard boundaries and vigilant defenders. In the context of urban informal sovereignties, territoriality is very often expressed in localized geographic terms, as control over a given street, neighborhood, or marketplace. However, it may also be expressed in corporal terms, as possession of a body as a territory, and in more abstract terms, as a claim of ownership of a particular market segment, bus route, or bureaucratic office. In the Indonesian context I have examined here, such claims are frequently elaborated through a culture of leadership and power that emphasizes prowess. Oliver Wolters (1999, 18) identified "men of prowess" as one of the shared features of precolonial polities in Southeast Asia, arguing that while these societies were hierarchical, they did not have states in the usual sense. Kinship was for the most part bilateral, and instead of power being passed from generation to generation through lineage, authority was achieved through the actions of charismatic leaders, and attributed to magical or spiritual potency. People of prowess could become ancestors and might therefore continue to be worshipped by subsequent generations, but they needed to earn such a status during their lifetimes. Their authority, in other words, was not so much institutionalized over time as bounded by individual biography: each generation might see the rise of a new leader with a new constellation of followers. The polities that came into being around people of prowess were thus highly personalized and very fragile.

The story of the emergence of more conventional and durable states in Southeast Asia is generally told as a Weberian narrative about the routinization of this early form of charismatic authority, first through Indianization, and later, through colonialism.[18] Indianization provided an encompassing ideology of divine kingship that attached spiritual potency to lineage as well as to divine power.[19] Colonialism deepened this routinization through the introduction of enduring bureaucratic structures and patterns of succession. However, a great deal of scholarship on colonial and postcolonial Southeast Asia emphasizes that this putative routinization of charismatic authority was never definitive. Examples of more charismatic forms of authority continue to be found within modern states.[20] More importantly, people of prowess claiming spiritual potency, invulnerability, and the like reappear again and again at the edges, and in the interstices, of formal state power.[21] Rather than being superseded by modern state forms, charismatic authority remains an enduring force. With each new generation of leaders there is at least the potential that new figures of charismatic authority will emerge, throw into doubt the sovereignty of the state, and pose anew the question of how such power can be routinized.

Figures like the *jago* of the colonial period, the youth of the revolutionary period, the local gangs of the 1970s, and the *jegger* of the 1980s and '90s were all associated with these long-standing notions of prowess. In 1990s Bandung, this was evident in the kinds of territorial claims made by the *ronda* and by *jegger*, which depended on performances that demonstrated a mastery of violence, such as beatings and duels, and which drew attention to conventional attributes of spiritual potency, such as the possession of *ilmu* and the sporting of tattoos. Everyday discourse about crime and security, which often focused on magic and the spirit domain, reinforced this association. The tight connection between informal sovereignties and cultural constructions of prowess is important because it means that informal sovereignties in Indonesia have an aura of perennialism about them. In contrast to the formal state apparatus—which since colonial times has often been viewed as something distant, alien, and modern—informal sovereignties evoke a sense of proximity, indigeneity, and tradition. This adds to their legitimacy.

That informal sovereignties have an aura of tradition and indigeneity about them should not blind us to the fact that they are deeply structured by their relations with the modern state. Although the *ronda* may have precolonial origins, it is an institution that was nurtured by the colonial state, which saw it as an efficient and effective tool for policing Java's villages and cities.[22] In the postcolonial era, the New Order regime further entrenched the *ronda* by placing it under the supervision of the police and extending its use to other parts of the archipelago. Similarly, although urban *jegger* from the revolutionary period onward have tended to adopt a leadership style that appeals to traditional notions of prowess, their territorial power has historically derived in large part from backing they received from elements in the army and the police. At the local level, police used *jegger* to enforce a strong-arm order and to extract rents from criminal enterprises and neighborhood businesses. Thus, although historically the state has surrendered some of its authority to the *ronda* and the *jegger*, it has also played a decisive role in shaping the forms that such "traditional" informal sovereignties can take, has circumscribed their spheres of activity, and has helped sustain them through time.

While the modern state has at times played an important role in cultivating informal sovereigns, it is also true that informal sovereignties have tended to emerge and gain strength under conditions of state weakness. Periods of political transition, like the anticolonial revolution, the shift from Sukarno's to Suharto's rule, and the end of the New Order regime, were times when informal sovereigns asserted their authority more strongly and gained a new importance. Similarly, places in Bandung with a relatively marginal relationship to state power, such as "native" quarters during the colonial period and poor *kampung* in more recent decades, provided fertile grounds for informal sovereigns to establish themselves.[23] Yet the history of the *ronda* and *jegger* also shows that the state is not always as "weak" as it might appear to be. The modern state in Indonesia has grown accustomed to working through proxies. Once conceived of in terms of "indirect rule," this approach to governance has been maintained well into the postcolonial period and has thoroughly informed practices of everyday policing, particularly the policing of urban informality. Under some circumstances, such arrangements have provided an opening for informal actors—whether individual or collective—to emerge and stake their own claims to sovereign power. At other times, even when state power appears to be weak, it continues to be evoked by informal sovereigns as an absent presence—for example, through performances like the donning of quasi-military uniforms or the claiming of police backing.

While state weakness, or at least patchiness, in part explains the emergence and maintenance of informal sovereignties in Bandung, the spread of capitalism and the growing penetration of the market have also been important factors. *Jegger* and their gangs sometimes got their starts in *kampung*, but they quickly fought to take control of larger places of commerce. Up until the 1970s, this mainly meant marketplaces, cinemas, and transport terminals, but as industrial and market forces gradually reshaped the cityscape, it came to include other spaces like factories, shops, malls, discotheques, bars, billiard halls, and illicit casinos. Enmeshed as it was in a global system operating at multiple scales, capitalism in the city did not always obey a territorial logic. However, capitalist forces at some point need to alight on places, and in these places, they are susceptible to reterritorialization. In Bandung, as in many other large Indonesian cities in the 1970s and early 1980s, the initial agents of this reterritorialization were *jegger*, who used threats, violence, and promises of protection to assert control over emerging industries and markets. Gradually, the provision of security itself became an industry, albeit one based on a foundation of extortion.

The Petrus killings and the advent of Siskamling in the 1980s allowed the state to wrest back some degree of control over the lucrative local security industry. The killings of *preman* in the Petrus campaign effectively eliminated and displaced existing territorial powers and provided an opening for the police, the army, and private security guards to replace them. Siskamling provided a rubric for greater state involvement in privatized policing and encouraged the expansion of the security industry to all sectors of the formal economy. The massive rollout of private security since the 1980s thus has two aspects. First, it represents a franchising out of the state's policing powers, since the explosion in the numbers of Satpam means that much preventive policing work can be delegated to the private sector. In this regard, Siskamling can be viewed merely as an early iteration of the sort of privatization that is now evident in cities all over the world. Second, however, Siskamling emerged in a context where most policing was already conducted by private entities, albeit informal ones that were only starting to formalize. Siskamling aimed to effect the formalization of informal sovereignties within channels that could be controlled by the state.[24] Thus, while policing powers remained in private hands, they were shifted away from *jegger* and their ilk to people working under the formal oversight of the police. In this regard, the state was asserting rather than ceding greater control. The shift was not universal, of course, and *jegger*—particularly in the informal sector and in black markets—continued to work in the shadows.

Informal sovereignties also played a role in helping extend capitalism and the market. In Bandung in the last decades of the twentieth century, informal sovereigns like the *jegger* and Satpam set themselves up as (sometimes predatory) guardians of the growing number of industries, markets, malls, and middle-class housing developments that were spreading across the urban landscape at the time.[25] Partly they were protecting capital and its owners from the specter of crime, but implicitly they were also anticipating and trying to prevent assertions of more collectively articulated territorially based claims. After all, "security" can refer to the security of private property, but as my analysis of the *ronda* showed, it can also be understood as a collective good provisioned, shared, and claimed in common by all who inhabit a particular territory. Over the years, this more collectivist orientation has provided the basis for countless neighborhood protests pitting communities against outside developers and business owners.[26] Seen in this light, the *jegger* and the Satpam were needed in part because they could help protect private ownership against such charismatic collectivist claims.[27]

In sum, informal sovereignties in Indonesia have been highly malleable entities. While they have enjoyed the legitimacy conferred upon them by their aura of perennialism and indigeneity, they have also shown themselves to be highly adaptive to changing circumstances. At their collective and collectivist extreme, they have sometimes seemed like examples of societies "against the state" (Clastres 1987) that could pose a challenge to government authorities and private property, while at other times they have served as state proxies and protectors of capitalist expansion. Whatever shape they have taken, however, their authority has been defined primarily in territorial terms. They have thus played an important role in constituting Bandung—as well as other Indonesian urban centers—as territorial cities.

If, historically, Bandung's informal sovereigns have been characterized as traditional and closely associated with the logic of territoriality, both the colonial and the postcolonial state have served as the primary agents of a self-consciously modern effort to govern the city according to a logic of surveillance. The modern mode of surveillance, as it emerged in Bandung in the late-colonial era, sought to reorder the city in such a way that the real world of bodies, places, and things corresponded to their official representations—to the maps, photographs, lists, and statistics of the state's archive. It was a logic that involved three kinds of work: acquiring knowledge useful to governance, creating a blueprint for an ideal urban order, and establishing mechanisms for making that blueprint of order a reality. The telos of this logic was what Michel Foucault described as panopticism: a mode of power that controls populations through technologies of individualization, registration, spatial partitioning, and regulation aimed at placing the governed subject in "a state of conscious and permanent visibility" (1995, 201).

When we think about the logic of surveillance, it is often in static terms, as an already constituted regime, like Jeremy Bentham's designs for the panopticon prison. As a form of governmentality in Bandung, however, it did not come into being all at once. The gaze unfolded in a step-by-step fashion, mediated by specific subjects, technologies, and domains of knowledge. It started with acts of imagination on the part of government officials, who had a vision for a new city and a reorganized agricultural export economy in this highland region. The vision entailed opening up agriculture to private plantations, bureaucratizing government, sedentarizing the population, refashioning rural and urban landscapes, and building infrastructures to facilitate and regulate traffic. By surveying, mapping, registering, counting, planning, and ordering, surveillance directly facilitated the deterritorialization of institutions, people, places, and flows from prior political economies and modes of life and their reterritorialization within the new economic regime.

As Bandung modernized and grew, the colonial gaze adopted a series of distinct, and progressively encompassing, perspectives on the cityscape.

Initially, with what I have called *the view from the carriage* (and from cars and trains), the gaze remained at a distance from its objects and was concerned primarily with ordering the surfaces that could be seen by officials traveling along roads and railways. With the construction of elevated buildings and the advent of aerial photography, it then progressed to *the view from above*, which focused on mapping and shaping the overall morphology of the city to reflect colonial social divisions. Finally, mediated by the science and technologies of modern hygiene, it came to encompass *the view in depth*, focusing on ordering what were—from the standpoint of European officials—the darkest and most interior spaces in the colony: non-European homes. It was in this view in depth that colonial surveillance most closely approached the ideals of panopticism, while at the same time revealing its limits in the fetishistic conviction that an apparatus that can make things visible will also offer its operator a kind of remote social control.

The desire for a mechanism of remote control was strong in the Bandung context, in part because of the real and perceived social distance between the colonial state and colonized subjects. In the late nineteenth and early twentieth centuries, a number of factors contributed to this sense of distance, including an increased rationalization of the bureaucracy, a growing racialization of colonial culture, and the rise of anticolonial movements. Even in noncolonial contexts, governmental rationalities based on surveillance developed as a means to facilitate centralized forms of rule at a distance (cf. Scott 1998). In colonial contexts, these rationalities—particularly the fascination with identifying, classifying, counting, registering—were arguably more pronounced as they were also key elements in establishing "an illusion of bureaucratic control" over indigenous reality (Appadurai 1993, 317). This was evident in colonial Bandung, where officials—as well as at least one local novelist (see chapter 3)—fantasized about regimes of total panoptic knowledge and control over the people and spaces of the city. As Takashi Shiraishi (2021) has shown, the late-colonial Dutch East Indies state went to considerable lengths to modernize and refashion the policing apparatus to make such panoptic knowledge an institutional reality.

However, the pronounced social distance between rulers and ruled in this context had another effect too, which was to give the surveillance regime a sense of seemingly perennial incompleteness. Whether because government resources were too limited to build out a complete surveillance regime or because officials felt there was something inherently inscrutable about indigenous society, the fantasy of total control was belied by the conviction at the level of policy that, to be practical and effective, the modern surveillance apparatus would need to be coupled with more traditional policing practices. Within the logic of colonial surveillance there was thus a tendency to work with, and to retool, existing practices and technologies, rather than build an entire regime from the ground up.

The sense of incompleteness undoubtedly also contributed to the fascination with spectacles and performances aimed at visually demonstrating the effectiveness of modern surveillance. In the colonial period, the quintessential form such performances took was before-and-after photos, showing how a piece of the cityscape was transformed by a particular governmental intervention. The photos demanded that viewers identify with the aesthetic values of a gaze that saw the preintervention cityscape as disorderly and old-fashioned and the postintervention one as orderly and modern. Ideally, viewers would also gain an appreciation of the hidden power required to effect such a dramatic transformation.

These core features of the colonial logic of surveillance survived into the postcolonial period and became ensconced within formal practices of everyday policing. The New Order regime in particular placed a great deal of emphasis on this aspect of rule. By the late 1990s, those near the bottom of the police hierarchy, and even those in para-state institutions like Siskamling, had become experts in sustaining the state's illusion of bureaucratic control. This was evident in the almost ritualized performances in which high-level police officials would "go down to the field" (*turun ke lapangan*) and be shown—as they looked upon the streets from their car windows, or inspected the precinct's data room—the image of an effectively surveilled urban order. Indeed, the art of maintaining the illusion of bureaucratic control had by then reached such a level of sophistication that the apparatus of surveillance seemed to have diverged from the ideal of the panopticon and morphed into an optical regime with its own distinctive qualities.

The contrast between this optical regime and Bentham's panopticon as analyzed by Foucault is instructive. The panopticon consists of a watchtower surrounded by individualized cells whose occupants are continuously bathed in light. Guards in the watchtower can see but cannot be seen, so inmates must imagine they are being watched, whether or not this is indeed the case. As a result of their total visibility, they end up disciplining themselves. By contrast, within the optical regime I have delineated in this book, there is no total visibility. Rather, it is as if the windows of the watchtower are mirrored on both sides. What the mirrors reflect back is not the viewer but the view or scene the people working the mirrors believe the viewer wishes to see. Those working the mirrors for the benefit of people who wish to see like a state—such as prison guards and police officials—imagine that those looking out from the watchtower desire a view that corresponds to their blueprints of order. Those on the reverse side, in contrast, imagine that subjects looking back at the watchtower wish to see a reflection of themselves as figures of territorial power and prowess, and an image of the state as a site of "unseen powers"[28] whose effects are periodically made spectacularly visible.

These two imaginaries were not without points of intersection or communication. The informal police fraternities, situated precisely at the interface between the state bureaucracy and the territorial city, served to mediate between the two. With roots in police training academies, these fraternities were structured by the bureaucratic logic of successive graduating classes (*angkatan*) and organized into a hierarchy that emphasized the authority of elder over younger "brothers." Founded in a masculinist culture of hazing and violence similar to those found in gangs, such fraternities provided their members with a sense of impunity by promoting the idea that "Seniors can do no wrong."[29] Within the context of everyday policing, they were sustained by an illicit economy consisting of flows of goods, gossip, information, money, and, at least notionally, women. This economy depended in part on extracting value from the performance of routine policing functions and in part on accessing tributary flows through connections into predatory institutions of territorial authority, such as local gangs and security services. In effect, fraternities thus facilitated the deterritorialization of informal sovereignties, on the one hand, and the territorialization of bureaucratic authority, on the other. In doing so, they gave shape to a kind of neopatrimonialism within the police that recognized, and was infused by, territorial practices and ways of thinking.

In their different ways, Siskamling, Petrus, and fraternities each provided points of articulation between the evolving bureaucratic regime of surveillance and territorially based regimes of community protection. Siskamling sought to formalize existing territorial security regimes and integrate them within a larger system of surveillance controlled by the police; the Petrus campaign sought to demonstrate the state's power of surveillance by using secret blacklists to target and eliminate criminalized figures of territorial power; and fraternities sought to leverage the power of local toughs and gangs to support a corrupt economy within the police bureaucracy. But state efforts to encompass, eliminate, appropriate, or subordinate the power of informal sovereigns were only ever partially successful. In part this is because institutions of territorial power at the neighborhood level continued to endure and to produce new figures of informal authority whose relation to the police had yet to be settled. But it was also because the logic of territoriality could be applied to other domains, including—as in the case of fraternities—to the bureaucracy itself.

The dynamics, tensions, and mediations between territoriality and surveillance—and their implications for ordinary urban dwellers—have been very much on display in the years since the end of Suharto's New Order regime and the rise of a more decentralized and democratic polity. We see this explicitly in the case of the plaza in front of Gedung Sate. While the *reformasi* movement successfully pushed back against state authority over the plaza, opening it up to a new array of people and activities, this opening was soon exploited by market forces. The first movements in this direction took place in the informal sector, where commercial activities were quickly subordinated to the territorial logic that had long pertained to the city writ large. However, the withdrawal of Mr. Ayi, the locality's most well-known *jegger*, from the daily life of the plaza meant that the pattern of authority became more fragmented and competitive than it had been in the past. Such fragmentation was presumably exacerbated by the more divided and competitive landscape of authority within the post–New Order state, in which different fraternities positioned themselves to offer *bekking* to particular territorial groups in return for access to protection rackets (Wilson 2015), and by a reorientation of the policing economy toward other forms of off-budget revenue, such as those arising from legal conflicts and patronage relationships with ethnic Chinese businesspeople (see Baker 2010, 2013, 2015). While the resulting pattern of authority that took shape on the plaza was somewhat unruly, it enabled the pop-up market and other commercial activities to grow over a period of more than a decade to a scale and level of intensity that it had never reached in New Order times.

When the mayor and the governor finally intervened to try to get a handle on these developments, they reverted to certain New Order tropes and methods. Putting forward a modernist vision oriented to the aesthetics of the view from above, they sought to cleanse the main part of the plaza of its informal, unruly elements and to give the place a facelift. Without saying so explicitly, they made it clear that they had lists of the *preman* who dominated the plaza, and offered them an ultimatum that, while undoubtedly softer in tone than that used in the era of Petrus and Siskamling, was similarly framed: either submit to formal state power, accept a more circumscribed sphere of activity, and receive a degree of official recognition, or face harsh repression. Conspicuously, as the Kodim commander's statements made clear, this ultimatum was linked not just to a desire to materialize abstract ideas of urban order but also to a desire to address the threat posed by tributary flows that bypassed "the government."[30] In the case of the plaza, then, the modernizing facelift thus entailed the use of surveillance as a way of constraining the growth of informal territorial power by displacing it in some areas and circumscribing it in others, all while bringing it under the overall umbrella of the state.

The story of Gasibu plaza is in many respects a microcosm of Bandung's broader trajectory over the past two decades, which have seen the opening of the public realm to new kinds of popular participation, followed by the encroachment of the market, first under the informal protection of toughs and then under the watchful gaze and disciplinary control of state authorities. This transformation continues to be shaped by the struggles and tensions between territorial modes of authority, which seek to localize and subordinate market forces, and modernist aspirations to transcend territoriality and establish a mode of urban order based on surveillance.

Panopticism and Prowess in Comparative Perspective

The dynamics of urban policing I have described in this book are particular to Bandung and other cities in Java in many of their specifics, but they are also part of a broader story that extends well beyond Indonesia. Consider, for instance, the history of how new techniques and technologies of surveillance were incorporated into policing. The late nineteenth and early twentieth centuries were a time when countries around the world were modernizing and professionalizing their police forces. Techniques and technologies like anthropometry, fingerprinting, filing systems, and mapping were being developed, shared, and adopted widely—so much so that it makes sense to see this as a period when the governmental logic of panopticism began to achieve a global reach. At the same time, historians have shown how various colonial and national genealogies shaped how surveillance regimes were incorporated into the modern state: the kinds of surveillance technologies they used, the kinds of data they collected, and the purposes to which surveillance was put. In the colonial Philippines, for example, "the surveillance state" emerged quite quickly, over the course of the first two decades of the twentieth century, sooner and more systematically than in the Dutch East Indies. As Alfred W. McCoy (2009) has shown, by combining techniques developed for military intelligence with an array of new information technologies, and grafting these onto policing institutions created by the Spanish colonial regime, the American colonial state was able in just a few years to create file cards on the equivalent of 70 percent of Manila's population and to develop "a covert capacity that included media monitoring, psychological profiling, surveillance, disinformation, penetration, manipulation, and, when required, assassination" (28–29). This stood in contrast to developments in the Dutch East Indies, where the surveillance regime grew more incrementally out of the emerging bureaucratic state and took shape comparatively late. The infrastructures were also put to different purposes by the respective colonial powers; whereas in the Dutch East Indies local forms of surveillance were aggregated into a system that became focused on repressing radicalism and policing a "no trespass" zone of political crime, in the Philippines, surveillance was used in support of American efforts to co-opt and subordinate elements of the local political elite (Shiraishi 2021, 8–10). Thus, despite relying on many of the same techniques and technologies, the form and function of these early surveillance regimes also reflected the particularities of the colonial state formations in which they were being deployed. The same can be said for subsequent developments within these regimes during the postcolonial era.

The logic of territorial authority arguably shows an even greater degree of variation across countries and cities globally. As Kivland (2020b, 14) has argued, there has been a global proliferation of informal, or street, sovereignties, and these need to be understood analogically, while accounting for how each one is shaped by global and national forces as well as local cultural dynamics. In many cities in North America, for example, the neighborhood watch amounts to little more than a household commitment to calling the police in the event one witnesses a suspected crime. In settings like this, neighborhood territoriality and the informal domain of authority are weak. In Tanzania, in contrast, territorial groupings similar to the *ronda* have been given state recognition and incorporated into the broader criminal justice system, such that they perform not just a recognized policing function but also a judicial one (Heald 2006). Perhaps the closest analog to the Indonesian case that I have read about is in fact Nigeria, where a volunteer night guard system using patrols, bells, and charms was cultivated by a dualistic colonial state and then later bifurcated into violent marketplace gangs and political thugs, such as the Bakassi Boys, on the one hand, and a reinvented system of privatized security and community policing, on the other (Fourchard 2008; Harnischfeger 2003). As in Indonesia, these groups asserted their rights and spiritual legitimacy based on a masculinist claim to being "sons of the soil" and community protectors (Pratten 2008). While the cultural content and specific institutional dynamics of the two cases undoubtedly differ, it is quite striking how many similarities there are in their colonial and postcolonial histories.

Even where analogical forms of informal sovereignty seem to be more divergent, considering possible parallels between cases can be illuminating. For example, in Jamaica, as described by Deborah A. Thomas (2019, 12), contemporary garrison communities have a kind of political cohesiveness and instrumentality vis-à-vis outside powerholders that one would not likely find in an Indonesian *kampung*. Yet Thomas's account of the central importance of racial assemblages to the formation of garrison communities serves as a forceful reminder that the dualism in urban policing that helped constitute and empower *kampung* institutions like the *ronda* was similarly rooted in a colonial racial divide. While in the postcolonial era this divide has been largely overcoded by distinctions based on socioeconomic class and residential pattern, what originally distinguished such neighborhoods was the fact that they were part of the "native" quarters in the city, and therefore subject to more indirect forms of rule. Furthermore, while the Indonesian experience may not fully bear out Thomas's thesis that "the dominant logic of the plantation . . . undergirds all modern sovereignty projects," it is certainly the case that key figures of Indonesian territorial authority like the *jago*, the *jegger*, the *jawara*, the *preman*, and the *ronda* all have historical genealogies that lead back to the colonial plantation and village. This genealogy is also reflected in the mythology that surrounds such figures, which often highlights the moment they "plant their flag" in the city after their arrival from the countryside (see chapter 2). In these respects, widely shared structural features of colonial political economies may well help explain many of the numerous parallels that can be observed between informal sovereignties across a range of national and urban contexts.

At the same time, it is also important to avoid reifying territorial authority within a given urban or national context. A key argument of this book has been that the logic of territoriality that underpins informal sovereignties is highly malleable and should not be reduced to its manifestation in a particular institutional form. As described in chapter 1, the slit gong, the guard house, and the neighborhood watch may under some circumstances constitute the neighborhood as a rigid territory whose inhabitants are tightly knit into a defensive community, but in other circumstances, they may serve merely to express presence and activate ties, establishing a loose gathering of residents through collective practices that are mainly "just for fun." In this sense, territoriality exists along a continuum from more forceful and more bounded to lighter-touch and more loosely defined; and while at a given historical moment it may manifest in one place along that continuum, as circumstances change, its position on the continuum may also change. Furthermore, territoriality can vary along other axes as well. As a form of institutionalization, the *jegger*-led gang is highly hierarchical and coercive, while the *ronda* is comparatively egalitarian and voluntary. Even in times and places where hierarchy and gangs are seemingly the order of the day, one will find examples of territorial authority being asserted in a more egalitarian, collectivist fashion (and vice versa). This means that each institutional form remains haunted by the ongoing potentiality of other possible forms, which adds to the sense that territorial authority is always open to question, requiring continual attention and maintenance to be effective.

Beatrice Jauregui (2016, 13–14) has described how in India, a key characteristic of police authority is that it is understood to be "provisional," subject to pushback and questioning, and therefore requires continual negotiation with other actors and the navigation of a complex social field. This is likewise true in Indonesia, in part because the police participate—both directly and indirectly—in the claims and counterclaims of the territorial city and therefore are subject to its vicissitudes. But the uncertainty of their authority is also due to the fraught role the police have as mediators between the demands of the territorial city and the demands of the bureaucratic state. This involves more than just mediating between social groups; it involves mediating between differing logics, cultural institutions, performances, and practices (Garriot 2013; Haanstad 2012, 2013). In Bandung, precinct-level police in particular found themselves caught between the two logics, two sets of expectations and two modes of legitimacy. Their response was to stage-manage the demands of surveillance and territoriality in ways that would allow the two logics to coexist, while exploiting the powers they derived from each. Arguably, the contradictions and corruption this entailed only intensified the provisionality of their authority.

In the opening to this book, I described how I felt crossing the Sukamiskin Prison yard, the sense of menace that came from finding myself exposed to two diverging but overlapping forms of authority and their attendant cultures of fear. I also cited Didier Fassin's (2017) observation that the ethnographer who studies policing "experiences fear at the same time as he learns how social control works" (12). For me, the experience of fear was indeed the affective basis for learning how Indonesian social control works, but the analysis came much later, only after living with the fear for some time, tracing its sources, and exploring its ramifications. Understanding this state of fear does not mean being able to escape from it. Even years later, as I write this, I still feel dread in the pit of my stomach when I recall the prison guard's whistle. At the same time, my analysis has also shown that the territorial city contains within it a range of other possibilities beyond those that came to the fore when territoriality was placed into articulation with the fraternities and surveillance regime that came to dominate the New Order state. One in particular stands out for me: that form of Indonesian territoriality that offers a grounded collectivism, loosely structured, caringly maintained, playful, artful, and resilient. In settings where this form of territoriality is manifest, instead of fear, one finds a way of gathering and a way of dwelling that is no less potent for being "just for fun."

GLOSSARY

Adat Custom; customary law

Alat Instrument; penis

Alun-alun Central square

Aman Safe; secure; untouchable

Anak buah Underling; subordinate

Angkatan Generation; graduating class

Anthropometry Biometric system of human identification

Audzubillah May God protect me

Babakan (Sundanese) Subdivision of Kampung

Badjingan Squirrel; scoundrel; thief

Bale-bale Bed

Bangsat Rascal; scoundrel; thief

Barang bekas Used goods

Basa okem *Preman* language; prokem

Bau Measure: 7,096 meters square

Bekas jari/bekas jeridji Finger trace; fingerprint

Bekas kopi Coffee grinds

Bekas pacar Former boyfriend/girlfriend

Bekking Backing (from military, police)

Benteng Fortification; wall

Bersih lingkungan Clean of environment; uncontaminated by "communist" contagion

Besar Large

Bromocorah Recidivist; professional criminal

Calo Agent; ticket scalper; intermediary

Calung Sundanese musical band performance

Camat Subdistrict head

Cap Stamp

Centeng Guard on private land; thug; foreman

Clurit Sickle (often used as a weapon)

Cultuurstelsel (Dutch) Culture system

Dekking See *bekking*

Desa Village

Diisi Filled

Dijaga Guarded

Dikagumi Admired

Disegani Respected

Disiplin Discipline

Diskresi Discretion; euphemism for police violence

Djahat Evil; criminal

Djalan Travel; road

Djoeara Champion

Doersilo Unethical; recidivist; professional criminal

Duits Colonial-era currency

Dukun Sorcerer

Gali-gali Gang member; criminal

Gardu Guard post

Gardujati Guardhouse

Gerakan tutup mulut Closed-mouth movements; "wall of silence"

Golok Machete

Hajj Pilgrimage

Halal Permitted (Islam)

Hancur Wrecked

Haram Forbidden (Islam)

Hati Heart; inner voice

Ilmu Magical science, mystical sciences

Imah (Sundanese) House

Iseng "Just for fun"

Jaga Guard; watch over

Jago(an) Local tough; charismatic leader; a champion in fights; game cock

Jantan (Bahasa prokem) Duel; (Indonesian) male; masculine

Japrem (Bahasa prokem) *Preman*'s allotment

Jawara See *jago*

Jegger See *preman*

Jimat Amulet

Jurukunci Gatekeeper; superintendent

Kakak Elder brother/sister

Kakak asuh adik asuh Elder sibling trains and cares for younger sibling

Kaliwon A secretary to the *patih*

Kampung Neighborhood/quarter

Kapok "Learned a lesson"

Keamanan Security; security forces

Kebal Invulnerable

Kebal hukum Invulnerable to law

Kelemahan Weakness; fatal flaw

Kelengahan Inattentiveness

Keluarga besar Extended family (e.g., of the armed forces)

Kemasukan Entry; possession (by spirit)

Kenal Know; be familiar with

Kenong-kenong Gongs

Kentongan Wooden gong or bell

Kentonganisasi Government program to put *kentongan* in every village

Kepalasuku Tribal leader

Keramat Sacred spot; shrine

Keras Violent; harsh

Kesitan Quick, hasty

Khas Specific; exclusive

Kobokan Dishwater

Koenang-koenang Fireflies; recidivists; professional criminals

Kohkol (Sundanese) see *kentongan*

Koprek (Sundanese) see *kentongan*

Kosong Empty

Kota City

Kriminalitas Criminality

Kris Sacred dagger

Kronco/Kroco (Bahasa prokem) Underlings

Letjet Blister, scratch; professional criminal

Main hakim sendiri "Play judge oneself"; take justice into one's own hands

Maling Thief

Maling doerdjana Professional thief

Maling pitnahan Slandering thief

Maling sebab sakit hati Revenge thief

Maling tipoean Swindler thief

Mantri Government official of low rank

Mantri ukur Surveyor

Masuk Enter; break in

Masyarakat People; society

Mata-mata Eyes; spies

Mayat bertato Tattooed corpse

Melamun Daydream

Membina Develop; cultivate; reform

Menak (Sundanese) aristocracy

Menembus Go through; penetrate

Moetawatir Inherited; passed on from generation to generation; professional criminal

Munjung **stories** Stories about sacrifices made to spirits to attain one's desires

New Order Period during which General Suharto's regime was in power in Indonesia (1966–98)

Niat Desire; intention; plan

Oknum Government official not acting on behalf of the government but on behalf of oneself

Operasi Operation

Orang Person

Orang asing Foreigner; stranger

Orang tidak kenal Foreigner; stranger

Otat (Bahasa prokem) tattoo

Paal/pal Measure: approx. 1 mile

Pancasila Five principles of Indonesian nationhood: belief in one's God; humanity that is just and civilized; unity of Indonesia; democracy guided by the wisdom of representative deliberation; social justice

Pangreh praja "Native" territorial officials

Patih Assistant to regent

Penjahat Criminal; evildoer

Permisi "Excuse me"

Perpanjangan tangan Extended arms; informants

Pesantren Islamic boarding school

Petrus Mysterious Killings

Piket Picket

Pintar Wise (e.g., in the mystical sciences)

Polisi pamong praja "Native" police officials

Pos kamling/pos keamanan Security post

Pos ronda Security post for *ronda*

Prajurit Soldier; a body of armed men responsible for maintaining security in rural areas

Preman A tough (criminalized)

Preman berdasi Suit-wearing *preman*

Pribumi "Native"; indigenous

Punten (Sundanese) see *permisi*

Raja King

Rakyat The people

Razia Operation; police raid

Rijnlandse roede (Dutch) Rhineland birch

Ronda A Portuguese loanword meaning a night watch or neighborhood watch

Rukun Harmonious state of being

Rumah House; home

Rupiah Indonesian currency

Sadis Excessively violent

Sasakgantung Hanging bridge

Satpam Satuan Pengamanan, or Security Unit

Sawah Wet-rice field

Semoet gatel Itchy ant; professional criminal

Setoran Rent; deposit

Sidik jari Finger examination; fingerprint

Sikim (Bahasa prokem) knife

Siluman Invisible; a human who has taken the appearance of an animal

Sirep Fall into a deep sleep (induced by a spell)

Slametan A Javanese communal purification or good-luck ritual

Surat sakti Magically powerful letter

Tahu Know

Tanah Abang A region in Jakarta

Tantangan Challenge

Tetangga Neighbor

Tjap doemoek Touch stamps; fingerprints

Tradisi corps Corps tradition

Trontongan Slits made in the bamboo between the knots, for joining purposes

Tumbak Measure: 3.7674 meters

Tumpeng A ceremonial dish of yellow rice

Ulak goman (Bahasa prokem) see *golok*

Upeti Tribute

Veldpolitie (Dutch) Field Police

Verbetering (Dutch) Improvement

Vrijman (Dutch) Free man

Wadana See *wedana*

Warga Member/citizen; resident

Warung Food stall

Wedana District chief, under supervision of the regent and the *patih*

Wegloopen (Dutch) run away; desert; elope

Weri Spy; evildoer; professional criminal

Woning (Dutch) House

NOTES

Introduction

Epigraph: Benedict Anderson (1990c) "Old State," 95.

Epigraph: Didier Fassin (2017). "Introduction," 12.

Earlier versions of some portions of this introduction were published in Joshua Barker, 2006, "Vigilantes and the State," *Social Analysis: The International Journal of Cultural and Social Practice* 50 (1): 203–7.

1   Foucault developed the concept of governmentality in his later work. It may be defined as "a form of activity aiming to shape, guide or affect the conduct of some person or persons" (Gordon 1991, 2), or as "all those more or less calculated and systematic ways of thinking and acting that aim to shape, regulate, or manage the comportment of others, whether these be works in a factory, inmates in a prison, wards in a mental hospital, the inhabitants of a territory, or the members of a population" (Inda 2005, 2). It generally operates less through force and more through the cultivation of people's desire to govern themselves and others. See also Dean (1999).

2   The idea that there is a gap between the world "out there" and the world of representations, and that there ought to be isomorphism between the two, is integral to a correspondence theory of truth.

3   The territorial vision is certainly not exclusive to these groups. The modern nation-state is a thoroughly territorial entity, and even at the level

of cities, there are many examples of state actors seeking to define their authority in territorial terms.

4   "Informal sovereigns" resonates because very often such groups take shape within the so-called informal sector, such as among street vendors and others working at the margins of the legal economy, and it is there where their base of authority is strongest. It also reflects a discourse within the institution of the police, which highlights the need to engage with "informal leaders" as a means of enhancing law enforcement and security. However, the shortcoming of this term is that it does not fully capture an important aspect of such parastate power: that it is periodically subjected to, and sometimes seeks out, formalization. The lines between formal and informal are thus shifting, which does not mean they do not matter, but it does mean one needs to keep a critical eye on processes of formalization and informalization and not take these categories for granted. The term "street sovereigns" does not carry this connotation and nicely reflects an aspect of parastate power that is a key focus of this book: its territoriality and the fact that it emerges from the street and spaces associated with the street, such as the neighborhood and the marketplace. Furthermore, the term's ties to street economies and street politics are very often what endows it with its force, even if it comes to take on broader identities based on religion, ethnicity, or political stripe. In what follows, I use the terms "informal sovereigns" or "informal sovereignties" when I am describing the general phenomenon and "street sovereigns" when I wish to make explicit the connection to the street.

5   On the history of this gaze in Thailand, see Winichakul (1994) and Vandergeest and Peluso (1995). On its history in Indonesia, see Mrázek (2002).

6   To take just a few further examples: in urban Haiti, *baz*, a kind of social club of neighbors that can serve as a locus of local political power and help manage everyday infrastructures such as garbage collection and informal access to the electrical grid, while also brokering relationships with politicians and NGOs (Kivland 2020a, 503); in Jamaica, "dons" take on a variety of governmental functions: taxing businesses, policing, assisting in relocating informal vendors, mediating conflicts, getting out the vote at election times, and providing welfare (Jaffe 2013, 2015); and in Port Elizabeth, South Africa, the Amadlozi are based on a form of charismatic leadership; they investigate a wide range of crimes and petty disputes, and hold regular public sessions that function much like a court (Buur 2005).

7   Much scholarship on state power outside the Indonesian context has drawn a distinction between the myth, image, or imagination of state power and actual technologies or practices of rule (Migdal 2001; Hansen and Stepputat 2001). Whereas the state presents an image of itself as an

entity that is unified and all-powerful, standing above and ruling over society, practices of rule would seem to belie this myth. On the undermining of this myth in the postcolonial Indonesian state, see Geertz (2004) and Klinken and Barker (2009).

8 Rutherford (2012) has shown how the authority of the state relies on performances of sovereignty that always run the risk of serving to undermine its sovereign claims.

9 Following the end of the New Order, the media interest in crime has grown, fed in part by a growth in the numbers of newspapers and private television stations. Virtually all television stations now have programs dedicated to crime reporting, many of which are modeled after the American reality television show *Cops*.

10 On the use of *rawan* to describe whole regions of the country during Suharto's rule, see G. Robinson (1998).

11 The modern forms of legibility and visual order I am referring to here correspond to those described by Mitchell (1988, 2002) and Scott (1998).

12 My understanding of the logic of territoriality is heavily influenced by the discussion of territory and milieu found in Deleuze and Guattari (1991, chap. 11).

13 For a more comprehensive discussion of theories of the Indonesian state, see Barker and Klinken (2009).

14 For definitions of deterritorialization, see Deleuze and Guattari (1991, 61, 141–44, 453–56). My use of the term is analogous to Weber's use of the term "transpose," as in the following: "Bureaucratic and patriarchal structures are antagonistic in many ways, yet they have in common a most important peculiarity: permanence. In this respect they are both institutions of daily routine. . . . The patriarch is the 'natural leader' of daily routine. And in this respect, the bureaucratic structure is only the counter-image of patriarchalism *transposed* into rationality. As a permanent structure with a system of rational rules, bureaucracy is fashioned to meet calculable and recurrent needs by means of a normal routine" (Weber 1968, 18; emphasis added).

15 On the use of figures as both signs and personifications of broader social transformations, see Barker, Harms, and Lindquist (2013a, 2013b).

16 Indonesian law (UU No. 2 tahun 2002) enshrines the notion that policing is the responsibility of all citizens, stating that "the police function, which encompasses the maintenance of security and social order . . . be carried out by the Indonesian National Police as the instrument of the state, assisted by society." See also Rajab (2003, 2).

17 Indeed, the government has encouraged the emergence of a private-sector security industry in part because it is easier to regulate and surveil the activities of formal businesses as compared with the activities of gangs and toughs.

18 Since heads of households were generally assumed to be men, this also served to reinforce the tight connection between the New Order's militarism and its patriarchy (Suryakusuma 2004a).

19 In an analogous way, Tom Boellstorff (2007, 37) discusses the "coincidence" between systems of meaning deployed by Indonesian gay publications and those found in broader discourses of national belonging.

20 Population figures are based on 2020 data. See "Jumlah Penduduk (Jiwa), 2018–2020," Badan Pusat Statistik Kota Bandung, accessed August 9, 2022, https://bandungkota.bps.go.id/indicator/12/32/1/jumlah-penduduk .html; "Bandung, Republic of Indonesia," Global Future Cities Programme, accessed August 9, 2022, https://www.globalfuturecities.org /republic-indonesia/cities/bandung.

21 Territoriality and bureaucratic state power share a reliance on masculinist ideology, and this ideology is integral to the culture of fraternities.

22 "Cilengka" is a pseudonym.

23 However, it may not differ that much. Sexist ideologies about women and their sexuality were core features of the New Order state and extended into the social fabric. See Suryakusuma (1996); K. Robinson (1998); and Sen (1998).

24 This is a study of policing in a broad sense, not an ethnography of policing within a particular neighborhood. For a study that presents an account of transformations to policing and informal sovereignties within the context of a specific Bandung neighborhood, see Barker (2009c).

Chapter 1: *Ronda*: The Neighborhood Watch

Epigraph: Robert E. Park (1968). "The City: Suggestions," 26–27.

Epigraph: Marc Augé (1995). "From Places to Non-Places," 61.

Earlier versions of some portions of this chapter appeared in Barker, 1999, "Surveillance and Territoriality in Bandung," 95–127.

1 I've seen other substitutes used, including the rim of a car wheel and an empty rocket shell dating from the Second World War.

2 Following Deleuze and Guattari, consistency here is understood "not in the sense of homogeneity, but as a holding together of disparate elements" (Massumi 1992, 7).

3   The gendered division of labor, in which men are militarized and women are constructed as housewives (e.g., by being put in charge of Family Welfare Guidance programs at the neighborhood level), has been a prominent feature of Indonesian state authority, particularly under the New Order (Suryakusuma 2004b, 161–73).

4   Although residents of neighborhoods in Indonesian cities and towns usually claim a high level of territorial solidarity, the communities can be quite diverse and divided. Suzanne Brenner (1998, 222), studying Laweyan, a community in Solo known for its batik entrepreneurship, found that beneath the "unruffled pattern of life that everyone worked so hard to maintain on the surface" was a great deal of status competition and class division.

5   The basic idea of the *ronda* is not peculiar to Indonesia. In Peru, for example, the so-called *rondas campesinas* (peasant rounds) of the 1980s had an important role to play in rejecting the efforts of both the Sendero Luminoso and the Peruvian military to force villagers to take sides in the civil war (Starn 1999). These guards, originally formed by members of local communities to defend against thieves and rustlers, evolved into an armed civil defense force that rejected encroachments by both the military and the guerrillas.

6   *Rukun* means harmonious, *tetangga* means neighbor, and *warga* means citizen. Each Rukun Tetangga consists of a few dozen households (*rumah tangga*), while each Rukun Warga consists of a handful of Rukun Tetangga.

7   An analogous strategy of traffic surveillance was used on a larger scale in old Palembang, where the sultan positioned his palace between the ocean and the hills so that he could keep an eye on foreign visitors, while also monitoring people bringing goods from the highlands to market (Colombijn 2002, 287).

8   The distinction between the milieu and the territory is elaborated in Deleuze and Guattari (1991, 311–22).

9   Among the Anakalang, in eastern Indonesia, exchange processions are often accompanied by the sound of gongs, which carry "distinctive tones capable of indexing the particular village that owns them" (Keane 1997, 82).

10   As in much of Southeast Asia (Errington 1989, chap. 2; Schefold, Domenig, and Nas 2003; Waterson 1990), buildings in Java were often built on piles or stilts. One of the ways thieves would enter into houses was by coming up through the floor. For some stories about the social function of this kind of forced entry in the highland Philippines, see Barton (1963).

11   For a discussion of *ilmu* and its gendered dimensions among the Negeri Sembilan, see Peletz (1996, chap. 4).

12 The specific characteristics of Javanese mystical power are described in Anderson (1990b); Errington (1989); Keeler (1987); and Moertono (1981). In terms of the analysis presented here, what Anderson describes as "Javanese power" could be defined as "the capacity to territorialize." *Ilmu* provides a theory or map of particular territories.

13 The structure of these narratives bears some resemblance to the genre of Javanese travelogues described by Quinn (1992, 6), in which "the world beyond Javanese culture became a kind of new domain of pseudo-supernatural power which individuals could visit, in actuality as narrator and vicariously as reader, and from which they could return with knowledge and personal authority that might benefit Javanese society at large, and at the same time give power and privilege to themselves."

14 Translated into Indonesian by Ajip Rosidi with the title *Memuja Siluman*. *Memuja* means "to worship," while *siluman* means both "invisible" and "a human who has taken the appearance of an animal."

15 For an account of inner power that emphasizes the importance of intersubjective and hierarchical ties between gurus and disciples, see Wilson (2011).

16 An early compilation of *primbon* was published by the Dutch scholar H. A. van Hien, who collected texts from various parts of Java and published them under the title *De Javaansche Geesten Wereld* (*The Javanese Spirit World*). His study provides a kind of encyclopedia of the Javanese spirit world, complete with the names and characteristics of demons and ghosts, descriptions of various calendrical systems in use, and explanations of how to use the divination manuals he includes. Van Hien (1912, 3) distinguishes between four types of magical texts (*petangan*): *pawoekon*, *ngelmoe*, *tengeran*, and *primbon*. These different texts are variously Hindu Buddhist, Hindu Parsi, animist, or Islamic in character. In common usage, however, all are now referred to as *primbon*.

17 The following description is based on van Hien 1912, 330–34.

18 Examples of additional cycles abound in the *primbon* literature; some are based on the human life cycle and on agricultural seasons, and days and nights are divided into various numbers of hours, ranging from as few as three (for a day) to as many as thirty (day and night). Van Hien uses ninety-five pages (1912, 330–425) to describe examples of these systems. See also Ammarell (1988) and Kumar (1985).

19 *Primbon Djawa Bekti Djamal* (n.d.), 12, quoted in Quinn 1975, 43.

20 This "four-five" (center and four points) spatial pattern was so ubiquitous in Dutch East Indies villages that early Dutch structuralists took it to be the basis of a "primitive classification system" (Ossenbruggen 1977).

21 The idea of empty thoughts is also found in Yogyakarta. Steve Ferzacca (2002, 107) found a connection between empty thoughts and empty spaces as they both "put the person at risk for exposure to spirit possession or an anxiety that can lead to madness." Shelly Errington (1989, 90) also claims that in South Sulawesi, it is commonly understood by people that it is dangerous to "stare vacantly into space" because of the risk of entry by spirits. See also James T. Siegel (1986, 56) and his discussion of vagueness of mind and *Sore*, the attempt to rectify this situation.

22 The importance of attentiveness and the dangers of inattentiveness are an enduring theme in the discourse on thieves in Java. For more examples of this line of thinking, see Keeler (1987, 234–42).

23 This system, known in the colonial period as the *girig-stelsel*, is described in Boekhoudt (1908) and Dutch East Indies (1907, 49–50).

24 In the Bandung area in the 1920s, communists, Islamic groups, and local government authorities all struggled to bring *ronda* groups under their control (Lubis 2005, 177–78).

25 It is a "thing" rather than an "object" as the latter implies too much of a subject-object relation. It ought to be thought of as capable of a "becoming." On the becoming of things, see Heidegger's (1971) *Poetry, Language, Thought*, especially "Building, Dwelling, Thinking," and "The Thing."

26 In his classic study of Javanese culture, Clifford Geertz (1976) argued that a simple neighborhood communal meal and prayer, known as the *slametan*, was the elementary ritual of Javanese religion. The *slametan* allowed people of diverse religious beliefs to come together and share in a ceremony aimed at creating a condition of health, security, and well-being (*slamet*). As Andrew Beatty (1999) subsequently observed, the *slametan* continues to be an important part of Javanese religion. What makes it so effective is that it encompasses diversity without making people dwell on it. Participants in the ritual gather together and share something and then return home with their different interpretations of how the ritual fits into their broader set of beliefs. The ritual allows for unity in form while remaining deliberately vague about meaning. In Muslim-majority Java, this studied vagueness is what allows for a measure of unity in the face of what can sometimes be rather stark differences between those whose religious beliefs are a syncretic combination of Islamism and Javanism, and those who aspire to a purer form of modern Islamic belief. If the *slametan* is the elemental ritual of Javanese religion, the *ronda* is the central microregime of Indonesian territoriality and policing.

27 The fact that territorial subjects are privileged over other subjectivities is perhaps not surprising when we consider that scholars of Southeast Asia

have long recognized the importance of spatial metaphors in organizing consciousness (e.g., Errington 1989; Traube 1986).

28 I use the term "legitimate" here, but one might also simply say "powerful." As Anderson (1990b) has shown, charismatic claims do not depend on legitimacy; legitimacy is rather seen as an effect of the force of such claims.

29 Part of the power of the idea of the neighborhood undoubtedly comes from how it articulates with other subjectivities at other socio-spatial scales. As Tom Boellstorff remarks (2005, 35), "One's sense of self as a youth could be global, as a man local, and as a laborer national, all at the same time. Or to be a youth could be both local and global at the same time, intersecting." Seen in this light, the *ronda* is part of a system that produces a social imaginary of locality that has at times intersected with larger-scale collective subjects, like that of the nation.

Chapter 2: Neighborhood Fears, Vigilantism, and Street Toughs

Epigraph: Benedict Anderson (1990c). "Old State," 5.

Earlier versions of some portions of this chapter appeared in Barker, 1999, "Surveillance and Territoriality in Bandung,"

1 Indonesians use a variety of terms to describe the figure of the tough. In Bandung, the most common terms people used were *jegger*, *jawara*, *jago*, and *preman*. The Indonesian term *preman* is sometimes used to refer to any ex-convict or criminal, or to mean "civilian," but these are not the senses in which I use it here. *Preman* has acquired a very charged, negative connotation (see chapter 5) and is therefore not suitable as a purely descriptive term. Outside the Sundanese context, the local tough is often referred to as the *jago*, or fighting cock (Geertz 1973). In Bandung, *jago* tends to be used in its adjectival form rather than as a noun, probably in part because it sounds like a Javanese word, which for Sundanese listeners runs counter to the notion that these are the preeminent figures of locality. The terms *jegger* and *jawara* are common among Sundanese speakers in Bandung. *Jawara* is a more traditional Sundanese term, and, in the Bandung context, it is generally used to refer more restrictively to adepts in martial arts (e.g., *pencat silat*). The term *jegger* is more modern and can encompass a scrappier and less cultured kind of street tough. It is thus well suited to the Bandung city context discussed here. For historical analyses of these types of figures, see Onghokham (1978, 112–57); Rush (1990); Schulte Nordholdt (1991); and Smail (1964, 88–89). On the genealogy of the term *preman*, see Ryter (2005, 2001, 124–55) and Anderson (1999, 6–9).

2   Kayu Agung, a region in southern Sumatra, is one of the most famous places for Robin Hood–type characters. Its form of *merantau* (circular migration) has often been tied up with professional thievery. According to Apriana Z. Rachman (1985), people in Kayu Agung can recount stories about criminality from all over Indonesia, and indeed the world. They call their thieves *duta keliling* (roving ambassadors), and there are rules about whom one may steal from (i.e., outsiders) and why. On the tradition of "great" or "noble" thieves in Java, see Keeler (1987, 236–37).

3   For a discussion of the Mysterious Killings campaign, see chapter 5.

4   Jérôme Tadie (2002, 414) provides an excellent description of the ways that criminal gangs in the Senin area of Jakarta divide up urban space into "micro-territories," expressed by the saying "Every forest has its tiger." His research also shows that many gangs in Jakarta define themselves and their territories in explicitly ethnic terms (or sometimes by the place of origin of their members).

5   Indonesian newspapers and novels often refer to thieves as "uninvited guests" (*tamu yang tidak diundang*).

6   In the nineteenth century, the neighborhood watch apparently had a whole kit of tools for the purpose of catching thieves. One observer offers the following description:

> The three implements which are seemingly indispensable for constabular use are the *bunday*, the *kumkum*, and the *toyah*. The first is a short pole, about four feet in length, upon the top of which are tied two pieces of wood, so placed as to meet in an acute angle, and open towards the ends, like the distended jaws of an alligator; the resemblance being made greater by the addition of dried stems of sharp thorns, tied on the two pieces of wood, and looking somewhat like rows of teeth. These effectually serve the purpose of detaining any runaway around whose neck they are fixed, lacerating the flesh to a terrible extent should he offer the slightest resistance.
>
> The man into whose keeping the *bunday* is confided is called upon to act on the escape of the prisoner. In pursuing him he runs at full speed, endeavouring to fix the instrument round the neck, waist, arm, or leg of the pursued, who, as soon as he feels the sharp thorns encircling his body, generally comes to a full stop. Should he prove, however, one of those determined ruffians who are dead to all feelings of pain, another instrument, the *kumkum*, is brought into play. This heavy-looking weapon, which is of a very formidable aspect, consists of a bar of iron in the shape of a small sword, attached to the top of a stave some five feet long. The third of these singular instruments is the *toyah*, which is as simple in its construction as the use to which it is put is novel. It is in the shape of a

pitchfork, the points of which are purposely made blunt. This is certainly the most humane-looking of the three, and it is to be hoped therefore the one first tried against the delinquent. The object for which it is used is that of bringing the pursued down on his knees, and thus effectually stopping his further progress. This is accomplished by thrusting the open space between the prongs against the knee-joint—from the back of course—and so compelling the man by the force and suddenness of the attack, to make a genuflexion; the result of which is, that he becomes an easy prey to the pursuer. In the interior of some guardos [guard posts] there are some other weapons, or *sunjata*, such as the *tomba*, or long spear, but none of them so ludicrously novel as those I have just described. (D'Almeida 1864, 22–24)

In present-day Bandung, people normally capture the thief with their bare hands or use implements that they find at hand.

7   I am unaware of cases in which female thieves have been beaten in this way, but it may well happen.

8   On the jumping eye, see Deleuze and Guattari (1984, 204).

9   On the importance of audiences for spectacles of sovereignty, see Rutherford (2012).

10   In his study of mock head-hunting rituals in South Sulawesi, Kenneth George (1996, 186–87) describes how such competitive displays of territorial power shape political relationships through time. He notes that villagers in Sulawesi rehearse the scenes of violence over and over, not only for their mythic value but also as a way of "keep[ing] *collective memory* moving through time" (187).

11   *Munjung* translates to "heaping." It connotes excess and is used to describe the practice of seeking out and making a pact with a spirit in return for receiving what one desires.

12   This method of disposing of corpses was used in the Mysterious Killings campaign during the 1980s (see chapter 5).

13   Andrea Corsini Harjaka Hardjamardjaja (1962, 32–35) describes a less moralizing—and more messianic—variant of this kind of story in Java. In this story, based on the actual biography of a famous religious teacher in Java in the 1920s, a humble *ronda* guard sought spiritual power through fasting and meditation. Rather than submitting to an outside state, he received a gift of supernatural spiritual potency (*wahyu*) and was proclaimed by his followers to be the coming of the righteous prince (*ratu adil*). His disciples built a palace for him, which was modeled on the *kraton* of Solo. Fearful of his growing power, the authorities arrested him and used a powerful dagger (*kris*) from the real *kraton* to subdue his followers.

14   For a discussion of the difference between these terms, see note 1 of this chapter.

15   For other accounts of the biographies of various *jago* and *jawara*, see the studies by Cribb (1991); Tadie (2002); Wilson (2002); Fauzi (2004); Barker (2009b); and Wilson (2011).

16   The vast majority of such communal violence is precipitated by what are recognized as "tiny problems" (*masalah sepele*) like an offhand insult.

17   For a rich discussion of the role of *calo* and the changing culture of brokers in Indonesia, see Lindquist (2012).

18   The terms *otat, jantan, ulak goman,* and *sikim* are not in fact Indonesian but what's called basa okem or prokem, a slang language used by criminals and youth (Chambert-Loir 1983) that likely started in the country's prisons.

19   Tadie (2002, 417) describes the various senses of *pegang* when used in this kind of context as follows: to control, to hold, to master, and to run affairs.

20   These quotes, and the subsequent ones, reflect mostly verbatim written notes I took while reviewing a routine police report, or BAP. The report was based on interviews by the police with suspects and victims, which were then typed up as first-person narratives by the investigating officer.

21   In this regard, the *jegger* is analogous to the large-bodied slit gong discussed in chapter 1, which incorporated smaller territories into a larger whole.

22   See John T. Sidel (1999) on "bossism" for a larger-scale, more formalized instance of "strongman rule" in the Philippines. In Indonesia, this kind of authority generally remains more nascent and informal (see also Bourgois [2003] for an ethnographic parallel in the United States).

23   Ian Wilson (2015) has used the lens of the protection racket to understand changes in the character of large militias in Jakarta in the post-Suharto period.

24   The presumption that penis implants increase female sexual pleasure apparently dates back to their emergence in Southeast Asia. Anthony Reid (1988, 148–50), who has documented this history, suggests that the interest in female sexual gratification is reflective of the power enjoyed by Southeast Asian women in the fifteenth and sixteenth centuries. Laurie J. Sears (1996, 31) provides a different interpretation, noting that men gain status by virtue of their willingness to endure the operation of inserting the implants. In a study of penis implants among working-class men in contemporary Southeast Asia, Terence Hull and Meiwita Budiharsana (2001) found that men most commonly list female sexual

pleasure as the reason for obtaining an implant. However, interviews with female sex workers revealed that many women find these implants to be "strange and uncomfortable" (64).

25 Historically, both tattoos and penis inserts have been widespread forms of body modification in South and Southeast Asia (Anderson 2004; Brown, Edwards, and Moore 1988; McCabe 2003; Tannenbaum 1987, 1993). On the use of tattoos as a form of punishment in various Southeast Asian societies, see Andaya (2005). On the use of tattoos in India to deter convicts from escaping, see Anderson (2004).

26 On tattoos as a sign of criminality, see also chapter 5.

27 The association of tattoos with the magic of invulnerability is also found in Burma (Tannenbaum 1987).

28 The term for spies in Indonesian, *mata-mata*, also means "eyes."

29 On the etymology of *preman* and its relation to the Dutch *vrijman*, see Ryter (2001, 129–30).

30 The history of the *jago* in the context of the colonial state and monopoly capitalism has been discussed by James R. Rush (1990).

Chapter 3: Urban Panopticon

Epigraph: Walter Robert van Hoëvell (1852). "Tjoeroek penganten," 427.

1 Allen Feldman (1997, 30) describes scopic regimes as "the agendas and techniques of political visualization: the regimens that prescribe modes of seeing and object visibility and that proscribe or render untenable other modes and objects of perception. A scopic regime is an ensemble of practices and discourses that establish the truth claims, typicality, and credibility of visual acts and objects and politically correct modes of seeing."

2 This story appears in Ido (1949) (cited in Kunto 1984, 13–14) and in a political pamphlet entitled *Poeseurna Paseondan* (Pagoejoeban "Pasoen-dan" 1925, 9). An alternate story claims that the regent at the time, a man by the name of Wiranatakusumah II, chose the location after having it pointed out to him by a ray of light (Lubis 2005, 116–17).

3 For an account of the gradual bureaucratization of indigenous government in Java, see Sutherland (1979).

4 The earlier case is described in the following works: Ekadjati, Kartikasari, and Masduki 1993; Drewes 1985; Hilman 1982; and Kartadinata 1921.

5 This act should also be seen in the context of an international wave of terror attacks and assassinations at the turn of the twentieth century (Anderson 2005).

6   On the Bandung plan, see Lubis (2005, 131). For discussions of old-style Java-
     nese town plans, see H. J. van Mook's ([1926] 1958) description of Kota Gede
     and H. F. Tillema's ([1922] 1958) description of "an average regency seat."

7   Not all *kampung* in Bandung were named after the places from which
     their inhabitants had migrated. Some were called by the name of the
     kampung's founder (especially in Chinatown), by the name of crops that
     were harvested there, or by the name of a local landmark (e.g., Gardujati
     = guardhouse, Cukangjati = small bridge, Sasakgantung = hanging bridge,
     Regol = side door) (Ekadjati, Hardjasaputra, and Marlina 1985, 60–62).

8   The plural society is a society in which ethnic groups are culturally, lin-
     guistically, and often residentially divided, but meet in the marketplace
     (Furnivall 1956, 304–5). Bandung did come to stand as a relatively stark
     example of such a society, but its enclaves were undoubtedly more mixed
     than Furnivall's theory might lead us to assume. This was certainly the
     case in the towns of Makassar and Semarang, where Heather Sutherland
     (1986) and Theo Stevens (1986) found that actual residential patterns dur-
     ing the colonial period showed a rather more complex social morphology
     than that suggested by the image of the plural society.

9   It was during this period, in the year 1900, that the first steam-powered
     automobile made its appearance in Preanger. The smooth, rolling view
     afforded by such conveyance would become even more important as au-
     tomobiles became more common.

10   See Kunto (1984, 94) and Dutch East Indies (1936, 78). The first compre-
     hensive census of Bandung's population took place in 1920. According
     to W. Brand (1958, 227), Bandung was the only town in the colony that
     maintained a reliable register of the indigenous population.

11   This plan was proposed by H. F. Tillema, a Dutch expert on health and
     an obsessive photographer. On Tillema, see Mrázek (1997, 21–23) and Coté
     (2002).

12   In the prewar period aerial photography was quite popular around Ban-
     dung, but it was only in the 1970s that it came to be used explicitly for
     the purposes of *kampung* improvement. The impetus for this later use
     of aerial photography came from engineers at the Bandung Institute of
     Technology (Pollé and Hofstee 1986). On the question of how the aerial
     view came to be associated with ideas of command and control, see Dor-
     rian (2007).

13   Although the primary audience for this modern urban architecture was
     European, it left a powerful impression on some early nationalists. One
     of these was Indonesia's first president, Sukarno, who graduated from the
     Bandung Institute of Technology and designed a few buildings around

town. It was Sukarno who went on to promote monumental building projects after independence, and it was he who chose Bandung as the site for the famous Asia-Africa Conference in 1955. That conference was arguably the last time Bandung would be envisioned as a prototype for the future, though as a prototype of a national-modern rather than a colonial-modern form of development and of equality rather than hierarchy.

14 Chief among these reports was the multivolume *Onderzoek naar de mindere welvaart der inlandsche bevolking op Java en Madoera* (Dutch East Indies 1905–14). Others focused more specifically on problems of welfare in urban areas (cf. Coté 2002, 324–31).

15 On the growing racism of the late-colonial period and its effect on social boundaries between groups in the Dutch East Indies, see Taylor (1983) and Stoler (1991).

16 For a discussion of how these anxieties manifested during an exhibition on hygiene in Bandung in 1927, see Honggare (2021).

17 This gave rise to a veritable "culture of improvement" (Pollé and Hofstee 1986, 117), or what Tania Li (2007) describes as a form of governmentality based on "the will to improve."

18 Not all these changes resulted from fear of the plague. There were also the mosquitoes that carried malaria and the bacteria that caused dysentery, for example, which was the impetus for a complete reorganization of the water system (filling in fishponds and turning them into wet-rice paddies, the building of latrines, restrictions placed on river use).

19 Foucault describes a similar arrangement in nineteenth-century European hospitals as follows: "It was necessary to avoid undue contact, contagion, physical proximity and overcrowding, while at the same time ensuring ventilation and circulation of air, at once dividing space up and keeping it open, ensuring a surveillance which would be both global and individualising while at the same time carefully separating the individuals under observation" (1980b, 146).

20 According to Foucault, this distinction between the dream of total visibility and the surveying gaze is what characterizes the difference between Jean-Jacques Rousseau and Jeremy Bentham. For Rousseau, "it was the dream of a transparent society, visible and legible in each of its parts, the dream of there no longer existing any zones of darkness," whereas for Bentham it was "a visibility organised entirely around a dominating, overseeing gaze" (Foucault 1980b, 152).

21 For a rich textual analysis of these films and their use of microscopy and before-and-after visualizations, and the qualities as spectacles, see Stein (2006).

22 For a discussion of how photography in the Dutch colony served two main aims, one concerning scientific legibility, the other aesthetics, see Siegel (2011, 76–96).

Chapter 4: Subjects of Surveillance

1 Women's sexuality has been an important site for defining relationships between the colonizer and the colonized in colonial and postcolonial settings. This was true not just of native women's sexuality but also for European women in colonial settings (see Stoler 2010).

2 In Indonesian newspapers, brothel districts in cities are called *lokalisasi*, or "localizations." The way the state controls prostitution has remained largely unchanged since the mid-nineteenth century.

3 Schoute (1937) is referring to a brothel set up in 1843 by the resident of Bagelen in Purworedjo.

4 For an account of a more recent use of cards to monitor prostitution in Batam, see Lindquist (2009, 80, 164).

5 In addition to driving the development of new surveillance regimes, the fear of impostors may have had the ironic effect of teaching those being surveilled that they possessed the power to become someone else when (not having intended to pose as someone else) they themselves had never thought they were anyone other than themselves (see Siegel 1997, 80–84).

6 A very similar quote, which Bertillon attributed to Belgian prosecutor Edmond de Ryckère, is cited in Cole (2001, 53): "To fix the human personality, to give each human being an identity, a positive, lasting and invariable identity, always recognizable and easily demonstrable, such seems to be the broadest aim of this new method" (Bertillon 1896, 80, cited in Cole 2001, 53).

7 "To find [a definition of the word 'bread'] in the dictionary, for instance, I look first for the letter B, eliminating the 25 other letters of the alphabet; then I find R as a subdivision of B, then E as a subdivision of BR, then A and D in a similar way, until I find that very word in the only place in the dictionary where—if correctly spelled—it can properly be filed. Similar analyses and eliminations are made in searching for a description in an anthropometrical file, with results almost as favorable" (Bertillon 1977, 9). Similar comparisons to the dictionary were also made in discussions of the classification system used for fingerprinting. See Mrázek (1997, 18).

8 On the role that the "myth of racial homogeneity" (126) played in the adoption of fingerprinting in other countries, such as India and the United States, see Cole (2001).

9   On the paranoia that resulted from the inscrutability of "native" society for colonial administrators in Java, see Onghokham (1978).

10   In the late 1970s, Ward Keeler (1987, 238–39) also observed that people he knew in Central Java were particularly fearful of thieves during festive occasions like shadow puppet performances.

11   The same system was used in a modified form for the supervision of health workers in the hygiene program (see chapter 3).

12   In this period, local police were unsalaried and few and far between. In case of a theft in which an initial search did not turn up the culprits, the victim would usually hire local people to track down the thieves and recover the stolen goods.

13   According to Soeropringgo (1906), it was usually only professional thieves who were recognized as criminals in the legal sense. The other forms of theft involved the destruction or hiding of evidence, so no legal case could be made. This did not mean nothing was done about the other cases, but resolution did not take place through the courts.

14   On this fear, see Henk Schulte Nordholt (1991, 74–92) and Onghokham (1978, 112–57).

15   In this regard, the assassination attempt on the resident and regent of Bandung is a case in point (see chapter 3). Although the resident was informed of the attack before it took place, his immediate reaction was to call Martanagara, who then had to mobilize all the spies in the region to find the culprits. Even though Martanagara had only taken office that same day, he still had more access to what was going on in the town than the resident.

16   The village *ronda* was variously called the *ronda kota* (city ronda), *ronda djalan prijaji* (*priyayi* street *ronda*), or *ronda besar* (big *ronda*).

17   The recording of criminal reports required literacy, so most of the *mantri polisi* were drawn from the ranks of the *priyayi*. The first handbooks were directed at this class of persons. For examples, see Djajanegara (1911) and Hesselink (1911).

18   See Sutherland (1979, xix).

19   The following account is based on Sutherland (1979, 92–93) and Oudang (1952, 12–32).

20   Batavia was an exception to this, as it had long used a combination of Dutch police and "native" subordinates.

21   The following account is based on Oudang (1952, 12–32). For an account of how these reforms unfolded in the city of Surabaya, see Bloembergen (2007).

22 The following account is based on Poeze (1994, 229–46) and Sutherland (1979, 92–93).

23 For an account of this history of overhearing and its role in the national awakening, see Siegel (1997, chaps. 1–3).

24 Simon A. Cole (2001, 166) explains the broader enthusiasm for finger-printing as follows: "Anthropometry looked like a science; fingerprinting looked like a technology. Anthropometry was observational; fingerprint-ing was mechanical. Anthropometry evoked the rigors of scientific ob-servation; fingerprinting evoked the efficiencies of mass production."

25 Mrázek's article shows beautifully how dactyloscopy fit into the larger pattern of technological surveillance in the late-colonial Indies.

26 The term *bekas* is territorial, I would suggest. In addition to meaning "trace," it also connotes the residue or remainder of other types of con-tacts (e.g., *bekas pacar* = former lover; *bekas kopi* = coffee grinds; *barang bekas* = used goods). It can also refer to a "receptacle" of some kind. On the differences between the trace and the scientific fingerprint, see Ginzburg (1990).

27 On this point, Michael T. Taussig (1993, 222) cites Sir Francis Dalton, who reported that he was informed by Sir William Herschel that "because it was so hard to obtain credence to the signatures of the natives . . . he thought he would use the signature of the hand itself, chiefly with the intention of frightening the man who made it from afterward denying his formal act." For an account of how the Bertillon method was used in India, see also Anderson (2004).

28 More precisely, the only interaction it says anything about is the interac-tion between light, the operator, the subject, and the measuring tools.

29 "A person's fingerprint, John Henry Wigmore, the leading US scholar on legal evidence, famously asserted in 1923, 'is not testimony about his body, but his body itself'" (Cole 2001, 167, citing Wigmore 1923, 874).

30 Such birth certificates are the precursors of the identity card in use in Indonesia today. For a fascinating analysis of how photographic identity cards mediate relations between citizen and state in Indonesia, see Stras-sler (2010, 124–63).

31 As Pemberton (1994) has shown for Central Java, local rulers were mas-ters at deploying *adat* custom and etiquette as a means of culturally subordinating—through language and bodily comportment—both the populations they ruled and the colonizing Dutch. As a form of disciplin-ary power, *adat* was thus of central importance. At times, Dutch surveil-lance encroached on spheres normally governed by *adat*. In the hygiene program, for example, disciplines were imposed that required people to

adopt new practices, such as brushing their teeth, washing their hands at particular times, using outhouses, and so forth. Moreover, books were published that specifically addressed the hygienic aspects of traditional ceremonies, like teeth filing in western Java, and forms of healing (see, for example, Sangkanningrat [n.d.]).

32 For an insightful analysis of the discourse of modernity in Indonesia as bringing "light" to the colony, see Mrázek (2002).

33 Other identities, far more important to early twentieth-century society than those bodies recognized by scientific identification, included various ethnic identities. John Pemberton and Tsuchiya Kenji, for example, have described various Javanese identities available through the languages of the Solonese *kraton* and Dutch ethnography. Moreover, James T. Siegel has shown that the Indonesian "I" was highly mobile during this period and that the most powerful mediator of identities was not in the Dutch or Javanese spheres, but rather in the sphere of the lingua franca with its seemingly limitless capacity to defer recognition. From the standpoint of a national identity consolidated through the state, however, Benedict Anderson has noted the central importance of the colonial state's use of surveillance to overlay a grid on what would become the national domain (Anderson [1983] 1991; Pemberton 1994; Siegel 1997; Tsuchiya 1990).

Chapter 5: State of Fear

Epigraph: W. P. Nainggolan (1984). *Pengunaan lokasi pertokoan yang dilaksanakan oleh Satpam dalam rangka menunjang tugas Poltabes Bandung*, 44.

An earlier version of this chapter appeared as Joshua Barker, 1998, "State of Fear: Controlling the Criminal Contagion in Suharto's New Order," *Indonesia* 66: 7–44.

1 In the Sukarno era, the army had also been used to put down regional rebellions against Jakarta's rule. It frequently cultivated local militias to aid in these efforts.

2 Also referred to by the names Mysterious Shootings (*Penembakan Misterius*) or Mysterious Shooters (*Penembak Misterius*).

3 Among the police, it is also frequently called the Sistem Swakarsa (Self-Help System). The police have defined it as "Unity and sameness of people's understanding, attitude, behavior within various living environments that arise in the shape of care toward preventing, prohibiting, tackling, and responding in an appropriate and speedy way to tendencies and/or cases of disturbance of order, crime, and calamities that could or

are striking at their interests, themselves, or their surroundings, along with being able to take care of themselves in accordance with changing circumstances" (*Laporan akhir penelitian industrial* 1994, 4).

4 This is reminiscent of the Dutch fears of rats in Bandung's houses that were "perfectly content to nest in perfectly visible positions" (see chapter 3).

5 On the way in which the solar eclipse of 1983 was used to justify the Mysterious Killings, see Pemberton (1994, 314–16). On the shadowy world of crime during the colonial period, see Schulte Nordholt (1991, 74–92).

6 According to Jeffery Winters (1996, 122), 1981 saw the peak in availability of the New Order state's discretionary funds.

7 For a detailed account of tensions between members of the political elite and how they played themselves out in the Petrus campaign, see the excellent analysis by Bourchier (1990).

8 According to Siegel (1998), contemporary newspaper accounts of Petrus portrayed *gali-gali* as having the following characteristics: they were excessively violent (*sadis*), they were organized, they took in a lot of money, they had an uncontrolled force of expression, and they desired what everyone else desired. *Preman* and *jegger* are similar types. For a discussion of the different valences of the terms, see note 1 in chapter 2.

9 For the most part, however, the police regarded such gangs as a problem of juvenile delinquency and not as a serious threat.

10 For the statistical characteristics of this crime wave, see Bourchier (1990).

11 For an account of how this emphasis on violence also serves to advance the interests of Indonesian elites, see Collins (2002).

12 Kopkamtib was a structure of command initiated in 1965. Headed first by Suharto, and later by Sumitro and Sudomo, its aim was to "restore national security and order" by establishing a group within the military that had extraordinary powers and did not have to follow laws of criminal procedure. During the 1960s and '70s, Kopkamtib was primarily used to eliminate, or at least frighten, "communists" and to suppress political dissent. Siskamling and Petrus marked a shift in Kopkamtib away from political threats to "criminal" threats.

13 In South Jakarta alone in 1970, the police listed thirty-nine gangs. The names of some women's gangs: the Fu Man Chu, the Single Girl, the Pretty Doll, Monalisa, the Hunter Boys, Amigos. Regional gangs: Banten Boy, Batak Boy, AMS (Ambon-Maluku-Seram). ABRI (Armed Forces of the Republic of Indonesia) gangs: Gang Siliwangi, Gang Beerland, Gang Panser. Mixed gangs: Santana, the Trouble, SBC (Santa Barisan Setan), MBC

(Manggarai Boy's Club), Sarlala (Sarang Laba Laba), Kasko (Kami Selalu Kompak), Kobel, Tjablak, Scarlet BCD, Motor Scarlet, Flamboyant, Devil Kids, the Casanova SK 700, Provost, Chabreek, 9 AK, Mr. Lonely Heart, the Bat Boy MDC, the Flaming Gos, Leo Patra, the Legos. In Bandung: Mexis, AMX, BBC (Buah Batu Boy's Club), Melos (Menak Lodaya Sadis), Megas (Menak Galunggung Sadis), Amek (Anak Muda Emong Karapitan), Hippies Dago, Dollar, Patorados, Bexis, TXC. See Soenarjo (1970, 59-63).

14   For a discussion of the dynamics of urban gang life in Bandung prior to the New Order, see Barker (2009c).

15   For a study of a *jegger*-based gang, see chapter 2 and Muflich (1979).

16   See, for example, the study of Gang "X," which showed strong tendencies toward bureaucratization (Tomasoa 1981).

17   On Pemuda Pancasila, see also Anderson (2001, 15-16).

18   On Massa 33, see Mappalahere (1995, 2) and *Surabaya Post*, March 18, 1995.

19   Satpam is an abbreviation of Satuan Pengamanan (Security Unit). Hansip is an abbreviation of Pertahanan Sipil (Civil Defense), a kind of civilian guard that is sometimes also called Kamra (from Keamanan Rakyat, or People's Security). Both Satpam and Hansip have entered the lexicon of everyday speech to refer to the guards both as individuals and as social types.

20   In addition to its work with Siskamling, the Guidance Unit is also involved in training and working with youth groups.

21   *Centeng* is translated by the journalist as "thugs," but in pre-Siskamling terminology it meant simply "night watchman" (e.g., of warehouses).

22   In Bandung in 1996, more than half of the Satpam guards working had attended these.

23   *Residivis* has a broader sense than the English word "recidivist": it refers not just to "repeat offenders" but often to "ex-convicts" as well.

24   Much of this mirrors the type of intelligence apparatus set up in East Timor. Compare, for example, the account found in Tanter (1990, 244-45).

25   Surat Keputusan Kapolri No. Pol. SKEP/220/VI/1982, June 14, 1982.

26   The police-issued "letter of good behavior" was a required document for almost any employment outside the informal sector (with the exception of foundations and businesses set up for employing and reforming ex-convicts). This regulation thus closed off one of the few avenues ex-convicts had to regain the rights of ordinary citizens, condemning them to a life of economic—as well as social—exile.

27 *Surabaya Post*, February 22, 1982; *Surabaya Post*, March 8, 1982.

28 On the role of the *calo*, see Lindquist (2012).

29 One of the reasons the armed forces were in favor of Satpam was that it would provide an employment opportunity for low-ranking retirees whose pensions were very small (and perhaps keep them out of trouble).

30 The nongang guards that were hired were initially mostly low-level armed forces retirees, but as the program expanded, the guards came to include young men and women, almost all of whom were either villagers or people who came from the poorer areas of towns.

31 In September 1982, before Petrus began, the family of a military commander in East Java had been murdered by thugs. The military's response to this was to avenge the killings by executing the suspects and throwing their corpses in a river (Schulte Nordholt 2002). It is likely that this event and similar killings in the Jember-Bondowoso area some months before were the immediate models for the Petrus killings (see Bourchier 1990, 185). One wonders, however, if these East Java commanders got their idea from a wave of killings they had overseen in Jember in 1981. The victims of these killings, of which there were twenty-seven, were accused of being sorcerers and *bromocorah*, and were killed by the "masses" from villages where they lived. They, too, were tied up or placed in sacks and thrown into rivers. See *Surabaya Post*, March 2, 1981.

32 For more on the colonial genealogy of such public order operations, see chapter 6.

33 Pemberton (1994, 312), describing the killings in Solo, notes that the Solonese morgue during this period, which was inundated with corpses, had a kind of open-door policy for people to come and look. For more about police spectacles, see chapter 6.

34 Adding names, because of local and personal politics, was probably more acceptable.

35 See Rochijat (1985).

36 In Yogyakarta, the people *Tempo* mentioned as being worried about this ultimatum were all members of protection rackets and gangs (i.e., *calo*, *petugas keamanan*) (*Tempo*, April 16, 1983, 54).

37 Of course, there was no guarantee that those who reported to the authorities would not themselves be killed (for a case of this in Yogyakarta, see *Tempo*, April 16, 1983). Furthermore, we will never know how many people failed to report because they were *too* frightened of being killed, or how many failed to report because they did not see themselves as suspect and thus were not frightened at all.

38 This story was recounted in a police college thesis by Sumarwoto (1984, 77). This thesis itself raises the question of whether a person wearing a tattoo is necessarily a criminal. It indicates that the association between the two— and their life-or-death implications—did not always sit well with the police.

39 Indeed, tattoos have at various times been interpreted as an index of criminality. Nineteenth-century criminal anthropologist Cesare Lombroso and his Italian School of criminology believed that a predilection for criminality could be gleaned from the body, and compiled a list of physical characteristics, including tattoos, said to be typical of the "born criminal" (Cole 2001, 23–24, 57–58; Gell 1993, 11–18).

40 On the various meanings of the game cock, see Geertz (1973).

41 This respondent also noted that he did not put the tattoos on all at once because there was no way he would have been able to stand the pain.

42 My terminology, not Bourchier's. On fraternities, see chapter 6.

43 The appropriation of the power represented by criminals took place through imitation. The tendency of killings during the Petrus campaign to mimic the violence attributed to the figure of the *gali* has been analyzed by Siegel (1998, 108–9). According to Siegel, this mimicry is especially apparent in the excessive violence used to kill the campaign's victims.

44 For cases of mimicry after Petrus, see, for example, "Two Corpses in a Sack Turn Out to Be Recidivists Killed by Villagers," *Media Indonesia*, September 20, 1996; "Accused of Stealing Piggy Bank, Village '*Jegger*' Dead by Mass Punishment," *Suara Karya*, December 15, 1995; "*Preman* Thrown in River," *Suara Karya*, August 20, 1996.

45 Because of the nature of Petrus, it is difficult to obtain first-hand accounts of what those who conducted the killings thought about it. For the most part, the police I asked denied any knowledge about the campaign or made it clear that it was not something that should be discussed. Nonetheless, I was told some stories about similar events.

46 The impression I was given was that Petrus-like killings have become a standard police tool for fighting violent crime.

47 I could not be sure I had caught the actual code number. In my original field notes I tentatively recorded it as "486," but have since learned that "86" is an American slang term for getting rid of someone, so perhaps this was the code being used.

48 On the role of secrets in the culture of shadow police hierarchies, see chapter 6.

49 As Joni talked about his orders, I got the sense that he did not really know where exactly they came from, only that he must obey them. And at no

time during our discussions did he mention any of the ideological reasons behind the war in East Timor or the operations against *preman*. For him the "reasons" for these wars never even entered the picture; he was concerned merely with the power and danger associated with his own role in them.

50 In fact, as noted above, estimates of the number of people killed as a result of Petrus are in the range of about five to ten thousand people.

51 Other cases of these Petrus impostors: "Wanita Pemeras yang Mengaku Penembak Misterius Ditangkap" [Woman extortionist claiming to be Mysterious Shooter arrested], *Surabaya Post*, January 14, 1984; "Memeras dengan Dalih 'Petrus'" [Extorting with 'Petrus' subterfuge], *Surabaya Post*, June 2, 1984.

52 By 2022, there were an estimated one million Satpam guards across Indonesia, making them far more numerous than the police, whose personnel reportedly numbered approximately 450,000. See M. Mahmud, "Wow jumlah Satpam 1 juta orang, dua kali jumlah polisi," iNewsDepok.id, February 2, 2022, https://depok.inews.id/read/38562/wow-jumlah-satpam-1-juta-orang-dua-kali-jumlah-polisi.

53 At the same time, the police were given oversight not just of security guards but of youth groups, Islamic boarding schools, motorcycle-taxi drivers, and "informal" local leaders. Many of these received training and coordination from the police and became what the police referred to as their "extended arms" (*perpanjangan tangan*).

54 Some gangs continued to operate with *bekking* from elements in the army or the police.

55 These foundations catered to ex-convicts and escaped Petrus through connections to the right powers in Jakarta. Sometimes trained by the military, the individuals who exited these organizations were useful for political purposes like instigating riots since they could always be threatened with being killed or imprisoned if they did not cooperate. For example, one such group was used in the violent takeover of the PDI (Indonesian Democratic Party) headquarters in July 1996.

56 On *bekking*, see chapter 2.

Chapter 6: The Police Precinct

1 See Loekman Soetrisno quoted in *Merdeka*, January 5, 1996; and A. Muis, *Media Indonesia*, June 22, 1996.

2 For an analysis of fraternities in Germany before the First World War—delivered in a tone not dissimilar to Sadikin's—see Max Weber (1968, 215–16).

3   Or elsewhere: "It's hogwash that the police can order other people if they themselves are not ordered. . . . Sometimes there's a thief who has already been handcuffed and is then beaten. Or only because a car won't stop after committing an infraction a police officer does as he pleases, drawing his gun only in order to scare the driver. It is happenings such as these that must be eliminated" (*Suara Karya*, March 13, 1996).

4   Many scholars have discussed the patriarchal nature of the New Order state. See, for example, Sen 1998; Suryakusuma 1996; Lev 1996; K. Robinson 1998. Kathryn Robinson, in particular, writes that "the project of the New Order has also rested on a refashioning of the gender order. In this an 'emphasised' femininity (see Connell 1987) has been promoted as part of a social order in which the domination of a hegemonic masculinity is fundamental to its authoritarian character, manifested in militarism, and the elevation of the power of the patriarch as an aspect of state power" (1998, 67). Krishna Sen (1998) and Julia Suryakusuma (1996) have explored the ways in which the New Order state attempted to institutionalize specific gender ideologies. Sen charts the role of groups like Dharma Wanita (a national organization that serves as a sort of sorority, or "sisterhood," for wives of civil servants) in promoting the Indonesian woman as wife and housewife. Suryakusuma (1996, 98) uses the term "State Ibuism" to describe an ideology through which women are cast as "dependent wives who exist for their husbands, their families and the state."

5   As noted in the introduction, Cilengka is a pseudonym.

6   During my time there, the holding cell was used only for male prisoners.

7   While for more than a decade following independence, the Indonesian police had a status independent of the army, navy, and air force, in 1962, the police were integrated into the armed forces. During the New Order, this integration was deepened, such that police ranks came to follow the nomenclature of military ranks. As part of the reforms that followed the end of the New Order, in 2000, the police were pulled out of the armed forces and placed under the direct authority of the president. As part of this change, a new system of ranking was introduced whereby captains assumed the title of senior inspector.

8   The way I met Andi in the first place is relevant here. I was at the provincial headquarters doing research when I met a man who wanted to study English. I told him I could help, and to return the favor, he introduced me to a friend of his from the academy who headed a precinct in the Bandung area (i.e., Andi at Cilengka).

9   This endurance is partly attributable to the discourse of kinship, which itself is meant to transcend territorial or linguistic ties.

10 Within educational institutions there are organizations and informal groupings defined in ethnic terms. Among police in Bandung, however, such forms of ethnic solidarity were largely inconsequential.

11 Other requirements include religiosity, health, fitness, minimum height, being "clean" of communism, and proof that one has had no problems with the law. I was told that of the ten thousand men who took the entrance exam, only six hundred were admitted in 1996. The exam included the following sections: physical test, mental test, health test, psychology test, and Pancasila (national ideology) test. It was also rumored that applicants had to pay a fee to ensure their acceptance, but this was denied by academy leaders.

12 The question of whether to allow military men to marry has been answered in different ways over time and across countries. For a discussion of these variations, see Enloe (2000, 154–57).

13 Surat Keputusan Gubernur AKABRI Bagian Kepolisian, Number Skep/P/97/XII/1978, December 30, 1978.

14 From 1967, when the police first began training with the army cadets, to 1971, this orientation was particularly violent and on at least one occasion resulted in the death of a cadet. Since 1972, the orientation has been toned down somewhat, but it is nonetheless remembered by post-1972 graduates as one of the most difficult periods in their lives.

15 I do not know how pickpockets would respond to the hazing death of an initiate, but I suspect it would be treated as unfortunate and sad rather than as natural or accidental.

16 Pickpockets, too, might expect to rise in status within their gang over time, but these shifts would be less predictable since they are not underpinned by the institutional logic of schools, which take in a new generation of students each year and spit out graduates.

17 Errington (1989, 52) notes that there are two main ways in which difference is figured in island Southeast Asia: as hierarchical and as complementary. Describing seniority as one type of difference, Errington also notes that generally "people of senior generational layers are supposed to protect and advise those who are younger, while those who are younger are supposed to respect and obey those who are senior" (49). We could thus see "Seniors can do no wrong" as being a bureaucratized version of what happens in this type of hierarchy. About complementary difference, Errington notes that it "is often imaged and elaborated as the contrast between brother and sister, which stands as the icon of male-female difference generally" (52–53). The fraternity in this case deviates from a complementary model since women figure as symbols of exchange and

one's ability to sexualize and objectify women signifies one's own power and prestige in the hierarchy of the fraternity.

18 It is important to distinguish between how women and men describe each other and how they actually interact with each other (Keeler 1990, 128). Indeed, my account is based on how men at the precinct articulate conceptions of gender. Had I focused on women's accounts and their relations more closely I may have found an alternative account (see Brenner 1995).

19 Tom Boellstorff (2004, 470) observes that "in the new Indonesia, men who publicly appear to make improper choices threaten this gendered and sexualized logic of national belonging." This can make them targets of violence.

20 Feminine identity was promoted in a similar manner by the New Order state. Suryakusuma (1996) has described the functions of Dharma Wanita. Membership is obligatory, and a woman's position within the organization is determined by the position held by her husband; as Suryakusuma notes, her skills and educational level are "of no consequence, only the husband's position counts" (99). While men are absent from Dharma Wanita, their presence is ubiquitous; Dharma Wanita espouses a female identity that cannot be separated from its members' roles as wives and mothers.

21 "Tripping" on ecstasy was the fashion in expensive discotheques throughout Indonesia in the mid- to late 1990s. It was signified not so much by the inner state of being produced by the drug as by the shaking back and forth of the head to the rhythm of house music. On the meaning of ecstasy use in Indonesia, see Lindquist (2004, 2009).

22 Suryakusuma (1996, 114), in her discussion of high-ranking officials and the military, insightfully notes that "women are a source of pleasure and wives a necessary inconvenience, but women are also a threat and annoyance. When a soldier marries, he requires the approval of his superiors to ensure that his loyalty to his wife does not supersede that of his military command. Prostitution helps to maintain the loyalty of soldiers by satisfying their 'needs' while on duty." The discourses and activities of fraternities help sustain this gender ideology.

23 Unlike at the City Police and Provincial Police headquarters, there was no unit for traffic and no separate unit for intelligence.

24 While in principle, Reserse at the precinct level were also responsible for performing criminal intelligence work, in practice, there was little correspondence between these agents and the Criminal Intelligence sections at the higher levels of the police hierarchy.

25   For an in-depth study of the use of language as an index of gender among the police in Pittsburgh, Pennsylvania, see McElhinny (1993).

26   On the meaning of *anak buah* within the context of gangs, see chapter 2.

27   On the role of *calo* in bus terminals and cinemas, see chapter 2.

28   If the incentive was good enough, agents at Reserse would bend over backward to assist someone. For example, they would change the story of a theft to make it sound more plausible, or even invent a story so that a loss was transformed into a theft.

29   Case reports are known as BAP (*Berita Acara Pemeriksaan*). A criminal case file consists of BAPs that report the results of interviews with suspects, witnesses, victims, and experts, along with reports on physical evidence and copies of letters authorizing detention of the suspect, the confiscation of evidence, and so forth.

30   These stories were even more common for deals worked out with public prosecutors who claimed to the families of the accused that they would ask for less than the maximum sentence allowed by law (often misrepresenting the maximum to families who were unfamiliar with the statutes).

31   In the case of the *pamong praja*, trucks and bulldozers were brought around and unfortunate victims watched as their sources of livelihood were destroyed or carted away. Then, the street curbs were painted with their white and black checks and everything looked "clean." For a detailed description of how such public order operations impacted on the livelihoods of their victims, see Van Bruinessen (1988).

32   One might expect that the police would have close ties to prosecutors and judges, but at lower and middle levels of the hierarchy, this was not the case. Police officers almost never went to court to testify, and prosecutors rarely came to visit precincts. The police aimed merely to provide prosecutable cases and only rarely did they have any contact with cases after they finished their reports. Furthermore, they showed little interest in what happened to cases after they had been sent to the prosecutor, except on occasions when they had made a mistake and the report had to be done again. For example, they did not gripe about criminals getting off lightly, as one might expect. The police, in effect, operated a different racket than did the prosecutors and judges, the latter forming the backbone of what the Indonesian media often refers to as the "court mafia."

33   The reported number of Chinese Indonesians seems too low, particularly when compared with the number of Buddhists.

34   More revealing, however, was the use of a special code within an individual's identity card number to indicate that he or she was Chinese. In the late 1970s this took the form of a zero before the rest of the identification

number (for naturalized citizens or "foreigners" the number was written in red ink). Despite protests, this practice was justified as necessary
"to facilitate administration and computer registration" (*Kompas*, February 21, 1979, cited in Suryadinata 1992, 200). In 1990 the minister of home
affairs again justified the practice by saying that it was needed "because
they want to monitor the Chinese" (*Straits Times*, March 13, 1990, cited in
Suryadinata 1990, 201). Since then, however, this overt code reportedly
has been replaced by a surreptitious one that allows the state to maintain
its lists but hides people's "real" identities from the public.

35 Siskamling provided a rubric for extending this logic of surveillance beyond
the police and into the local security "system" of *ronda* patrols, Hansip
guards, and Satpam. One of the duties of the Guidance Unit was to go out
into the precinct and check in with the various civilian guards, or "control"
(*kontrol*) them as the officers described it, to make sure they were doing
their job and to gather any information they might have about suspicious
happenings in the area. They would sometimes also inspect guard posts and
make recommendations for how they might be improved, such as by adding equipment or by posting maps of the neighborhood on the guard post's
walls. As part of this activity, they sometimes held regional competitions for
best guard post. These competitions were spectacles in which police brass
"went down to the field" (*turun ke lapangan*) to inspect the posts, rank them,
and provide prizes to the most exemplary posts. In one neighborhood in
which I lived, the Hansip guards talked about this for a couple of weeks
before the event. The year before, they had won second prize, which they
attributed to the fact that their guard post was "complete" except that it
still had no toilet. To prepare for the upcoming inspection, the post was
repainted and cleaned up and banners extolling Siskamling were hung out.
On the day of the visit, the guards wore smart uniforms and shiny boots.
On this particular occasion, however, the officials did not end up coming,
to the great disappointment of the guards. After a little while, the banners were taken down and things returned to normal.

36 Andi himself lived very modestly, so if this figure is true, he may well have
passed most on to higher-ups, keeping only a small portion for himself.

37 For a debate about the best way to translate the term *oknum*, see Kammen
(2003); Kingsbury (2004); and Reid (2006, 208, 222)

Conclusion

1 On citizen forums, see Antlöv (2003) and Chandra et al. (2003).

2 Ian Wilson (2015, xvii) eloquently describes this period in Bandung as
one in which the authoritarian New Order state had "fractured into a

complex menagerie of rival groups competing for territory, resources and rents amongst preman, the poor and unemployed young men." See also Barker (2006, 205–6).

3   Interestingly, this was also a time when growing numbers of countercultural youth embraced tattoos as a fashion trend, thereby weakening the stigma that had long linked tattoos with criminality.

4   The Sundanese term the parking attendant used to describe the territory he was allocated, *lapak*, is indicative of how territoriality functioned in this context. *Lapak* is a word used to describe the mat on which people sit while they are gambling, fishing, or performing some other kind of specific activity (see Tamsyah et al. 2003, 148). In this case, the term would presumably have derived from the mats used by street vendors for laying out their wares on the pavement.

5   Edward Aspinall (2013) describes the effects of democratization and neoliberal entrepreneurialism on Indonesian state patronage networks in terms of fragmentation. Jacqui Baker (2015) has examined in detail the effects of such post-Suharto fragmentation on policing patronage networks in particular.

6   Mr. Ayi was reportedly responsible for this innovation. Although his regular spot for business was the Gasibu plaza, he would sometimes also sell snacks and food at a nearby military field, particularly when special events were being held. Such events were often enclosed by fences constructed out of bamboo. Ayi noticed that after such events the bamboo lengths were thrown away, so he started scavenging these and stockpiling them at his home, which was located in a neighborhood around the corner from Gasibu plaza. Once he had enough bamboo, he started renting it out to event organizers who wanted to build their own enclosures. As the business grew, he replaced the bamboo with metal fencing and gradually added generators, sound equipment, and even security personnel to his offerings.

7   "Setelah PKL, Pemda Tertibkan Preman di Gasibu," *Republika*, April 16, 2014, https://www.republika.co.id/berita/nasional/jawa-barat-nasional/14 /04/16/n447lp-setelah-pkl-pemda-tertibkan-preman-di-gasibu.

8   "Emil Gandeng Kodim Tertibkan PKL Gasibu," *Tribun Jabar*, April 16, 2014, http://jabar.tribunnews.com/2014/04/16/emil-gandeng-kodim-tertibkan -pkl-gasibu.

9   "Emil Gandeng Kodim Tertibkan PKL Gasibu."

10 "Gasibu Akan Dijadikan Taman Rekreasi Monumental," *Berita Satu*, October 26, 2014, https://www.beritasatu.com/destinasi/220286-gasibu-akan -dijadikan-taman-rekreasi-monumental.html.

11   Tya Eka Yulianti, "Mulai Besok Lapangan Gasibu Kota Bandung Ditu-
     tup untuk Umum," *detikNews*, August 27, 2015, https://news.detik.com
     /berita-jawa-barat/3003049/mulai-besok-lapangan-gasibu-kota-bandung
     -ditutup-untuk-umum.

12   "Renovasi Gasibu, Jawa Barat Siapkan Rp 16 M," *Tempo*, August 19,
     2015, https://nasional.tempo.co/read/693391/renovasi-gasibu-jawa-barat
     -siapkan-rp-16-m.

13   "Perlunya Etika di Lapangan Gasibu," *Jawa Pos*, January 16, 2017, https://
     www.pressreader.com/indonesia/jawa-pos/20170116/282153585976614.

14   "Perlunya Etika di Lapangan Gasibu."

15   Video, accessed December 20, 2018, https://commandcenter.bandung.go
     .id/videografis/page/2/.

16   At least some of the CCTV cameras were equipped with speakers, so moni-
     tors in the Command Center could speak directly to those on the street
     who were observed doing something wrong.

17   Agie Permadi, "Antisipasi Begal, Kota Bandung Butuh 600 CCTV," *Kom-
     pas.com*, September 7, 2018, https://regional.kompas.com/read/2018/09
     /07/11173131/antisipasi-begal-kota-bandung-butuh-600-cctv.

18   The routinization of charisma is the process whereby charismatic lead-
     ership becomes stabilized and incorporated into enduring institutional
     structures (Weber 1968). Benedict Anderson's (1990a, 1990b) essays on
     Javanese power analyze cultural conceptions of charisma in Java, how
     such power was routinized in Javanese tradition, and how it was drawn
     upon by President Sukarno. Sutherland (1979) describes the history of
     bureaucratization of rule in late-colonial Indonesia.

19   On divine kingship as a characteristic of precolonial states in Southeast
     Asia, see Heine-Geldern (1942). On the Indianization of Southeast Asian
     states, see Coedès (1968).

20   For example, Benedict Anderson's (1972) study of Indonesian revolu-
     tionaries emphasizes the continuing importance of "men of prowess"
     culture within the nascent Indonesian Army. Similarly, Loren Ryter
     (2001, 2009) has shown how Indonesian *preman* first created a mass youth
     organization in support of Suharto's regime and later reinvented them-
     selves as parliamentarians in the post–New Order period. Elsewhere in
     Southeast Asia, John T. Sidel (1999) has argued that although the rise of
     local Philippines "bosses" is a modern effect of the political economy of
     American colonialism and electoral democracy, the "big man" aspects
     of these bosses is something perennial to the Philippines and part of the
     broader phenomenon of "men of prowess." Ryter (2012) points out that
     the concept of prowess is relevant for understanding modern power in

places like Indonesia even if one does not subscribe to more essentialist arguments about its precolonial Southeast Asian origins.

21 Jeremy Kingsley's (2012) work on *kyai* leadership in Lombok, Ian Wilson's (2006) work on religious and ethnic militias in Jakarta, and Kari Telle's (2009) work on the Dharma Wisea security group, also in Lombok, are just a few examples of scholarship showing the continuing importance of claims of spiritual potency, invulnerability, and charismatic authority for leaders operating at the margins of state power. For further examples, see Barker (2016).

22 As Baker (2010, 99) has rightly pointed out, the fact that the *ronda* goes by a Portuguese name casts some doubt on the idea that the institution has precolonial origins.

23 On the history of state weakness in Bandung's *kampung,* see Reerink (2015).

24 As discussed in chapter 5, toward the end of the 1970s, *jegger* gangs were already starting to formalize on their own, by establishing themselves as security companies. Siskamling prohibited such initiatives and established rules for private security companies that ensured they would remain under the close watch of the police.

25 Case studies of informal sovereignties in other countries indicate Indonesia is not unique in this regard. In Nigeria, for example, the Bakassi Boys protected traders and markets during times of state weakness (Harnischfeger 2003); in post-Soviet Ulan-Ude, gangs played a role in the shift from a state-led economy to a market economy (Humphrey 2004); and in Nicaragua, gangs facilitated the shift from locally based economies to narco-capitalism (Rodgers 2006). For a rich analysis of the relationship between predatory privatized violence and Indonesia's changing political economy, see Mudhoffir (2022).

26 In Bandung, the development of new factories, shopping malls, flyovers, hotels, and apartment buildings almost always takes place on land claimed by *kampung* dwellers. Resistance to such development is thus framed in terms of the rights of territorial communities. For a discussion of such conflicts in post-Suharto Bandung, see Reerink (2006).

27 The role of the *jegger* in this respect is similar to that of the rural *jago* of colonial Java. Java in the nineteenth century was for the most part ruled indirectly through regents and their underlings. Javanese cultural constructions of social hierarchy emphasized that leaders—who were a part of the nobility—should remain aloof from their followers, who were seen as commoners. This social distance between rulers and ruled was one of the factors that created a space for *jagos* to emerge as key power brokers between regents and the village world, since leaders could appear

aloof, while *jagos* worked in the shadows to impose a strong-arm order (Onghokham 1984). The strong arm was important because rural Java was undergoing a process of capitalist enclosure and a deepening of market penetration. With these changes, the colonial regime became increasingly concerned with "tranquility and order" (*rust en orde*) at the village level. As local enforcers and spies, *jagos* were one of the main means of establishing this order. However, it was not always clear whose order they were establishing. James Rush's (1990) study of nineteenth-century opium farms in Java suggests that the entire apparatus for establishing law and order at the village level—the police, the courts, village heads, and, most importantly, *jagos*—was effectively hijacked by the Chinese owners of such farms in their competition over market share. A significant black market for opium had grown up alongside the legal market, and one way to handicap a competitor was by having their distributors arrested for black-market activities. Opium was not unique in this regard, as a similar dynamic was evident in the livestock market (cf. Schulte Nordholt 1991). In both cases, *jagos* appeared not just as power brokers moving into the gaps resulting from the patchiness of the colonial state but also as key mediators between legal and criminal realms.

28 The continuing fascination with the "unseen powers" of the state in post-Suharto Yogyakarta is perceptively analyzed by Sheri Gibbings (2013).

29 Such masculinist culture in the academy and its hazing practices could have had other outcomes. McCoy (1995) has traced how hazing in the early years of the Philippine Military Academy yielded a generation of leaders who prized honor and supported constitutional governance.

30 Whether it was the government as such being bypassed, as opposed to a particular fraternity within the state, remained unclear.

REFERENCES

List of Newspapers and News Sources

Beritasatu.com. Jakarta, Indonesia
detikNews. Jakarta, Indonesia
iNewsDepok.id. Jakarta, Indonesia
Jawa Pos. Surabaya, Indonesia
Kompas.com. Jakarta, Indonesia
Media Indonesia. Jakarta, Indonesia
Merdeka. Jakarta, Indonesia
Republika. Jakarta, Indonesia
Suara Karya. Jakarta, Indonesia
Suara Merdeka. Semarang, Indonesia
Surabaya Post. Surabaya, Indonesia
Tempo. Jakarta, Indonesia
Tribun Jabar. Bandung, Indonesia

Primary Sources

Ahadiat, Anto. 1994. *Nilai Dan Fungsi Kentongan Pada Masyarakat Bali*. Jakarta, Indonesia: Proyek Pengkajian dan Pembinaan Nilai-Nilai Budaya Pusat, Direktorat Jenderal Kebudayaan, Direktorat Sejarah dan Nilai Tradisional, Departemen Pendidikan dan Kebudayaan.

Akhmadi, Heri. 2009. *Breaking the Chains of Oppression of the Indonesian People.* Jakarta, Indonesia: Equinox Publishing.

Akip, Marlan. 1991. "'X': Sebuah organisasi pencopet profesional di Jakarta Barat (Studi kasus terhadap kelompok pencopet 'X')." BA thesis, Criminology Department, Universitas Indonesia.

Althusser, Louis. 1971. *Lenin and Philosophy, and Other Essays.* Translated by Ben Brewster. London: New Left Books.

Ambri, Moh. 1977. *Memuja siluman.* Translated by Ajip Rosidi. Bandung: Pustaka Jaya.

Ammarell, Gene. 1988. "Sky Calendars of the Indo-Malay Archipelago: Regional Diversity/Local Knowledge." *Indonesia* 45 (April): 85–104.

Andaya, Barbara Watson. 2005. "Regulating Marriage and Sexuality: States and Laws in Early Modern. Southeast Asia." Paper presented at the International Conference on the Early Modern World, University of Chicago, June 3.

Anderson, Benedict. 1972. *Java in a Time of Revolution: Occupation and Resistance, 1944–1946.* Ithaca, NY: Cornell University Press.

Anderson, Benedict. (1983) 1991. *Imagined Communities: Reflections on the Origin and Spread of Nationalism.* London: Verso.

Anderson, Benedict. 1990a. "Further Adventures of Charisma." In *Language and Power: Exploring Political Cultures in Indonesia,* edited by Benedict Anderson, 78–93. Ithaca, NY: Cornell University Press.

Anderson, Benedict. 1990b. "The Idea of Power in Javanese Culture." In *Language and Power: Exploring Political Cultures in Indonesia,* edited by Benedict Anderson, 17–77. Ithaca, NY: Cornell University Press.

Anderson, Benedict. 1990c. "Old State, New Society: Indonesia's New Order in Comparative Historical Perspective." In *Language and Power: Exploring Political Cultures in Indonesia,* edited by Benedict Anderson, 94–120. Ithaca, NY: Cornell University Press.

Anderson, Benedict. 1999. "Indonesian Nationalism Today and in the Future." *Indonesia,* 67 (April): 1–11.

Anderson, Benedict, ed. 2001. "Introduction." In *Violence and the State in Suharto's Indonesia,* edited by Benedict R. O'G Anderson, 9–19. Studies on Southeast Asia 30. Ithaca, NY: Southeast Asia Program Publications, Southeast Asia Program, Cornell University.

Anderson, Benedict. 2005. *Under Three Flags: Anarchism and the Anti-Colonial Imagination.* London: Verso.

Anderson, Clare. 2004. *Legible Bodies: Race, Criminality and Colonialism in South Asia.* Oxford: Berg.

Antlöv, Hans. 2003. "Not Enough Politics! Power, Participation and the New Democratic Polity in Indonesia." In *Local Power and Politics in Indonesia: Decentralisation and Democratisation,* edited by Edward Aspinall and Greg Fealy, 72–86. Singapore: Institute of Southeast Asian Studies, Singapore.

Appadurai, Arjun. 1993. "Number in the Colonial Imagination." In *Orientalism and the Postcolonial Predicament: Perspectives on South Asia,* edited by Carol A.

Breckenridge and Peter van der Veer, 314–40. Philadelphia: University of Pennsylvania Press.

Aspinall, Edward. 2013. "A Nation in Fragments: Patronage and Neoliberalism in Contemporary Indonesia." *Critical Asian Studies* 45 (1): 27–54.

Augé, Marc. 1995. *From Places to Non-Places: Introduction to an Anthropology of Supermodernity*. Translated by John Howe. London: Verso.

Baker, Jacqui. 2010. "The Rise of Polri: Democratisation and the Reorganisation of the Coercive Apparatus of the Indonesian State." PhD diss., London School of Economics.

Baker, Jacqui. 2013. "The Parman Economy: Post-Authoritarian Shifts in the Off-Budget Economy of Indonesia's Security Institutions." *Indonesia* 96 (October): 123–50.

Baker, Jacqui. 2015. "The Rhizome State: Democratizing Indonesia's Off-Budget Economy." *Critical Asian Studies* 47 (2): 309–36.

Bandoeng en de hygiëne. 1927. Bandoeng: Vorkink.

Barker, Joshua. 1999. "Surveillance and Territoriality in Bandung." In *Figures of Criminality in Indonesia, the Philippines, and Colonial Vietnam*, edited by Vicente L. Rafael, 95–127. Ithaca, NY: Southeast Asia Program Publications, Southeast Asia Program, Cornell University.

Barker, Joshua. 2001. "State of Fear: Controlling the Criminal Contagion in Suharto's New Order." In *Violence and the State in Suharto's Indonesia*, edited by Benedict Anderson, 20–53. Studies on Southeast Asia 30. Ithaca, NY: Southeast Asia Program Publications, Southeast Asia Program, Cornell University.

Barker, Joshua. 2006. "Vigilantes and the State." *Social Analysis: The International Journal of Cultural and Social Practice* 50 (1): 203–7.

Barker, Joshua. 2008. "Beyond Bandung: Developmental Nationalism and (Multi) cultural Nationalism in Indonesia." *Third World Quarterly* 29 (3): 521–40.

Barker, Joshua. 2009a. "Introduction: Ethnographic Approaches to the Study of Fear." *Anthropologica* 51 (2): 267–72.

Barker, Joshua. 2009b. "Introduction: Street Life." *City and Society* 21 (2): 155–62.

Barker, Joshua. 2009c. "*Negara Beling*: Street-Level Authority in an Indonesian Slum." In *State of Authority: State in Society in Indonesia*, edited by Gerry van Klinken and Joshua Barker, 47–72. Ithaca, NY: Southeast Asia Program Publications, Southeast Asia Program, Cornell University.

Barker, Joshua. 2013. "Epilogue: Ethnographies of State-Centrism." *Oceania* 83 (3): 259–64.

Barker, Joshua. 2016. "From 'Men of Prowess' to Religious Militias." *Bijdragen tot de taal-, land-en volkenkunde* 172 (2–3): 179–96.

Barker, Joshua, Erik Harms, and Johan Lindquist. 2013a. "Introduction." In *Figures of Southeast Asian Modernity*, edited by Joshua Barker, Erik Harms, and Johan Lindquist, 1–17. Honolulu: University of Hawaii Press, 2013.

Barker, Joshua, Erik Harms, and Johan Lindquist. 2013b. "Introduction to Special Issue: Figuring the Transforming City." *City and Society* 25 (2): 159–72.

Barker, Joshua, and Gerry van Klinken. 2009. "Reflections on the State in Indonesia." In *State of Authority: State in Society in Indonesia*, edited by Gerry van Klinken and Joshua Barker, 17–46. Ithaca, NY: Southeast Asia Program Publications, Southeast Asia Program, Cornell University.

Barton, Franklin Roy. 1963. *Autobiographies of Three Pagans in the Philippines*. New Hyde Park, NY: University Books.

Bateson, Regina. 2021. "The Politics of Vigilantism." *Comparative Political Studies* 54 (6): 923–55.

Beatty, Andrew. 1999. *Varieties of Javanese Religion: An Anthropological Account*. Cambridge: Cambridge University Press.

Bertillon, Alphonse. 1977. *Instructions for Taking Descriptions for the Identification of Criminals and Others by the Means of Anthropometric Indications*. Translated by Gallus Muller. New York: AMS Press.

Bertrand, Jacques. 2004. *Nationalism and Ethnic Conflict in Indonesia*. Cambridge Asia-Pacific Studies. Cambridge: Cambridge University Press.

Biantaro, Teguh. 1983. "Hubungan antar taruna di Akabri bagian kepolisian (Studi kasus terhadap ekses negatif yang timbul dalam proses interaksi)." BA thesis, Perguruan Tinggi Ilmu Kepolisian (College for the Science of Policing).

Bloembergen, Marieke. 2004. "Between Public Safety and Political Control: Modern Colonial Policing in Surabaya (1911–1919)." Paper presented at the 1st International Conference on Urban History, Surabaya, Indonesia, August 23–25.

Bloembergen, Marieke. 2007. "The Dirty Work of Empire: Modern Policing and Public Order in Surabaya." *Indonesia* 83 (April): 119–50.

Boekhoudt, W. 1908. *Rapport Reorganisatie van het Politiewezen op Java en Madoera (uitgezonderd de Vorstenlanden, de Particuliere Landerijen en de Hoofdplaatsen Batavia, Semarang en Soerabaia) 1906–07*. Batavia: Landsdrukkerij.

Boellstorff, Tom. 2004. "The Emergence of Political Homophobia in Indonesia: Masculinity and National Belonging." *Ethnos* 69 (4): 465–86.

Boellstorff, Tom. 2005. *The Gay Archipelago: Sexuality and Nation in Indonesia*. Princeton, NJ: Princeton University Press.

Boellstorff, Tom. 2007. *A Coincidence of Desires: Anthropology, Queer Studies, Indonesia*. Durham, NC: Duke University Press.

Bourchier, David. 1990. "Crime, Law and State Authority in Indonesia." In *State and Civil Society in Indonesia*, edited by Arief Budiman, 177–212. Clayton, Australia: Monash University, Asia Institute.

Bourgois, Philippe I. 2003. *In Search of Respect: Selling Crack in El Barrio*. 2nd ed. Cambridge: Cambridge University Press.

Bousquet, Georges-Henri. 1940. *A French View of the Netherlands Indies*. Translated by Philip E. Lilienthal. London: Oxford University Press.

Brand, W. 1958. "Differential Mortality in the Town of Bandung." In *The Indonesian Town: Studies in Urban Sociology*, edited by Willem Frederik Wertheim, 225–73. The Hague: W. van Hoeve.

Brenner, Suzanne. 1995. "Why Women Rule the Roost: Rethinking Javanese Ideologies of Gender and Self-Control." In *Bewitching Women, Pious Men: Gender and Body Politics in Southeast Asia*, edited by Aihwa Ong and Michael G. Peletz, 19–47. Berkeley: University of California Press.

Brenner, Suzanne. 1998. *The Domestication of Desire: Women, Wealth, and Modernity in Java*. Princeton, NJ: Princeton University Press.

Brown, Donald, James W. Edwards, and Ruth P. Moore. 1988. *The Penis Inserts of Southeast Asia: An Annotated Bibliography with an Overview and Comparative Perspective*. Berkeley: Center for South and Southeast Asian Studies, University of California, Berkeley.

Bubandt, Nils. 2005. "Vernacular Security: The Politics of Feeling Safe in Global, National and Local Worlds." *Security Dialogue* 36 (3): 275–96.

Butler, Judith. 1990. *Gender Trouble: Feminism and the Subversion of Identity*. New York: Routledge.

Buur, Lars. 2005. "The Sovereign Outsourced: Local Justice and Violence in Port Elizabeth." In *Sovereign Bodies: Citizens, Migrants and States in the Postcolonial World*, edited by Thomas Blom Hansen and Finn Stepputat, 153–71. Princeton, NJ: Princeton University Press.

Buur, Lars, and Steffen Jensen. 2004. "Introduction: Vigilantism and the Policing of Everyday Life in South Africa." *African Studies* 63 (2): 139–52.

Caldeira, Teresa P. R. 2000. *City of Walls: Crime, Segregation, and Citizenship in São Paulo*. Berkeley: University of California Press.

Certeau, Michel de. 1984. *The Practice of the Everyday Life*. Berkeley: University of California Press.

Chambert-Loir, Henri. 1983. "Those Who Speak Prokem." Translated by James T. Collins, *Indonesia* 37: 105–17.

Chandra, Eka, Diding, Ari Nurman, and Paulus Rudolf. 2003. *Membangun forum warga: Implementasi gagasan partisipasi dan penguatan masyarakat sipil di Kabupaten Bandung*. Bandung: Yayasan AKATIGA.

Clastres, Pierre. 1987. *Society against the State: Essays in Political Anthropology*. New York: Zone Books.

Coedès, George. 1968. *The Indianized States of Southeast Asia*. Honolulu: East-West Center Press.

Cole, Simon A. 2001. *Suspect Identities: A History of Fingerprinting and Criminal Identification*. Cambridge, MA: Harvard University Press.

Collins, Elizabeth. 2002. "Indonesia: A Violent Culture?" *Asian Survey* 42 (2): 582–605.

Colombijn, Freek. 2002. "The Ecology of Sumatran Towns in the Nineteenth Century." In *The Indonesian Town Revisited*, edited by Peter J. M. Nas, 283–95. Münster, Germany: Lit Verlag.

Connell, Raewyn. 1987. *Gender and Power*. Sydney, Australia: Allen and Unwin.

Coté, Joost. 2002. "Towards an Architecture of Association: H. F. Tillema, Semarang and the Construction of Colonial Modernity." In *The Indonesian Town Revisited*, edited by Peter J. M. Nas, 319–47. Münster, Germany: Lit Verlag.

Cribb, Robert. 1991. *Gangsters and Revolutionaries: The Jakarta People's Militia and the Indonesian Revolution, 1945–1949*. Sydney, Australia: Asian Studies Association of Australia in association with Allen and Unwin.

Crouch, Harold. 1988. *The Army and Politics in Indonesia*. Rev. ed. Edited by George McTurnan Kahin. Politics and International Relations in Southeast Asia. Ithaca, NY: Cornell University Press.

D'Almeida, William Barrington. 1864. *Life in Java with Sketches of the Javanese*. 2 vols. London: Hurst and Blackett.

Dean, Mitchell. 1999. *Governmentality: Power and Rule in Modern Society*. London: Sage Publications.

Deleuze, Gilles, and Félix Guattari. 1984. *Anti-Oedipus: Capitalism and Schizophrenia*. Translated by Mark Seem, Helen R. Lane, and Robert Hurley. London: Athlone Press.

Deleuze, Gilles, and Félix Guattari. 1991. *A Thousand Plateaus: Capitalism and Schizophrenia*. Minneapolis: University of Minnesota Press.

Derrida, Jacques. (1974) 1998. *Of Grammatology*. Translated by Gayatri Chakravorty Spivak. Baltimore: Johns Hopkins University Press.

Djajanegara, Raden Batin. 1911. *Boekoe nasehat aken priaji-priaji dalam mendjalanken kepolisiean*. Betawi: Pertjitakan Gouvernement.

Djamin, Awaloedin. 1995. *Pengalaman seorang perwira POLRI*. Jakarta, Indonesia: Pustaka Sinar Harapan.

Dorrian, Mark. 2007. "The Aerial View: Notes for a Cultural History." *Strates: Matériaux pour la recherche en sciences sociales* 13.

Drewes, Gerardus Willebrordus Joannes. 1985. "The Life-Story of an Old-Time Priangan Regent as Told by Himself." *Bijdragen tot de taal-, land-en volkenkunde* 141 (4): 399–422.

Dutch East Indies and Departement van Economische Zaken. 1936. *Volkstelling 1930. Deel VIII. Overzicht voor Nederlandsch-Indië. Census of 1930 in the Netherlands Indies Volume VIII. Summary of the Volumes I–VII*. Batavia: Landsdrukkerij.

Dutch East Indies and Koninklijk Instituut voor de Taal-, Land- en Volkenkunde van Nederlandsche-Indië. 1911. *Adatrechtbundel IV, bezorgd door de commissie voor het adatrecht (Java en Madoera)*. The Hague: Martinus Nijhoff.

Dutch East Indies and Welvaartcommissie. 1905–14. *Onderzoek naar de oorzaken van de mindere welvaart der Inlandsche bevolking op Java en Madoera*. Batavia: Landsdrukkerij.

Dutch East Indies and Welvaartcommissie. 1907. *Onderzoek naar de oorzaken van de mindere welvaart der Inlandsche bevolking op Java en Madoera. VIII. Samentrekking van de afdeelingsverslagen over de uitkomsten der onderzoekingen naar het recht en de politie*. Weltevreden, Dutch East Indies: Visser.

Echols, John M., and Hassan Shadily. 1989. *An Indonesian-English Dictionary*. 3rd ed. Revised and edited by John U. Wolf and James T. Collins in cooperation with Hassan Shadily. Ithaca, NY: Cornell University Press.

Ekadjati, Edi S., Sobana Hardjasaputra, and Ietjeu Marlina. 1985. *Sejarahkota Bandung 1945-1979*. Jakarta, Indonesia: Departemen Pendidikan dan Kebudayaan.

Ekadjati, Edi S., Tatiek Kartikasari, and Aam Masduki. 1993. *Wawacan carios Munada*. Vol. 8. Jakarta, Indonesia: Bagian Proyek Penelitian dan Pengkajian Kebudayaan Nusantara, Direktorat Sejarah dan Nilai Tradisional, Direktorat Jenderal Kebudayaan, Departemen Pendidikan dan Kebudayaan.

Enloe, Cynthia H. 2000. *Maneuvers: The International Politics of Militarizing Women's Lives*. Berkeley: University of California Press.

Errington, Shelly. 1989. *Meaning and Power in a Southeast Asian Realm*. Princeton, NJ: Princeton University Press.

Fassin, Didier. 2017. "Introduction: Ethnographying the Police." In *Writing the World of Policing: The Difference Ethnography Makes*, edited by Didier Fassin, 1-20. Chicago: University of Chicago Press.

Fauzi, Muhammad. 2004. "'Lain Di Front, Lain Di Kota': Jagoan Dan Bajingan Di Jakarta Tahun 1950-An." Paper presented at the 1st International Conference on Urban History, Surabaya, Indonesia, August 23-25.

Feldman, Allen. 1997. "Violence and Vision: The Prosthetics and Aesthetics of Terror." *Public Culture* 10 (1): 24-60.

Ferzacca, Steve. 2002. "A Javanese Metropolis and Mental Life." *Ethos* 30 (1-2): 95-112.

Foucault, Michel. 1980. *Power/Knowledge: Selected Interviews and Other Writings, 1972-1977*. Edited by Colin Gordon. Translated by Colin Gordon, Leo Marshall, John Mepham, and Kate Sopher. New York: Pantheon Books.

Foucault, Michel. 1995. *Discipline and Punish: The Birth of the Prison*. Translated by Alan Sheridan. New York: Vintage Books.

Fourchard, Laurent. 2008. "A New Name for an Old Practice: Vigilantes in South-Western Nigeria." *Africa* 78 (1): 16-40.

Furnivall, John. 1956. *Colonial Policy and Practice: A Comparative Study of Burma and Netherlands India*. New York: New York University Press.

Garriott, William. 2013. "Police in Practice: Policing and the Project of Contemporary Governance." In *Policing and Contemporary Governance: The Anthropology of Police in Practice*, edited by William Garriott, 1-15. New York: Palgrave Macmillan.

Geertz, Clifford. 1973. "Deep Play: Notes on the Balinese Cockfight." In *The Interpretations of Cultures*, 412-54. New York: Basic Books.

Geertz, Clifford. 1976. *The Religion of Java*. Chicago: University of Chicago Press.

Geertz, Clifford. 1980. *Negara: The Theatre State in Nineteenth-Century Bali*. Princeton, NJ: Princeton University Press.

Geertz, Clifford. 2004. "What Is a State If It Is Not a Sovereign? Reflections on Politics in Complicated Places." *Current Anthropology* 45: 557-91.

Gell, Alfred. 1993. *Wrapping in Images: Tattooing in Polynesia*. Oxford: Clarendon Press.

George, Kenneth M. 1996. *Showing Signs of Violence: The Cultural Politics of a Twentieth-Century Headhunting Ritual*. Berkeley: University of California Press.

Gibbings, Sheri. 2013. "Unseen Powers and Democratic Detectives: Street Vendors in an Indonesian City." *City and Society* 25 (2): 235–59.

Ginzburg, Carlo. 1990. "Clues: Roots of an Evidential Paradigm." In *Myths, Emblems, Clues*, translated by John Tedeschi and Anne C. Tedeschi, 96–125. London: Hutchison Radius.

Goldstein, Daniel M. 2004. *The Spectacular City: Violence and Performance in Urban Bolivia*. Durham, NC: Duke University Press.

Gordon, Colin. 1991. "Governmental Rationality: An Introduction." In *The Foucault Effect: Studies in Governmentality: With Two Lectures by and an Interview with Michel Foucault*, edited by Graham Burchell, Colin Gordon, and Peter Miller, 1–52. Chicago: University of Chicago Press.

Gupta, Akhil. 1995. "Blurred Boundaries: The Discourse of Corruption, the Culture of Politics, and the Imagined State." *American Ethnologist* 22 (2): 375–402.

Haanstad, Eric J. 2012. "'Ratchaprasong Is Alive': Bangkok's Decentralized Spaces of Security and Public Performance." *Internationales Asienforum* 43 (3–4): 279–99.

Haanstad, Eric J. 2013. "Thai Police in Refractive Cultural Practice." In *Policing and Contemporary Governance: The Anthropology of Police in Practice*, edited by William Garriott, 181–205. New York: Palgrave Macmillan.

Hansen, Thomas Blom, and Finn Stepputat. 2001. *States of Imagination: Ethnographic Explorations of the Postcolonial State*. Durham, NC: Duke University Press.

Hansen, Thomas Blom, and Finn Stepputat. 2006. "Sovereignty Revisited." *Annual Review of Anthropology* 35 (October): 295–315.

Hardjamardjaja, Andrea Corsini Harjaka. 1962. "Javanese Popular Belief in the Coming of Ratu-Adil, a Righteous Prince: An Attempt at Assessing Its Theological Value and an Inquiry into Its Adaptability to the Incipient Stages of Evangelization in Present-Day Java." PhD dissertation, Pontifical Gregorian University, Rome.

Harnischfeger, Johannes. 2003. "The Bakassi Boys: Fighting Crime in Nigeria." *Journal of Modern African Studies* 41 (1): 23–49.

Heald, Suzette. 2006. "State, Law, and Vigilantism in Northern Tanzania." *African Affairs* 105 (419): 265–83.

Heidegger, Martin. 1971. *Poetry, Language, Thought*. New York: Harper and Row.

Heine-Geldern, Robert. 1942. "Conceptions of State and Kingship in Southeast Asia." *Journal of Asian Studies* 2 (1): 15–30.

Herbert, Steve. 2017. "Accountability: Ethnographic Engagement and the Ethics of the Police (United States)." In *Writing the World of Policing: The Difference Ethnography Makes*, edited by Didier Fassin, 23–41. Chicago: University of Chicago Press.

Herriman, Nicholas. 2006. "The Killings of Alleged Sorcerers in South Malang: Conspiracy, Ninjas, or 'Community Justice'?" In *Violent Conflicts in Indonesia: Analysis, Representation, Resolution*, edited by Charles A. Coppel, 90–105. London: Routledge.

Hesselink, W. F. 1911. *Hadlir paling doeloe pada tempat dilakoekennja perboewatan djahat. Pemimpin ringkas boewat orang-orang jang hadir paling doeloe.* Batavia: Hoa Siang In Kiok.

Hilman, Imam. 1982. "Peristiwa pembunuhan Assisten Residen Nagel tahun 1845." *Seminar sejarah nasional III. Seksi sejarah perlawanan terhadap Belanda.* Vol. 1, 37–46. Jakarta, Indonesia: Direktorat Sejarah dan Nilai Tradisional, Departemen Pendidikan dan Kebudayaan.

Hoadley, Mason C. 1994. *Selective Judicial Competence: The Cirebon-Priangan Legal Administration, 1680–1792.* Ithaca, NY: Southeast Asia Program Publications, Southeast Asia Program, Cornell University.

Hoffman, Danny. 2011. *The War Machines: Young Men and Violence in Sierra Leone and Liberia.* Durham, NC: Duke University Press.

Honggare, Robin Hartanto. 2021. "Disease on Display: The First Hygiene Exhibition in the Netherlands Indies Revisited." *Southeast of Now: Directions in Contemporary and Modern Art in Asia* 5 (1–2): 97–116.

Hull, Terence H., and Meiwita Budiharsana. 2001. "Male Circumcision and Penis Enhancement in Southeast Asia: Matters of Pain and Pleasure." *Reproductive Health Matters* 9 (18): 60–67.

Humphrey, Caroline. 2004. "Sovereignty." In *A Companion to the Anthropology of Politics,* edited by David Nugent and Joan Vincent, 418–36. Malden, MA: Blackwell.

Husein, Teuku Ashikin. 1983. "Jasa-jasa keamanan oleh Yayasan prems di wilayah pertokoan Blok M." BA thesis, Perguruan Tinggi Ilmu Kepolisian (College for the Science of Policing).

Hydrick, John Lee. 1939. *Intensive Rural Hygiene Work and Public Education of the Public Health Service of Netherlands India.* Batavia: Public Health Service.

Ido, Victor [Hans van de Wall]. 1949. *Indië in de goeden ouden tijd.* 2 vols. Bandung: Nix.

Inda, Jonathan Xavier. 2005. "Analytics of the Modern: An Introduction." In *Anthropologies of Modernity: Foucault, Governmentality, and Life Politics,* edited by Jonathan Xavier Inda, 1–20. Oxford: Blackwell.

International Crisis Group. 2001. *Indonesia: National Police Reform.* ICG Asia Report No. 13 (20 February). Jakarta/Brussels: International Crisis Group.

Jaffe, Rivke. 2013. "The Hybrid State: Crime and Insurgent Citizenship in Urban Jamaica." *American Ethnologist* 40 (4): 734–48.

Jaffe, Rivke. 2015. "From Maroons to Dons: Sovereignty, Violence, and Law in Jamaica." *Critique of Anthropology* 35 (1): 47–63.

Jaffrey, Sana. 2019. "Leveraging the Leviathan: Politics of Impunity and the Rise of Vigilantism in Democratic Indonesia." PhD diss., University of Chicago.

Jauregui, Beatrice. 2016. *Provisional Authority: Police, Order, and Security in India.* Chicago: University of Chicago Press.

Kammen, Douglas. 2003. "Recent Scholarship on the Indonesian Military." *Indonesia* 76 (October): 215–19.

Kartadinata, Mas. 1921. *Rasiah Priangan.* Weltevreden: Bale Pustaka.

Kartodirdjo, Sartono. 1973. *Protest Movements in Rural Java: A Study of Agrarian Unrest in the Nineteenth and Early Twentieth Centuries*. Singapore: Oxford University Press.

Keane, Webb. 1997. *Signs of Recognition: Powers and Hazards of Representation in an Indonesian Society*. Berkeley: University of California Press.

Keeler, Ward. 1987. *Javanese Shadow Plays, Javanese Selves*. Princeton, NJ: Princeton University Press.

Keeler, Ward. 1990. "Speaking of Gender in Java." In *Power and Difference: Gender in Island Southeast Asia*, edited by Jane Atkinson and Shelly Errington, 127–52. Stanford, CA: Stanford University Press.

Kingsbury, Damien. 2004. "Letters to the Editors." *Indonesia* 77 (April): 181–83.

Kingsley, Jeremy. 2012. "Peacemakers or Peace-Breakers? Provincial Elections and Religious Leadership in Lombok, Indonesia." *Indonesia* 93 (April): 53–82.

Kivland, Chelsey L. 2020a. "The Spiral of Sovereignty: Enacting and Entangling the State from Haiti's Streets." *American Anthropologist* 122 (3): 501–13.

Kivland, Chelsey L. 2020b. *Street Sovereigns: Young Men and the Makeshift State in Urban Haiti*. Ithaca, NY: Cornell University Press.

Klinken, Gerry van, and Joshua Barker. 2009. "Introduction: State in Society in Indonesia." In *State of Authority: State in Society in Indonesia*, edited by Gerry van Klinken and Joshua Barker, 1–16. Ithaca, NY: Southeast Asia Program Publications, Southeast Asia Program, Cornell University.

Kumar, Ann. 1985. *The Diary of a Javanese Muslim: Religion, Politics and the Pesantren 1883–1886*. Faculty of Asian Studies Monographs, New Series, 7. Canberra: Faculty of Asian Studies, Australian National University.

Kunto, Haryoto. 1984. *Wajah Bandoeng tempo doeloe*. Bandung: P. T. Granesia.

Kunto, Haryoto. 1993. *Riwayat kota di tatar Sunda*. Bandung: Badan Perencanaan Pembangunan Daerah Propinsi Daerah Tingkat I Jawa Barat.

Kusno, Abidin. 2006. "Guardian of Memories: Gardu in Urban Java." *Indonesia* 81 (April): 95–150.

Lambourne, Gerald. 1984. *The Fingerprint Story*. London: Harrap.

Laporan akhir penelitian industrial security dan permasalahnya. 1994. Jakarta, Indonesia: Pusat Pengembangan Ilmu dan Teknologi Kepolisian.

Lev, Daniel S. 1996. "On the Other Hand?" In *Fantasizing the Feminine in Indonesia*, edited by Laurie J. Sears, 191–202. Durham, NC: Duke University Press.

Levi-Strauss, Claude. 1969. *The Elementary Structures of Kinship*. London: Eyre and Spottiswoode.

Li, Tania. 2007. *The Will to Improve: Governmentality, Development and the Practice of Politics*. Durham, NC: Duke University Press.

Lindquist, Johan. 2004. "Veils and Ecstasy: Negotiating Shame in the Indonesian Borderlands." *Ethnos* 69 (4): 487–508.

Lindquist, Johan A. 2009. *The Anxieties of Mobility: Migration and Tourism in the Indonesian Borderlands*. Southeast Asia: Politics, Meaning, and Memory. Honolulu: University of Hawai'i Press.

Lindquist, Johan. 2012. "The Elementary School Teacher, the Thug and His Grandmother: Informal Brokers and Transnational Migration from Indonesia." *Pacific Affairs* 85 (1): 69–89.

Low, Setha M. 2002. "Introduction: Theorizing the City." In *Theorizing the City: The New Urban Anthropology Reader*, edited by Setha M. Low, 1–33. New Brunswick, NJ: Rutgers University Press.

Lowe, Celia. 2007. "Recognizing Scholarly Subjects." In *Knowing Southeast Asian Subjects*, edited by Laurie S. Sears, 109–38. Seattle: University of Washington Press.

Lubis, Nina H. 2005. *Kajian sejarah Bandung selatan*. Bandung: Dinas Kebudayaan dan Pariwisata Babupaten Bandung.

Mamdani, Mahmood. 2018. *Citizen and Subject: Contemporary Africa and the Legacy of Late Colonialism*. Princeton, NJ: Princeton University Press.

Mappalahere, Farid. 1995. "Organisasi Massa 33 (studi kasus organisasi pengamanan swasta di Surabaya)." *Surabaya Post*, March 18.

Martin, Jeffrey T. 2013. "Police as Linking Principle: Rethinking Police Culture in Contemporary Taiwan." In *Policing and Contemporary Governance: The Anthropology of Police in Practice*, edited by William Garriott, 157–79. New York: Palgrave Macmillan.

Massumi, Brian. 1992. *A User's Guide to Capitalism and Schizophrenia: Deviations from Deleuze and Guattari*. Cambridge, MA: MIT Press.

Mayer, Leendert Theodorus. 1889. *Peratoeran hoekoeman policie jang oemoem atas orang bangsa Jawa dan sebrang di tanah Hindia-Nederland: Menoeroet salinan jang soedah kaloewar dari Kangdjeng Goebernement dengan di pindahken kapada hoeroef Ollanda dan di tambahken katrangan*. Samarang: G. C. T. Van Dorp and Co.

McCabe, Michael. 2003. *Tattoos of Indochina: Magic, Devotion, and Protection*. Atglen, PA: Schiffer.

McCoy, Alfred W. 1995. "'Same Banana': Hazing and Honor at the Philippine Military Academy." *Journal of Asian Studies* 54 (3): 689–726.

McCoy, Alfred W. 2009. *Policing America's Empire: the United States, the Philippines, and the Rise of the Surveillance State*. Madison: University of Wisconsin Press.

McElhinny, Bonnie Sue. 1993. "We All Wear Blue: Language, Gender and Police Work." PhD diss., Stanford University.

Meijer, D. H. 1926. "Dactyloscopie voor Nederlansch-Indië." *Koloniale Studiën* 10 (2): 909–47.

Migdal, Joel S. 2001. *State in Society: Studying How States and Societies Transform and Constitute One Another*. Cambridge Studies in Comparative Politics. Cambridge: Cambridge University Press.

Milner, Anthony Crowthers. 1982. *Kerajaan: Malay Political Culture on the Eve of Colonial Rule*. Tucson: Association for Asian Studies, University of Arizona Press.

Mitchell, Timothy. 1988. *Colonising Egypt*. Berkeley: University of California Press.

Mitchell, Timothy. 2002. *Rule of Experts: Egypt, Techno-Politics, Modernity*. Berkeley: University of California Press.

Moertono, Soemarsaid. 1981. *State and Statecraft in Old Java: A Study of the Later Mataram Period, 16th to 19th Century*. Rev. ed. Ithaca, NY: Modern Indonesia Project, Southeast Program, Department of Asian Studies, Cornell University.

Mrázek, Rudolf. 1997. "From Darkness to Light: Optics of Policing in Late-Colonial Netherlands East Indies." Paper presented at the Conference for Crime and Punishment: Criminality in Southeast Asia, Amsterdam, March 20–22.

Mrázek, Rudolf. 2002. *Engineers of Happy Land: Technology and Nationalism in a Colony*. Princeton, NJ: Princeton University Press.

Mudhoffir, Abdil Mughis. 2022. *State of Disorder: Privatised Violence and the State in Indonesia*. Singapore: Palgrave Macmillan.

Muflich, Ayip. 1979. "Mardy pelingung gang (Suatu studi kasus)." BA thesis, Criminology Department, Universitas Indonesia.

Nainggolan, W. P. 1984. "Pengunaan lokasi pertokoan yang dilaksanakan oleh Satpam dalam rangka menunjang tugas Poltabes Bandung." BA thesis, Perguruan Tinggi Ilmu Kepolisian (College for the Science of Policing).

Netherlands Indies Medical and Sanitary Service, ed. 1929. *Control of Endemic Diseases in the Netherlands Indies*. Weltevreden: Landsdrukkerij.

Niessen, Nicole. 1995. "Indonesian Municipalities under Japanese Rules." In *Issues in Urban Development*, edited by Peter J. M. Nas, 125–27. Leiden: Research School, CNWS.

Onghokham. 1978. "The Inscrutable and the Paranoid: An Investigation into the Sources of the Brotodiningrat Affair." In *Southeast Asian Transitions: Approaches through Social History*, edited by Ruth T. McVey, 112–57. New Haven, CT: Yale University Press.

Onghokham. 1984. "The *Jago* in Colonial Java, Ambivalent Champion of the People." In *History and Peasant Consciousness in South East Asia*, edited by Andrew Turton and Shigeharu Tanabe, 327–43. Osaka: National Museum of Ethnology.

Ossenbruggen, F. D. E. van 1977. "Java's Monca-Pat: Origins of a Primitive Classification System." In *Structural Anthropology in the Netherlands: A Reader*, edited by P. E. de Josselin de Jong. The Hague: Martinus Nijhoff.

Oudang, M. 1952. *Perkembangan kepolisian de Indonesia*. Djakarta, Indonesia: Mahabarata.

Pagoejoeban "Pasoendan." 1925. In *Poeseurna Paseondan (Soend-Hollandsch)*. Bandoeng: N. V. Mij. Vorkink.

Park, Robert E. 1968. "The City: Suggestions for the Investigation of Human Behavior in the Urban Environment." In *The City*, edited by Ernest W. Burgess, Robert E. Park, and Roderick D. McKenzie, 1–46. Chicago: University of Chicago Press.

Peletz, Michael G. 1996. *Reason and Passion: Representations of Gender in a Malay Society*. Berkeley: University of California Press.

Pemberton, John. 1994. *On the Subject of "Java."* Ithaca, NY: Cornell University Press.

Pinto da França, Antonio. 2000. *Pengaruh Portugis di Indonesia*. Jakarta, Indonesia: Pustaka S. H.

Poeze, H. A. 1994. "Political Intelligence in the Netherlands Indies." In *The Late Colonial State in Indonesia: Political and Economic Foundations of the Netherlands Indies 1880-1942*, edited by Robert Cribb, 229–45. Leiden, Netherlands: KITLV Press.

Pollé, Victor E. L., and Paul Hofstee. 1986. "Urban Kampung Improvement and the Use of Aerial Photography for Data Collection." In *The Indonesian City: Studies in Urban Development and Planning*, edited by Peter J. M. Nas, 116–35. Dordrecht, Netherlands: Foris Publications.

Pratten, David. 2008. "The Politics of Protection: Perspectives on Vigilantism in Nigeria." *Africa* 78 (1): 1–15.

Purwanto, Andreas A., and Mohamad Subroto. 1997. "Kalau preman yang dituding." *Detektif dan Romantika* 25–28 (8).

Quinn, George. 1975. "The Javanese Science of Burglary." *Review of Indonesian and Malayan Affairs* 9 (1): 33–54.

Quinn, George. 1992. *The Novel in Javanese: Aspects of Its Social and Literary Character*. Leiden: KITLV Press.

Rachman, Apriana Z. 1985. "Dimensi kebudayaan dalam perilaku pencurian (Dengan minat khusus pada masyarakat Kayu Agung)." BA thesis, Criminology Department, Universitas Indonesia.

Rafael, Vicente, ed. 1999. *Figures of Criminality in Indonesia, the Philippines, and Colonial Vietnam*. Ithaca, NY: Southeast Asia Program Publications, Southeast Asia Program, Cornell University.

Rajab, Untung S. 2003. *Kedudkan dan fungsi Polisi Republik Indonesia dalam sistem ketatanegaraan (Berdasarkan UUD 1945)*. Bandung: C. V. Purnomo.

Reerink, Gustaaf. 2006. "The Price of Uncertainty: Kampung Land Politics in Post-Suharto Bandung." International Institute for Asian Studies, Leiden University. https://scholarlypublications.universiteitleiden.nl/handle/1887/12716.

Reerink, Gustaaf. 2015. "From Autonomous Village to 'Informal Slum': Kampong Development and State Control in Bandung (1930-1960)." In *Cars, Conduits, and Kampongs: The Modernization of the Indonesian City, 1920-1960*, edited by Freek Colombijn and Joost Coté, 193–212. Leiden, Netherlands: Brill.

Reid, Anthony. 1988. *Southeast Asia in the Age of Commerce, 1450-1680*. New Haven, CT: Yale University Press.

Reid, Anthony. 2006. *Verandah of Violence: The Background to the Aceh Problem.* Singapore: NUS Press.

Robinson, Geoffrey. 1998. "Rawan Is as Rawan Does: The Origins of Disorder in New Order Aceh." *Indonesia* 66 (October): 127–57.

Robinson, Kathryn. 1998. "Love and Sex in an Indonesian Mining Town." In *Gender and Power in Affluent Asia,* edited by Krishna Sen and Maila Stivens, 63–86. London: Routledge.

Robison, Richard. 1986. *Indonesia: The Rise of Capital.* Sydney, Australia: Allen and Unwin.

Rochijat, Pipit. 1985. "Am I PKI or Non-PKI?" *Indonesia* 40: 37–56.

Rodgers, Dennis. 2006. "The State as a Gang: Conceptualizing the Governmentality of Violence in Contemporary Nicaragua." *Critique of Anthropology* 26 (3): 315–30.

Roosa, John. 2006. *Pretext for Mass Murder: The September 30th Movement and Suharto's Coup d'État in Indonesia.* Madison: University of Wisconsin Press.

Rush, James R. 1990. *Opium to Java: Revenue Farming and Chinese Enterprise in Colonial Indonesia, 1860–1910.* Ithaca, NY: Cornell University Press.

Rutherford, Danilyn. 2012. *Laughing at Leviathan: Sovereignty and Audience in West Papua.* Chicago: University of Chicago Press.

Ryter, Loren. 2001. "Pemuda Pancasila: The Last Loyalist Free Men of Suharto's Order?" In *Violence and the State in Suharto's Indonesia,* edited by Benedict Anderson, 124–55. Studies on Southeast Asia 30. Ithaca, NY: Southeast Asia Program Publications, Southeast Asia Program, Cornell University.

Ryter, Loren. 2005. "Reformasi Gangsters." *Inside Indonesia* 82 (April–June 2005). https://www.insideindonesia.org/reformasi-gangsters.

Ryter, Loren. 2009. "Their Moment in the Sun: The New Indonesian Parliamentarians from the Old OKP." In *State of Authority: State in Society in Indonesia,* edited by Gerry van Klinken and Joshua Barker, 181–218. Ithaca, NY: Southeast Asia Program Publications, Southeast Asia Program, Cornell University.

Ryter, Loren. 2012. "Privateers, Politicians, Prowess and Power." In *Southeast Asian Perspectives on Power,* edited by Liana Chua, Joanna Cook, Nicholas Long, and Lee Wilson, 121–32. London: Routledge.

Sangkanningrat. n.d. *Iets over hygiëne: In verband met adat, geloof en bijgeloof van het Soendaneesche volk.* Bandoeng: Nix.

Schefold, Reimar, Gaudenz Domenig, and Peter Nas. 2003. *Indonesian Houses: Tradition and Transformation in Vernacular Architecture.* Leiden: KITLV Press.

Schoute, Dirk. 1937. *Occidental Therapeutics in the Netherlands East Indies during Three Centuries of Netherlands Settlement (1600–1900).* Batavia: Netherlands Indies Public Health Service.

Schulte Nordholt, Henk. 1991. "The Jago in the Shadow: Crime and 'Order' in the Colonial State in Java." *Review of Indonesian and Malaysian Affairs* 25 (1): 74–92.

Schulte Nordholt, Nico. 2002. "Violence and the Anarchy of the Modern Indonesian State." In *Violence and Vengeance: Discontent and Conflict in New Order*

Indonesia, edited by Frans Hüsken and Huub de Jonge, 52–70. Saarbrücken, Germany: Verlag für Entwicklungspolitik.

Scott, James C. 1998. *Seeing like a State: How Certain Schemes to Improve the Human Condition Have Failed.* New Haven, CT: Yale University Press.

Sears, Laurie J. 1996. "Introduction: Fragile Identities: Deconstructing Women and Indonesia." In *Fantasizing the Feminine in Indonesia*, edited by Laurie J. Sears, 1–44. Durham, NC: Duke University Press.

Sen, Krishna. 1998. "Indonesian Women at Work: Reframing the Subject." In *Gender and Power in Affluent Asia*, edited by Krishna Sen and Maila Stivens, 35–62. London: Routledge.

Shiraishi, Takashi, ed. 1990. *An Age in Motion: Popular Radicalism in Java, 1912–1926.* Ithaca, NY: Cornell University Press.

Shiraishi, Takashi. 2021. *The Phantom World of Digul: Policing as Politics in Colonial Indonesia, 1926–1941.* Singapore: NUS Press; Japan: Kyoto University Press.

Sidel, John T. 1999. *Capital, Coercion, and Crime: Bossism in the Philippines.* Stanford, CA: Stanford University Press.

Siegel, James T. 1986. *Solo in the New Order: Language and Hierarchy in an Indonesian City.* Princeton, NJ: Princeton University Press.

Siegel, James T. 1997. *Fetish, Recognition, Revolution.* Princeton, NJ: Princeton University Press.

Siegel, James T. 1998. *A New Criminal Type in Jakarta: Counter-Revolution Today.* Durham, NC: Duke University Press.

Siegel, James T. 2011. *Objects and Objections of Ethnography.* New York: Fordham University Press.

Smail, John R. W. 1964. *Bandung in the Early Revolution, 1945–1946: A Study in the Social History of the Indonesian Revolution.* Ithaca, NY: Southeast Asia Program, Department of Asian Studies, Cornell University.

Soe, Lie Piet. 1931. *Bandoeng di waktoe malem.* Bandoeng: Minerva.

Soenarjo. 1970. "Suatu analisa tentang tumbuhnya anak-anak pemuda di Djakarta." BA thesis, Perguruan Tinggi Ilmu Kepolisian (College for the Science of Policing).

Soeropringgo. 1906. "Penjelidikian dari djalannja pentjoeri dan gogol-gogol. Tijdschrift voor het Binnelandsch Bestuur." *De Indische Gids* 28 (2): 1368–73.

Spyer, Patricia. 2006. "Some Notes on Disorder in the Indonesian Postcolony." In *Law and Disorder in the Postcolony*, edited by Jean Comaroff and John L. Comaroff, 188–218. Chicago: University of Chicago Press.

Starn, Orin. 1999. *Nightwatch: The Politics of Protest in the Andes.* Durham, NC: Duke University Press.

Steedly, Mary Margaret. 1993. *Hanging without a Rope: Narrative Experience in Colonial and Postcolonial Karoland.* Princeton, NJ: Princeton University Press.

Stein, Eric A. 2006. "Colonial Theatres of Proof: Representation and Laughter in 1930s Rockefeller Foundation Hygiene Cinema in Java." *Health and History* 8 (2): 14–44.

Stepputat, Finn, and Thomas Blom Hansen. 2005. "Introduction." In *Sovereign Bodies: Citizens, Migrants, and States in the Postcolonial World*, edited by Finn Stepputat and Thomas Blom Hansen, 13–48. Princeton, NJ: Princeton University Press.

Stevens, Theo. 1986. "Semarang, Central Java and the World Market 1870–1900." In *The Indonesian City: Studies in Urban Development and Planning*, edited by Peter J. M. Nas, 56–70. Dordrecht, Netherlands: Foris Publications.

Stoler, Ann Laura. 1991. "Sexual Affronts and Racial Frontiers: National Identity, 'Mixed Bloods' and the Cultural Genealogies of Europeans in Colonial Southeast Asia." *Transformations*. Comparative Study of Social Transformations Working Paper no. 64, 1–43.

Strassler, Karen. 2010. *Refracted Visions: Popular Photography and National Modernity in Java*. Durham, NC: Duke University Press.

Sumarwoto, Arief. 1984. "Latar belakang kebiasaan pelaku kejahatan tertentu memakai tatto sebagai salah satu ciri penampilannya." BA thesis, Perguruan Tinggi Ilmu Kepolisian (College for the Science of Policing).

Suryadinata, Leo. 1992. *Military Ascendancy and Political Culture/Golkar Dan Militer: Studi Tentang Budaya Politik*. Jakarta, Indonesia: Lembaga Penelitian, Pendidikan dan Penerangan Ekonomi dan Sosial.

Suryakusuma, Julia I. 1996. "The State and Sexuality in New Order Indonesia." In *Fantasizing the Feminine in Indonesia*, edited by Laurie J. Sears, 92–119. Durham, NC: Duke University Press.

Suryakusuma, Julia I. 2004a. "Bayonnetting the Vagina: Militarism and Violence against Women." In *Sex, Power and the Nation: An Anthology of Writings, 1979–2003*, 237–53. Jakarta, Indonesia: Metafor Publishing.

Suryakusuma, Julia I. 2004b. "State Ibuism: Appropriating and Distorting Womanhood in New Order Indonesia." In *Sex, Power and the Nation: An Anthology of Writings, 1979–2003*, 161–88. Jakarta, Indonesia: Metafor Publishing.

Sutherland, Heather. 1979. *The Making of a Bureaucratic Elite: The Colonial Transformation of the Javanese Priyayi*. Singapore: Heinemann Educational Books, published for the Asian Studies Association of Australia.

Sutherland, Heather. 1986. "Ethnicity, Wealth and Power in Colonial Makassar: A Historiographical Reconsideration." In *The Indonesian City: Studies in Urban Development and Planning*, edited by Peter J. M. Nas, 37–55. Dordrecht, Netherlands: Foris Publications.

Svensson, Thommy. 1991. *State Bureaucracy and Capitalism in Rural West Java: Local Gentry versus Peasant Entrepreneurs in the 19th and 20th Centuries*. Copenhagen: NIAS.

Tadie, Jérôme. 2002. "The Hidden Territories of Jakarta." In *The Indonesian Town Revisited*, edited by Peter J. M. Nas, 402–23. Münster, Germany: Lit Verlag.

Tamsyah, Budi Rahayu et al. 2003. *Kamus Lengkep Sunda-Indonesia, Indonesia-Sunda, Sunda-Sunda*. Cetakan 3. Bandung: Pustaka Setia.

Tannenbaum, Nicola. 1987. "Tattoos: Invulnerability and Power in Shan Cosmology." *American Ethnologist* 14 (4): 693–711.

Tanter, Richard. 1990. "The Totalitarian Ambition: Intelligence Organisations in the Indonesian State." In *State and Civil Society in Indonesia*, edited by Arief Budiman, 244–45. Clayton, Australia: Monash University, Asia Institute.

Taussig, Michael T. 1993. *Mimesis and Alterity: A Particular History of the Senses*. New York: Routledge.

Taylor, J. G. 1983. *The Social World of Batavia: European and Eurasian in Dutch Asia*. Madison: University of Wisconsin Press.

Telle, Kari. 2009. "Dharma Power: Searching for Security in Post–New Order Indonesia." *Social Analysis* 53 (1): 141–56.

Telle, Kari. 2013. "Vigilante Citizenship: Sovereign Practices and the Politics of Insult in Indonesia." *Bijdragen Tot de Taal-, Land- En Volkenkunde* 169 (2–3): 183–212.

Thomas, Deborah A. 2019. *Political Life in the Wake of the Plantation: Sovereignty, Witnessing, Repair*. Durham, NC: Duke University Press.

Tillema, Hendrik Freerk. (1922) 1958. "Lay-Out of an Average Regency Seat." In *The Indonesian Town: Studies in Urban Sociology*, edited by Willem Frederik Wertheim, 79–84. The Hague: W. van Hoeve.

Tio, Ie Soei. 1958. *Lie Kimhok 1853–1912*. Bandung: L. D. Good Luck.

Tomasoa, Leonard. 1981. "Kepemimpinan dalam Gang X (Suatu studi terhadap kehidupan di gang di dareah Kebayoran Baru)." BA thesis, Criminology Department, Universitas Indonesia.

Traube, Elisabeth G. 1986. *Cosmology and Social Life: Ritual Exchange among the Mambai of East Timor*. Chicago: University of Chicago Press.

Tsing, Anna. 2003. "Cultivating the Wild: Honey Hunting and Forest Management in Southeast Kalimantan." In *Culture and the Question of Rights: Forests, Coasts and Seas in Southeast Asia*, edited by Charles Zerner, 24–56. Durham, NC: Duke University Press.

Tsuchiya, Kenji. 1990. "Javanology and the Age of Ranggawarsita: An Introduction to Nineteenth-Century Javanese Culture." In *Reading Southeast Asia: Translation of Contemporary Japanese Scholarship on Southeast Asia*, 75–108. Ithaca, NY: Southeast Asia Program, Cornell University.

Valette, G. J. P. 1896. *De herkenning van misdadigers door anthropometrische identificatie volgens het stelsel van Alphonse Bertillon en de wenschelijkheid der toepassing daarvan in Nederlandsch-Indië: Een memorie*. The Hague: De Swart en Zoon.

Van Bruinessen, Martin. 1988. "'Duit, jodoh, dukun': Observations on Cultural Change among Poor Migrants to Bandung." *Masyarakat Indonesia* 15: 35–65.

Vandergeest, Peter, and Nancy Peluso. 1995. "Territorialization and State Power in Thailand." *Theory and Society* 24 (3): 385–426.

van Hien, H. A. 1912. *De Javaansche geestenwereld en de betrekkingen, die tusschen de geesten en de zinnelijke wereld bestaat, verduidelijkt door petangan's bij de Javanen en Soendaneezen in gebruik*. 1ste deel de geschiedenis der godsdiensten op Java. Batavia: G. Kolff and Company.

van Hoëvell, Walter Robert. 1852. "Tjoeroek penganten." *Tijdschrift voor Nederlandsch Indië* 14 (1): 425–27.

van Mook, Hubertus Johannes. (1926) 1958. "Kuta Gede." In *The Indonesian Town: Studies in Urban Sociology*, edited by Willem Frederik Wertheim, 274–331. The Hague: W. van Hoeve.

Wardoyo, Danang Kukuh. 2004. "Trial by Fire." *Inside Indonesia* 79 (July–September). https://www.insideindonesia.org/trial-by-fire?highlight=WyJ3 YXJkb3lvIiwid2FyZG95bydzIlo%3D.

Waterson, Roxanna. 1990. *The Living House: An Anthropology of Architecture in Southeast Asia*. Singapore: Oxford University Press.

Weber, Max. 1968. *On Charisma and Institution Building*. Edited by Shmuel Noah Eisenstadt. Chicago: University of Chicago Press.

Welsh, Bridget. 2008. "Local and National: Keroyokan Mobbing in Indonesia." *Journal of East Asian Studies* 8 (3): 473–504.

Widjojoatmodjo, Abdulkadir. 1927. *Riwajat Kepolisen di Hindia Ollanda Dengan Ringkas. Lesing deng hadlirat j. m. toean Resident Prijangan-Tengah dalam Congres Ilandsche Politie Bond ke-tiga di Bandoeng pada boelan April 1927 tanggal 17*. Semarang: Typ Khouw Beng Wan.

Wigmore, John Henry. 1923. *A Treatise on the Anglo-American System of Evidence in Trials at Common Law*, Vol. 4. 2nd ed. Boston: Little, Brown.

Wilson, Ian Douglas. 2002. "The Politics of Inner Power: The Practice of Pencat Silat in West Java." PhD diss., Murdoch University.

Wilson, Ian Douglas. 2006. "Continuity and Change: The Changing Contours of Organized Violence in Post–New Order Indonesia." *Critical Asian Studies* 38 (2): 265–97.

Wilson, Ian Douglas. 2015. *The Politics of Protection Rackets in Post–New Order Indonesia: Coercive Capital, Authority and Street Politics*. London: Routledge.

Wilson, Lee. 2011. "Beyond the Exemplary Centre: Knowledge, Power, and Sovereign Bodies in Java." *Journal of the Royal Anthropological Institute* 17 (2): 301–17.

Winichakul, Thongchai. 1994. *Siam Mapped: A History of the Geo-Body of a Nation*. Honolulu: University of Hawai'i Press.

Winters, Jeffrey. 1996. *Power in Motion: Capital Mobility and the Indonesian State*. Ithaca, NY: Cornell University Press.

Wolters, Oliver. 1999. *History, Culture and Region in Southeast Asian Perspectives*. Ithaca, NY: Southeast Asia Program Publications, Southeast Asia Program, Cornell University.

INDEX

Page locators in italics refer to figures

thief's body, 63; territorial subject prone to, 58; and war against rats, 107–108, 137, 265n4. *See also* national fears

Feldman, Allen, 84, 258n1

Field Police (Veldpolitie), 129

film, used in educational campaigns, 110–11

fingerprinting, 26, 132–35, 263n24, 25

folktales, 46–47, 64–70

Foucault, Michel, 2, 14, 90, 109, 136, 207, 231, 247n1, 260nn 19, 20

France, 59, 118–19

fraternities, 26, 177–78, 232; and bureaucratic hierarchy, 196; and common local languages, 180–81; co-optation of informal sovereignties, 213–14; defined, 185; fraternal economy, 186–98; gangs comparable to, 185–86, 271n16; historical context, 213; institutional origins of, 180; military, 161, 167–69, 177; patrimonialism distinguished from, 210–11; and police precinct house, 178–86; "secrets" of, 166, 199, 204, 209, 215. *See also* police

free man (*vrijman*), 77

A French View of the Netherlands Indies (Bousquet), 131–32

Freud, Sigmund, 43

gali-gali (gangs), 144, 152, 265n8

gangs: *calo* (go-betweens), 71, 149–50; fraternities comparable to, 185–86, 271n16; *gali-gali*, 144, 152, 265n8; hierarchy of in prison, 2; integration into state surveillance machine, 146; names of, 265–66n13; organization of, 60–61; patterns of recruitment, 71; and retreat of neoliberal state, 11–12; spiritual potency of members, 26; of thieves, 60–61; turf warfare, 145. See also *jegger* (*preman*) (street toughs); prowess

gatekeeper (jurukunci), 46–47, 64–69

gaze, 17; interiorization of, 109; and police precinct, 204–10; "scopic regime," 84; and tattoos, 75; view from above, 99–102, *101*, 222, 230, 233; view from the carriage, 84, 96–98, 102, 113, 230; view in depth, 102–112, 230. *See also* panopticon; surveillance

Gedung Sate (Satay Building and plaza, Bandung), 100, *103*, 217–24, 233; festive events, 221, *223*; Gasibu field, 223, 234; *lapak* (microterritories), 218, 220, 275n4; pop-up markets, 219–20; protests at, 219, *220*, *221*; revitalization program, 222–23. *See also* Bandung (Java, Indonesia)

Geertz, Clifford, 253n26

Gell, Alfred, 76–77

General Investigation Bureau (Algemeene Recherche Dienst, ARD), 130–31

George. Kenneth, 256n10

ghost-guards, 50–52

Goldstein, Daniel M., 11

Golkar (Golongan Karya, or Functional Groups), 149

governmentality, 5, 229, 247n1

Great Post Road, 85, 86, 97–98

guardhouses, *34*, 38–41, *40*, 55–57, 128, 130; as communications posts, 55; folktales told at, 46; milieux of, 42, 56; music played at, 42, 53, 56; names for, 38; political uses of, 55; revamped as *pos kamling* (security system posts), 147–48

Guattari, Félix, 42, 249n14

Guidance of Society Unit (Guidance Unit), 146–47, 174–75, 190, 266n20, 274n35

gurus, imprimatur of, 47

Hansip (uniformed guards), 146–48, 173, 266n19, 274n35

Hasbi, Mohammad, 155, 164

hazing, 182–85, 232, 278n29

health and hygiene, 84, 230, 263–64n31; educational campaigns, 108–11; and ethnic divisions, 207–208; film and slides used in educational campaigns, 110–12; houses rationalized, 98–99; policing of, 19; racist logic of, 103; sanitary cordon, 91–92; vaccination, 116–18. *See also* contagion/disease

health workers (*mantri*), 109–10

Henry, Edward, 133

"Henry system," 133

Hoadley, Mason C., 85

housing, 251n10; certification program, 107; location of, 49–50, 98–99; penetration and reconstruction of to prevent rats, 104–7; surveyability of, 107

human rights groups, 150–51

Hydrick, John Lee, 109–10

identity, 11, 119; individual, and vaccination, 116–18; of neighborhood, 62n11; *nekad* (determination), 160, 161; notions of, 127; tattoos and self-identity, 159–61

identity cards, 13, 118, 135, 263n29; codes for Chinese, 273–74n34; for *gali*, 152; as marks, 119; used for extortion, 171–72

Ie Soei Tio, 94–95

ilmu (mystical knowledge and spells), 44, 162, 165, 167, 169, 226, 252n12

"imagined community," 56

imitation: of Petrus by extortionists, 171–72; of police by guardhouses, 148; state mimicry of territorial power, 161–73

impostors, 118–20, 127, 131–32, 261n5; 269n51; "false" correspondence, 137

inattentiveness (*kelengahan*), 50

India, 237

Indianization, 225

indigeneity, 226, 228

indirect rule, 9, 18, 87–88, 227, 236, 277n27

Indonesia: corruption of, 176–77, 232; coup and political killings, 1965–66, 181, 207; economic growth of 1970s, 143, 148; military-bureaucratic elite, 23; nationalism, 11, 22, 55, 130–32, 137, 143, 213, 259n13; secessionist movements, 11. *See also* Bandung (Java, Indonesia); Batavia (Dutch East Indies); Dutch East Indies; Jakarta (Indonesia); Java; New Order (*Orde Baru*)

informal sovereignty, 142, 248n4; and brokers against outside threats, 14, 59–60; developed during times of state weakness, 226–27; global proliferation of, 235, 277n25; increase in after Suharto ouster, 216–17; police co-optation of, 26, 213–14; reciprocal performances with state, 10–11; "traditional," 226, 229; underlying commonalities between institutions, 12. *See also* sovereignty; territorial authority

inner power (*tenaga dalam*), 18

insecurity (*rawan*), 16–17

Instructions for Taking Descriptions for the Identification of Criminals and Others by the Means of Anthropometric Indications (Bertillon), 119–20

interiority, 56–57; architectural, 100; of discipline, 109, 231

interpellation, 53–56; of community by neighborhood watch, 53–56; of view by *jegger* tattoos, 76

invulnerable body (*kebal*), 44–45, 71, 72, 163, 168

Islamic boarding schools (*pesantren*), 170, 173

Islamic Defenders Front, 221

jago (colonial-era strong men), 226, 236, 254n1, 277–78n27

Jakarta (Indonesia), 20–21, 161; Kayu Agung, thieves from, 60–61, 255n2; megacity region, 24; Prems

Jakarta, 149. *See also* Batavia (Dutch East Indies)

Japan: occupation of Java, 38, 55; Yakuza gang, 144–45

Jauregui, Beatrice, 237

Java, 16, 18, 88; Japanese occupation of, 38, 55; opium farms, 278n27; slit gong codes, 54; street toughs, 70. *See also* Bandung (Java, Indonesia); Indonesia

Java Sugar Syndicate, 134

jegger (*preman*) (street toughs), 13; community description of, 158; duels (*jantan*), 72, 75, 77, 78, 161; and force of territorialization, 70–75; as local heroes, 162–63; *munjung* compared with, 77; from outside neighborhood, 59–60; *preman berdasi* (former street *preman* impersonating civil servants), 172; process for setting up territory, 72; rents extorted by, 72–75; tattoos, 75–78; terms for, 254n1; turf wars, 71–72; underlings of (*anak buah* or *kronco*), 71–72, 74, 77. *See also* gangs

"just for fun," 42, 53, 57

"juvenile delinquent," categories of, 59

Kalimantan, Borneo, 52

Kamil, Ridwan, 222

"karang songo" calculations, 49

Kayu Agung, West Sumatra, thieves from, 60–61, 255n2

Kediri, Java, 54

Keeler, Ward, 18, 262n10

kentonganisasi, or "slit gongization process," 148, 165, 174

khas (specific or exclusive character), 42

kinship structures, 18, 62, 90, 94, 161, 225; fraternal, 187

Kitab Mantra Yoga, 42–43

Kivland, Chelsey L., 235

Komando Distrik Militer, Kodim, 222, 234

Kopkamtib (Komando Pemulihan Keamanan dan Ketertiban, or Command for the Restoration of Security and Order), 144–45, 149, 151, 265n12

Kunarto, General, 193

Kunto, Haryoto, 107

land, territory defined in terms of, 73–74

land tenure, 52

lapak (microterritories), 218, 220, 275n4

law, diminished by police academy hierarchy, 184–85

"letter of good behavior," 149, 193, 196, 266n26

letters of permission for public meetings, 204

Liberia, 11

Lie Kimhok, 92, 94

Lie Piet, Soe, 114

linguistic order, 62–63, 107, 127

localization, 117–18, 261n2

Lombroso, Cesare, 268n39

magic: beheading as means to counter, 166, 168; divination manuals (*primbon*), 48–50, 252nn16, 18; fingerprinting as, 133; gatekeeper (*jurukunci*), 46; ghost-guards, 50–52; guardian figures, 49; *ilmu* (mystical knowledge and spells), 44, 162, 165, 167, 169, 226, 252n12; invulnerable (*kebal*) body, 44–45, 71, 72, 163, 168; obstruction of modernization, 94–96; power of territories, 44–50; rituals to ward off threats, 15, 42–43, 47–48; sacred spot (*keramat*), 44–47; "sixth sense," 44, 47, 50, 96; and spatial orientation, 49–50, 252n20; specialists, 44, 47–48; spells (*sirep*), 48; *surat sakti* (magically powerful letters), 172. *See also* spirits

main hakim sendiri ("play judge themselves"), 9, 58, 76, 163–64, 170

preman berdasi (former street preman impersonating civil servants), 172

Prems Jakarta, 149

presence, 50–53; "metaphysics of," 57

pribumi (indigenous population), 72, 97, 130

primbon (divination manuals), 48–50, 252n16, 18

private security services, 14–15, 144–45, 148–49, 175, 250n17, 277n24; state franchising of, 203, 228. See also businesses

protection rackets, 71–75, 77–79, 144–45, 161; bekking (dekking), 77–78, 218, 233; long-term ties with offenders, 197–99; payment to avoid police violence, 197–98; and police cooperation, 193–94; police protection from other police, 201–202. See also debt relation

protests, 123, 219, 220, 221

provincial congress (Dewan Perwikilan Rakyat Daerah), 149

Provincial Police, 149, 208

prowess: comparative perspective, 234–38; historical perspective, 224–34; "men of prowess," 17, 225, 276–77n20; spiritual potency, 26, 225–26; and tattoos, 160; tattoos used to assess, 26. See also gangs

Public Health Service, 108

public order police (polisi pamong praja), 199–200, 273n31

Quinn, George, 43, 50, 252n13

Rachman, Apriana Z., 255n2

racist discourses, 103

Raden Saleh, 88

rationality, bureaucratic, 19, 89–90, 230, 249n14

rats, 102–108, 136, 137, 265n4

recidivists (residivis), 148, 158–59, 162, 266n23

recognition, 154, 166–69; anthropometric, 122, 127; and police academy, 181–85; and violence, 183–84

The Recognition of Criminals by Anthropometrical Identification According to the Laws of Alphonse Bertillon and the Desirability of Their Application in the Netherlands Indies (Valette), 122–23

reform (reformasi) movement, 24, 216, 221

regents, 85, 92–94, 128

Regional Investigations Unit (Gewestelijke Recherche), 130

rents. See debt relations

Reserse (Criminal Investigation Unit), 156, 165, 190–201, 211–12, 272n24

reterritorialization, 66, 171, 173, 206, 227, 229

revenge, 169–71, 267n31

riots, 170, 269n55

roads and railways, 84–87; Great Post Road, 85, 86, 97–98; Preanger line, 94–96, 98

Rockefeller Foundation, 109

Rodgers, Dennis, 11–12

ronda. See neighborhood watch (ronda)

Rousseau, Jean-Jacques, 260n20

routinization, 27, 84, 125, 218, 225–26; of charisma, 276n18; of killings, 151–52

Rukun Tetangga/Rukun Warga (neighborhood and residents' associations), 38, 147–49, 173, 251n6

rule of law, suspension of, 151, 214

rust en orde (tranquility and order), 16

Rutherford, Danilyn, 10

Ryter, Loren, 145, 276n20

sacred spot (keramat), 44–47

Sadikin, Ali, 176–77, 215

São Paulo, Brazil, 59

Satpam (uniformed guards), 146–50, 173, 228, 266n19, 267n29, 269n52

Satpamsus (Satuan Pengamanan Khusus), 149

School for Police Administration, 188, 189

Schoute, Dirk, 118

scientific knowledge: fetishization of, 136–37; fingerprinting, 132–35, 263n24, 25; internalization of, 113. *See also* anthropometry

"scopic regime," 84, 258n1

Scott, James C., 12, 206

security, 3; *aman* as root word for, 16; collective, 228; different senses of, 20; "vernacular" concepts of, 16–17

Security and Crowd Control Unit (Sabhara, or Samapta Bhayang-kara), 190

Seeing Like a State (Scott), 206

"seeing like a state," 12, 79, 206, 232

Serang (coastal town), 98–99

Shiraishi, Takashi, 55, 230

shops and stalls (*warung*), 36–37

Sidel, John T., 276n20

Siegel, James T., 15, 62, 163, 265n8

Siskamling, *sistem keamanan lingkungan* (environment security system), 13, 19–20, 142, 277n24, 190, 228, 232, 274n35; and businesses formed by ex-convicts, 145, 148–49; Guidance of Society Unit (Guidance Unit), 146–47; Hansip (uniformed guards), 146–48, 173, 266n19, 274n35; *kentonganisasi*, or "slit gongization process," 148, 165, 174; massive expansion of, 150; as new way of organizing local security, 142; volunteer residential security, 145–46. *See also* Satpam (uniformed guards)

Sistem Swakarsa (Self-Help System), 264–65n3

"sixth sense," 44, 47, 50, 96

slametan ritual, 95–96, 253n26

slit gong, 38–39, 40, 50, 250n1, 251n9; electricity poles as stand-ins for, 36; interpellation by, 53–54, 76; *kentonganisasi*, or "slit gongization process," 148, 165, 174; *kohkol*, 56;

koprek, 56; pragmatic and artistic applications, 41–42; territoriality and place defined by, 41–44; translocal uses of, 54–56; used to keep people awake, 36, 43–44; used to mobilize against thieves, 55. *See also* neighborhood watch (*ronda*)

Smail, John, 55

social order: modernist vision of, 5–6, 12–13, 233–34; territorial vision of, 5–6, 233–34, 247–48n3

"societies against the state," 5, 70, 228–29

Soeropringgo, 125, 262n13

sovereignty: colonial, franchised to other entities, 8; as performative, 8, 10–11, 249n8; state and informal, relationship between, 142; "street sovereigns," 6, 9, 248n4. *See also* informal sovereignty

spatial orientations, 14, 92, 99, 218–19; directionality, 49–50, 252n20; *naga* (dragon-like creature), 49–50

speed bumps (sleeping policemen), 41

spirits, 126; and *keramat*, 45–47; *munjung*, 64–70, 77–78, 256n11; phantom state compared with *munjung*, 64–70; possession by, 45, 50–51. *See also* magic

Spyer, Patricia, 17

spy networks, 116, 126–28, 131–32

state: absentee, 11–12; authoritarian, 4, 6–7, 12–13, 26, 270n4; *bekking* (protection of *jegger*), 77–78, 218, 233; "bifurcated" authority of, 8–9; and blacklists, 153–54; building blocks of, 6–7; extrajudicial violence sponsored by, 4, 142, 164; impulses of, 7, 12–13; as institution, 7–8; *jegger*'s debt to, 77–78, 226; mimicry of territorial power, 161–73; myth of, 12–13, 248–49n7; neopatrimonial dynamics of power, 210–13, 232; phantom, 59, 64–70; and police power, 173–75, 228; post-Suharto weakening of, 63; potency of, 166; pyramidal image of power, 13; reciprocal performances with informal sovereigns, 10–11; revenge against, 169–71; "seeing like a state," 12, 79, 206; "society against the state," 5, 70, 228–29; and "truth," 137, 154–55, 174; unitary conception of, 8–9; violence, monopoly on, 4–5, 7–9, 164, 213–14

"street sovereigns," 6, 9, 248n4. *See also jegger (preman)* (street toughs)

Suharto, 1, 6, 27, 161, 227; monopolistic control over military, 144; Petition of Fifty opposition to, 143; resignation of, 13, 176, 216. *See also* New Order (*Orde Baru*)

Sukamiskin Prison (Bandung), 1–2, 28, 60, 82

Sukarno, 22, 227, 276n18; buildings designed by, 259–60n8

Sumarwoto, Arief, 158–59

Sundanese ethnic group, 20–21; aristocracy, 88; *calung* musical performances, 42; outside power in folklore, 64; seminomadic swidden cultivation, 87, 92

surat sakti (magically powerful letters), 172

surveillance, 14–20; anthropometry, 118–23; birth certificates, 135, 263n30; of brothels and prostitutes, 117–18, 261n2; bureaucratization of, 3, 27, 96–97, 146; CCTV cameras, 223–24, 276n16; and colonial economy, 85–88; of criminals, 55; defined, 17; emergence of in context, 25; fetishization of the tools of, 136–37, 230; fingerprinting, 132–35; and gaze, 84; interpellation of community, 53–56; lanterns required at night, 124–25; limitations of, 230–33; line of sight, 98, 113, 123; lists, 13, 26, 143, 148, 152–54, 159; local leaders' monopoly on identification, 122–23; local techniques of, 123–28; "looking the other way," 200–201,

204; modernization of, 88–94, 229; optical regime, 231–32; and pandemics, 7; Petrus rooted in tradition of, 151; of policing practices, 19, 25; of populations, 25; prototypes, 117; sedentarization of population, 86–87, 91; spy networks, 116, 126–28, 131–32; subjects of, 115; surveyability, 107, 113, 200; technologies of, 25; territoriality distinguished from, 6, 13, 17–18, 26; two independent processes of, 136; two-pronged apparatus of, 115; urban panopticon, 112–14; view in depth, 102–112, 230. *See also* gaze; Petrus (paramilitary operation); Siskamling, *sistem keamanan lingkungan* (environment security system)

Suryakusuma, Julia, 187, 272nn20, 22

suspicion, 17

Tadie, Jérôme, 255n4

Tangkubanparahu, (mountain), 222

Tanzania, 235

Tasikmalaya riot, 170

tattoos, 13, 26, 72, 75–78; as aid in appropriation of territorial power, 75–78; and being tough ("game cock," *agoan*), 160; considered sign of criminality, 76, 155–61, 268n39; magical powers of, 160; new types of, 172; penis implants, 75–76, 257–58n24; Polynesian tattooing, 76–77; removal of, 156, 159; and self-identity, 159–61; thief's scars comparable to, 76. *See also* body

Taussig, Michael, 133, 263n27

territorial authority, 5–8, 13, 26, 232, 235–37; current spread of, 7; at Gedung Sate plaza, 216–22; multipolar structure of, 218–19; outsiders, response to, 17, 43–44, 50; range and flexibility of institutions, 25, 236–37; state mimicry of, 161–73; visibility of, 76. *See also* authority; informal sovereignty

with, 163–64; "play judge them-selves" (*main hakim sendiri*), 9, 58, 76, 163–64, 170; rationales for, 78–79; by state actors, 3–4

Villa Isola, Bandung, 100, *101*

violence: bystander role in, 63–64; col-lective, 59, 62; disapproval of meth-ods, 167–68; *diskresi* (discretion), 196; eradicating (*menggulung*), 62, 63; extrajudicial, 4; hazing, 182–85, 232, 278n29; increased severity of, 63; killings of 1965–66, 144, 207; lack of as territorial weakness, 64; law identified with, 184–85; mass killings, 6, 25, 26; order restored by, 62–63; in police academy, 181–85; by police against suspects, 196–98; pummeling (*menggebuki*), 62; and recognition, 183–84; "shock therapy," 142; Siskamling attempts at monopolization of, 145–46; spec-tacular, 63–64; state and popular intertwined, 4–5; state monopoly on, 4–5, 7–9, 164, 213–14; swarming (*mengeroyok*), 62; against thieves, 3, 6, 11, 51, 58; vigilante, 3; word-punch, 63. *See also* Petrus (Mysteri-ous Killings, *Pembunuhan Misterius*)

vision, 112

Wardoyo, Danang Kukuh, 63

Weber, Max, 8

wedana (district chief), 88–89, 91, 128, 131

Wigmore, John Henry, 263n29

Wilson, Ian, 274–75n2

Wolters, Oliver, 17–18, 225

women, 251n3, 259n23, 261n1, 270n4, 271n18; Dharma Wanita member-ship, 270n4, 272n20; and military, 272n22; and neighborhood watch, 37; police officers, 28; as symbols of exchange, 187, 271–72n17

woning (house), 107

word-punch, 63

wuku calendar, 48–49

Yakuza gang (Japan), 144–45

Yogyakarta (central Java), 150, 152, 267n36

www.ingramcontent.com/pod-product-compliance
Lightning Source LLC
Chambersburg PA
CBHW020825270326
41928CB00006B/440